MONEY DYNAMICS FOR THE NEW ECONOMY

Venita VanCaspel, CFP

President,
VANCASPEL & CO., INCORPORATED

SIMON AND SCHUSTER   NEW YORK

Published by Simon and Schuster
A Division of Simon & Schuster, Inc.
Simon & Schuster Building
Rockefeller Center
1230 Avenue of the Americas
New York, New York 10020
SIMON AND SCHUSTER and colophon are registered trademarks of
Simon & Schuster, Inc.
Designed by Irving Perkins Associates
Manufactured in the United States of America
10 9 8 7 6 5 4 3 2 1

Library of Congress Cataloging-in-Publication Data

VanCaspel, Venita, date.
  Money dynamics for the new economy.

  Includes index.
  1. Finance, Personal.   I. Title.
HG179.V363   1986   332.024   86-3761
ISBN 0-671-61435-5

Dedicated to
Lyttleton Tazwell Harris IV

Contents

Chapter 3   53

Inflation and the New Economy

Chapter 4   66

Stock Dynamics in the New Economy

Chapter 5   92

Professional Money Management
for the New Economy

Chapter 6   **134**

Real Estate in the New Economy

Chapter 7   **175**

Home Sweet Home—To Rent or Buy?

Chapter 8   **201**

Energy Dynamics

The World of Equipment Leasing, Cable Television, and Cellular Telephones

Tax-Saving Opportunities in the New Economy

Investing in Hard Cash and Hard Assets

Chapter 15   **417**

Investing in a College Education

Chapter 16   **435**

Taking Your Financial Inventory

Chapter 17   **451**

Selecting Your Financial Planner

Chapter 18   **464**

Repositioning Your Assets for Maximum Gain in the New Economy

Preface: The Challenge of Change

We are living in an exciting new era in American history, an era of dynamic and far-reaching change, a time of restructuring when this mighty nation shifts from a giant industrial society to one based upon the creation and distribution of services and information, a time of dramatic movement in the dual directions of high tech and high touch, where each new technology is matched with a compensating human response!

You are indeed fortunate to be living in this exciting era and to have selected this particular book at this time. As a principal economy moves from one major era to a new major era, a parenthesis develops between the two, creating immense opportunities for financial gains to those who are well informed and have the knowledge and courage to act.

No longer do you have the luxury of ignorance of financial affairs, for you are now being thrust headlong into the most sophisticated money era our world has ever known. To prosper, or even to survive in this New Economy, it is paramount that you become fully equipped with timely financial knowledge and possess the right mental attitude, agility, determination, and the acute sense of timing necessary to adjust to this rapid change. In the New Economy you will find that it will not be change, but your reaction to change, that will determine your financial standing over the next several years.

Will you eagerly accept the challenge of change at this time? Change can greatly enhance your fortune, or it can destroy it; make you a millionaire or a pauper; delight or disappoint you; exhilarate you or depress you. History tells us that change brings with it heightened potential on the one hand and devastating crevasses of danger on the other. And how you cope with the inevitable changes going on around you will, in large part, determine whether you will win or lose the vital money game. But you must remember that the money game is not like any other game. You do not have the luxury of choosing whether you will play or not, because the money game is the *only* game in town! And since you have no choice but to play, it is vital that you learn to play the game very well. Losing the money game could mean spending the remainder of your life in a state of frustrating, devastating financial insecurity.

But let's look on the bright side and move forward with a positive mental attitude and a determination to accept the challenge of change. Financial independence can rightfully be yours if you have an average ability to earn, a little discipline to save, apply the information you will learn in this book, and if you are granted enough time. You have control over the first three principles above, and I will show you how to buy the fourth.

The exciting and encouraging thing for you to know is that today there are avenues of investment available to you which just a few years ago were open only to the rich. Today you can benefit, as they have, by investing directly in American industry, real estate, energy, communications, technology, commerce, and a vast array of other areas of our American free enterprise system.

As you pursue this wide range of investment options offered by the New Economy, you will find that there will be an investment for every season, but there will be *no* investment for *all* seasons. Agility and diversification will become your keystones as you learn from this book how to take advantage of the opportunities and dynamics of the New Economy, and how to position your assets effectively where demand is greater than supply in order to compound your money more rapidly.

This is a *personal* book. Financial planning is by necessity personal, because you are different from any other person. You are a unique creation and have developed in your own unique way. You have different financial objectives, assets, tax bracket, temperament, emotions, and time schedules than even your closest friend. Your financial program, therefore, must be created and designed for you and you alone.

If I could sit down with you to help you plan your financial future, I would ask many searching and pertinent questions about you, your money, your needs, goals, desires, feelings, and prejudices. We would then work together to design a program that would fit not only your financial needs but your emotional needs as well. Designing a program for your financial needs is relatively simple, once I have all the facts. But mapping a course that fits your temperament and your prejudices and then communicating these ideas to you in such a way that you will understand and then act upon them is a continuous challenge.

Since you and I may never have the opportunity to sit and discuss your personal financial plans, I have designed this book to give you a step-by-step guide to use in creating your own financial blueprint, and I challenge you to keep it updated constantly to fit these dynamic and ever-changing times.

I will be sharing with you the knowledge I have acquired over the past twenty-three years as an economist, stockbroker, and Certified Financial Planner. During that time it has been my joy to watch the assets of my clients grow and see their dimensions for living expand through the application of the money and living skills that I have taught them and helped them apply.

Many of my clients and friends have asked why and how I became a financial planner. For many years I was a stockbroker for a large brokerage firm that was a member of the New York Stock Exchange. However, I found myself frustrated by the feeling that I was just not doing enough for my clients. I found that what most people needed was not someone to tout them on a particular stock that they felt might go up a few points; what they really needed was someone to sit down with them and help them analyze where they were and where they wanted to be at a certain period in their lives, and then to help them arrive at their desired destination and buy the time to acquire this desired living estate. I found at the time that most of the so-called money experts were extremely specialized and that each of them was only interested in promoting his or her own particular products, such as stocks, bonds, life insurance, savings accounts, and so on. There seemed to be a great need for a person or a team that was competent and caring to provide a much-needed service that would offer all-encompassing, objective financial planning and bring people who needed financial assistance together into a coordinated, guided, and functioning whole.

I soon became convinced that this was a calling worth all my life and talents. So in 1968, at a very low spot in the stock market and at a time when nearly all the small brokerage houses were merging into large ones, I left a large one to open a small one. This was a scary move at the time, but the need was so great and my dedication so strong that I forged ahead and started the business. Our success over the past years proves that there really was an important void in the financial services industry that needed to be filled, and we were instrumental in offering a service that people in need of financial help responded to. And I personally have the satisfaction of knowing that I have made a truly worthwhile contribution to the financial future of thousands.

It continues to be my privilege to be in daily contact with some of our nation's top policymakers, the most expert observers of the money scene, our leading financial planners, and a large number of successful business and professional people who make decisions that affect us all.

Through my seminars, speeches, books, and counseling, I take joy in believing that I have helped raise the level of financial independence of my fellow Texans, and through the enormous sale and use of my past four books—*Money Dynamics, The New Money Dynamics, Money Dynamics for the 1980s,* and *The Power of Money Dynamics*—the financial independence of a nation. Financial planners, stockbrokers, and enthusiastic readers across the nation continue to recommend my books to their clients and friends. My daily mail, enthusiastically detailing successful results from the books, is an avalanche of joy to me. Nothing delights me more than receiving stories of success from my readers and valued clients. A large number of colleges and universities have also adopted the books as texts for their business schools.

My National Public Television shows, "Venita VanCaspel's MoneyMakers," now in its fifth year, and "Profiles of Success," in its first year, are carried on more than 160 stations. My radio shows, my national newsletter, *Money Dynamics Letter,* my cassette albums, and my computer program are helping keep listeners and subscribers on the exciting edge of investment opportunities. Through them Americans are learning how to profit from taking advantage of a vast number of opportunities offered by our free enterprise system. "Profiles of Success" vividly highlights those who have succeeded under this system, and it is my hope that it will be an inspiration to my viewers.

It is now time for you to reach out with your hands and let me grasp them firmly as I lead you down the road to financial independence. To provide you with a solid foundation it will be necessary from time to time to introduce you to tables, charts, and graphs that may not be as exciting as we would both like them to be. But please do persevere! Devour them. Let them seep deeply into your subconscious mind. You will find them invaluable in the attainment of your predetermined worthwhile goal of financial independence. And now let's begin our exciting journey together into the New Economy and learn how you can financially benefit from the dynamic and far-reaching changes that are taking place in our society.

Acknowledgments

So many have touched my life and helped me toward my goals that this page could not possibly thank them all. But I would like to express my special thanks to Helen Fourmy, who has been my faithful, motivating, and excellent associate for many years; to JoLieta Davis, whose immense talent and personal dedication smooth the ripples of my personal and business life; and to her very talented assistants, Yvonne Villman, Rachel Curry, and Elinor Becker; to Susan Prickett, whose calm and lovely competence gives me a sense of continuity; to Betty Henderson, whose enthusiasm for the task at hand makes being around her a delight; to Christina Rohde, my beautiful and efficient secretary; to Donah Shaw, who brings fun combined with efficiency to our lives, to Nancy Claire, the voice and warmth of our companies; to Jennifer Harris, Sharon Head, Betty McLeod, Kathryn Shoff, and Diana Hale, the very talented group of associates that does so much to make our financial planners an asset to our clients; to John Weatherston, who brings us the wise maturity that comes from experience; and most especially to Walt Burton, Wally Garrett, Mike Thompson, and Dwayne Baugus, who, along with Helen, make up the most talented team of financial planners in the country today.

Chapter 1

The New Economy

Welcome to the New Economy

Welcome to the exciting world of the New Economy and its kaleido-scope of change. Dynamic, challenging, and sometimes frustrating changes are taking place in our family relationships, our living styles, our technology, our international affairs, and especially in the nurture and investment of our money.

As you observe the world around you and as you read this book, you may find that many of the old money rules that you have learned just do not work in today's rapidly changing environment. But don't despair. Instead, keep a positive mental attitude and you'll discover that the New Economy is opening up a vast new array of investment options with superb potential for the small and large investor alike.

Rejoice and take pleasure in the fact that you are living at a time in the nation's history when our economy is shifting and moving from one major era to the next. In my many years as a Certified Financial Planner, I have never seen so many viable opportunities for investors to make money. To participate, you will need discipline, knowledge, agility, and a positive mental attitude. Your role is to supply the discipline and positive mental attitude. My role will be to supply you

The New Economy   23

with the knowledge, the motivation, and the new thinking patterns that will be essential for winning the money game in the New Economy. To tap into this new world of opportunities, you must first fling open the windows of your mind, throw out many of your preconceived ideas about money, reexamine those that are salvageable, and learn to accept the reality and concepts of the New Economy.

But just how do you begin to reorient your thought patterns to these exciting changes? Your first step is to obtain and devour John Naisbitt's book *Megatrends*. Within its covers you will discover that a major restructuring of America is occurring at a rapid pace and that new directions are transforming our lives in ways that will affect all of us into the twenty-first century. From the vast array of statistics Naisbitt has gathered, I have concluded that there are eight major trends now taking place that will have the greatest impact on our investment strategies as we prepare to enter the next century. These are:

1. America, which moved from an agricultural-based society in the early 1900s to an industrial-based society, is now moving into a communication society based upon the creation and distribution of information.

2. Both the high tech and the high touch of this new communication society will greatly affect human responses and interrelationships.

3. No longer are we living in an isolated, self-sufficient national economic system, but we are rapidly becoming part of a new global economy.

4. We will no longer be the world's industrial leader.

5. We are shifting from relying on institutional help to more self-reliance in all aspects of our lives.

6. We are restructuring our business endeavors from short-term considerations to long-term time frames.

7. More Americans are moving to the South and West, away from the industrial cities of the North.

8. We are exploding into a free-wheeling multiple-option society.

Naisbitt points out that the most reliable way to anticipate the future is to understand the present. I have designed this book to enable you to understand the present money world while at the same time anticipating what the exciting money world of the future might hold for each of us based upon these major trends. You learned in Basic Economics 101 that one of the keys to good investing is to put your money where demand will be greater than supply. You will find that the New Economy will repeal many of our old money rules, but this is one that I believe will stand and become even more viable.

To determine where demand will be greater than supply, we must become good students of trends—in fact, megatrends. Trends tell us the directions in which our society and economy are moving. And when we make decisions compatible with these trends, the trends will tend to help us along. As Naisbitt states, "Trends, like horses, are easier to ride in the direction they are already going."

In the New Economy, we have entered an era when we are mass-producing knowledge as we once mass-produced things. Knowledge will become the driving force of our economy and will become the new source of power. Power will no longer be money in the hands of a few, but rather information in the hands of many. Knowledge then becomes the key to productivity, which in turn creates economic value.

We must realize that as an economy moves from one major economic era to another, changes do not occur overnight. In fact, a parenthesis occurs during the transition, and it provides the potential for extraordinary economic gains to those who are knowledgeable about the changes taking place in the economy. We are now in this parenthesis period, so with a little applied discipline and a positive mental attitude on your part, let me help you make some rewarding discoveries as we travel down the road to financial independence together. I truly believe that if you apply the techniques clearly defined in this book, you can make the next ten years the most profitable you have ever experienced.

Your Role as an Investor

No matter what your occupation, background, personality, or present financial status may be, you are an investor. You are either investing all of your wealth in today's goods and services or you are reserving a portion of it to invest in tomorrow's goods and services. You do not have the choice of whether or not you will invest, but you do have the choice of *how* you will invest. The wisdom you bring to bear on these choices will have a greater influence on your financial future than the actual amount of money that comes your way.

Do you want to consume all that you earn today and hope that somehow tomorrow will take care of itself? As shortsighted as this might seem, it is the course being taken by the vast majority of your fellow citizens.

Your Sources of Income

If you stand back and objectively analyze your potential sources of future income, you will find that there are essentially three. These are:

1. *You at work.* Most of us can expect to have an income for some forty to fifty years from work at our chosen professions. Unfortunately, we cannot work forever, and at some point in our lives we will have to retire.

2. *Your money at work.* If you apply discipline, knowledge, agility, and a positive mental attitude and actively participate in the vast array of investment options open to you, a time will come when you no longer have to work for your money. It will work for you. Experience has taught me that income from capital is immensely more secure than income from labor!

3. *Charity.* This is an option that has rarely brought happiness, but instead an existence based upon "handouts" from friends, relatives, or the government.

Which source of income do you want to depend upon when you retire? Since work may not be an option open to you and charity is not palatable to many, apply your intelligence toward assuring yourself that there is sufficient money at work to live the lifestyle of your choice and, when the time comes, to retire in financial dignity. This is not only the wisest course for you to pursue in your financial life, it is also, in fact, an obligation that you owe to yourself and your loved ones. It is no secret that the majority of our citizens who reach retirement age find themselves in a pronounced state of financial *in*security.

Reasons for Financial Failure

Why do so many fail to become financially independent? During my many years as a financial planner, I have searched for the answer and I now believe I have found the reasons. There are six, and here they are:

PROCRASTINATION

Procrastination can be the greatest deterrent to reaching your goal of financial independence. It is a deadly enemy of your obligation to retire in financial dignity. I have observed that in the early years of life, when spending habits are formed, thoughts of retirement are far away and have little relationship to current needs and even less to future needs. The habit becomes reinforced with the same passing of time that brings retirement closer. Then when retirement time is so near as to be of immediate concern, it is often too late to make adequate preparation. Don't procrastinate with your financial future. Make "Do It Now" your slogan for the rest of your life!

FAILURE TO ESTABLISH A GOAL

It has been said that if you aim at nothing in life, you are likely to hit nothing! I have never had anyone come to me and say, "Venita, I plan to fail." Yet I have observed many who failed to plan and who unfortunately met with the same dismal results.

Through the delightful experience of moderating my television shows, and after listening to the life stories of the other recipients who were honored, as I was, with the Horatio Alger Award for Distinguished Americans, I have reached some conclusions about the necessary ingredients for success in life and in money matters under our free enterprise system. Successful people differ in appearance, voice, height, weight, education, and family background, but they all have one thing in common: They know where they are going. Each has a goal. If anything sidetracks a goal, or if something doesn't work the way they planned, they just dust themselves off and go right back in the direction of their goal. After many years of observation, I am in complete agreement with the famous psychologist William James, who said, "Anything the mind can believe and conceive, it can achieve."

Visualize your financial goal right now. Your mind will not let you conceive what you cannot achieve. Write out your immediate, intermediate, and distant goals in a clear and concise manner. State exactly what your goals are, and your timetable for accomplishing each of them. This will crystallize your dreams and cause you to develop a different style of life in which more power and energy are devoted to each day's activities. You will become a different person. Problems will appear to you in a different light, and you will find that you can focus on their solutions. A by-product of goal-setting is determination. It is already a force inside of you, and goal-setting releases the power of determination so that it can propel you to financial levels that were, before, beyond your reach.

Success in money management is not a windfall that comes to some and not to others because of fate, chance, or luck. Success in money management can be predicted (yes, *predicted*!), if you have a plan and if you follow that plan.

One more thing about goals: Set them now, and act on them now. Time can be your greatest ally in the achievement of your goals, especially your financial ones. If you have a sufficient amount of time, you will not need as much money to put to work. The less time you have, the more money it will take to achieve your goals. Don't waste this precious commodity.

IGNORANCE ABOUT MONEY

A third reason for failing is ignorance of what money must do to accomplish a financial goal. There is an educational void in our nation, and unfortunately we are raising a generation of financial illiterates. Even many college graduates cannot figure simple percentages. Our schools and universities often do a tremendous job of teaching the know-how of a vocation, but they are not teaching students the one subject that they will need to live well in our free enterprise system—*how to manage their money*. This vacuum is so great that the average couple cannot begin to confront the financial uncertainties and the multitude of choices they face in our complex society.

This lack of financial know-how is destroying the American Dream for many. And if Americans do not own and participate in the fruits of the free enterprise system, they might vote to destroy it. Any person will be against something that he doesn't understand, or that he feels he can't participate in. The destruction of this system, especially in this new era of prosperity and opportunity which it has made possible, would be one of the greatest tragedies ever to beset our world. We all realize that the free enterprise system is not perfect, but it is the best system yet devised for bringing the greatest good to the greatest number of people.

FAILURE TO LEARN OUR TAX LAWS

The fourth reason many fail to achieve financial independence is that they fail to learn and apply our tax laws. The only money you will ever get to spend at the grocery store is what the government lets you keep. Every investment you make must be carefully correlated with your tax bracket or you are making the wrong investment. You must learn to avoid taxes, not evade them (the difference could be ten years!). Learn to defer taxes, convert to classifications where the taxes are lower, and learn to think in terms of tax equivalents. Throughout this book you will find how to invest for "keepable" income.

Contrary to any headlines you may be reading, your total tax bill will not be cut appreciably this decade. Even with the much lauded so-called tax cut provided by the Economic Recovery Tax Act of 1981, taxes were increased, not decreased. They were increased less than they would have been had the act not been passed; however, each tax year since, Congress has taken back most of the cuts, so that taxes have gone up, not down. Social Security taxes alone have added a large amount to your tax bill. Another massive tax increase, which came in the guise of a mislabeled "windfall profits tax," was really a sales tax on gasoline, heating oil, and other petroleum products. It was called a tax on "windfall profits" to make it more palatable to a public ignorant of basic economics. Remember that the purpose of taxes is to pay for government expenditures. If the government spends more than it takes in (which it has been doing with great regularity), then you and I pay the difference in the form of inflation and the interest expense on the national debt.

Learn the rules of the money and tax game. You are playing a very serious game of financial survival, and this book is designed to teach you how to win.

THE WRONG KIND OF LIFE INSURANCE

The fifth reason that people fail to become financially independent is that they have been sold the wrong kind of life insurance. I say "sold," because if they had received sufficient information about the purpose of life insurance, and how each policy was put together, they would not have made the tragic mistakes that they have made.

When my first book was published, I requested that my publisher make Chapter 13—"Life Insurance, The Great National Consumer Fraud?"—available in booklet form. We estimate that over four million copies are now in circulation, and I have been delighted with the fantastic impact this chapter has made and is continuing to make on the life insurance industry. Thousands of families have had a better opportunity to achieve financial independence, and widows and orphans have been able to live in financial dignity rather than poverty because of this chapter. You will learn more about life insurance in Chapter 13 of this book.

FAILURE TO DEVELOP A WINNING MENTALITY

The sixth reason that people fail to win the money game is that they fail to develop a winning mentality. The demarcation line between success and failure is often very narrow. It can be crossed if the desire can be stimulated, if competent guidance is available, and if sufficient encouragement and incentive are provided. There are many vital parts to the psychology of winning, but some of the most important for financial independence are attitude, effort, lack of prejudice, persistence, enthusiasm, the ability to make a decision, and self-discipline.

Attitude is truly a magic word that you should place not only in your vocabulary but also in the very fiber of your being if you desire to be successful in the realm of money or in any other important area of your life. You will shape your own financial life by the attitudes that you hold each day. If you have a poor attitude about studying money management, you won't learn very much until you change that attitude. If you have an attitude of failure, you are defeated before you start. Look around you and study successful people. You will find that they go sailing through life from one success to another. These people have the attitude that they can accomplish whatever they set out to do. And because of this attitude, they do accomplish their goals and achieve some remarkable things in life.

Effort on your part is vital, because to become a good investor you must seriously apply your intelligence, use your ability to acquire knowledge, and give your attention to details and timing. If you cannot, will not, or do not have the ability to do these things successfully for yourself, don't take a distorted ego trip by not admitting that someone may be able to do something better than you can do it. Put the professionals to work for you.

Luck is something that I do not believe in. I have found that luck happens when preparedness and opportunity get together. If you are prepared, you will be lucky. You will find that the more you place yourself in the path of opportunity, the luckier you will become. In my own experience, I have found that I have never learned a new tax law or mastered a new investment concept that I haven't had a chance to use it for the benefit of my clients or myself almost immediately. A close and cherished friend of mine, who is a well-known and respected business consultant, once studied a particular company and bought shares of its stock while the firm was still in its infancy. These shares grew in value tremendously and made him a wealthy man. There are those who would scoff and say, "I should be so lucky." It wasn't luck. He was prepared.

Free Lunches do not exist along the road to financial independence. If I were to distill all the wisdom I have learned into nine words, they would be: There is no such thing as a free lunch. I have observed two drives where this is evident. One is the gambling instinct, which has driven many to failure in the market. Investing, properly approached with constant supervision, is in my opinion the safest long-term option for money. Speculation, on the other hand, can be risky. This desire for a free lunch can be seen working in the opposite way by those who leave their funds in a savings institution because they refuse to pay a brokerage commission or pay for investment advice on how best to put their money to work. The money that they save is often very costly in the end. When you make an investment decision, don't consider what it "costs." You don't care what it "costs." But you are truly concerned with what it *pays*.

Lack of prejudice is also an important attribute of the psychology of winning. We all have prejudices, but we should continuously work to rid ourselves of them. In counseling, I sometimes encounter a couple who seem to be saying to me, "Please don't confuse us with the facts." They don't want to know the truth, for the truth will not make them free, regardless of how carefully or intelligently it may be presented to them. They are prejudiced.

Persistence and follow-through are attributes most winners possess. If you begin a financial planning program and happen to experience a temporary setback, don't give up! I have observed this many times. A client will start a monthly investment program. If the market goes up after he starts the program, he will happily make his investment each month. But if the market goes down, he will abandon the program, no matter how hard I try to explain that he can actually benefit from long-term stock market fluctuations. There is absolutely no substitute for persistence.

Enthusiasm is contagious. If you have it in sufficient quantities, others will welcome you into their group. You will be more in touch with the needs and thinking of the people around you, and you can profit from the investment opportunities that will become obvious to you. I believe that I can forgive almost any shortcoming a person might have except lack of enthusiasm. It is the greatest enemy of a winning attitude, and is especially damaging in the acquisition of money.

The ability to make a decision is another characteristic of a winner in money matters. I have found over and over again that those who succeed in making large sums of money reach decisions very promptly and change them, if at all, very slowly. I have also found that people who fail to make money reach decisions very slowly, if at all, and change them frequently and quickly. Procrastination and indecision are twins. Pluck this grim pair out of your life before they bind you to the treadmill of financial failure.

Yesterday is past. Tomorrow is only a promise. Only today is legal tender. Only this moment of time is yours. Where you will be financially next year or ten years from now will depend upon the decisions that you make today, or on the decisions you don't make. Of the many studies I have made of successful people, near the top of the list of their characteristics is their ability to be decisive. Of the many studies of failures, at the top of the list of reasons for failure is procrastination. Study, think, plan, and *act!*

Self-Discipline must be practiced if you expect to be a winner in the money game. The secret of financial independence is not brilliance or luck, but the discipline to save a part of all you earn and to put it to work in shares of American industry, real estate, natural resources, communications, agriculture, tangible assets, and others. Self-discipline helps you to achieve goals. It is also a mental and physical process. It's your own visualization of your predetermined worthwhile goal of financial independence.

The successful people I know seem to find their accomplishments not too difficult and often surprisingly easy, simply because it seems so few are really trying. Winners look at life as a game—a game they expect to win, are prepared to win, desire to win, and know how to win. They have conscientiously nurtured and developed the habit of winning. They affirm and reaffirm to themselves each day that they are self-determined.

Overcaution is the enemy of success. It should be avoided whenever possible if you expect to be a winner. The person who takes no chances must usually take what is left over after the others have finished choosing. Overcaution is as bad as, if not worse than, lack of caution. Since life will always contain an element of chance, both should be avoided. Not to win is not a sin, but not to try is a tragedy. As Tom Peters and Bob Waterman point out in their book *In Search of Excellence,* the companies that are the most successful have a bias toward action. They are willing to take risks because they realize there is no reward without risk.

If you have never missed when investing, you haven't been in there trying. Or you have been holding your losers much too long for maximum profits. Play the money game well, but never safely. Avoid a life of no hits, no runs, no errors! The reason that many people are not successful investors is that they are afraid to do anything at all with their money. So they just leave it in a fixed "guaranteed" position for years, where the ravages of inflation and taxation destroy it. That's not playing it safe—that's just playing it dumb!

Knowledge is crucial to success. Think as you build your financial plan around your goals. Don't guess. Information in our communication society is available on almost any subject that you need to be informed about. So put as much accurate information together as possible, and then act on it.

Every financial plan is different. But, in general, there are two rules that always apply:

Build your capital and add to your nest egg while you are young. Remember to pay *yourself* first. And don't spend the nest egg. Use your accumulated assets for collateral for building a larger egg and then a larger one. Never consider any of your earnings on investments as spendable until you have reached your goal of financial independence. This is how to develop your money power. Your banker will welcome you with open arms if you have collateral to back your bankable ideas.

Be an owner and acquire equity as you invest. Own the thing that owns the thing. Own the assets that create wealth. If you are (or remain) a lender, you will receive only a portion of the earning power on your money. The owners of things will be the big winners, and this book will teach you how to be an owner of a vast array of assets in the New Economy.

Finally, as we continue together down the road toward financial independence for you and your family, you need to rid yourself of the old myth, if you have been flirting with it, that money is not important. Money *is* important—vitally important! It is just as important as the food it buys, the shelter it provides, the doctors' bills it pays, and the education it helps procure for you and your family. Money is important to you because you live in a civilized society. To split hairs and say that it is not as important as other things is just arguing for the exercise. Nothing—absolutely nothing—will take the place of money in areas in which money works.

What is money? Money is a medium of exchange and it is the harvest of your production. The amount of money you receive will always be in direct ratio to the need for what you do, your ability to do it, and the difficulty of replacing you. I am amazed at the number of people who tell me that they want money but don't want to take the time and trouble to qualify for it. Until they qualify for it, there's no way they can earn it.

It is important, however, to keep money in its proper place. It is vital to your well-being, but it is only a servant, a tool with which you can live better and enjoy more of the world around you. Granted that money is necessary to modern life, but you only need so much of it to live comfortably, securely, and well. Too much emphasis on money can reverse your whole life and make you the servant and money the master.

You want to have money and the things it buys. But you must also continually make sure that you haven't lost the things that money can't buy.

Summary

To accumulate enough money to achieve financial independence, all you need is a plan—a road map—and the courage, the knowledge, and self-discipline to arrive at your destination. There will no doubt be problems and setbacks as you make your journey. But nothing can stand in the way of your plan's successful completion if it is backed by persistence and determination.

APPLICATION

All the knowledge in the world will do you no good unless you apply it to your own particular circumstances. So at the end of each chapter I'll give you some questions to answer, some financial data to collect, and some specific tasks to perform.

May I suggest that you obtain a loose-leaf notebook and that you paste these words on the outside:

___(Your name)'s___ Progress Report Toward Financial Independence

Begin your notebook by listing the following objectives:

1. In the years ahead, my financial goal is to have a net worth of:

No. of Years	Net Worth
_____	_____
_____	_____
_____	_____
_____	_____

2. Books I will read to help me develop a positive mental attitude about money and sharpen my ability to detect opportunities to achieve financial independence:

_____

_____

_____

SUGGESTED READING LIST:

Psycho-Cybernetics, by Dr. Maxwell Maltz
Think and Grow Rich, by Napoleon Hill
Tough Minded Faith for Tender Hearted People, by Dr. Robert Schuller
Megatrends, by John Naisbitt

Chapter 2

The Dynamics of Money

Now that you understand the dynamics and great challenges of the New Economy, understand your role as an investor in this exciting new era in American history, know what you need to develop a winning mental attitude about money, and have placed money in its proper perspective, it is time to examine the major financial periods of your life and determine the steps necessary to accomplish your goal of financial independence.

The Financial Periods of Your Life

The financial lives of most people usually fall into three distinct periods: the "Learning Period," the "Earning Period," and the "Yearning" or "Golden Period" (depending on the decisions you make in your "Earning Period"). In terms of age, the three periods normally break down as follows: Learning Period—age 1 to 24 years; Earning Period—age 25 to 64 years; Yearning or Golden Period—age 65 to ?. Now let's closely examine each of these periods.

THE LEARNING PERIOD

You began to learn at birth, and I hope you will never cease to learn until you bid this world goodbye. Just the fact that you are reading this book indicates that you are still learning and willing to learn. Even though your formal learning period will probably be your first 25 years (depending upon your choice of vocation), in the New Economy, with its shifts from the short-term to the long-term approach, there will be a transformation in the way we look at education and vocational selection. The notion of lifelong learning will replace the popular short-term approach to education, whereby you went to school, graduated, and were finished. This long-range perspective may mean that you will need more of a generalist education. If you specialize too much, you could soon find your specialty obsolete. If you become a generalist, committed to lifelong education, you can be more flexible as times change.

If you are considering whether a college education is a good investment for yourself, your children, or your grandchildren, the answer is still yes. It will cost between $15,000 and $50,000 depending upon the choice of schools, vocation, and the number of years before entering college. But the investment can yield an excellent return. Studies show that a college graduate earns $250,000 to $400,000 more during his life than does a person with only a high school diploma. Time, money, and effort invested in education increase the productivity of the individual. This investment in human capital is similar to an investment in capital equipment for a plant that increases productivity, which in turn yields an increase in profits. And a college education can bring more than just financial rewards. The ability to think and to plan is stimulated in college. There are fewer divorces among college graduates. A college education can also add a greatly enlarged dimension to life. And it is an asset that cannot be confiscated through taxation or other means. So, one of the first investments you should make is an investment in education—an investment in yourself.

Education is preparation, and you must be prepared to win in this rapidly changing New Economy when opportunities arise for financial gain. Don't be like the man who stood in front of a wood-burning stove and said, "Give me some heat and I'll give you some wood." That's just not the nature of the wood-burning stove. The wood must come first. The same is true for preparation, so don't skimp on this important ingredient. Put adequate wood in your burner, and it will yield the warmth of financial security. However, never make the mistake of thinking that you can rest on your laurels of accumulated knowledge, for you are living in a dynamic world of change that makes it absolutely essential to obtain new information every day. I hope you did not end your education upon your graduation but that you have made a total commitment to continual and lifelong learning.

THE EARNING PERIOD

The second period of your financial life will be your earning period. This period will probably last for around 40 years, from age 25 to age 65. This is the time when you apply the knowledge that you learned previously to the vocation that you have selected to earn you a living. It is also the time when you acquire the new knowledge and experience that will increase your earning ability. Have you ever thought of how much money will come your way during those 40 earning years, or have you just thought of your earnings as so much money a month? Add it up and you will see that you will earn a tremendous amount of money during this period. Even if you never earn more than $525 a month, over a quarter of a million dollars will pass your way. If you earn as much as $1,050 a month, over half a million dollars will pass your way. And if you earn as much as $2,500 a month, over a million dollars will pass your way during this period. Just examine the chart below.

As you can see from the chart, there is no question that a considerable amount of money will come your way. The problem with most

MONTHLY INCOME	10 YEARS	20 YEARS	30 YEARS	40 YEARS
$ 500	$ 60,000	$120,000	$ 180,000	$ 240,000
600	72,000	144,000	216,000	288,000
800	96,000	192,000	288,000	384,000
1,000	120,000	240,000	360,000	480,000
1,500	180,000	360,000	540,000	720,000
2,000	240,000	480,000	720,000	960,000
2,500	300,000	600,000	900,000	1,200,000
3,000	360,000	720,000	1,080,000	1,440,000

people is how to keep some of it from passing through their fingers and have it available to invest toward their financial independence.

Let me share with you a very simple secret for the accumulation of wealth. The secret has only ten words in it and is so simple that you will be tempted to discard it. But if you remember it and put it to use, it will be of great value to you for the remainder of your life. The secret is this: *A part of all I earn is mine to keep.* Now you may be tempted to say, "Everything I earn is mine to keep," but that is not exactly so. It belongs to the IRS, the grocer, the mortgage company, the church, and so on. If you were to place in a line, in the order of their importance to you, all those whom you wanted to receive a portion of your paycheck, would you place yourself at the head of the line? Is that where you are putting yourself now? If you are like so many others, you have put yourself at the end of the line, trying to save what is left over and finding that your ability to spend up to and beyond your income is utterly amazing. You must learn to pay yourself *first* or, if not first, at least along with the others. If you were to save one-tenth of all you earned every year for ten years, you would have accumulated a whole year's salary. And if you put that money to work, before long you would have much more working for you.

Are you a good steward of your money? In 1748 Benjamin Franklin wrote, "Money is of a prolific, generating nature. Money can beget money, and its offspring can beget more." His was a definition and practical explanation of the nature of money and one that can be of great value to you. Franklin's words have an almost biblical ring to them, an echo of the story of the talents in the Book of Matthew that makes us aware that we are required to be good stewards of money. I firmly believe that every dollar that comes your way comes there for a purpose. A portion of that dollar should be spent for the necessities of life, a portion for luxuries, a portion should be given away, and a portion should be invested for tomorrow's goods and services. I am also thoroughly convinced that you are the steward of every dollar that comes your way; and if you are not a good steward of that money, it will be taken away from you.

THE YEARNING PERIOD OR GOLDEN YEARS

The third period in your life will be your retirement years. These will either be your "yearning" years or your "golden" years, depending on the financial decisions you make during your "earning" years.

If you are a male age 65, you will probably live to be around 79 years of age. If you are a female age 65, you can probably look forward to living well into your eighties. My oldest client was in her nineties when I was finally able to convince her to stop investing for growth!

Will this period of your life just take care of itself? The answer is *no*. The future belongs to those who prepare for it; and, unfortunately, tragically few are preparing! Why, in a nation with a high per capita income and unrivaled prosperity, do the vast majority of our citizens reach age 65 without having made adequate preparations for retiring in financial dignity? Perhaps they, and you, have been lulled into a false sense of security by the cozy sound of the words "Social Security." You may find out all too soon, as so many have, that it should have been called "Social *In*security." But by the time you make that discovery, it may be far too late to alter your financial fate.

Actually, Social Security was never meant to provide you or anyone else with financial independence. It was enacted in the midst of the Great Depression of the 1930s to prevent mass destitution. If you can count on it at all, which I don't recommend, treat it as a very minuscule part of your financial plan. The probability of it making a meaningful contribution to your retirement is slim. It may surprise you to learn that when you reach the age to qualify for Social Security benefits, if your income from it and other sources is insufficient for you to live in financial dignity, thus making it necessary for you to continue to work, then you will have to forfeit part of your Social Security benefits until you reach age 70.

The startling fact about Social Security is that, with the passing of each year, the chances that it will be able to provide for even a fraction of your financial needs when you retire are becoming less and less. Congress has as much as admitted its own true estimate of Social Security's long-term prospects by passing laws enabling you to provide for your own retirement needs through tax-deferred Individual Retirement Accounts (IRA's) and other retirement plans. The message is clear: "Don't blame us if Social Security is no longer in existence when you retire. We made it possible for you to have your *own* retirement plan." This move is another trend of the New Economy as we move each year from dependence on institutions to self-reliance. You must be aware of this trend and prepare to move with it in the years ahead.

You may be able to decide how long you will work, or it may be decided for you. But the decision about how long you will live is not in your hands. Present-day medical science is getting so good at prolonging our lives that we now hear people speaking of the "graying of America." Medical science may be adding years to your life, but it is still up to you to add some life to those years. You must be prepared to take care of yourself financially, and, like it or not, money will be a necessity. It will not in itself bring happiness, but it will give you options in life you won't have without it. Until you are financially independent, you are an economic slave. No matter what our ages, slavery does not bring the self-esteem each of us must possess.

Retiring in Financial Dignity

Since one of your objectives is to have sufficient funds to retire in financial dignity, you might ask how much it will take? I really don't know, but let's see if we can make some intelligent projections.

The amount of money you will need at retirement time will depend upon the standard of living you wish to maintain, the number of years before you retire, the destruction that inflation will have brought to the purchasing power of money, your ability and willingness to apply what you will learn in this book to produce the maximum income and growth during retirement, and the number of years you will live.

To get some idea of the amount that may be required, let's begin with what you would need if you were retiring today, and then adjust your figures by what you think the future rate of inflation will be. Nobody really knows what the effects of inflation will be in the future. Inflation could subside with the other economic trends of the New Economy. But it is a judgment you must make for yourself. Table 1-1 (p. 42) can help you relate that judgment to dollars.

Read across the top of the chart and find the rate of inflation you think it is safe to assume. Then follow the column down until you find the line that corresponds with the number of years left until you retire. There you will find how many dollars it will take then to buy the same amount of groceries one dollar buys today. For example, assume that you would need $2,000 per month if you were retiring today, that you are age 45, that you plan to retire in 20 years at age

TABLE 1-1. ADDITIONAL INCOME NEEDED (IN DOLLARS) AT RETIREMENT, WITH VARIOUS INFLATION RATES

YEARS UNTIL RETIREMENT	5%	8%	10%	12%	15%
10	1.63	2.16	2.59	3.11	4.05
11	1.71	2.33	2.85	3.48	4.65
12	1.80	2.52	3.14	3.90	5.35
13	1.89	2.72	3.45	4.36	6.15
14	1.98	2.94	3.80	4.89	7.08
15	2.08	3.17	4.18	5.47	8.14
16	2.18	3.43	4.60	6.13	9.36
17	2.29	3.70	5.05	6.87	10.77
18	2.41	4.00	5.56	7.69	12.38
19	2.53	4.32	6.12	8.61	14.23
20	2.65	4.66	6.73	9.65	16.37
21	2.79	5.03	7.40	10.80	18.82
22	2.93	5.44	8.14	12.10	21.64
23	3.07	5.87	8.95	13.55	24.89
24	3.23	6.34	9.85	15.18	28.63
25	3.39	6.85	10.83	17.00	32.92
26	3.56	7.40	11.92	19.04	37.86
27	3.73	7.99	13.11	21.32	43.54
28	3.92	8.63	14.42	23.88	50.07
29	4.12	9.32	15.86	26.75	57.58
30	4.32	10.06	17.45	29.96	66.22
31	4.54	10.87	19.19	33.56	76.14
32	4.76	11.74	21.11	37.58	87.57
33	5.00	12.68	23.23	42.09	100.70
34	5.25	13.69	25.55	47.14	115.80
35	5.52	14.79	28.10	52.80	133.18

65, and that you think inflation will average 5 percent. Find the 5 percent column, follow it down to the line for 20 years, and find your retirement factor, 2.65. Now we adjust: $2,000 × 2.65 = $5,300. That is the amount you would need per month in 20 years to obtain the same housing, food, and clothing as you do with $2,000 today.

However, inflation will probably not cooperate with you by stopping when you retire, so you should also plan for an additional amount to cover continued inflation throughout your retirement years.

How much capital will you need in order to produce $5,300 per month for your retirement? Shall we use a conservative 6 percent yield? If so, you will need $1,060,000 of capital [$5,300 × 200 (12 months ÷ .06 yield) = $1,060,000]. At an 8 percent yield, you can reduce this amount to $795,000; at 12 percent to $530,000; at 18 percent to $353,333; and at 24 percent to $265,000. That's a lot of capital, but before you become discouraged, remember that you have 20 years before you need these funds for retirement. And if you decide to use a portion of your principal each month during retirement, this amount can be further reduced. Remember that although there can be some risk in using a portion of your income-producing capital, there's nothing sacred about principal. The important thing is that you have provided yourself with financial dignity and security upon retirement and that you and it come out together.

SAVINGS REQUIRED TO RETIRE IN FINANCIAL DIGNITY

As you build your principal, how much will you need to save each month if you are averaging, say, a 6 percent yield on your investment? Look at Table 1-2 (p. 44). If your goal is $300,000 and you begin saving when you are age 25, you can reach it by saving just $153 per month. If you wait until you are age 40, you will have to put in $429 a month. If you put your money to work at 12 percent, and shame on you if you do no better after applying what you will learn in this book, you can reduce the amount you must invest by more than half. Or better, you can increase your goal.

As you can see, time is a powerful ally in the accomplishment of your goal, but use it to your advantage and don't try to reach your goal too fast, as tempting as it may be. But you will be tempted, for we live in an age of "instants." We drink instant coffee and eat instant pudding, take instant pictures, make instant withdrawals from our bank accounts and have instant replays on our television sets. But don't make the mistake of trying to carry this over into your money world. It takes *time* to accumulate a living estate. You and many others may have difficulty accepting this fact of life. Many have adopted an attitude of impatience, craving instant gratification, perhaps at the cost of serenity and physical and mental well-being. On the other hand, impatience to get things done deserved much of the credit for the achievements of Americans in building the wealthiest

TABLE 1-2. **MONTHLY SAVINGS NEEDED AT 6% INTEREST (COMPOUNDED ANNUALLY) TO ATTAIN PREDETERMINED AMOUNT OF CAPITAL**

AGE NOW	YEARS TO RETIRE- MENT	MONTHS TO RETIRE- MENT	*Desired Amount*			
			$200,000	**$300,000**	**$500,000**	**$1,000,000**
25	40	480	$ 102	$ 153	$ 255	$ 510
30	35	420	140	210	350	700
35	30	360	198	297	495	990
40	25	300	286	429	715	1430
45	20	240	426	639	1065	2130
50	15	180	674	1011	1685	3370
55	10	120	1192	1788	2980	5960

nation in the world. But time is important in building an estate, and as a matter of fact it is the first ingredient of my formula for financial independence.

Formula for Financial Independence

I have used this formula for many years and it has been extremely valuable to me and my clients:

Time + Money + American Free Enterprise =
The Opportunity to Become Financially Independent

Time—Ingredient Number One. If you are young and have only a small amount of money to invest, don't despair. You possess one of the most important ingredients for financial independence—*time*. It doesn't take very much money to add up to a tidy sum *if* you have time for it to grow. Savings of just $30 per month started at age 25 can equal $90 per month started at age 35, $300 at age 45, and $1,275 per month started at age 55. If we calculate the importance of time in reverse, savings of $50 per month for 10 years at 12 percent will add up to a sum that is less than savings of $25 a month for 15 years.

Perhaps you are fortunate enough to already have a lump sum of $10,000. Let's look at the difference time makes in the amount of capital you will accumulate (exclusive of taxes):

YEARS	AT 12%
10	$ 31,058
20	96,462
30	299,599
40	930,509

These figures point to the importance of starting as early as you can to reach your predetermined goal of financial independence. I hope you are granted a large amount of the first ingredient of my formula, and that you learn at an early age the importance of putting each day to maximum use.

Money—Ingredient Number Two. The second ingredient of my formula for financial independence is money. You have it every payday, or you have acquired it through previous paydays of your own or your industrious and generous ancestors. Your next challenge is to put this money to work for yourself as hard as you had to work to get it. To become financially independent, you must save regularly and make your money grow. Unfortunately, I observe many people who save and let savings institutions grow, building magnificent skyscrapers that add impressively to our skylines.

American Free Enterprise—Ingredient Number Three. This brings us to the third ingredient of my formula for financial independence. By investing your money in American free enterprise, you can benefit directly from the enormous productivity, growth, and wealth of the New Economy. The ultimate purpose of this book is to provide you with the knowledge and the tools to do just that—to teach you how you can own your share of American industry, energy, real estate, communication systems technology, agriculture, and a wide variety of other viable investments.

Rate of Return on Your Investments

You have seen how important time is in the accomplishment of your goal. Now let's introduce another important factor, the rate of return. The rate of return that you receive on your funds will be determined by how skillfully you, or the professional adviser who helps you, are in putting your money to work. Let's look at the difference an additional 5 percent per year return can make in your results:

$100 Per Month Invested at 10% and 15%

YEARS	AT 10%	AT 15%	DIFFERENCE
10	$ 21,037	$ 28,018	$ 6,981
20	75,602	141,372	65,770
30	217,131	599,948	382,817
40	584,222	2,455,144	1,870,922

Are you amazed at the difference an additional 5 per cent can make? One of the best ways to obtain a graphic picture of the importance of the rate of return is to study compound interest tables. Compound interest tables are fascinating. In my opinion, the "Eighth Wonder of the World" is not the Astrodome in Houston, Texas, but compound interest. Learn to use Tables 1 through 6 in the Appendix and you will find them to be of enormous help in reaching your financial goal. Take a moment now to study them and you will be surprised to find some real jewels of information. And I will help you apply the information so you won't have to go it alone.

LUMP-SUM INVESTMENT

Appendix Table 1 shows you how much a $10,000 lump sum will grow over the years at various rates of return. If you haven't yet saved $10,000, just keep dropping zeros until you've reached your category. If you are fortunate enough to have $100,000, just add a zero. For example, if you have $10,000 to invest for a goal that is 20 years away and you can average 12 percent on your money, you will have $96,462 when that time arrives, exclusive of taxes. If you have 30 years, that $10,000 will grow to $299,599. In 40 years it will be

$930,509. Note that this last figure is almost a million dollars, produced from an original investment of only $10,000 by mixing the ingredients of time and compound interest to make your money work for you.

THE MONTHLY INVESTMENT PLAN

Let's now assume that you don't have a lump sum, but can invest just $1,200 per year (or an average of $100 per month). Appendix Table 2 shows that if you average 12 percent over a 20-year period, your results will be $96,838. In 30 years, $324,351, and in 40 years, $1,030,970. As you can see, the secret of financial independence really isn't brilliance or luck, but rather the discipline to save a portion, no matter how small, of all you earn and put it to work intelligently.

Perhaps your timetable does not fit into neat little five- and ten-year segments, and the money you have to invest is not in blocks of a $10,000 lump sum or $100 per month. In the Appendix you will find tables that give you the necessary numbers to calculate a lump-sum investment at various rates of return from 2½ to 15 percent and from one to fifty years (see Table 5) and also tables that give you goals that can be reached by investing a variety of amounts on a regular monthly basis (see Table 6).

What Can You Do with a Dollar?

There are only three things you can do with a dollar: spend, loan, or own. If you decide to spend your dollar, I hope you have a good time, but you have just cut off our conversation. The only money that I can help you invest is the money that you decide to keep. If you decide not to spend it now but to spend it later (not ever to spend it at all is just too cruel a thought!), then there are just two things you can elect to do with your dollar—loan or own. You may "loan" it to a savings institution, thus placing it in what is commonly called a "guaranteed" fixed position. Or you may elect to place your dollars in a position so that you can "own." You may own shares of American industry, real estate, commodities, energy, communication systems, gems, rare stamps, art objects, and so on. Since "owning" is the most profitable way to invest your hard-earned dollars, we will explore the many ways you can own as we proceed through this book.

The Rule of 72

The Rule of 72 can be extremely useful and valuable to you as an investor, yet I have a degree in economics and finance and I was never taught this rule in college. The Rule of 72 gives you the answer to the question of how long it will take to double your money, or to make $1 become $2, at various rates of return. The rule tells us that if you obtain 1 percent on your money, it will take 72 years for $1 to become $2. If you obtain 1.3 percent, it will take you 55.4 years. (You may be saying to yourself that no one in this enlightened society would loan at that rate, but when you read Chapter 13 you may find that you are doing just that.) If you obtain 4 percent, it will take 18 years. If you obtain 6 percent, it will take 12 years. If you obtain 12 percent, it will take 6 years; at 18 percent, 4 years; and at 24 percent (which is quite possible, by the way) it takes just three years.

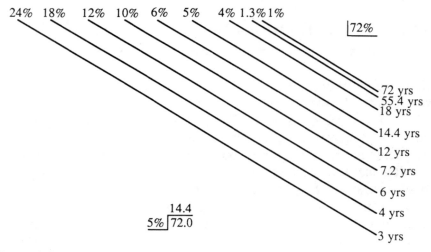

Figure 1.1.

As you can clearly see, it does make a difference how well you invest your money.

Is It Safer to Loan or Own?

So what is the "safest" thing to do with your money, "loan" or "own"? In the past, has it generally been safer to "loan" your money to a savings institution at 4 to 6 percent (or for brief periods of time at 18 percent), or to "own" shares of American industry, real estate, and energy with the hopes of *averaging* 15 to 40 percent or even higher? We shall take an in-depth look in this book at the ways that have truly been the "safest" long-term approaches to money management. Suffice it to say here that if you have to wait 18 years at 4 percent or 12 years at 6 percent for $1 to become $2, you have lost the fight, because inflation has doubled your cost of living in just the past 10 years, to say nothing of your loss through the tax bite. Even at 10 percent, you were losing the battle, just like the little frog that was trying to hop out of the well. Every time he hopped up one foot, he slid back two. If you ignore change, inflation, and taxes, then your money exercises may prove to parallel those of the little frog, but without the lovely princess to give you the kiss that miraculously turns you into an affluent prince!

Clarifying Stability vs. Safety

One of the most common mistakes I see people make in the investment of their money is to confuse two very similar words that have very different meanings. These two words are "stability" and "safety." Stability is the return of the same number of dollars at a point of time in the future. Safety is the return of the same amount of food, clothing, and shelter. You can be "stable" and be far from "safe." This book is dedicated to helping you become a *safe* investor.

Reaching for a $300,000 Estate

I encourage my clients to have as their very minimum goal a $300,000 estate. I must admit, though, that as soon as they reach it, I raise the ante. Although your goal should be a minimum of this amount, the younger you are the higher your goal must be, because inflation will continue to erode your purchasing power. A 6 percent yield on $300,000 is only $1,500 per month, and that's not exactly living on Easy Street today. A 12 percent yield gives you $3,000 per month.

Let's assume that you can average a 12 percent total return on your investments (this book should help you to far exceed this rate). How much would you have to save each month at that rate to arrive at a $300,000 estate by age 65? If you begin at age 25, it will require $30 a month; at age 35 you will need to invest $90 per month; at 45 the sum is $300 a month; and if you wait until you are 55 years of age, it will require an investment of $1,275 per month. Lump sums required at these respective ages to reach $300,000 are $3,225, $10,020, $31,101, and $96,501. As you can see, time and your rate of return are two of your greatest allies for reaching your goal of financial independence.

Your Pennies Can Become Millions

It is possible that you have heard this vivid example of compounding before, but I feel it is prudent to repeat it. Let's assume that you had a choice of working 35 days with a pay of $1,000 per day, or working for a penny the first day and doubling the amount each day for 35 days. Which job offer would you take?

If you took the first choice, at the end of the thirty-fifth day you would have received $35,000. What would you have received if you had made the second choice? You would have received $339,456,652.80! As you can see, one penny compounded at 100 percent per day produces over a third of a billion dollars in just 35 days. I realize that this is an exaggerated example, but your rate of earnings is very important in your continuing quest for financial independence.

You might be interested to learn, by the way, that most of the extraordinary figure in the above example was created during the last five days of compounding. Even here, time proves to be a crucial element. In this book you will get to know and fully comprehend rates of return and how to compound your capital through prudent, well-planned investments.

Summary

You and I have now come a long way toward determining what your goal must be to attain financial independence. We have had to look at some charts and tables in order to give you a real perspective of your challenge, but also to provide you with the knowledge you need to be able to win the money game. You have learned that it will be necessary for you to save for the future so that you can fulfill your obligation to yourself, to your family, and to society. But you have also learned that you already have all the requirements for financial independence, and that you don't have to go it alone. Your dollars can have fantastic earning power, and it is up to you to become informed and knowledgeable about how you can invest those dollars in order to reap the highest returns possible.

APPLICATION

1. Source or sources of income I will depend on at age 65: _____

2. Number of years before I plan to retire: _____

3. Monthly income I would need if I were retiring today: _____

4. The average rate of inflation I feel it is safe to project between now and

   retirement: _____

5. If we have this rate of inflation, I will need $_____ per month (use Table 1-1, p. 42).

6. If I average the following rates of return, I will need to save per month:

Rate of Return	Save per month
_____%	$_____
_____%	$_____
_____%	$_____

7. My minimum objective for rate of growth on my investments is _____%

8. Amount I can put to work today: (a) lump sum $ _____;

(b) per month $ _____

Inflation and the New Economy

Inflation Is Still with Us

No matter what you may read or hear about the demise and disappearance of inflation in our economy, the truth is that this menace is still lurking in the shadows, poised and ready to strike again with full force at any time. Even though the government reports that the inflation rate is now somewhere above 3 percent, many economists feel that the "real" inflation rate may be around 10 percent or more, depending on whom you talk to or whose report you read. Raymond Devoe publishes the *Devoe Report,* which includes his "Trivia Index." This index calculates the median price increase for some 45 different small items most Americans buy regularly, such as cigarettes, gum, canned soft drinks, dry cleaning, and magazines. The index has risen 21.6 percent in the past two years, or 4.32 times the official 5 percent gain of the consumer price index. Many feel that the consumer price index includes many commodities that the average American rarely purchases and that these items tend to keep the government index low, whereas other barometers such as the

"Trivia Index" may be more reflective of the "real" inflation rate today.

In this chapter, we will take an unemotional look at inflation and the devastating path it has cut across the face of the United States, bringing havoc to many a financial plan. In order to deal with this situation, you must learn how to put inflation to work *for* you instead of against you.

There are four prime reasons you must learn to invest:

1. To put inflation to work for you
2. To increase your income
3. To make your capital grow
4. To learn to turn your tax liabilities into assets

Inflation—Be Its Victim or Its Beneficiary

I like to think of inflation as the clever pickpocket who lies in wait for us all. Through the efforts of the Reagan administration, its rate has decreased; but the direction is still upward, even if it has been slowed to a decreasing rate. Four to six percent inflation is admittedly better than 15 percent, but even at a 6 percent rate our cost of living will double in twelve years.

Accept inflation as a fact of life and make your decisions about money accordingly. If I can leave only one thought with you after you have read this book, it is this: Deal with life as it truly is and not the way you wish it were. This chapter will give you the facts about inflation. This book will enlighten you as to ways that you can make inflation work for you rather than against you. There is probably nothing in your economic life that can make as much money for you as inflation if you understand how it works, learn to embrace it rather than fear it, and harness its energy to work for you.

Inflation does not destroy wealth. It does not reduce the number of houses that builders can build, the amount of wheat that farmers can produce, or the number of telephones that can be installed. Inflation redistributes wealth—it takes wealth from those who do not understand how it works and gives it to those who do. Inflation takes from the ignorant and gives to the well-informed. You will be either its victim or its beneficiary; it will make you a winner or a loser. The choice is yours. It is much more fun being a winner. All you need to do is recognize that inflation is a fact of your life—an economic force in the world in which you live—and that you must protect yourself against it or suffer its dire consequences. Inflation has been your constant companion since the day you were born, and from all indications it will continue to be with you for the remainder of your life. This problem does not belong to the United States alone but has been felt worldwide. Tolstoy chronicled that every civilized nation that has ever existed has experienced the ravages of inflation.

Why Do We Have Inflation?

Your government has been the chief cause of inflation. Inflation came about because the government felt "obligated" to give you all the little "extras" of life that you wanted, such as full employment and health insurance that many wouldn't buy for themselves. The word "entitlement" has been a favorite with politicians for the past ten years. They have equated entitlement to being "entitled to" support from the cradle to the grave, often without any relationship to effort on the part of the recipients, just because they were fortunate enough to have been born in the United States.

If our forefathers were writing the Bill of Rights today, after having lived in our environment for a number of years, they might very well add a clause to the bill saying that every person is entitled to a job. Before World War II, this was not a commonly held belief. Before then, prices often went up, but they also went down rather quickly, so in effect prices remained essentially stable. Now, many believe in their right to job security regardless of changes that have occurred in our economy. They are supported by the philosophy of a host of congressional members that any problem can be solved if enough money can be thrown in its direction. These concepts have caused inflation to rampage, not only here but abroad, for we have exported this philosophy.

The year after World War II ended, Congress passed the "full employment act," which declared that our government would vigorously promote both price stability and full employment. Even a college freshman with one semester of Economics 101 should know that those are two inconsistent goals. The Employment Act of 1946 was to be the embodiment of Utopia, and brilliant government administrators would do a balancing act whereby high employment rates could be generated by accepting higher inflation. But what has the implementation of this theory wrought? We have found that employment that results from inflation lasts for only a short period of time, and in order to restimulate employment, inflation must again be accelerated. Always remember that full employment brings the politicians more votes than does licking inflation; therefore the majority of politicians will opt for full employment.

Put Inflation in Perspective

If you will learn to substitute the word "dilution" every time you see the word "inflation," you will come to have a better understanding of inflation. If the government printed and circulated a million dollars for every million already in circulation, twice as many dollars would be chasing the same amount of goods and services, so they would rise to twice their original price. The true value of goods and services has not risen, but rather the value of the currency has been cut in half by doubling its quantity—hence dilutions have occurred.

To put these thoughts in perspective, let's think of bread as just one example of what has happened. In 1940, you could buy ten loaves of bread for $1. By 1950 you could buy only six loaves. By 1960, you could buy only four, by 1970 only three, and by 1980 only one. How many loaves will your dollar buy today? It is the same dollar, but it has lost the major portion of its only value. If I can do nothing else for you in this book but help you to convert your thinking from dollars into bread, I will have done you an immense favor. I warn you, it is an emotional transition that only a few can make. If you can make it, you will be in the minority; but remember, it is only the minority that will become financially independent.

Between 1940 and 1985, the dollar held its own in only two years, and then by less than 1 percent. Not even a professional gambler would bet against those odds. Yet, if you are holding a dollar today, you are betting against those odds. If you are a saver, placing your savings in a "guaranteed" position, you are a gambler, and if the past is any indication of the future, you are "guaranteed" to lose!

An Investment Recommended by Many

What if I were to say to you, "I want to recommend a stock for your serious consideration. I know that its record has not been very good, but I have faith that it will improve. It was selling for $100 in 1955; by 1960 it had dropped to $96; by 1965 to $88; by 1970 to $79; by 1975 to $50; and by 1980 it was $35. Today it is at $25, but don't let that discourage you from investing in it." If I were to make such a "buy" recommendation to you, what would you say to me? Before you say, "You've got to be kidding!" I want you to know that this investment is recommended by most of our state and national banks, by all of our savings and loan institutions, by all of the nation's life insurance companies that sell cash surrender value policies, by your city, and by the federal government itself. What is this investment? It is the U.S. dollar! Figure 3-1 will illustrate to you what has happened to the purchasing power of the U.S. dollar over the last few decades.

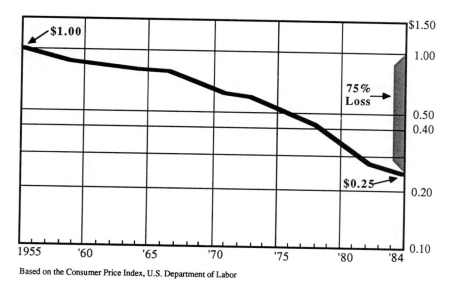

Based on the Consumer Price Index, U.S. Department of Labor

Figure 3-1. *Purchasing power of the U.S. dollar, 1955–1984.*

If "guaranteed" dollars are recommended as a good, "safe" investment for you by banks, savings institutions, and insurance companies that sell cash surrender value life insurance, you can bet they never want a "guaranteed" dollar for themselves. They want to "guarantee" your principal, "guarantee" your rate of return, and "guarantee" that your dollar will work for *them*—usually harder than it works for you. You will receive a "guarantee" that you can always get back each deflating dollar you have placed with them (excluding "your" savings account with the life insurance company). You are also guaranteed that you will never receive any more than that dollar, plus any compound interest you may have left with them, regardless of how much your money has earned for the institution to which you loaned it, and regardless of what the cost of living has become.

Inflation averaged 2 percent in the 1950s, 2.3 percent in the 1960s, 6.1 percent in the first half of the 1970s, 8.8 percent in the latter part of the 1970s, reached an intermittent high of 19 percent in the early 1980s, and then slowed during the Reagan years. If, however, you assume an annual inflation rate of 7 percent in the 1980s, Table 3-1 shows you what you will have to earn in 1990 to keep pace with what you had to earn in 1970 and 1980 in order to maintain the same standard of living.

TABLE 3-1. **INFLATION'S EFFECT ON INCOMES**

IF YOU HAD THIS INCOME IN 1970	YOU NEEDED THIS MUCH TO BE AS WELL OFF IN 1980	YOU WILL NEED THIS MUCH (IF INFLATION RUNS AT THE SAME PACE) IN 1990
$ 5,000	$ 10,676	$ 25,697
7,500	16,188	39,188
10,000	22,552	55,941
20,000	34,349	87,708
25,000	59,855	188,689
30,000	73,171	148,658
35,000	86,036	204,795
40,000	98,356	231,024
50,000	121,556	280,417
100,000	221,677	493,574

SOURCE: *U.S. News and World Report,* July 14, 1980.

What Is Ahead for Inflation?

What will actually happen with inflation during the remainder of the 1980s? Much depends on the rate of federal spending over the next few years. If government spending as a percentage of our nation's economic output (our Gross National Product) is reduced, then there is hope that inflation will moderate. If this does not occur, then the inflationary spiral will continue.

We must watch Congress and the President closely for signs of which direction inflation will take. If inflation should average 4 percent, before you rejoice you should realize that in 18 years you will lose one-half of the only value your money has—its purchasing power. At 7 percent you will lose it in ten years and at 12 percent in just six years. If we continue to have inflation, one of the things you will want to avoid is "guarantees," for the "guaranteed" dollar can be a guaranteed loss. You'll especially want to avoid guaranteed monthly incomes of annuities and endowment policies.

Have you read advertisements for endowment policies that proclaim "an income that you can never outlive," and then go on to promise you an income of $1,000 a month for as long as you live? Let's assume that we can keep inflation at an average rate of 8 percent. What future dollars would you need to equal the current purchasing power of $1,000? ("A" on Table 3-2, p. 60.) Or looking at it another way, what will be the future purchasing power of $1,000? ("B" on Table 3-2.)

How to Obtain a Real Income of 2 Percent

If you were to say to me, "Venita, I think I deserve a 'real' income after income taxes and inflation of 2 percent," how much would you have to obtain on your investment to reach what you have decided you deserve? My answer to you would be influenced by two factors: the rate of inflation and your tax bracket. Table 3-3 (p. 61) will probably be an eye-opener to you. As you will see, if we have inflation at 6 percent and you are in a 20 percent tax bracket (I jokingly tell my

TABLE 3-2. **8% INFLATION**

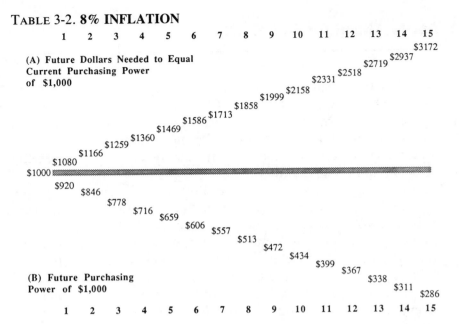

| | 1 | 2 | 3 | 4 | 5 | 6 | 7 | 8 | 9 | 10 | 11 | 12 | 13 | 14 | 15 |

(A) Future Dollars Needed to Equal
Current Purchasing Power
of $1,000

$3172 (15)
$2937 (14)
$2719 (13)
$2518 (12)
$2331 (11)
$2158 (10)
$1999 (9)
$1858 (8)
$1713 (7)
$1586 (6)
$1469 (5)
$1360 (4)
$1259 (3)
$1166 (2)
$1080 (1)
$1000
$920 (1)
$846 (2)
$778 (3)
$716 (4)
$659 (5)
$606 (6)
$557 (7)
$513 (8)
$472 (9)
$434 (10)
$399 (11)
$367 (12)
$338 (13)
$311 (14)
$286 (15)

(B) Future Purchasing
Power of $1,000

| | 1 | 2 | 3 | 4 | 5 | 6 | 7 | 8 | 9 | 10 | 11 | 12 | 13 | 14 | 15 |

seminar audiences that they're at least in a 20 percent tax bracket if they're warm!), you must receive 10 percent on your money. If you are in a 30 percent bracket and we have inflation at 7 percent, you must earn 12.9 percent. In a 40 percent bracket and at 8 percent inflation, you must earn 16.7 percent; and in a 50 percent bracket and 9 percent inflation, you must earn 22 percent. As you can see, you really have to run very fast today to be 2 percent ahead.

The New Math of Inflation

In an inflationary economy, inflation rewards those who owe money, not those who pay cash. I am not talking about plastic money—your Visa, MasterCard, or American Express card. Never charge anything you can't pay for in thirty days, and never borrow for your daily living or luxuries. Only borrow long-term for investing—never for spending—and only if you can sell your investment for as much as you paid for it. Always be solvent.

TABLE 3-3. **RATE OF RETURN REQUIRED TO PRODUCE A "REAL" 2% INCOME AFTER INCOME TAXES AND INFLATION**

INCOME TAX RATE	Inflation Rate										
	2%	3%	4%	5%	6%	7%	8%	9%	10%	11%	12%
50%	8.0	10.0	12.0	14.0	16.0	18.0	20.0	22.0	24.0	26.0	28.0
40%	6.7	8.3	10.0	11.6	13.3	15.0	16.7	18.4	20.0	21.7	23.3
30%	5.7	7.1	8.6	10.0	11.4	12.9	14.3	15.7	17.1	18.6	20.0
20%	5.0	6.3	7.5	8.8	10.0	11.3	12.5	13.8	15.0	16.3	17.5

INSTRUCTIONS:
1. First select the column that matches the inflation rate (2% to 12%).
2. Second, select the line that matches the income tax rate (20% to 50%).
3. The number that appears at the intersection of the column and line indicates the rate of return necessary to offset the combined effect of income taxes and inflation. (For example, if you assume inflation will be 6%, a 50% taxpayer must earn a 16% rate of return per annum in order to show a 2% real growth after adjusting for both income taxes and inflation. At 10% it goes to 24%.)

Let's look at the balance sheet of three families and see which family was the most prudent in an inflationary economy:

The Anderson family's balance sheet looks like this:

Cash	$10,000	Mortgage	$ 5,000
Home	10,000	Net Worth	15,000

Net worth is the difference between your assets and your liabilities and is a measure of how rich you are.

Now let's assume that prices double as they have over the past ten years. The Andersons' balance sheet will now look like this:

Cash	$10,000	Mortgage	$ 5,000
Home	20,000	Net Worth	25,000

The Andersons' net worth has now increased from $15,000 to $25,000, which at first glance appears good; however, their net worth has not doubled as prices did. Therefore, this family has fallen behind in the inflation race. Their wealth or purchasing power has been reduced by inflation.

Now let's examine the Barton family's balance sheet:

| Cash | $ 5,000 | Mortgage | $ 5,000 |
| Home | 10,000 | Net Worth | 10,000 |

A doubling of prices has this effect on their balance sheet:

| Cash | $ 5,000 | Mortgage | $ 5,000 |
| Home | 20,000 | Net Worth | 20,000 |

The Bartons have held their own. They have exactly kept pace with inflation.

Now let's look at the Calloway family's balance sheet:

| Cash | $ 3,000 | Mortgage | $10,000 |
| Home | 12,000 | Net Worth | 5,000 |

When prices doubled, the Calloways' net worth looked like this:

| Cash | $ 3,000 | Mortgage | $10,000 |
| Home | 24,000 | Net Worth | 17,000 |

The Calloways' net worth increased from $5,000 to $17,000, or more than tripled, while prices only doubled. The Calloways beat inflation.

What lesson about inflation have you learned from these three families? Is it this sad commentary: "Inflation often rewards those who owe long-term debt, not those who pay cash"? This does not mean that you should overborrow. The inflation rate also fluctuates, and there will be times when it is increasing at a decreasing rate. When you receive such indications, reduce your borrowing until the trend reverses.

You don't have to be on the verge of bankruptcy to benefit from inflation. You can and should have cash, but you will want to have a large amount of your assets invested in things that can inflate with the cost of living. Again, I emphasize, own the thing that owns the thing. To win the inflation game in the years ahead, you will have to learn to borrow money wisely. Your assets must be primarily in investments that can rise as fast as the general price levels at each stage of the inflation cycle. There was a time when families did not feel comfortable unless they had cash. Today, money has such earning potential that they may not feel comfortable with much of it idle and will be actively searching for the best way to make every dollar work hard for them.

With Inflation, Knowledge Is Power

Inflation will not hurt you if you become knowledgeable and act to protect yourself from it. But you will be saddened as you look around and see the tragic faces of the hardworking, thrifty, sacrificing persons who have faithfully saved and put their money where they have been told it would be safe and have lost their money's only true value —its purchasing power. With it they have also lost the privilege of retiring in financial dignity. During their working years, their raises usually matched or exceeded their cost-of-living increases; but when they got off the inflation train and it went on without them, they had no chance of keeping up with the inflationary spiral.

To take advantage of the transfers that inflation makes in wealth, you must begin by thinking in terms of a full range of investments that you will have positioned efficiently at the proper time to beat inflation. Your investments must maximize your after-tax return balanced against a level of risk that provides you with peace of mind. You will want to avoid fads unless you are equipped emotionally to act rapidly. As inflation pushes up the price of your assets, faddists will start jumping in with both feet. At this point prices will begin to overdiscount inflation. The faddist will be selling as prices drop. You will want to be in a position to buy at this time.

To beat inflation, you will always want to be holding the right combination of assets. As I have pointed out previously, and let me reemphasize again, there is an investment for each season, but not an investment for all seasons. This means that nothing you have can be just put away in your safe-deposit box and forgotten. You must learn to be flexible and alert. You should classify all the investment vehicles available to you as to their appropriateness for accelerating inflation or decelerating inflation. Then decide whether inflation is about to accelerate or decelerate.

Many who come to me for financial counseling have already accumulated sufficient assets, or could easily do so within a few years, to enable them to reach or work toward financial independence, if these assets were properly put to work. This may be true for you. You may be working extremely hard for your money, but unfortunately once it is obtained, instead of putting it to work for yourself, you have unknowingly given away its earning power. You cannot afford to have your money working for others. If you do, you will lose the money and the tax game!

Summary

Inflation will be a part of your life for as long as you live. You can fear it, hide your head in the sand, and say that it doesn't exist or that it will go away or that it is slowing down, but you are only kidding yourself and inviting financial disappointments. Inflation can be your valuable ally if you make it work for you instead of against you. Learn to embrace it rather than fear it, and use it to increase your wealth by applying your intelligence and energy to studying the inflation cycles and positioning your assets at the proper location at the proper time. You must face the reality that you will probably never own an asset that is immune to the inflation cycle.

Remember that you can be either inflation's victim or its beneficiary. Get on the right side of inflation and harness its energy to work for you. The facing of this reality and your determination to use these forces in your best interest can be a challenging and profitable undertaking.

APPLICATION

1. Have you mentally made the necessary transition from dollars into bread?

   _____

2. Do you think the Full Employment Act of 1946 will be repealed?

   _____

3. Are you still living under the *Poor Richard's Almanac* theory of working hard, saving, and not borrowing? _____

4. What steps will you take today to throw off Poor Richard's shackles and move into the real world? _____

_____

_____

5. What steps will you take to put inflation to work for you rather than against you? _____

_____

_____

Chapter 4

Stock Dynamics in the New Economy

Timing is a critical ingredient when considering an investment in the stock market; and, in my opinion, the timing for this book could not be better! As we move into the exciting atmosphere of the New Economy and its kaleidoscope of change, I firmly believe that we are entering a bull market environment unprecedented in the last sixteen years and that the Dow Jones Industrial Average could very easily be above 3,000 before the end of this decade. I have never claimed to have a crystal ball, nor do I now, but I see the future convergence of so many factors in the New Economy that are already in motion that I can reach no other conclusion.

While studying the stock market and the opportunities that it holds, it is vital that we review my formula for financial independence:

Time + Money + American Free Enterprise =
The Opportunity to Become Financially Independent

Now let's substitute "shares of American corporations" for "American free enterprise." Once you have done that, your next questions should be: Which companies and in which industries should I invest? What can I reasonably hope to gain if I do invest?

And how much of my assets should I commit to this area of investing? Before you can answer these questions and others, we must take a look at the terminology of the marketplace and understand how the stock market operates. And you must realize that investing in the stock market is not a game. You don't just "play the market." Investing is a very exacting science that requires skill, training, knowledge, and discipline. And even with these qualifications, you will not always be right; for the dynamic and fast-moving world of the New Economy changes every minute of every day. Successful investing is a skill that you must either learn yourself or hire professionals to do for you. You have no other choice.

Terminology of the Market

To become a successful investor, you need to know the language of investing and the kinds of securities that you will find in the marketplace.

There are three basic types of securities. These are:

1. Common stock

2. Preferred stock

3. Bonds and debentures

COMMON STOCK

All corporations have common stock. If you organized a corporation for the purpose of buying a magazine stand at the corner of Broadway and Market Street, and sold one share of common stock to nine persons at $100 per share and one share to yourself at $100, the corporation would be capitalized at $1,000 and would have ten stockholders. In buying one of these shares, you became a shareholder or part owner of the corporation. You took an equity position and will participate in the future gains or lack of gains of the corporation for as long as you hold your share.

PREFERRED STOCK

Preferred stocks are equities in a corporation senior to the common stock and on which a fixed dividend must be paid before the common shareholder is entitled to a dividend each year. The dividend is usually higher, and if it is a cumulative preferred stock, any past dividends that have been omitted must be paid before the common shareholder is entitled to a dividend. If the preferred stock is also convertible to common stock, it will have a conversion ratio into the common.

There is much confusion about preferred stock. The uninitiated seem to think that "preferred" automatically means "better," but this is rarely true. Unless it is convertible, it has neither the growth potential of a common stock nor the relative stability of a bond. The word "preferred" relates to dividend precedence only. Since 85 percent of the dividends from an American corporation are exempt from taxation when received by another American corporation, the market price of higher-yielding preferreds tends to rise, making them less attractive to individual investors. You will normally receive a higher rate of return from a high-quality corporate bond than from a preferred stock.

BONDS AND DEBENTURES

The third type of security is bonds and debentures. A corporate bond may be a mortgage bond; and if, for example, you were to invest in equipment trust certificates, you would hold a mortgage on specific assets such as freight cars, heavy equipment, buses, or airplanes.

A much larger area of the bond market is debentures, where your security for this type of bond is the general credit rating of the issuing corporation. For example, you may buy an American Telephone and Telegraph debenture at 8.70 percent due in 2002. In this instance, you do not acquire a mortgage on specific telephones or equipment, but instead your security is based on the tremendous assets and credit standing of AT&T.

Characteristics and differences of common stocks and bonds can be oversimplified by stating them in this manner:

STOCKS

1. Not guaranteed as to principal

2. Not guaranteed as to rate of return

3. Guaranteed to participate in the future destiny of the company

BONDS

1. "Guaranteed" as to principal if assets are available at maturity

2. "Guaranteed" as to rate of return if funds are available

3. Not guaranteed to grow, regardless of any increase in the profits of the corporation

Bonds will be covered in more detail in a later chapter.

Convertible Bonds. There are those who think that convertible bonds give the best of two worlds—offering you the third characteristic under stocks, and the first two under bonds; however, they frequently fall short on both scores.

A convertible bond is a bond that usually carries a lower interest rate than a regular corporate bond, but is convertible into common stock at a specified ratio. For example, if a convertible is bought at par, which in a bond is usually $1,000, and is convertible into 100 shares of common at the holder's option, and the common is selling at $10, there would be no incentive to exchange, for the bond will usually carry a higher yield than the common. However, if the market price of the common should increase to $15, you would now have a bond with a value of $1,500. If, on the other hand, the common goes below $10, you still have your bond with its higher yield acting as a cushion under the bond.

Since convertibles have not performed that well over the years, emphasis in this chapter will be placed on common stocks, as they will offer you the greatest potential for gain (or loss). The vast array of them in the marketplace may seem confusing to you at first, but we will take a step-by-step approach, and your learning should progress rapidly. In the next chapter you will also learn how to let the professionals in the market do your investing for you.

To be successful in the stock market, you should know how to use the mass network of facilities available to you for trading securities and you should keep accurate records. Figures 1 and 2 in the Appendix are suggested forms for keeping records of your buys, sells, and dividends.

Stock Exchanges and Listed Stocks

Stocks that are publicly held are classified as either listed or unlisted (commonly referred to as over-the-counter). "Listed" means that a stock is listed and traded on a national or regional exchange. Listed stocks represent, in dollar assets, the largest segment of the American economy. There is probably no asset that you will ever own that you can so readily turn into cash as a stock that is listed on a national exchange. Thus it offers almost instant liquidity. Our four largest exchanges are the New York Stock Exchange, the American Stock Exchange, the Pacific Stock Exchange, and the Midwest Stock Exchange.

THE BIG BOARD

The New York Stock Exchange is the oldest and largest. It began very informally near the time of the birth of our nation when our first Secretary of the Treasury needed to set up a monetary system. To have a monetary system in this new nation, he needed to establish banks. And to establish banks, he needed stockholders who were willing to invest capital. However, no one was willing to invest capital in bank stocks if there was no way to sell their shares. So to make a market for these bank stocks and other issues, a group of eleven men would meet under a buttonwood tree at the foot of a street in New York called Wall, and trade among themselves and as agents for their clients. They eventually moved inside, and from this humble beginning grew the mighty New York Stock Exchange.

The Over-the-Counter Market

Another vast area of the stock market is the "unlisted" market, called the over-the-counter (OTC) market, which actually has no "counter" or official meeting place. (Once, I had a client become confused and ask me for an "under-the-counter" stock. After he told me of the stock he had in mind, I decided he had accidentally hit on a good description. It was a very speculative stock.)

For many years there was no central marketplace for over-the-counter stocks. Various brokerage houses would "make a market" in a particular stock by inventorying the stock they bought and sold. There are now over 50,000 stocks traded in the over-the-counter market through a network of telephone and teletype wires linking the various brokerage houses. There is a daily "pink sheet" giving "bid" and "asked" quotations of the market makers from the previous day reporting to the National Daily Quotation Service. ("Bid" means what someone is willing to pay for the stock and "asked" is the amount for which someone is willing to sell, subject to confirmation or change in price.) When you see a market report on a listed stock in the newspaper, you know that a trade actually took place at that price. In the over-the-counter market, you could have a quote with no trade taking place.

There is a wide variety and range of quality in the stocks traded in the over-the-counter market. Traditionally, bank and insurance company stocks have been traded there, even though they have substantial assets. On the opposite end are "penny stocks" (those that sell for a nominal amount per share), which also trade there. Often a stock is traded over-the-counter for years, and as it grows in assets and popularity, it may apply for listing on a national exchange and be accepted.

In the past, I have warned that if you are new to the market, you probably should avoid the over-the-counter market until you become more knowledgeable, but with the establishment of the National Association of Security Dealers Advanced Quotations (NASDAQ), the whole complexion of this market has changed. Since it was founded in 1971, NASDAQ has had a profound effect on the OTC market, making current markets available to all parts of the country at the same time and enabling dealers to give prompt and accurate service.

Establishing Your Brokerage Account

Opening an account with a stockbroker can be as easy as opening a charge account with a local retailer. Establishing an account with a financial planner (a financial planner is a stockbroker, but a stockbroker is not necessarily a financial planner—unless he or she is trained to treat your complete financial planning needs) will be more comprehensive, since you will need to provide more information about your assets, your tax bracket, your financial objective, and your temperament.

Once your account is opened, you can make a purchase or sale. A confirmation is mailed to you showing the number of shares of stock purchased or sold, the price, commission and fees, net amount due, and settlement date. Within five business days from the trade date, you must pay for the stocks you have bought or, in the case of a sale, you must deliver your stock certificate and receive payment. Stock commissions vary, depending upon the type of stockbroker you use, but they are generally low and average around 1½ percent.

After your account has been opened, you may place your orders by telephone with your broker and ask him to buy or sell securities for you.

Setting Your Financial Objectives

Prior to embarking upon your stock investment program, it is vital that you assess your own personal financial situation and decide whether you need to invest for growth, income, stability, or some kind of combination of these factors. The Triangle of Finance shown below will enable you to see where you should place yourself for your mental comfort or temperament and for the best correlation with your financial objectives.

At the top of the triangle I have placed Growth, at the left Income, and at the right Stability. (By stability I mean a guarantee of the same number of dollars at a future date, not the return of the same purchasing power.) As you can see, the further you move toward

Growth, the further you move away from Stability and Income. You may be in your accumulation period and should be investing for Growth, but when you move in that direction, you could have increased volatility. This may disturb your peace of mind, and peace of mind is a good investment, too. If you came to me as a client, I would try to determine your peace-of-mind level, because regardless of how well the investment fits your financial objective, if you are uncomfortable with it, it is not right for you and you may abandon it before it has had time to achieve the desired goal.

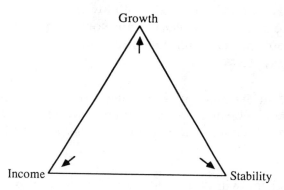

Now that you have learned some of the basics of how the stock market works, just how do you approach the selection of individual stocks in the New Economy?

Investing in the Inevitable

One of the basic tenets of investing is to invest in the inevitable. What are some of the trends we see developing in the New Economy that appear to come as close to the inevitable as possible?

Demographics. Our population is rapidly aging. We are seeing what many call "the graying of America." Those citizens over age 55 control a larger portion of discretionary income than did earlier generations. They will place a strain on our medical delivery system, making us search for ways of lowering our medical costs in the years ahead. At the same time that the aging of America is occurring, on the opposite end of the spectrum we have a new baby boom in the making.

Business Conditions. Business will become more highly competitive, forcing them to reduce costs and improve productivity. Capital spending for technology will be necessary for survival in this competitive climate.

Transportation. Our transportation system must be improved so that companies can operate efficiently with lower inventories—one of the secrets of the Japanese success. Enormous sums must therefore be spent to repair and maintain our infrastructure—highways, bridges, water supplies, etc.

Decentralization. Technology is forcing a return to decentralization. There will be a rebirth of cottage industries, with short customized production runs becoming the norm. It will no longer be necessary to build large plants to gain economies of scale.

Housing. Housing will command a smaller share of our resources as our homes become smaller and manufactured housing comes of age.

Reallocating Capital. A shrinking of the need for large amounts of capital will cause a movement of capital out of tangible assets into financial assets.

Litigious Society. During our agricultural era it was man against nature. Then the industrial era pitted man against fabricated nature. In the new information society, the game will be people interacting with people. This will increase personal transactions, which in turn will produce a litigation-intensive society. With more personal transactions, there will be more to go sour. At the same time, the number of lawyers that are being produced by our law schools is dramatically increasing. In 1960 there were 250,000 lawyers in the U.S. The American Bar Association predicts the number will reach 750,000 by 1987 and a million by the mid-1990s. And the paralegal profession is growing even faster.

Longer Time Frames. We are restructuring our business endeavors from short-term considerations to long-term time frames.

Global Economy. No longer are we living in an isolated, self-sufficient national economic system, but we are rapidly becoming a part of a global economy. Today we are faced with shrinking markets abroad. There is, however, a great demand for our expertise. Knowledge creates economic value.

Rapid Change. The shift in America from an agricultural society to an industrial society took over a hundred years. The shift from an industrial society to an information society is taking only two decades; and with changes occurring so rapidly, you will not have time to react. Instead, you will have to anticipate the future.

The trends of the New Economy that we have just discussed must affect your stock selections regardless of whether you are investing for income or investing for growth. Though they will more heavily influence your selections if your objective is growth, they cannot be ignored if your objective is income.

Let us assume that your financial objective is for income. Just how do you go about selecting stocks for income?

How to Select Income Stocks

YIELD

Before we look at the basic requirements for the selection of income stocks, let's discuss yield and how it is calculated. The yield on stock is the relationship of the dividend it pays to its market price. Every shareholder is entitled to the same dividend per share. However, the price you have paid for your stock may differ from the price paid by another shareholder. If you paid $50 for a share of stock and the dividend is $2, the yield on your original investment is 4 percent ($2 divided by $50). If you paid $35, the $2 represents a return, or yield, on your original investment of slightly more than 5.7 percent. You should, however, continue to calculate your yield on current market price, because you have the option of repositioning your assets.

DIVIDENDS THAT KEEP INCREASING

If you are dependent on dividends for your groceries and if the price of food continues to rise, you must increase your income or reduce your intake. Most of us would probably be a lot healthier if we did the latter, but we have a tendency to reject this alternative. Therefore, you will want to select stocks that not only pay good dividends now but also have had a good record of increasing their dividends consistently. I prefer stocks that have raised their dividends in at least eight of the past ten years and whose dividends today are 100 percent higher than they were ten years ago. I also prefer those that have held their dividend payout to less than 60 percent of earnings and have kept their debt under 25 percent. A record of strong and consistent dividends points to companies that are committed to similar performance in the future. Holding payouts under 60 percent of earnings helps eliminate companies that don't retain enough earnings to sustain growth. Keeping long-term debt low protects future earnings. But don't reach too far for yield and jeopardize your capital. Often I have calls from people who spot a stock paying a 12 to 14 percent yield and they want to buy it, assuming that no one else has been observant enough to spot this "bonanza." Usually the reason for the high yield is the poor evaluation that the market has given to the future prospects of the company, or it may be paying out an inordinately large percentage of its earnings, which could adversely affect future earnings.

So in selecting stocks for dependable income, it is obvious that you will want to choose quality issues with long established dividend records rather than younger, less tested companies that have not been in business long enough to establish extended dividend payment records. However, as change will be occurring rapidly in the New Economy, do not become complacent, but be ever vigilant to determine if the companies in which you have invested are staying on the cutting edge of change.

During times of market corrections, I often have calls from less sophisticated holders of income stocks who are worried that their dividend will be cut because the market price is down. If all is well with their company, I try to calm them with the explanation that short-term market prices often have no relationship to earnings. In the long term, however, they usually do.

BLUE CHIPS, RED CHIPS, WHITE CHIPS?

The stocks I have just described would generally be called blue chips. What is a "blue chip" stock? First, the name can be traced to the game of poker, in which there are three colors of chips: blue for the highest value, red for the next in rank, and white for the lowest value. Sometimes people say to me, "I only invest in blue chip stocks and throw them in a drawer and forget about them." They are asking for my approval of this practice, but I consider this approach a risky one. I would prefer to see them invest in more volatile stocks and watch them carefully than to have them "plant their garden and not tend it." The blue chips of today may be the red chips of tomorrow, the white chips of the next day, or merely the buffalo chips. (I'm a rancher. You do know what a pasture Frisbee is, don't you?) In the New Economy, be constantly aware of the changing color of your chips.

In summary, if your desire is for income from stocks, you should:

1. Look for companies that have a long, unbroken dividend record.

2. Don't reach too far for yield and jeopardize principal.

3. Remember that too high a yield can be dangerous and misleading.

4. Favor companies producing consumer goods and services.

5. Select sound companies that continue to increase their dividends.

Income stocks are not too difficult to select after you have conscientiously done your homework. If you do not need income now, consider companies with slightly lower yields. Often these companies are plowing back a larger portion of their earnings into expanded facilities that should in time yield higher earnings that would allow them to pay out higher dividends.

One of the most common mistakes I see investors make, whether they are interested in income or growth, is asking, "What does it pay?" If I could select a stock for you that doesn't pay you anything today, but just grows rapidly, this could be an excellent investment, even if you need income now. You could always sell a few shares for your living expenses and lose a smaller portion of your proceeds to taxes, since they would most likely be taxed as a capital gain.

Investing for Growth in the New Economy

Growth stocks can be your most rewarding investments and yet be your most challenging and frustrating, especially as we swiftly move into the New Economy. In Chapter 1 we looked at some of the characteristics of the New Economy. Now let's determine how these may influence your selection of growth stocks.

In 1956, for the first time in U.S. history, white-collar workers in technical, clerical, and managerial positions outnumbered those in blue-collar jobs. Industrial America crossed over to the New Economy, and since that time most of us have worked with information rather than in the production of goods. During the time of the industrial society, the most important resource was capital. There were many who knew how to build brick factories, textile mills, and automobile plants; but there were only a few who had access to the necessary capital to do so. In the New Economy, the new source of power will be information in the hands of many rather than money in the hands of a few. Value will be increased by knowledge rather than by labor, making access to the system much easier.

This parenthesis between eras that we are now experiencing, combined with the lowering of our capital gains taxes, has brought about an explosion of entrepreneurship in America; and new companies are being formed at the rate of over 600,000 a year. These new companies and others offer a number of new opportunities for investing in growth.

GROWTH STOCKS

What are growth stocks, and why should you consider investing in them? A growth company is usually one that is increasing its sales and earnings at a faster rate than the growth of the national population and business in general. The long-term growth rate of our population has been about 3 percent; and a growth company, as a rule of thumb, should be increasing its sales and net earnings at least as fast as the combination of the two, and preferably much faster, and it usually produces goods and/or services in new and dynamic industries.

To become an expert at selecting for growth, you must be aware of current events: current trends, supply and demand, psychology, and money markets. In fact, you must be truly current in all respects. One of the most stimulating characteristics of my profession is that every day is a new day in the market. Nothing remains static. There is no way you can be a truly top-notch investor by buying blue chips and throwing them in a drawer and forgetting them. This only increases your risk and lowers your opportunity for gain.

There appear to be two irreversible structural changes occurring in the U.S. that are permanently transforming our economic base. First, our transformation from a smokestack to a microchip economy. Second, the U.S. is no longer an economic fortress unto itself, but rather now a part of a global economy. And its potential for growth is boundless because its new thrust comes from our richest and most renewable resource—the human mind.

SELECTING THE RIGHT INDUSTRY

If I were to choose the most important consideration for selecting growth stocks, I would have to say that it is to be in the right industry at the right time. There is always an industry moving up, regardless of the general overall trend of the market, and you should endeavor to predict a trend before it happens and move out before the trend runs out.

In this New Economy, the emphasis will be on providing an endless array of customized services rather than producing massive amounts of standardized goods. As a result, the service and information industries will become more and more dominant, and by 1995 it is projected that these industries will account for more than 60 percent of our nation's Gross National Product and employ seven out of every ten working Americans. And in addition to growing faster than the economy as a whole, the service and information industries tend to hold up much better than others when business activity falls off. This sweeping transformation is creating a flood of investment opportunities in areas that include computer systems, services, and software; telecommunications; health and personal-care services; broadcasting and publishing; business and financial services; entertainment and leisure; merchandising; transportation services; public services; and many others. Changing your thinking about companies in which you invest may be difficult, but you must. As the railroad industry forgot that it was in the transportation business and did not or could not change because of being overregulated, it may now be just as difficult for you to accept the fact that we are now in the process of losing some of our heavy capital-intensive industries that have been our economic backbone for so many years.

SELF-GENERATING AND GROWING EARNINGS

It is important to select a company that has self-generating rising earnings and reserves with expectations for continued increases over the foreseeable future. Remember that few companies really shine solely by acquisitions. Pretax earnings on assets of growth companies should be between 10 and 30 percent.

A growth stock is not just a stock that has gone up in price, but rather one that has shown a consistent year-after-year superior growth in earnings, even in the face of business reverses, and that has a consistent year-in, year-out market for its products or services.

A growth company must retain a large portion of its earnings for research and development that will produce a salable product that offers excellence in quality, design, or performance, and preferably all three. A growth company must have a dynamic, aggressive sales department to promote its products or services in the competitive marketplace. And you will want to search for the companies that dominate their markets or are leaders in fast-growing fields. These can be companies in emerging fields or companies that have developed new ideas in established fields.

Special Situations and New Ventures

In addition to looking at growth stocks, you will also want to be on the lookout for special situations that may occur from time to time in the marketplace. Special situations could come about because of an expected merger, the launching of a new product, the sudden increase in the price of a valuable asset, a new mineral find, and so on. Your success will depend greatly on your getting accurate information ahead of the pack and reacting accordingly.

If you are considering buying stock in a new venture, it is vital to determine if the company is well capitalized and if it is being managed by competent people. Innovators may have a highly functional idea or patent, but they may not know how to run a business. Creative design people often are very poor at manufacturing techniques, cost control, merchandising, financing, and recordkeeping. Check to see if those who will run the business are personally solvent and have adequate practical or technical backgrounds. The third thing to consider in a new company is superiority of product or service. New products should be advanced, unusual, and ahead of the field. Finally, can you afford to lose everything you put into the new company and not miss the money? On the record, the chances of a new company's growing from zero to great substance are very slim. But if this kind of speculation adds zest to your life and you can afford it, happy hunting!

Investing in Foreign Markets

Since there is such a wide variety of stocks to choose from in the U.S., should you ever consider investing abroad? Of course you should if you have or can develop the expertise to do so. Search for bargains worldwide. Limiting yourself only to the United States could be like limiting yourself to only those stocks that begin with the letters "A" through "M."

As we move into the New Economy, our society continues to become more global. By broadening your horizons you can participate in economies that are expected to report impressive gains. At almost any point in time you will find some overseas markets expanding more rapidly than ours; and some countries have government policies that encourage capital formation and promote investment. Diversification can, if properly handled, moderate your risk and enhance your overall results.

Speculation

Speculating in the stock market is like playing the casinos in Las Vegas—never do it with serious money, money that you cannot afford to lose. But, on the other hand, if you have discretionary funds that are not necessary for your financial security, then go ahead and give it a try. But before you do, pay close attention to some of my basic rules of speculation:

1. Don't be greedy. One characteristic I have observed about the timing of all good speculators is that they never try to squeeze out the last point in a stock. When the great financier Bernard Baruch was questioned on how he made so much money in the stock market, he answered, "I always sold too soon." He always tried to leave a little in it for the next buyer.

2. Cut losses quickly. In trading, it is absolutely necessary to cut your losses quickly; and if you have made an error in judgment, don't wait around to find out just how wrong you really were. It may be that the market is just wrong or it may be that you have made an error in your calculation. In other words, get out while the getting is good!

3. Be objective and flexible. Don't fall in love with a stock and don't marry it. And don't be guilty of prejudices in stock. We all have them occasionally, but the sooner you recognize them and shed stocks that hinder your investment judgment, the better investor you will become.

4. Don't consider taxes. Tax considerations should be the furthest from your mind. When speculating, you are only trying to use $1 to make $2, not trying to do tax planning while in front of a stock board watching the "horses" run.

5. Don't cry and don't look back. If you don't make your objective in one arena, lick your wounds and charge forward to other more promising arenas.

Flexibility—A Key to Selecting Stocks

Common sense will be your greatest ally in selecting your stock portfolio. You probably will not be able to produce a superior investment performance all of the time. Some of the most respected professionals do not, and they occasionally lag behind the averages. First of all, you will want to search for bargains, because if you can buy stocks at a fraction of what you think they are worth, in the long run most of them should turn out better than if you had paid all you thought they were worth.

In order to evaluate what a stock is worth, you will want to conduct a security analysis. The best book on this subject is *Security Analysis* by Graham and Dodd. And after you have used standard security analysis to decide the value of a stock, you will want to compare it with the price of other stocks and buy those issues that have the lowest price in relation to what you think they are worth.

When evaluating your potential stock portfolio, you definitely need to be flexible. I know some investors who buy only famous stocks, while others tend to buy only those stocks that the analyst designates as fast-growing stocks. Be flexible enough not to be "charmed" by a particular stock or industry, because superior performance over the last few years does not insure the same kind of performance in the future. Get out if you feel that the time is right.

Flexibility also means searching the market to find the cheapest stock in relation to value. Remember that it is extremely difficult to buy a bargain if you are buying what other people are buying. If you are going to have superior performance, you need to be buying what other people are not buying, or even what other people are selling. Therefore, you will want to search for those areas that are extremely unpopular and then determine if that unpopularity is permanent. You will want to search for those stocks that other people are selling, and then if you determine that this problem or adverse outlook is only temporary, you will want to buy them and patiently hold them until the public changes its mind.

Buying Stocks on Margin

From years of observing margin account investors, my answer to you in this area of investing is no. Leave this area to the large, sophisticated (whatever that means) investors who are active in the market and who understand the risks as well as the rewards of this type of account. I find that it is usually best if you discipline yourself to the use of only your own investable funds. To lose some of your savings in the market is one thing, but to lose your future savings as well is another. And it is not that I don't believe in borrowing for investment, because I do in real estate and in other areas. But buying stocks on margin can be risky; and if the market moves against you, you could end up owing your broker a lot more than you can afford to lose.

Buying and Selling Options

An option is the right to buy or sell specific securities at a specified price within a specified time. The use of options has increased greatly in recent years, and many aggressive brokers promote them as the way to lock in additional income if you are on the selling side and to make a large return on a small investment if you are on the buying side. It is not all that easy, but in order for you not to feel left out when the conversation turns to "puts" and "calls," let's take a brief look at the world of options.

A "call" option is a contract that gives you the right to buy 100 shares of a given stock at a fixed price for a fixed period of time. The period of time usually runs nine months and ten days (for tax reasons), but you can also run 30, 90, 120 days, or other lengths of time. The premium that you pay for the option usually runs about 10 to 15 percent of the value of the stock.

A "put" option is the reverse of a "call" option. You now have the privilege of selling 100 shares of the stock at a fixed price within the option period. These usually cost a few percentage points less than call options and are not as popular.

Why would you ever buy an option? The main reason is that it gives you a chance to make a sizable profit on the move of a stock while limiting the amount of possible loss. If your expectations on the stock don't materialize and the stock drops in price, you simply let your option expire. Your loss is limited to the cost of your option, and you can be thankful that you did not buy additional shares, only to watch your investment shrink.

Your overall objective when you sell call options is to utilize various strategies to produce higher current income, lessen your portfolio's volatility, and reduce your risks in down markets.

Choosing and Maintaining a Profitable Portfolio

There are three important areas in choosing and maintaining a profitable portfolio of stocks: diversification, proper selection, and constant supervision.

DIVERSIFICATION

Diversification means spreading the risk. The old adage of not putting all your eggs in one basket has considerable merit in assembling a good investment portfolio. Don't put all your faith in one company or in one industry, for it may disappoint you. If you buy a diversified group of fundamentally sound stocks with good earnings and growth, the chances are that in a good market you will catch at least some of the big winners, since most big money in a diversified portfolio comes from one or two big winners. Don't be deceived into thinking that ten oil stocks or ten computer stocks constitute diversification. They do not. You should strive for a portfolio covering a wider range of industries. For example, you may have some stocks in the soft drink industry, the retail area, drugs, home furnishings, electrical equipment, brewing, electronics, computers, and others.

When managing your own portfolio, you may find it extremely helpful to limit yourself to ten stocks, regardless of the amount of money you have to invest. I am often surprised to find that investors think they can own only 100 shares of each company's stock. If the capital you have available for investing is sufficiently large, perhaps you should consider owning 1,000 or more shares of each stock.

Don't overdiversify, because you may find that you are unable to be current on a large number of companies or industries. If you limit your holdings to ten to fifteen stocks and a stock comes to your attention that you feel you should buy, what will this force you to do? Probably to eliminate one. In order to move to strength, it would now be prudent to go through your list and sell the one that is doing the poorest job for you. The way to upgrade a portfolio is to sell your losers and keep your winners, as this allows you the possibility of continuously moving to a position of strength.

TIMING AND PROPER SELECTION OF STOCKS

There is a time to buy and a time to sell, and the old adage about buying low and selling high is easy to say and very hard to do. Often you never know what the high or low is until it is too late for maximum advantage. But how do you determine when to buy and when to sell? Let's look at buying first.

When to Buy. First of all, buy stocks only when you think you can make a profit. The only reason to be in the market is to make money. And buy only when you anticipate a substantial rise within one year. Aim for a percent appreciation per year and buy for investment gain, not dividends.

To make money in the market, you may have to learn to buy ice cubes in the winter—in other words, learn not to run with the pack. Although you may find it extremely hard to go against the crowd, learn to buy stocks that others are selling and sell what others are buying.

When to Sell. I have a simple rule for judging when to sell a stock I own, and it is so simple that you will probably dismiss the whole idea. I do not look at what price I paid for a stock unless it would cause me to incur a large capital gains tax liability. I simply ask myself, "If I had the money this stock would bring in my hands at this moment, would I buy this stock at this price?" If my answer is yes, I hold. If it is no, I sell. The only difference between my owning this stock and having the money is a small amount of commission, which I should not let affect my judgment.

You may have great difficulty selling. Most people do. If you have a gain, you may hope for an ever greater gain or you may not be able to bear the thought of selling and paying the capital gains tax. But when you analyze the situation, there are only two ways to avoid eventually paying that tax, neither of which you are going to like. You can hold it until it goes back to what you paid for it; or hold it until your death, and let your heirs worry about the tax when they sell it. On the other hand, if you have a loss, you may say, "I won't sell, for I just can't afford to take a loss." You already have the loss and there are only two questions now that you should ask yourself. Can you deduct the loss advantageously on your income tax, and where are you most likely to make up your loss—where you are or in another stock? Lay your hand over the cost basis of your stocks and judge them individually on their potential over the next six months. When you no longer anticipate a worthwhile rise, when the outlook for earnings is no longer favorable, when the stock is clearly overpriced in relation to its normal price-earnings multiple or to that of companies of similar quality in the same industry, sell.

When Will the Dow Hit 3,000?

As I stated in the opening of this chapter, I am excited about the stock market and I am convinced that we will see a Dow above 3,000 by the latter part of the 1980s. I have many reasons for these convictions and let me now give you a few of the chief ones.

Incidentally, when I say "the Dow," I'm referring to the Dow Jones Industrial Average. There are actually four Dow Jones Averages—the Industrial, the Composite, the Utility, and the Transportation. However, the best known is the Industrial Average, which reflects the value of the stocks of 30 industrial companies. This time-honored index accounts for about 25 percent of the value of all New York Stock Exchange shares.

The first average was published in 1884 and included 12 stocks. It has had a long climb to its present height. It is also no longer an average. When it first began, the average was computed by adding the prices of the stocks in the average and dividing by the number of issues. The divisor has been changed over the years to adjust for stock splits and stock dividends. Eighteen stocks have been added, and there continue to be substitutions in an effort to make it truly reflect the market.

The Dow Jones Industrial Average may not be the most accurate indicator of the market, but when someone asks me "How's the market doing today?" I know they mean how is the Dow doing. It has been with us a long time and will probably be with us for a long time in the future.

It has taken over a hundred years for the Dow to reach its present level. Why do I think it will double over the next fourteen years?

Price-Earnings Ratio. The current price-earnings ratios of stocks are below what they have averaged over the past 90 years, which is an average of 14 times earnings. Indications are that we should return to this P/E ratio in the foreseeable future; and while the market values of the majority of stocks have not increased, the corporations behind them have prospered and their earnings have climbed. I currently see the stocks of many sound and profitable companies selling at drastic discounts.

Stocks are bargains when compared to other investment possibilities. Over the past decade, real estate and oil and gas have provided a hedge against inflation because their prices have increased. Stocks have not participated as much in these increases. Yet stocks are not just pieces of paper called stock certificates. They represent shares of ownership in real businesses that have assets that can produce growing earnings and dividends.

Shares below Book Value. There have only been three times in history when stock prices were below book value, and all three proved to be very short and ideal times to begin accumulating stocks for investment. These were 1932, 1942, and 1948.

Replacement Book Value. Because of inflation, it costs approximately 70 percent above stated book value to replace most American plants and equipment. Because shares have been selling below replacement costs, many corporations are now buying the shares of other corporations as a cheaper way of acquiring plants and equipment than building and acquiring new ones. Some of the smartest and best-qualified investors in the world know that these stocks are a bargain. How do I know? I know because these same businessmen are using their cash to repurchase their own stock at a fraction of what they know the shares are worth.

Political Environment. With the passage of the Economic Recovery Act of 1981, our country officially entered into a new era. No longer would it be the government's role to solve everyone's economic problems. Alas, it had attempted to do so for over twenty years and in the process had consumed an ever-increasing share of our finite productive resources. "Free enterprise" was now to be given a second chance, and government was to provide a supportive environment by finally decreasing government intervention in the system.

The act eliminated some of the disincentives for investing, such as lowering the capital gains tax, the elimination of the distinction between earned and unearned income; and it provided other incentives to earn and invest. This was vital to our economy, because it is through the stock market that increased savings are channeled into industry for investment in new plants and equipment; and it is through the stock market that the necessary research and development for technological advances and productivity enhancement are financed.

Movement from Hard Assets. It appears that inflation, though still present, will be increasing at a decreasing rate. In the past, for every 1 percent increase in inflation, $100 billion went out of stocks and into various hard assets and tangibles. Now that the rate of inflation has declined, the reverse is occurring, and funds which once went into hard assets are flowing back into the stock market.

Deleveraging. Our economy is in the process of being deleveraged. This means that future growth will be financed more with equity rather than with as much debt.

Demographics. We are entering a period of labor shortages, which in turn will accelerate technology. A new phase of the industrial revolution based on a technology of substituting capital for labor is getting under way.

Semiconductors—"The Chip." "The Chip" will continue to be the basis for our revolution in productivity. It will no doubt be as important a factor in our economy as were the development of the steam engine and mass production in their times.

Allocation of Capital. Funds for the exploitation of technology must come from the securities market. The principal role of the market has always been to allocate capital. Every economic system requires investment choices; and in a planned economy, such as socialism or communism, capital decisions are made by the bureaucrats. In a free enterprise capitalistic economy, the markets make those choices; and they determine which industries and companies will get capital and which will not. One of the principal differences between the economy of the United States and the economy of the Soviet Union is the stock market.

Pension Funds. Private pension plans alone are projected to be $4 trillion by the end of the 1980s, and the public pension funds could add another $2 trillion. If only 50 percent of the private pension funds (historically it has averaged 55 percent) goes into common stocks, that would amount to $2 trillion, and there are only around $2 trillion worth of stocks in the United States today.

Foreign Investors. There is an enormous amount of foreign money available for investment in the United States. Foreign investors' interest is twofold: 1) our stocks are attractive values, and 2) our country is the safest haven in the world for their capital. There has also been a change in foreign legislation; and the citizens of many countries, such as England, can now more easily invest in U.S. securities. Even Japan is allowing its pension funds to go outside the country to make 10 percent on their investments.

Individual Investors. There are large cash reserves in the hands of investors that are available to go into the stock market.

Now every person who has earned income can set up for himself his own pension fund, called an ''Individual Retirement Account'' (discussed later), and can contribute 100 percent of income up to a maximum of $2,000 per year. Over 100 million Americans are eligible, and if only one-fourth participate (that is, 25 million people) at $2,000 per participant, that amounts to $50 billion per year. And if only one-half of this amount goes into common stocks, that is $25 billion of new money into the market. Since this is more than the new supply of common stocks, this alone could have a large effect on pushing stock prices higher.

The New Economy may very well be the beginning of people's capitalism; and instead of only 33 million people in our country owning shares, we may soon have 100 million people participating in the free enterprise system through the stock market.

Summary

You should be prepared to participate in one of the most exciting eras for common stocks. The rewards can be substantial. If your objective is income now, carefully choose income stocks. If your objective is income later, growth stocks should be the most rewarding. The stock market is assumed by many to be a high-risk place to put your money. It certainly can be, but it can also be a conservative investment vehicle. There is "something for everyone" there, and it is up to you to learn all you can about the market and take advantage of everything it has to offer.

APPLICATION

1. A good way to become knowledgeable about growth industries is to be alert to current trends. To which areas should you be attuned as you read the daily newspaper?_____

2. How will you become informed about the management of the corporations in the industries that you feel offer the most growth potential?_____

   _____

3. How do you determine the right time to invest?_____

4. How will you time your sales?_____

5. What is the Gross National Product today?_____

6. What is your prediction of what the GNP will be in ten years?_____

7. What is your prediction of the price-earnings ratio of the stocks included in the Dow Jones Industrial Average in ten years?_____

8. What action will you take to apply your predictions to benefit your own financial future?

   a. _____

   b. _____

   c. _____

9. Sit down and draw the financial triangle. Place yourself on the triangle. Are you emphasizing income when your real objective is growth of capital?

Chapter 5

Professional Money Management for the New Economy

Now that you have had a good look at some of the basic requirements for becoming a successful investor in the stock market, you may be saying to me, "I'm an engineer (or accountant, salesman, or doctor). And I'm good at what I do because I devote many hours a day to my vocation, but I have neither the time nor inclination to study the stock market. Yet I know that I need to have my money working for me, since I may have children who will need funds to go to college and I'll need to have funds to retire in financial dignity someday. What can I do?" If you don't have what I call the three T's and an M, put professional money managers to work for you.

Time

The first T is for time. Do you truly have the time that it takes to study market trends on an ongoing basis? Do you really have the time to spend studying balance sheets, profit and loss statements, economic indicators, changes in monetary policies, increases in government expenditures, decreases in other areas of government expenditures, shortages, surpluses, consumer buying trends, international competition due to lower labor costs, access to raw materials, and so forth?

If you can answer that you do have this time and feel that it would be more rewarding financially and emotionally to spend it being a professional in the market than spending it developing more expertise in your profession, pursuing a hobby, or engaging in recreational activities, then you have the first T.

Training

The second T is for training. What is your educational background—accounting, statistical analysis, money and banking, marketing, economics, finance, psychology? Even if you do have the first T of time, can you properly translate this knowledge into action? If you can, and if you are thoroughly schooled in these areas and have developed some reasonable expertise in them, then you qualify for the second T.

Temperament

The third T is for temperament. Are you temperamentally suited for successful investing in the stock market? Have you worked very hard for your money? Were you a child of the Depression? Does your memory of hard times make you squeeze every dollar until the eagle screams loudly?

Among my clients, I have observed that those from such backgrounds sometimes tend to make their emotional decisions about money more black and white than they should be. Money decisions must often be various shades of gray. If a person has experienced bad times, he may either clutch a dollar very tightly to his bosom for fear of losing it, or decides that once he gets a dollar he is going to put it to work aggressively to see if he can turn that dollar into an additional dollar. The latter, in my opinion, is the temperament necessary for successful investing. Money is like a flower. If you squeeze it, you will crush the life out of it.

Analyze your own personality and determine if you can act immediately and unemotionally when you have reasonable cause to do so. If you wait until you are 100 percent sure, your decision will invariably be too late. I have found that most investment decisions are made far too late rather than too soon. The difference between mediocre and superb performance in the market is the ability to evaluate and then take the appropriate action quickly. There is a time to buy and a time to sell—regardless of which stocks you own. Can you unemotionally move when it is time to do so? If so, you have the third T, temperament.

Money

Now that you have analyzed the three T's, let's look at how you fit the M, which represents money. Do you have enough money to diversify your holdings? As you have already learned, diversification is one of the first rules of successful investing, but you may find that it is difficult to obtain the necessary diversification on your own with less than $100,000 to commit to the stock market. However, if you pooled your funds with others who had the same financial objective, you could obtain the necessary diversification with a relatively small amount of money. This can be accomplished through a mutual fund. A mutual fund should do for you what you would do for yourself if you had sufficient time, training, the right temperament, and sufficient funds to diversify.

If you have the three T's and an M, you will find that being your own pro can be fun and rewarding. Therefore, you should plan to devote considerable time and energy to this important facet of your financial future. If not, don't take an ego trip. Let the pros do it for you.

PRIVATE PROFESSIONAL MANAGEMENT

If you are fortunate enough to have a sizable amount of money to commit to the market, you may want to consider using the services of a stock investment advisory service to manage your individual stock portfolio. The service will usually charge you a management fee of ½ to 2 percent of the portfolio. It will buy and sell stocks on your behalf on a discretionary basis and keep you informed quarterly regarding the performance of your portfolio. You are free to withdraw from the service any time you are not happy with its results.

PUBLIC PROFESSIONAL MANAGEMENT

If the amount you have for investing in equities is less than it would take to qualify for private professional management, don't let it bother you, for you may obtain even better performance with relatively small amounts of money through the investment medium of investment company trusts, commonly called mutual funds. "Mutual" means that you may mutually benefit from pooling your resources with others. For example, let's say that you have $1,000 and alone you cannot obtain diversification or professional management. But let's assume that there are 999 others who each have $1,000 and have the same financial objective that you do. If all of you pooled your funds, you would have a million dollars, and with a million dollars you would have sufficient money to spread your risk among a number of different industries. You would also have enough money to hire some top professional money managers to select and constantly supervise your holdings. A mutual fund, then, should do for you what you would do for yourself if you had sufficient time, the proper training, the right temperament, and sufficient money to diversify, It offers the same advantages to the small investor that the wealthy have always had. The wealthy have enough money to diversify and enough money to hire the pros.

There are now over 30 million shareholders investing more than 400 billion dollars in the many varieties of mutual funds. These funds have become the fourth-largest type of financial institution in the United States. In the previous chapter, we concluded that there are three basic requirements for successful investing: diversification, proper selection, and constant supervision. Let's reexamine these three to see if a quality mutual fund with excellent management could fulfill these requirements.

The Seminar Fund

For the past 23 years, I have conducted financial planning seminars in Houston, Texas. At the second session of each seminar, I discuss mutual funds and how they work; and as an example, but not necessarily as a recommendation, I usually use the same mutual fund. It is middle-of-the-road in its financial objectives, has a good 51-year record, and has averaged over 12 percent compounded during its lifetime with all distributions reinvested. It is not the top performer among funds, but its record is consistently good. I always use a fund that has averaged at least 12 percent over its life, for I am convinced that is the minimum long-term performance you should accept on your money. With inflation and taxes, this 12 percent may not be enough to keep ahead in the future, but during this 51-year period it would have been. I will show you a system that we use today that should still keep you considerably ahead.

I will call this fund the Seminar Fund, although that is not its real name. If I were to use its real name, I would have to hand you a prospectus before I could tell you about it, and send you a new one each year. Obtain the prospectus of a mutual fund and study it. Most prospectuses are pretty much the same, although the funds they describe differ as to financial objectives, investment advisers, and performance; but their fees, commissions, and structure are similar. In the previous chapter on selecting stocks, we agreed that one of the first requirements for successful investing is diversification—spreading your risk—and mutual funds fulfill this requirement.

Diversification. The Investment Company Act of 1940 provides that a mutual fund may not have more than 5 percent of its assets in any one company or own more than 10 percent of the outstanding shares of any one company. Because of this regulation, if you own a mutual fund you know that you will always have at least twenty stocks in your fund's portfolio, and also that any one of the twenty will not represent more than 10 percent of the outstanding shares of that company. This in itself insures a fair degree of diversification. You will find as you explore the large number of funds available that most of them have from 100 to 150 different stocks in their portfolios, and that they cover a wide spectrum of industry groups. Diversification such as this can permit you to own your slice of the U.S. economy by becoming a part owner of the major companies whose products and services you use regularly. At the end of 1984, the Seminar Fund's portfolio was diversified into 107 common stocks. Even if you had many thousands of dollars to invest, you would find it difficult to achieve diversification this broad.

Proper Selection and Constant Supervision. The Seminar Fund has a committee that meets daily to determine which stocks to add and which to take out of the portfolio, or to determine which stocks they presently hold fulfill the requirements that the shareholders designated when they chose this particular fund. A staff of anaylsts, each a specialist in his own field, constantly reports to this committee. The fund has specialists in the oils, the chemicals, the technologies, and so forth. Not only do they read, analyze, and project figures on each company in their industry specialty, but they also make on-the-spot studies and conduct fact-finding interviews with the top officers of these companies.

Successful investing is a full-time job; and in a dynamic and competitive economy, the fortunes of individual companies—often entire industries—can change very rapidly. Professionals who can stay abreast of these changes and capitalize on them are likely to achieve superior results in the New Economy. These financial analysts log hundreds of thousands of miles a year visiting corporations and talking with their key executives, their competitors, their suppliers, their bankers, and their customers. The analysts also study the industry, as well as the economic and regulatory climate in which each company operates.

Successful investing is a continuous problem-solving process. As in any problem-solving situation, the individual or group that, first, has access to the best information concerning the problem and, second, that can apply the best combination of judgment, experience, imagination, and financial resources to this information, is the one most likely to arrive consistently with the best solutions. The thoroughness and training of these specialists fulfill the two other requirements of successful investing—proper selection and constant supervision.

Kinds of Mutual Funds

In addition to the three requirements of successful investing, mutual funds can provide other valuable benefits. You can select a mutual fund to match your financial objectives. Do you remember our triangle of finance that we used in Chapter 4 when we were discussing individual stocks? It is applicable here, too. A mutual fund must state in its prospectus its financial objective, and this objective cannot be changed without the consent of the shareholders. The financial triangle looks something like this:

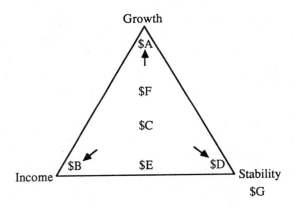

As you can see, you can't be a Paul Revere who hops on his horse and rides off in all directions. You must decide in which direction you want to go financially. When you maximize Income you move further away from Growth, and the same is true if you select Stability as your primary concern. A fund management group may offer a family of funds, attempting to provide a fund for each place on the triangle, or it may have only one or two funds.

There are eleven kinds of mutual funds available to you to choose: growth, growth with income, income, corporate bond, balanced, convertible bond, specialty, municipal bond, government securities, global, and money market funds.

GROWTH FUNDS

Under the growth designation, you could have three subheadings: "go-go," very aggressive growth, and quality growth.

If you invest in a quality growth fund, you will be placing your dollar nearer the top of the triangle at "A," because its objective is long-term growth. Intermittent volatility should not be of great concern, nor should you be interested in dividends. As a matter of fact, if it were possible for the fund managers to select stocks that paid no dividends and just grew in value, with no need to buy and sell and realize capital gains, this would be ideal for you. What you really want is for $1 to grow to over $4 in less than ten years. You would prefer not to have any tax liability in the meantime, if this were possible.

GROWTH WITH INCOME FUNDS

The middle-of-the-road fund that seeks growth with income is the stronghold of the mutual fund industry. It would fit in the middle of your triangle and is the place where most investors feel the greatest comfort. When deciding where you should be on the triangle, you should remember that your temperament is important in your investment program. In my counseling with a client, regardless of how much I think he should invest for maximum growth, if I detect that volatility would disturb his peace of mind, then the best investment for him will probably be in the middle. Peace of mind is a good investment, too.

Our Seminar Fund fits in the middle, and it is the letter "F" on the triangle. Let's say that "F" stands for "just fine" for most investors, because trying to make it too fast is what causes most failures. Remember, those who make it to their goal of financial independence have usually done it slowly. If you select your fund well from this category, you should be able to obtain your 12 percent compounded over a twenty-year period.

INCOME FUNDS

There are a number of quality income funds. Their portfolio managers choose stocks that have paid good dividends in the past, have a record of increasing dividends, and have a reasonable expectation of continuing good dividends and market stability of their shares. If your need is for income now, rather than later, then this is the type of fund you may want to consider. Your location on the triangle would be "B."

CORPORATE BOND FUNDS

When you invest in a corporate bond fund, you are placing your dollar in the lower right-hand side of the triangle (D). Bond funds have been around for many years; however, during the growth craze of the 1960s, they attracted very little attention. With the agonizing reappraisals that occurred in the stock market and the higher interest rates of the 1980s, they became popular again.

Bond funds invest most of their assets in debt-type securities such as corporate bonds and debentures, convertible bonds, treasury bonds and notes, or commercial paper. Instead of taking an equity position in the market, you become a lender of money when you choose these funds. When you invest in a bond fund, the price of the shares will fluctuate with interest rates. If you invest in a bond fund when the yield is 12 percent and the rate of interest goes to 14 percent, then the fund will not be able to sell its bonds at cost and, therefore, the price of your shares would decline. On the other hand, if the going rate drops to 10 percent, the fund probably can sell the bonds at a premium and the price of your shares will increase.

BALANCED FUNDS

You will find balanced funds in position "C" on the triangle. These are funds that invest approximately 60 percent of their funds in high-quality bonds and the remainder in high-quality income-producing blue chip stocks. In periods of market decline, if that decline has not been caused by extraordinarily high interest rates, they could experience less volatility than the growth funds. Conversely, in a rising market they usually lag behind.

CONVERTIBLE BOND FUNDS

In an effort to obtain the best of two worlds, some management groups established convertible bond funds a few years ago. These funds were designed to have a relatively good yield and some potential for growth. Any dollars you have placed in these funds would be placed around "E" on the triangle. As discussed earlier, convertible bonds are supposed to offer you the best of two worlds: the guarantee of principal and rate of return of a bond, and the potential for growth of common stock.

The theory runs that, even though you may be placing a bit of a damper on maximum growth potential, there is downside protection, for the convertible bond should drop in price only to a level where it will take on the characteristics of a bond yielding the current interest level. Unfortunately, we have had wildly gyrating and unusually escalating interest rates that have made these funds more volatile.

GLOBAL FUNDS

We have seen that the New Economy is becoming a global economy; and because of this, it would be prudent to investigate the number of outstanding funds that invest worldwide, especially since nearly 50 percent of the world's equity markets lie outside the United States.

Every day we are reminded of just how global our society has become and how dependent we all are on the technology and products of other countries. We drive German and Japanese cars; listen to Japanese stereos, radios, and television sets; wear sandals, blouses, and skirts made in Korea, Thailand, and Brazil. Everything from our most advanced communications and information systems to the small economy car sitting in our driveway comes from outside the United States.

In 15 of the past 25 calendar years, the Europe, Australia, and Far East Index, which is calculated by Capital International and reflects all of the major stock markets outside of North America, has done better than Capital International's U.S. Index, which tracks only the U.S. market. Since a basic principle of investing is to diversify, worldwide diversification seems to make good common sense.

SPECIALTY FUNDS

Specialty funds may concentrate on technology, health care, insurance, banking, utilities, or gold and other precious metals stocks. I have not placed them on the triangle because their characteristics are not easily categorized.

Mutual funds that invest in gold and silver mining companies both here and abroad can be a very interesting approach in times of worldwide economic instability and super inflation. To participate in gold you can buy gold coins, gold bullion, stocks of individual gold companies, or mutual funds concentrating in gold stocks. There are three basic reasons for buying gold mining shares in contrast to gold bullion. The first is that gold bullion does not pay dividends, while gold stocks have a historic record of paying relatively high dividends, especially South African shares. The second reason is that a government can confiscate gold when there is a danger of the citizenry losing confidence in its money. The third reason is you could expect gold mining shares to appreciate by a much larger percentage than gold bullion.

I use gold funds more as a fail-safe plan, like fire insurance on my home. If my home doesn't burn down, I don't cancel my fire insurance. If your gold shares do well, your other funds will not do as well.

MUNICIPAL BOND FUNDS

These funds provide tax-free income, permit additions in small amounts, and provide reinvestment privileges. They will be covered in detail in a later chapter.

GOVERNMENT SECURITIES FUNDS

In recent years, funds that invest chiefly in government securities have been attracting larger and larger amounts of capital, sparked by the decline in yields from savings accounts. These funds invest in government instruments such as mortgage-backed securities guaranteed by the Government National Mortgage Association (commonly called Ginny Maes), as well as Treasury bonds, note options, futures, and options on financial futures and repurchase agreements collateralized by U.S. government securities. Even though these funds offer relative stability and can offer higher income than money market mutual funds, their share values do change regularly with the fluctuations of market interest rates, just like those of any other fixed-income securities. The underlying government securities are guaranteed, but your share value is not.

MONEY MARKET MUTUAL FUNDS

In my opinion, there are only three places to have guaranteed liquid dollars—in a checking account, a money market mutual fund, or a bank money market account. You need funds in a checking account for convenience, but remember, that most checking accounts pay no interest unless you maintain a sizable balance. Money market mutual funds came about during the mid-1970s when high interest rates became available to those who had $100,000 to invest in savings. You probably remember seeing the ads back in 1974 offering 12 percent on $100,000 certificates of deposit. Well, not everyone had $100,000 in cash, so some of the funds established money market funds whereby investors with as little as $1,000 could take advantage of these higher rates by pooling their money with others in the fund.

When you place your money in one of these funds, there is no cost to put it in and no cost to take it out; it compounds daily; your rate will usually be comparable to that on a million-dollar certificate of deposit; you can write a check for $500 or more (some funds less); and you can even draw interest while the check is clearing.

Regular money market funds are invested in large-denomination, short-term money market instruments issued by the Treasury, government agencies, banks, and corporations. There are also money market mutual funds that must have 100 percent of their assets invested in either Treasury, federal agency obligations, or reposits backed by them. Their yield is generally ½ to 1 percent less, and some are exempt from state and local taxes.

I can see six advantages to money market mutual funds. The advantages are: 1) higher yields; 2) instant liquidity; 3) check-writing privileges; 4) funds draw interest while checks are clearing; 5) more safety; and 6) more privacy.

The "more safety" I have mentioned above may have surprised you. I know the argument that deposits in banks are protected by the FDIC (up to $100,000), while there is technically no insurance for money market funds. However, if there should be a tremendous run on the banks, the $100,000 could be hard to deliver. On the other hand, if you want added safety, you may use the funds that only invest in U.S. government paper, which is backed by the people who print our money.

Learn to use money market mutual funds for your business and personal use. You will need accounts with two different managements and you will learn why when we discuss "timing." On the triangle I have represented money market mutual funds by the letter "G" and have placed it outside the triangle, since it would be out of the market. Here "G" could represent "good" if money is attracting high interest rates or you are holding cash for reserves or until you make your next investment.

Other Mutual Fund Benefits

In addition to matching your financial objectives, properly selected mutual funds can provide other valuable benefits. These benefits include:

1. Convenience
2. Dollar-cost-averaging
3. Ease of recordkeeping
4. Passing on professional management
5. Ease of estate settlement
6. Lower Costs
7. Quantity discounts and rights of accumulation
8. Exchange privilege
9. Timing
10. Performance

CONVENIENCE—AN ESSENTIAL INGREDIENT

The first benefit is convenience. We all do what is convenient to us, and mutual funds can offer this convenience with a plan that will fit almost any pocketbook. You may start an investment program in a mutual fund with a relatively small amount of money; in fact, some funds have no minimum initial investment. Others will accept as small an amount as $100, and you may then add funds in any amount, which may be as low as $25. In addition, you have the privilege of automatically reinvesting both your dividends and capital gains, usually without commission. Some funds charge to reinvest dividends but none charge to reinvest capital gains. Since a mutual fund permits immediate reinvestment of small or large amounts of money, it gives you an opportunity to speed up your compounding potential.

DOLLAR-COST-AVERAGING AS YOU EARN

The second item on the list of additional advantages that a mutual fund may offer is that you can truly dollar-cost-average. This means putting the same amount of money into the same security at the same interval, which lets you invest as you earn. This guarantees that you will always buy more shares at a low cost than a high cost, giving you an average cost for your securities. If the market eventually goes up (it always has, though we don't know the future) you will make money. This system doesn't take brilliance or luck, just discipline to invest each month. One certainty of the stock market is that it will fluctuate, so put this benefit to work for you by putting an amount you can comfortably invest each month in your fund account and invest that amount on the same day each month.

You can also dollar-cost-average with larger lump sum investments. For example, you have $50,000 to invest but are not certain if it is the right time in the market to commit so large a portion of your assets. You could begin with $10,000 and add $10,000 each month for five months, or spread your investment over more months.

The mutual funds will carry your share purchase out to the third decimal point, which allows you to truly dollar-cost-average. And most funds will provide a bank draft authorization so that they can automatically draft your bank account each month. This is a good way to have a systematic investing program which insures that a deposit is made each month to the fund account without your having to remember to write a check. If you were to start early enough in your working career and did nothing but set up a bank draft system into a good mutual fund for a reasonable amount of your earnings, there is no doubt in my mind that you would become financially independent, probably many years before it is time for you to retire.

RECORDKEEPING MADE EASY

Another benefit of the mutual fund is that you have professionals doing your recordkeeping. You will have five choices when you open an account; and regardless of which choices you make, the fund will provide you with a historical record of your account.

1. Reinvest all distributions

2. Reinvest all distributions and add amounts systematically or as you desire

3. Receive dividends in cash and reinvest capital gains

4. Receive dividends and capital gains in cash

5. Receive a check a month

All you need to do is keep the last confirmation you receive each year, and you will have a complete record of your account. The mutual fund will also send you a Form 1099, showing the dividends and capital gains paid to you for the year. This you will want to keep for preparing your federal income tax return. You will also receive a confirmation statement every time there is any activity in your account.

PASSING ON PROFESSIONAL MANAGEMENT

The fourth benefit of a mutual fund is that it allows you to choose professional management for those dependent on you. This is a way that you can ''will some brains'' to your family so that they can continue to have professional management for their money in the event that you are not here to provide it for them.

EASE OF ESTATE SETTLEMENT

Another reason clients choose to place some of their assets in mutual funds as they grow older is the ease of estate settlement. Upon your death, the individual stocks in your portfolio will be frozen and can only be changed with the permission of the courts. This could be a time-consuming process, and in the meantime there may be a good reason to sell some of the individual issues to take advantage of conditions in the market. You do not purchase individual stocks when you invest in a mutual fund. Rather, you purchase shares in the fund that purchases the stocks. In the event of your death, mutual fund shares in your portfolio are frozen in the estate, but not the securities that make up the portfolio of the fund; and the fund's portfolio managers are free to buy and sell as market conditions dictate. Therefore, the mutual fund can provide professional management of the assets while awaiting settlement of the estate, which could take several years.

Another advantage that a mutual fund makes available is the ease with which an estate can be divided with no disruption of diversification. Let's assume that there are four heirs, that the benefactor wanted them to share and share alike, and that the securities in the estate were in the form of 4,000 shares of the Seminar Fund. Each heir would receive 1,000 shares and there would be no disruption of diversification in each of the four portfolios. Each would still own a proportionate share of 100 to 150 stocks, all professionally selected and managed as if they belonged to one billionaire.

LOWER COSTS

Mutual funds should not be used as trading vehicles, for the initial commission to buy shares of the fund can be higher than for individual stocks. However, there is no commission to sell, regardless of how much the shares may have grown in value. Also, most funds do not charge a commission to reinvest dividends or capital gains. This can result in lower commission costs to you in the long run when compared to buying and selling individual stocks.

It is interesting to compare the costs and commissions involved in dealing with mutual funds with other types of popular investments which are considered by many to be "free." As I said before, "there is no such thing as a free lunch." For example, let's assume that you had $10,000 to invest. A savings institution would not have charged you a commission to open a savings account; and, as a matter of fact, it may have given you a dandy toaster or a transistor radio for doing so. But how much does it really cost? Thirty years later, your $10,000 would have grown to $53,640 with the savings institution, if all the distributions had been reinvested. However, in that same period, had your $10,000 been in the Seminar Fund with all distributions reinvested, your results as shown below would have been $237,243. In the savings account you would have received back five times your original capital; in the Seminar Fund you would have received back over 23 times your original capital. If you deposited funds in a savings account to avoid paying commissions on the mutual fund, that "free" savings account cost you roughly $173,603. (Note Figure 5-1, p. 108.)

I call mutual fund commissions an "opportunity fee." My reason for doing so is this: let's assume that you want to travel from Houston to Dallas, and the only way to get there is by bus. So you go to the bus station and the clerk writes out your ticket and says, "That will be $14.65, please." You answer, "I'm not going to pay that." If you don't, you are just not going to Dallas. As I have said before, it is not

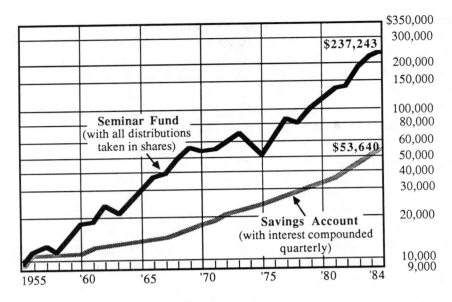

$350,000
300,000

$237,243
200,000
150,000

Seminar Fund
(with all distributions
taken in shares)

100,000
80,000
60,000
50,000
40,000
30,000

$53,640

Savings Account
(with interest compounded
quarterly)

20,000

10,000
9,000

1955   '60   '65   '70   '75   '80   '84

Based on data provided by the U.S. League of Savings Institutions.
Rates reflect both passbook and longer term certificate accounts.
A savings account offers a guaranteed return of principal and a fixed rate
of interest–but no opportunity for capital growth.

Figure 5-1.

what something costs you, but what it pays you that should be your chief concern.

There are, however, some mutual funds that do not make a sales charge. They are commonly referred to as "no load" funds. These are sold through direct mail and newspaper, radio and television ads. With these you will not have the help of a broker or financial planner to match your financial objective with the fund's objective, to select professional managers, to monitor their performance on an ongoing basis, or to time your purchases and exchanges. You will not have an original commission, but you may have costs you would not have with funds that do charge a commission.

Some funds, for example, use a version of a sales charge under a provision known as Rule 12b-1. Under this rule, they are allowed to charge a fee against the assets of the funds for distribution costs (a portion of which may be used to compensate brokers and financial planners) through a continuing annual charge against the assets of the fund, causing existing shareholders to bear the charge indefinitely. Some also have a contingent deferred charge which must be paid if the fund is redeemed before a certain number of years have passed.

QUANTITY DISCOUNTS AND
RIGHTS OF ACCUMULATION

Earlier I said that mutual funds enable the smaller investor to obtain the same advantages as the wealthier investor. The investor who has larger amounts does, however, obtain quantity discounts on his original purchases with a fund.

Perhaps you do not have a sufficiently large sum today to qualify for one of the higher quantity discounts, but you will during the next 13 months. Then you may want to consider buying under a letter of intent. The letter of inent is not a commitment to buy, but a privilege to buy at a discount during the 13-month period. If you decide later that you do not want to add the additional amount, that is your privilege. If the 13 months pass and you have not completed your letter, you have two choices: return the discount (which you would not have received anyway without the letter), or the custodian bank (which escrowed some of your shares when you signed the letter) will sell enough of your escrowed shares to return to the fund the additional discount you received and will send you the remaining shares. In effect, your discount would be adjusted back to the lower level. Therefore, the letter of intent never costs you more and it can save you money if you invest the additional amount.

Under what is called "rights of accumulation," you may also qualify for additional discounts. Let's assume that you own shares that have a value of $20,000 and that you have $5,000 you would like to add to your account. You may do so under the "rights of accumulation" at the $25,000 discount level. As your account grows, you may continue to add to it at progressively smaller "opportunity fees" as you cross each discount level.

THE EXCHANGE PRIVILEGE

Another valuable and important benefit of most mutual funds is that they can be exchanged for other mutual funds managed by the same company. Some companies offer as many as fifteen different funds for you to choose from. There is no commission for the exchange and either no charge or a $5 fee that would go to the transfer agent for his expense in making the exchange. This privilege could be of interest to you if your financial objective changed from, say, growth to income because you are nearing retirement age. You would simply move your assets from the growth fund to the income fund and start receiving monthly or quarterly distributions in cash for living expenses. Or instead of exchanging funds, you are also entitled to alter the terms of reinvestment or distribution of the fund you already have.

TIMING

The greatest advantage of owning mutual funds is that the exchange privilege gives you the ability to move in and out of the stock market without a commission. If, for example, the Federal Reserve is severely tightening the money supply, driving interest rates up and choking the market, you may want to move from a fund that invests in stocks to a money market fund for safer harbor, ride out the storm, and draw a tidy sum in interest in the meantime.

You may wonder why the fund managers do not take this action for you. They do move into as defensive a position as they can under the regulations by which they must operate. However, to qualify as a regulated investment company, which is important to you in terms of your taxes, less than 30 percent of their gross income in any fiscal year can be derived from holding securities less than three months. This regulation may inhibit them from moving from stock to cash on a short-term basis, which for your purposes may be the most prudent action to take. The exchange privilege gives you the opportunity to take advantage of the strength of top professional management while avoiding the weakness caused by these regulations. This can make it possible for you to exploit their offensive ability by holding their funds during rising markets and avoiding what may be short-term weakness by moving out of funds entirely during down markets. This process we call timing.

Timing Services. You can attempt to time your own moves in and out of the market, or you can use a timing service to do this for you at a fee. Our firm makes a timing service available to our clients. They can either avail themselves of this service or not. If they choose to do so, the timing firm will charge them 2 percent per annum of the net asset value of their shares under timing. The timing service company will either bill the client on a quarterly basis or the client can authorize the service to redeem sufficient shares of the fund to pay for the fee.

The timing service is superimposed on the fund. It is not done by the management of the fund. As a matter of fact, they prefer that you do not use timing, but leave everything in their hands. Timing services have become very viable considerations during the past few years, because the Federal Reserve has been "playing with" the money supply and causing great volatility in interest rates and available capital.

During the 20-year period between 1946 and 1966, we experienced an era of stability in our economy. Inflation was moderate, the fiscal authorities were not tampering unduly with the money supply, and for the most part the United States was dedicated to the profit system under free enterprise. Our standard of living was going up, and our gross national production was increasing steadily. Then in 1966, the Johnson administration attempted "welfare and warfare" without the courage to increase taxes. It wanted to create the "Great Society" without paying for it. This ended the era of stability and launched us into the era of pendulum economics.

Up until that time, our stock market indexes resembled a man with a yo-yo walking up a flight of stairs. The yo-yo went up and down, but the man eventually climbed the stairs. With the coming of pendulum economics, the market became like a man with a yo-yo *standing* on the stairs. You would make a profit from your investments and lose it, make it and lose it. It became more and more obvious that there were times when it might be too risky to be in the market and other times when it was risky to be out of it. If the drops could be avoided, the gains could be accelerated. This brought the birth of the timing services.

A sketch of what I have just described might look something like this:

Era of Stability   Era of Pendulum Economics

Our company and others went out to find a timing service that would get our clients out of the market at point "A" and back in at point "B." I wish I could report to you that we found one. We did not. We did find more than one service that had a good record of getting out in the "A" area and back in around the "B" area, but obviously, this would not guarantee against a loss. For example, if you went in at the high at $10 and the timing service triggered you out at $9, you would have suffered a $1 loss. What the timing service attempts to do is avoid your investment going to, say, $6 before you start your climb up again. Even if your climb starts at $9, your potential is greater than if you had come down to $6 before starting up again.

Timing services are not a panacea. In sideways markets they can be very disappointing. They should be used, if you so choose to use them, over at least a four-year period. Figure 5-2 shows the hypothetical results of using a particular timing service with a growth fund in the same family of funds as the Seminar Fund. As you will note, $100,000 grew during the eight years and five months on a buy/hold basis to $579,422, or 16.7 percent a year, and to $910,125 with timing, or 21 percent a year. The future may be better or, then again, it may be worse.

If you are convinced that a timing service can help in keeping you out of the market when you ought to be out and in the market when you ought to be in, then you should choose a family of funds that has an aggressive high-quality growth fund and a money market fund. The growth fund should go up faster in an up market when you are in and should go down faster in a down market; but if you are in when you ought to be in, and out when you ought to be out, this should work to your advantage.

You should, however, also be aware of the disadvantages of timing services. First, they can only try to get you out near the top and back in near the bottom, but they will not be infallible. Though the fund does not charge a commission to make the exchange, the IRS does get into the act. If a gain has occurred, you will have realized either a long- or short-term capital gain, and the IRS will want what they think is their share. However, if you are using timing with a tax-sheltered vehicle such as a Keogh, Individual Retirement Account, IRA rollover, pension, or profit-sharing plan, all of these compound tax-sheltered, and no tax will be due.

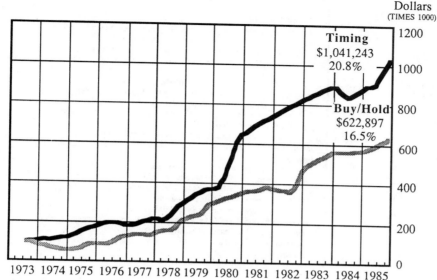

Dollars
(TIMES 1000)

Timing
$1,041,243
20.8%

Buy/Hold
$622,897
16.5%

1200
1000
800
600
400
200
0

1973 1974 1975 1976 1977 1978 1979 1980 1981 1982 1983 1984 1985

Figure 5-2.

PERFORMANCE

Another benefit of mutual funds is that their performance can be measured over the years. When investigating the numerous funds that are on the market, you can perhaps obtain some wisdom from the past, although there is no guarantee that it will be the same in the future. A well-managed fund should average in excess of 12 percent compounded over the next ten years. There will no doubt be times when this will be an unattainable goal and other times when you will vastly outperform this objective.

Figure 5-3 shows the 51-year record of the Seminar Fund without superimposing a timing service but using the expertise of their professional management. During this period, many seemingly catastrophic events occurred, as you can see by the notations titled "There have always been 'reasons' not to invest." You will also note, however, that during its 51 years from January 1, 1934, until December 31, 1984, it had a compound rate of return of 12.46 percent. You can see for yourself the years it did that well and the years it did not. As a matter of fact, 19 one-year periods were below that average and 32 one-year periods were above that average.

Results of a $10,000 investment
with capital gain distributions taken in shares[1]

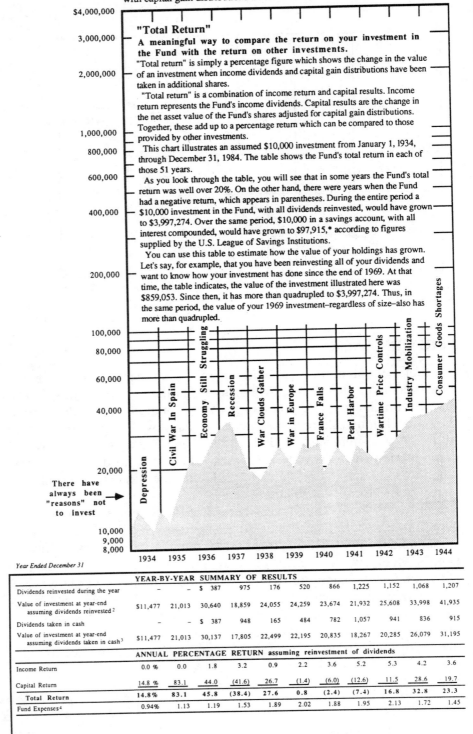

"Total Return"
A meaningful way to compare the return on your investment in the Fund with the return on other investments.

"Total return" is simply a percentage figure which shows the change in the value of an investment when income dividends and capital gain distributions have been taken in additional shares.

"Total return" is a combination of income return and capital results. Income return represents the Fund's income dividends. Capital results are the change in the net asset value of the Fund's shares adjusted for capital gain distributions. Together, these add up to a percentage return which can be compared to those provided by other investments.

This chart illustrates an assumed $10,000 investment from January 1, 1934, through December 31, 1984. The table shows the Fund's total return in each of those 51 years.

As you look through the table, you will see that in some years the Fund's total return was well over 20%. On the other hand, there were years when the Fund had a negative return, which appears in parentheses. During the entire period a $10,000 investment in the Fund, with all dividends reinvested, would have grown to $3,997,274. Over the same period, $10,000 in a savings account, with all interest compounded, would have grown to $97,915,* according to figures supplied by the U.S. League of Savings Institutions.

You can use this table to estimate how the value of your holdings has grown. Let's say, for example, that you have been reinvesting all of your dividends and want to know how your investment has done since the end of 1969. At that time, the table indicates, the value of the investment illustrated here was $859,053. Since then, it has more than quadrupled to $3,997,274. Thus, in the same period, the value of your 1969 investment–regardless of size–also has more than quadrupled.

There have always been "reasons" not to invest

Year Ended December 31

YEAR-BY-YEAR SUMMARY OF RESULTS

	1934	1935	1936	1937	1938	1939	1940	1941	1942	1943	1944
Dividends reinvested during the year	–	–	$ 387	975	176	520	866	1,225	1,152	1,068	1,207
Value of investment at year-end assuming dividends reinvested[2]	$11,477	21,013	30,640	18,859	24,055	24,259	23,674	21,932	25,608	33,998	41,935
Dividends taken in cash	–	–	$ 387	948	165	484	782	1,057	941	836	915
Value of investment at year-end assuming dividends taken in cash[3]	$11,477	21,013	30,137	17,805	22,499	22,195	20,835	18,267	20,285	26,079	31,195

ANNUAL PERCENTAGE RETURN assuming reinvestment of dividends

	1934	1935	1936	1937	1938	1939	1940	1941	1942	1943	1944
Income Return	0.0 %	0.0	1.8	3.2	0.9	2.2	3.6	5.2	5.3	4.2	3.6
Capital Return	14.8 %	83.1	44.0	(41.6)	26.7	(1.4)	(6.0)	(12.6)	11.5	28.6	19.7
Total Return	14.8%	83.1	45.8	(38.4)	27.6	0.8	(2.4)	(7.4)	16.8	32.8	23.3
Fund Expenses[4]	0.94%	1.13	1.19	1.53	1.89	2.02	1.88	1.95	2.13	1.72	1.45

Figure 5-3.

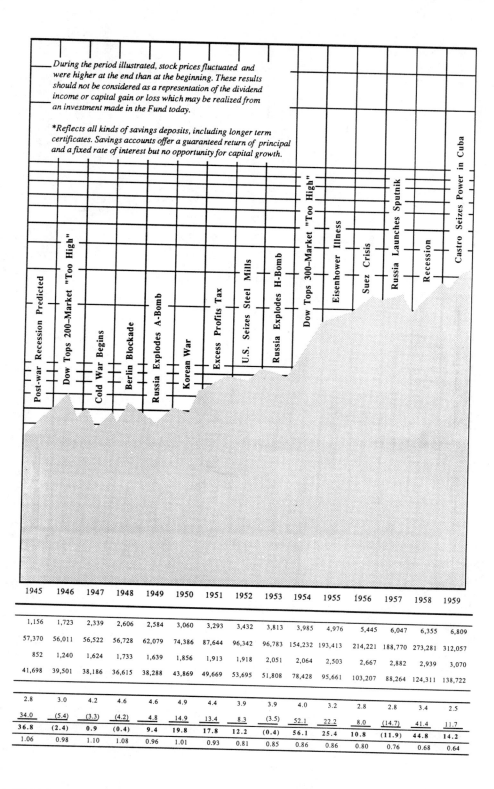

During the period illustrated, stock prices fluctuated and were higher at the end than at the beginning. These results should not be considered as a representation of the dividend income or capital gain or loss which may be realized from an investment made in the Fund today.

*Reflects all kinds of savings deposits, including longer term certificates. Savings accounts offer a guaranteed return of principal and a fixed rate of interest but no opportunity for capital growth.

Event labels (left to right): Post-war Recession Predicted · Dow Tops 200—Market "Too High" · Cold War Begins · Berlin Blockade · Russia Explodes A-Bomb · Korean War · Excess Profits Tax · U.S. Seizes Steel Mills · Russia Explodes H-Bomb · Dow Tops 300—Market "Too High" · Eisenhower Illness · Suez Crisis · Russia Launches Sputnik · Recession · Castro Seizes Power in Cuba

1945	1946	1947	1948	1949	1950	1951	1952	1953	1954	1955	1956	1957	1958	1959
1,156	1,723	2,339	2,606	2,584	3,060	3,293	3,432	3,813	3,985	4,976	5,445	6,047	6,355	6,809
57,370	56,011	56,522	56,728	62,079	74,386	87,644	96,342	96,783	154,232	193,413	214,221	188,770	273,281	312,057
852	1,240	1,624	1,733	1,639	1,856	1,913	1,918	2,051	2,064	2,503	2,667	2,882	2,939	3,070
41,698	39,501	38,186	36,615	38,288	43,869	49,669	53,695	51,808	78,428	95,661	103,207	88,264	124,311	138,722

1945	1946	1947	1948	1949	1950	1951	1952	1953	1954	1955	1956	1957	1958	1959
2.8	3.0	4.2	4.6	4.6	4.9	4.4	3.9	3.9	4.0	3.2	2.8	2.8	3.4	2.5
34.0	(5.4)	(3.3)	(4.2)	4.8	14.9	13.4	8.3	(3.5)	52.1	22.2	8.0	(14.7)	41.4	11.7
36.8	(2.4)	0.9	(0.4)	9.4	19.8	17.8	12.2	(0.4)	56.1	25.4	10.8	(11.9)	44.8	14.2
1.06	0.98	1.10	1.08	0.96	1.01	0.93	0.81	0.85	0.86	0.86	0.80	0.76	0.68	0.64

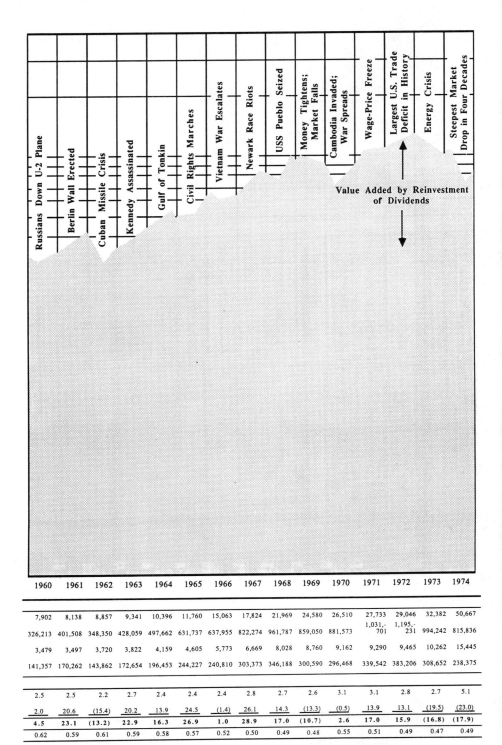

Russians Down U-2 Plane · Berlin Wall Erected · Cuban Missile Crisis · Kennedy Assassinated · Gulf of Tonkin · Civil Rights Marches · Vietnam War Escalates · Newark Race Riots · USS Pueblo Seized · Money Tightens; Market Falls · Cambodia Invaded; War Spreads · Wage-Price Freeze · Largest U.S. Trade Deficit in History · Energy Crisis · Steepest Market Drop in Four Decades

Value Added by Reinvestment of Dividends

1960	1961	1962	1963	1964	1965	1966	1967	1968	1969	1970	1971	1972	1973	1974
7,902	8,138	8,857	9,341	10,396	11,760	15,063	17,824	21,969	24,580	26,510	27,733	29,046	32,382	50,667
326,213	401,508	348,350	428,059	497,662	631,737	637,955	822,274	961,787	859,050	881,573	1,031,-701	1,195,-231	994,242	815,836
3,479	3,497	3,720	3,822	4,159	4,605	5,773	6,669	8,028	8,760	9,162	9,290	9,465	10,262	15,445
141,357	170,262	143,862	172,654	196,453	244,227	240,810	303,373	346,188	300,590	296,468	339,542	383,206	308,652	238,375

1960	1961	1962	1963	1964	1965	1966	1967	1968	1969	1970	1971	1972	1973	1974
2.5	2.5	2.2	2.7	2.4	2.4	2.4	2.8	2.7	2.6	3.1	3.1	2.8	2.7	5.1
2.0	20.6	(15.4)	20.2	13.9	24.5	(1.4)	26.1	14.3	(13.3)	(0.5)	13.9	13.1	(19.5)	(23.0)
4.5	23.1	(13.2)	22.9	16.3	26.9	1.0	28.9	17.0	(10.7)	2.6	17.0	15.9	(16.8)	(17.9)
0.62	0.59	0.61	0.59	0.58	0.57	0.52	0.50	0.49	0.48	0.55	0.51	0.49	0.47	0.49

[1] Results reflect payment of sales charge of 8 1/2% on the $10,000 investment. Thus, the net amount invested was $9,150. There is no sales charge on dividends reinvested or capital gain distributions taken in shares. Results shown do not take into account income and capital gains taxes. The total "cost" of this investment ($10,000 plus $1,273,117 in reinvested dividends) was $1,283,117.
[2] Total value includes reinvested dividends and capital gain distributions totaling $1,283,391 taken in shares in the years 1936-1984.

Clouded Economic Prospects · Economic Recovery Slows · Market Slumps · Interest Rates Rise · Oil Prices Skyrocket · Interest Rates At All-Time Highs · Steep Recession Begins · Worst Recession In 40 Years · Market Hits New Highs · Record Federal Deficits

$3,997,274 Total Value Assuming Dividends Reinvested[1,2]

$768,906 Capital Value Assuming Dividends Taken in Cash[3] (Total Dividends Taken in Cash $351,205)

$10,000 Purchase Price[1]

1975	1976	1977	1978	1979	1980	1981	1982	1983	1984	
48,349	45,088	48,387	54,338	67,923	88,644	112,525	141,850	142,870	155,775	
1,104,526	1,431,428	1,394,567	1,599,500	1,906,129	2,310,865	2,331,160	3,118,449	3,747,299	3,997,274	
13,901	12,429	12,892	13,967	16,843	21,113	25,651	30,668	29,384	30,756	
306,403	386,504	363,406	402,351	461,816	536,159	515,403	651,060	751,961	768,906	Compound rate of return for 51 years
5.9	4.1	3.4	3.9	4.3	4.6	4.9	6.1	4.6	4.2	3.36%
29.5	25.5	(6.0)	10.8	14.9	16.6	(4.0)	27.7	15.6	2.5	9.10%
35.4	29.6	(2.6)	14.7	19.2	21.2	0.9	33.8	20.2	6.7	12.46%
0.48	0.46	0.49	0.49	0.47	0.46	0.45	0.46	0.44	0.47	

[1] Capital value includes capital gain distributions taken in shares (total $387,463) but does not reflect income dividends taken in cash.

[2] Fund expense percentages are provided as additional information. They should not be subtracted from any other figure in the table because the income return figures already reflect their effect.

As you look at this record, you may be asking, "Is this investment guaranteed?" I'm happy to tell you it is not! If you want a "guaranteed" dollar, you should take your investment to an institution that has a gold emblem on the door that declares that your funds are "guaranteed" (up to $100,000) by the FDIC. What does FDIC stand for? That's right—the Federal Deposit Insurance Corporation, a guaranteeing arm of the government. Have you ever bought an insurance policy for which you did not pay a premium? What if I came to you and said, "I want to guarantee that you can always have your $10,000 back at any time regardless of what increases may have occurred in your cost of living and regardless of how much money I have made on your money, and all I will charge you is $1,240.04 per month, every month you leave it with me, or $14,880.48 per year"? You would probably say to me, "The cost is too high." In reality, that is what would have been your average cost the past 51 years to have had your $10,000 guaranteed, for a guaranteed dollar rarely pays —it usually costs dearly.

Now that you have studied the chart of the Seminar Fund, what are your reactions? Remember, it covers a long period of time—51 years from 1934 through 1984. Don't you agree that this is a fairly graphic picture of a man with a yo-yo going up the stairs? What difference did it make to him how many times the yo-yo yo-yo'd during the life of the fund? The stairs he climbed reached quite a height! If you had invested $10,000 on January 1, 1934, reinvested all your capital gains distributions (classified as part of capital by regulation), and on December 31, 1984, decided to cash in your shares, you would have received $768,906 net to you after all costs had been taken out, with the exception of your federal and state income tax responsibility. If you had reinvested both your capital gains and dividends, your $10,000 would have grown to $3,997,274.

What about inflation? Inflation is the economist's way of saying "rising prices." The experts can all explain how it happens and what it means, but no one has been able to make it go away. To keep even with rising prices, you will need a constantly rising income. In other words, you will need more take-home pay from your job and more dividends from your investments.

Look again at the chart in Figure 5-3 (p. 114) and find the line entitled "Dividends taken in cash." It shows how much cash, in income dividends, your $10,000 investment with capital gains reinvested would have generated during each of the past 51 years. Note that in 46 of the past 51 years, the dividends paid by the Seminar Fund increased over the prior year. From a modest $387 paid in 1936, the dividend payments have increased to $155,775 in 1984, more than 15 times your original investment.

Case Studies

THE BERKLEYS AND THE CAMPBELLS

Another way to examine the cost of the "guaranteed dollar" is to take the hypothetical case of Sally and Jim Berkley and Vicki and Jack Campbell. Both invested $50,000 on January 1, 1955, and each couple invested their funds for retirement and for some income to help with current expenses. The Berkleys placed their money in a "guaranteed position" where they could obtain a 12 percent return with the principal guaranteed. (This was no small feat, since the rate being paid by savings and loan associations in 1955 was 2.9 percent. Perhaps they invested in Lower Slobovia Sewer Bonds.) The first year, and every year thereafter, they earned $6,000 interest in their investment—$500 per month—never less, never more. The Berkleys felt safe and said, "With an investment that pays 12 percent a year, we have no worries and we are safe for life." But were they really? What happened to their purchasing power? In 1955 they could have bought a new luxury car for $6,000, but today they would have to spend that much on a used Volkswagen. Unfortunately, the Berkleys did not understand how savagely inflation could eat away at the purchasing power of their dollars. Their "safe" investment turned out to be not so safe after all.

The Campbells, on the other hand, understood that the only "safe" investment was one that would protect their purchasing power. They realized they would need more and more income in the years ahead and that their original investment would also need to grow. The Campbells decided to invest in the Seminar Fund; and, like the Berkleys, they took their income in cash. They knew that the value of their investment and the size of their income dividends would fluctuate, but they recognized the fact that a rising income is the best hedge against rising prices. And they felt that, over the long haul, an investment in the Seminar Fund and the income that it produced should continue to grow, reflecting the growing earnings and dividends of the companies in which the Fund invested.

Figure 5-4 shows what happened. Year after year, the Campbells received more income—rising income to help keep pace with the rising cost of living. By 1984, the Berkleys were still getting only $6,000 a year, while the Campbells received $18,731 in dividends from their Seminar Fund, which was 37.46 percent on their original investment of $50,000.

The Campbells had another enormous advantage over the Berkleys. At the end of 1984, The Berkleys' investment was still worth $50,000, since it was "guaranteed," but the Campbells' investment in the Seminar Fund had grown to $468,280 in addition to the $199,638 they had received in dividends. Perhaps you should think about the Berkleys and the Campbells as you plan your financial future, remembering that a fixed return, no matter how high it is, is never "safe" as long as prices keep going up. If you believe we will continue to have rising prices and feel that you will need rising income to offset them, maybe some of your investment dollars should be put to work in an investment like the Seminar Fund.

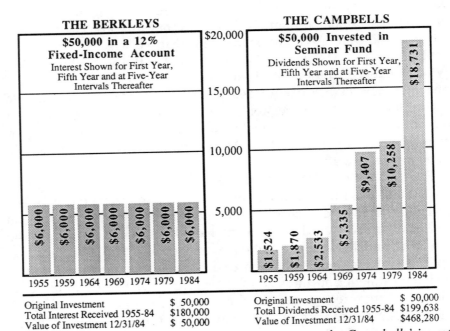

Original Investment	$ 50,000
Total Interest Received 1955-84	$180,000
Value of Investment 12/31/84	$ 50,000

Original Investment	$ 50,000
Total Dividends Received 1955-84	$199,638
Value of Investment 12/31/84	$468,280

Figure 5-4. *The Berkleys' "guaranteed" account vs. the Campbells' investment account.*

JOHN AND MARTHA DAWSON

John Dawson had worked for the telephone company for 25 years, but like many others, he and his wife Martha had not thought much about retirement and had saved very little. When John reached his fiftieth birthday, he and Martha began to wonder what his pension at the telephone company would be in 15 years, when he would be ready to retire. When he found out that it would only amount to $550 per month, he and Martha realized that even with Social Security their pension would not be enough to allow them to retire in dignity. After scrutinizing their budget, they decided they could save $100 a month, so each month after that John sent a check for $100 to the Seminar Fund. John and Martha did this for 15 years until John was ready to retire from the telephone company. When he retired, John instructed the fund to send him a check for his dividends each quarter and also to send him any capital gains made each year. This the fund did. John lived comfortably in retirement for another 20 years; and when he died, Martha looked at his records and discovered, much to her surprise, that they had received a total of $49,461 in dividends and $51,831 in capital gains distributions during the 20 years of John's retirement. Not only that, but the net asset value of their account in the Seminar Fund had grown to $100,198. And all John and Martha had ever done was to save $100 per month from age 50 to 65!

Table 7 in the Appendix gives the record of the Seminar Fund, showing a beginning investment of $250, adding $100 per month for 15 years for a total investment of $18,150, and then taking in cash the dividends and capital gains for the next 20 years. If you are 45 years of age, five years younger than John, you can see the 32 20-year periods of the fund in Table 8 in the Appendix. Perhaps you are only 40 and have 25 years to invest before retirement. Table 8 also shows you what has happened during each of the 27 25-year periods in the last 45 years. And if you are only 14 years of age, Table 9 in the Appendix is the total record that was attained by dollar-cost-averaging over a 51-year period. Beginning with $250 and adding only $100 per month, the total return for the period after all costs, with the exception of federal income taxes, was $3,371,100 from dollar-cost-average.

The secret of financial independence is not brilliance or luck, but the discipline to save a part of all you earn and to put it to work in a good cross section of American industry, energy, and real estate.

GEORGE GENIUS vs. SAM STEADY

You may be asking yourself, "Is this the right time to invest? If I wait, could I buy at a cheaper price?" To help answer these questions, let's look at two investors and, just for fun, let's call them Sam Steady and George Genius. Sam began investing $100 each month, reinvesting all his dividends and capital gains for 30 years in the Seminar Fund. When he calculated his results, he found that he had invested $36,000 and he held shares with a market value of $244,401.

George Genius, on the other hand, was truly a genius. After long, tedious hours of study and agonizing decision making, he successfully picked the absolute low of the year each year for 30 years and invested $1,200 at that point. When he calculated his results, he found that he had invested $36,000 and that the market value of his shares was now $276,103. He was sure that his performance would be so far superior to Sam Steady's that he was eager to tell him about it. When they sat down to compare their results, George was deflated to learn he had outperformed Sam by only $31,702 or less than $4/10$ percent per year. Moreover, Sam had done no agonizing over his investment and had enjoyed many hours of leisure that George had not had.

When is the best time to start a monthly investment program? Answer: as soon as possible.

Direct or Indirect Investing?

All money is invested in American industry either directly or indirectly. The direct method can be accomplished by putting your money to work in an investment similar to the Seminar Fund. An indirect method would be to lend your funds to a savings institution and let it invest in American industry. When you choose the latter method, you in effect place a filter between you and your investment. The screen in that filter has in the past been equipped with a very fine mesh, and very little has filtered through to you.

Remember, to become financially independent you must save and let your money grow. Many save and let savings institutions grow. Remember, to participate in the profits of American industry, you must get your eyes off the yo-yo and onto the stairs.

ALL ASSETS FLUCTUATE IN VALUE

Many choose indirect investing because they are worried about the fluctuations in value of direct investments. You should not let daily fluctuations bother you, because everything you own fluctuates in value. The market value of any asset you own is only what someone is willing to pay you for it. Your home fluctuates in value every day, but the newspaper doesn't carry a market page quoting its value, so you are unaware of the fluctuations. As a direct investment, mutual funds also fluctuate in value, but for the long-term investor who does not succumb to the yo-yo panic, those fluctuations have usually been to his benefit.

Consistency of Performance

Another benefit that we can find with mutual funds is consistency of performance over the years. Table 10 in the Appendix is a record of four time periods of the Seminar Fund, showing the span in each that was the best, the worst, and the median period.

For our purposes here, let's consider the median to be fairly typical. Here are the compound growth rates for each of the median periods:

MEDIAN PERIOD	ENDING VALUE	COMPOUND RATE
10 years (1955–64)	$ 29,537	11.4%
15 years (1933–49)	49,772	11.3%
20 years (1946–65)	100,743	12.2%
25 years (1958–82)	151,233	11.5%
Lifetime		
51 years (1934–84)	3,997,274	12.5%

In other words, for each long-term period the typical compound annual growth rate, when all dividends and capital gains distributions were taken in additional shares, was either slightly above or below 12 percent. And for the full 51-year lifetime of the fund, the actual—not median—compound growth rate was 12.46 percent. In today's environment of unusually high interest rates, 12 percent may not seem high, but remember that the current level of interest rates is a very recent phenomenon.

Your IRA Account and Mutual Funds

Mutual funds should make an excellent vehicle for your IRA account. It is simple to establish an IRA account by choosing the fund in which you wish to invest and completing an application form. The custodian cost is usually around $6 per year. The law provides that you may now contribute to an IRA account 100 percent of your earned income up to a maximum of $2,000 per year, deduct that amount from your taxable income, and let the earnings compound tax-deferred until you begin withdrawals from the account. If you have a non-working spouse, $2,250 can be contributed if at least $250 is registered in the latter's name. (This may be raised to $2,000. See Tax Addendum in the Appendix.) If both are working each can contribute $2,000 per year.

You may make your contribution any time before April 15 of the year following the year during which you made the income. If you have the $2,000 at the beginning of that year, you should consider making your contribution then, because that way you will have the entire amount compounding tax-sheltered for the longest possible period. If you choose to invest as you earn, a mutual fund is especially adaptable to this plan, in that you can add relatively small amounts to your account, and if you contribute the same amount each month or quarter, you will get the mathematical advantage of dollar-cost-averaging.

If you invested $2,000, $2,250, or $4,000 per year in the Seminar Fund, you would have had the following assets in your IRA account:

NUMBER OF YEARS	AMOUNT OF INVESTMENT		
	$2,000	*$2,250*	*$4,000*
10	$ 45,182	$ 50,888	$ 91,170
20	138,357	155,978	280,103
30	431,645	486,232	871,680
40	$1,590,491	$1,790,904	$3,210,962

The Check-a-Month Plan

Still another benefit you can derive from mutual funds is receiving a regular check every month from your fund account to help pay for your ongoing expenses. Let's assume that you began investing in the Seminar Fund on January 1, 1955, with a lump sum contribution of $10,000, and that you added $100 a month for the next 20 years. By December 31, 1974, you would have invested $33,900, plus dividends and capital gains, and you would own 20,124 shares with a market value of $93,174. (Details in Appendix, Table 11.)

Let's now assume you are ready to start relaxing and enjoying the fruits of your labor and investment program. You would then deposit your shares with the transfer agent of the fund (or you may have left them with him all along as unissued shares), and you would complete and send the fund a withdrawal application stating the amount each month or quarter you would like to receive. You would begin receiving a check a month or quarter, whichever you prefer, and are free to increase, decrease, stop, and start whenever you like. Each time, your check will be accompanied by a complete report on the status of your fund account.

If you had started a 6 percent withdrawal on December 31, 1974, you would have received monthly withdrawals of $465.87, or $5,590.44 per year. (Table 12 in Appendix.) Ten years later, on December 31, 1984, you would have withdrawn a total of $55,900, and your remaining number of shares would have increased to 30,182 with a market value of $332,003. Your net results would have been:

Amount withdrawn	$ 55,900
Amount remaining	332,003
Amount you contributed during 20 years	33,900
Amount contributed by American industry in 30 years	$354,003

Again, you don't have to fight the battle alone if you will let American industry work for you. The check-a-month plan can be an excellent way to use your accumulation in an orderly fashion while keeping the remainder at work in a diversified, continuously managed portfolio of common stocks. And as hard as it may be for you to believe, it was not until the mid-1960s that mutual funds were allowed by our regulatory agencies to show a check-a-month withdrawal record.

You might picture your withdrawal program as a kettle filled with nutritious broth. This broth represents housing, clothing, and food for your retirement years. As the fund needs dollars to send you your check each month, it will redeem shares. When the fund distributes dividends or capital gains, it reinvests them in additional shares. Therefore, the number of shares you own will change with any activity in your account. This is the reason that you deposit your shares with the transfer agent when you begin your withdrawal program. Your concern should not be with the number of total shares in your account but with the net asset value of the shares in the account. In this particular period, not only did you not use up your broth, but it grew to $354,003. You were taking out at a lower rate than American industry was putting in. You are free to increase or decrease your withdrawal any month you choose.

Let's assume that you decided to withdraw a little more from your account than was being added each year in the form of dividends and capital gains. After all, there is nothing sacred about principal and nothing that says that you are obligated to leave an estate to your heirs. You only have the obligation to take care of yourself for as long as you are on the face of this earth. If you used capital at 10 percent while it was only earning 9 percent, do you know how long your capital would last? Twenty-six years! If you begin your withdrawal program at age 65, in 26 years you will be 91 years of age!

Suppose you have $100,000 that is growing at the rate of 7 percent a year, and you withdraw at an annual rate of 8 percent—$8,000 a year or $666.67 per month. Look at the box where these two percentage figures intersect, and you will see that principal will last 30 years.

A check a month can be used in many ways. We have used it for making house payments, after encouraging our clients to make the minimum down payment on their houses, then to invest the difference in a fund and use a withdrawal program to make the additional payments. We have used it for alimony payments (it seems to make it less painful if the fund sends the check directly to the recipient). And we have used it for monthly college expenses.

Figure 5-5 is a handy chart to use in programming how long capital will last:

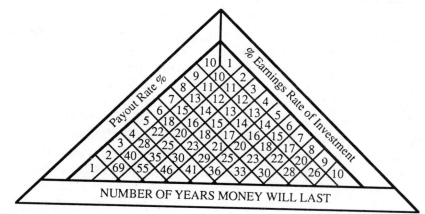

Figure 5-5.

Another way to visualize how long capital will last is to use Figure 5-6.

Withdrawal Rate	Annual Growth Rate of Fund									
	5%	6%	7%	8%	9%	10%	11%	12%	13%	14%
5%										
6%	36									
7%	25	33								
8%	20	23	30							
9%	16	18	22	28						
10%	14	15	17	20	26					
11%	12	13	14	16	19	25				
12%	11	11	12	14	15	18	23			
13%	9	10	11	12	13	15	17	21		
14%	9	9	10	11	11	13	14	17	21	
15%	8	8	9	9	10	11	12	14	16	20

Figure 5-6. *How Long Will Your Money Last?*

Who Invests in Mutual Funds?

A recent New York Stock Exchange study compared 22 million investors who owned only common stocks with nine million investors who owned mutual funds. (Five million owned both mutual funds and common stocks; four million owned funds only.) It contrasted the "stock only" investors with the fund investors and found:

1. Fund investors are the better-educated clients—65 percent are college graduates vs. 50 percent of the "stock only" clients.

2. Fund investors are the wealthiest clients with the largest assets —23 percent have portfolios of more than $25,000 vs. 15 percent of the other clients.

3. And to put away the idea that mutual fund investors lock up their money forever, fund investors are the most active clients, with 25 percent making more than six transactions per year vs. only 10 percent of other clients.

The Hindsight Game

For those considering an investment in individual stocks rather than a mutual fund, let's play a game to test your performance in stock selections. I am even going to let you choose the winners after the race has been run. Below are the thirty stocks in the Dow Jones Industrial Average. I grant you $30,000 and you are to select three stocks and invest $10,000 in each as of December 31, 1933. Now go down the list and make your selections:

DOW JONES INDUSTRIAL STOCK	YOUR SELECTION	ESTIMATED MARKET VALUE
Allied Signal	_____	_____
Aluminum Company of America	_____	_____
American Brands	_____	_____

American Can   _____   _____

American Express   _____   _____

American Telephone & Telegraph   _____   _____

Bethlehem Steel   _____   _____

Chevron   _____   _____

DuPont   _____   _____

Eastman Kodak   _____   _____

Exxon   _____   _____

General Electric   _____   _____

General Foods   _____   _____

General Motors   _____   _____

Goodyear Tire & Rubber   _____   _____

INCO   _____   _____

International Business Machines   _____   _____

International Harvester   _____   _____

International Paper   _____   _____

Merck & Company   _____   _____

Minnesota Mining & Manufacturing   _____   _____

Owens-Illinois   _____   _____

Philip Morris   _____   _____

Procter & Gamble   _____   _____

Sears, Roebuck   _____   _____

Texaco   _____   _____

Union Carbide   _____   _____

United States Steel   _____   _____

United Technologies   _____   _____

Westinghouse Electric   _____   _____

Woolworth, F. W.   _____   _____

Now look at Table 12 in the Appendix and you will find the amount each of your stocks would have grown to in that period of time. Add up their totals and divide by three to get your average. What is your figure? How close does it come to $768,906, the performance figure for $10,000 invested in the Seminar Fund? Are you surprised to find that only three stocks out of the thirty in the Dow Jones Industrial Average outperformed the Seminar Fund? Minnesota Mining & Manufacturing was the top performer of all—$10,000 in it grew to $9,435,000. The second-best performer was International Business Machines, which grew to $5,854,164. And the third was Merck, which grew to $4,230,003. The poorest, International Harvester, only grew to $12,188.

If you had been an investor at the end of 1933, do you think you would have chosen any one of these three stocks? Probably not, because Minnesota Mining & Manufacturing was a small manufacturer of sandpaper with one plant in St. Paul; IBM was a stodgy manufacturer of adding machines and typewriters whose net worth and profits had been declining for four years in a row. It was dropped from the Dow Jones for a number of years because our forefathers doubted if anyone was interested in office equipment. And Merck was a very closely held family business that was several payments behind in dividends to preferred stockholders.

The Seminar Fund during this time outperformed all but these three of the 30 stocks in the Dow Jones Industrial Average, and your $10,000 would have grown to $768,906 without reinvestment of dividends, and to $3,997,274 with reinvestment.

Mutual Funds for Income

At this point you might be saying, "So much for growth. I'm interested in income from my investment." Let's now look at dividends and compare the Seminar Fund to some popular individual stocks. Have you ever said, "If I had just invested in General Motors or American Telephone and Telegraph, I would have received a lot of cash dividends." After all, AT&T is the most widely held stock in the country and General Motors is second. However, had you been an investor in the Seminar Fund for the same period of time, you would have received more dividends. Here are the figures, assuming a $10,000 investment made on December 31, 1933:

	MARKET VALUE 12/31/84	TOTAL CASH DIVIDENDS	TOTAL RESULTS
Seminar Fund	$768,906	$351,205	$1,120,111
General Motors	$136,046	$212,857	$ 345,322
AT&T	$ 32,050	$ 64,873	$ 96,903

So when someone tells you he wished his grandfather had set aside some shares of GM or AT&T for him in the 1930s, tell him you would have preferred that your grandfather had put the same amount of money into shares of the Seminar Fund.

CAN YOU OUTPERFORM DOW JONES?

When investing on his own, the average person does not do as well as the Dow Jones Industrial Average. This does not mean, of course, that you are average. You should use the system that best serves your temperament, lifestyle, and pocketbook. Let's now take a look at Figure 5-7 and see how the Dow Jones Average of 30 Industrial Stocks, the Standard & Poor's 500 Composite Index, and the New York Stock Exchange Composite Index did in comparison to the Seminar Fund.

Note how the Seminar Fund's record compares with those of the leading unmanaged stock market indices. To keep the Seminar Fund's results comparable to those of the indices, we have assumed that all of the fund's distributions from long-term gains were received in additional shares.

UNDERLYING VALUE IS THE KEY

Companies create wealth; and in the past, successful investing in common stocks has resulted from becoming one of the owners of the companies creating this wealth. Stock prices in the long term are determined by the earnings and assets of these companies.

Do not make the mistake so many investors do of taking the short-term view of the stock market when providing for your long-term goals. I find that many predict the future by making straight-line

SUMMARY	LATEST 10 YEARS (to 12/31/84)	LATEST 20 YEARS (to 12/31/84)	LATEST 30 YEARS (to 12/31/84)	LATEST 51 YEARS (to 12/31/84)
Seminar Fund	+195.1%	+258.0%	+797.5%	+7,589.1%
Standard & Poor's 500 Composite Index	+143.9	+ 97.3	+364.8	+1,555.8
Dow Jones Average of 30 Industrial Stocks	+ 96.6	+ 38.6	+199.6	+1,112.8
New York Stock Exchange Composite Index	+166.8	+111.1	+396.8	na

Figure 5-7

extrapolations of the latest three- or five-year periods, and when the market has gone down over a period of several years, instead of welcoming it as a buying opportunity, they just sit on their hands. And when the market has been going up for a period of years, they assume the opposite and eagerly jump in with the full anticipation that this happy condition will continue for the next three to five years. Instead, watch for times in the market when good solid values are available, and have the courage to invest in the fund of your choice at bargain prices.

Summary

A mutual fund can do for you what you would do for yourself if you had sufficient time, training, and money to diversify, plus the temperament to stand back from your money and make rational decisions. It should make available to you what the very wealthy have always had: sufficient money to diversify and sufficient money to buy some of the best brains in the country.

If you can do better than the professionals and can spare the necessary time from your full-time vocation, by all means do your own buying and selling. If not, don't let your ego keep you from hiring these professionals to work for you and your money.

APPLICATION

1. Analyze your performance record on your individual stock holdings over the past ten years. What has been your percentage of gain?

   _____

2. Rate yourself with regard to the three T's and an M as they relate to investments: Time _____ Training _____ Temperament _____ Money _____

3. After rating yourself, should you manage your own portfolio or let the professionals do it for you? _____

   Should you manage a part and let the professionals manage a part?

   _____

4. Which type of fund best fits your financial objective and temperament? Growth stocks _____ Income stocks _____ Bonds and government securities _____

5. Should you hire a timing service? _____

6. How much can you invest today in a lump sum? _____

7. What amount can you add each month? _____

8. Should you use the convenience and discipline of the bank draft system to draft your account so that your investment schedule will be systematic? _____

9. Which day of the month will you invest each month? _____

10. What is the secret of financial independence? _____

Chapter 6

Real Estate in the New Economy

We have just taken an in-depth look at the vital role proper investing in stocks and mutual funds must play in increasing your net worth in the New Economy. The next important area you must become knowledgeable about is real estate and how it can add to your portfolio of investments and help propel you down the road to financial independence.

Since the early days of our civilization, ownership of real estate has been held in high esteem and often regarded as the primary yardstick in determining a person's wealth and stature in his community. Since real estate is a basic necessity in both prosperous and less prosperous times, investors have chosen it to achieve capital growth and attractive income levels over the years. Population growth and technological advances create an ongoing demand for living, working, and shopping space—demand which can often exceed available local supply. Real estate can benefit from inflation as inflation pushes up replacement costs, thereby enhancing existing property values. Income-producing properties, on the other hand, are sold in relation to their cash flow; and forces which increase revenues have a positive effect on the values of those properties at the time of sale.

Limited Partnerships

The advantages of investing in real estate, including large apartment complexes, office buildings, shopping centers, miniwarehouses, and well-located tracts of raw land, are well publicized, and you have probably wondered how you could participate, knowing that you didn't have the large amounts of capital required. In the past, this may have been true, but not today. With the advent of the limited partnership, you can, even if you only have a relatively small amount of investable funds, invest just like the multimillionaires in the vast array of potentially profitable major real estate projects. The limited partnership method of investing opens a wide range of investment opportunities to a large percentage of our population that were never available before. If you have never been an investor in a limited partnership, you have been missing some excellent potential.

A limited partnership is a legal entity formed for investment purposes composed of one or more general partners who have professional expertise, who are willing to assume unlimited liability, and who are the active partners responsible for administering the partnership, plus several or a large number of limited partners, usually without expertise, who do not want liability beyond the extent of their investment, but who have investable funds. The limited partners are treated as individuals, with all the tax advantages and the net income derived from the investments flowing directly through to them. This is called the *conduit principle*. A limited partnership may be diagrammed in this manner:

THE LIMITED PARTNERSHIP	
Limited Partners	**General Partners**
1. Provide capital	1. Provide management
2. Have limited liability	2. Have full liability

3. Enjoy benefits such as:
  a. tax-sheltered distributions
  b. excess tax write-offs
  c. no intermediate taxation of profits
  d. participation in any profits
	3. Profits usually subordinated to limited partners receiving a specified return and original capital

There are two types of limited partnerships with which you will want to become familiar: the registered limited partnership and the private placement limited partnership.

REGISTERED LIMITED PARTNERSHIPS

When a limited partnership is offered to the public on a national basis, it must be registered with the Securities and Exchange Commission and also with the securities commission of any state where it is offered. The syndicator, or general partner, must go to considerable expense and spend a tremendous amount of time to register the offering prospectus, which is a very long, complicated document written by lawyers in legal terminology. The Securities and Exchange Commission neither approves nor disapproves the offering. Nor does the SEC rule on its investment merits, but it does attempt to see that those making the offering make "full disclosure" of all material facts relative to the offering, which usually means full disclosure of all the negatives that could possibly occur. Rarely will you become aware of any positive attributes of the offering unless you read to the end of a very long document and have advanced degrees and extensive experience in financial analysis in the particular area being presented. After you have read the prospectus of a particular offering, you may be completely stunned and wonder how your financial planner or broker ever had the audacity to recommend such a "risky" investment. But don't stop there. Continue to study and investigate and find out if the potential profits from the investment outweigh the risk factors presented. Look to see if these are truly negatives, for often you will find they are not, despite the warnings.

After the offering has been registered with the SEC, the syndicators must then register it with each state in which the offering will be sold. Some state commissions determine who can be a "suitable investor" in their state, what is the minimum investment that residents of their state may make, and some even pass judgment on what is "fair, just and equitable." Any sales literature used, which must always be accompanied by the current prospectus, must also be cleared with the National Association of Securities Dealers. After the registered limited partnership has been cleared with all the regulatory authorities, then financial planners and stockbrokers registered with the National Association of Securities Dealers can offer by prospectus units of the partnership to suitable investors.

The offerings are usually quite large and may be for amounts well in excess of $100 million. Each unit is usually $250, $500, or $1,000, although some may be as high as $5,000, and the minimum amount of investment is usually $2,500 or $5,000 in an individual account and $2,000 in an Individual Retirement Account. In a registered offering you are not allowed to stage in your investment over several years; consequently your total investment must be made during the period the offering is open. You can, however, add units until it closes once you have made your initial investment. The offerings are usually open for several months, so you should have ample time to become familiar with an offering, unless you wait until near its closing date.

Because the size of most registered partnerships is large, you will own your proportional share of a number of different properties in different geographical locations. The kinds of properties may also be very diverse. The offering may specify which properties you will be investing in, or it may be a "blind pool," meaning that the general partners will select the properties and make the investments as the funds come in.

If you have funds that don't need to be liquid for several years and if you don't have the emotional need to tally up your net worth daily, you will want to consider having some of your after-tax dollars invested in registered limited partnerships.

PRIVATE PLACEMENT LIMITED PARTNERSHIPS

If only a relatively small amount of money is needed for an offering, or if the units are large and only a relatively small number of investors are needed, the general partner will not go to the considerable expense of registering the partnership with the SEC. The expense of registration can actually destroy the economics of a partnership unless the amount of the funds needed is relatively large. The general partner is allowed to have 35 "non-accredited" investors that meet the suitability requirements of the syndicator, plus an unlimited number of "accredited investors" that meet certain qualifications; or retain a "purchaser representative" who has the experience and knowledge to evaluate the merits and risks of the investment.

If some of your income will be taxed at 42 percent or above, you will want to investigate private offerings. These can be structured so your investments can be paid in over several years and can be made partially or completely with tax dollars that you would otherwise lose to the IRS. Your deductions or write-offs may run from 50 percent to over 200 percent in the year the investments are made. Registered offerings may also have write-offs of 100 percent, but this will usually take around five years to accomplish.

With private placement offerings, you will usually have only limited or no diversification, since most often there will only be one property in the partnership. Even though the partnership offering document is exempt from registration with the SEC, it must make "full disclosure" of all material facts. This document will probably be an inch thick, and a large portion of it will be devoted to dire warnings of the risks of the investment. The risks may be very high or they may be relatively low. Investigate the merits of the offering and then decide.

Benefits of Real Estate

The three major economic benefits of owning real estate are 1) the potential for income, 2) capital appreciation, and 3) tax advantages. If you place your emphasis on any one of these benefits, you will decrease the others, since they are interrelated. Therefore, before you begin to select the type of real estate investment that will be best for you, you must first determine your financial objective and your tolerance for risk. Do you need income now or do you need income later? If you need income now, you will want an investment that provides current cash flow. If your need for income is later, your emphasis should be on capital appreciation. If your income from other sources is presently being subjected to high taxation, you may want to emphasize tax advantages for current deductions.

Since tax advantages are present in real estate investing regardless of your emphasis, let us learn how you get deductions. Deductions come from two chief sources: depreciation and interest expenses. If your properties are operating at a loss, these losses are also deductible. The best way to learn about tax advantages is by using examples. First, let's look at indirect investing in real estate where you do not receive these tax advantages and then look at direct investing.

INDIRECT INVESTING

Even though you may have never made a commercial real estate investment, if you have had a savings account with a savings institution you have been an indirect investor. As you deposited your hard-earned money at the teller's window, the loan officer at a desk a few steps away in normal times has been lending out your money to be invested directly into real estate. You were "guaranteed" your sliver of the interest earned by that loan, plus your original deposit. Meanwhile, the institution and the borrower may have been the chief beneficiaries. Let's say, for example, that you have $100,000 and you place it in a savings account at 8 percent and you are willing to leave it there for one year. Also, let's assume that the portion of the interest you earn is taxed at 40 percent. At the end of the year, results could look something like this:

$100,000	Deposit
8,000	Interest for one year
$108,000	Total at the end of the year
(3,200)	Taxes due at 40% on $8,000
$104,800	Net after taxes
4.8%	After-tax return

And what was the rate of inflation for the past few years? Any time it was greater than 4.8 percent, you were like the little frog that hopped up one step and slid back two. You didn't make it out of the financial well.

DIRECT INVESTMENT IN
A NON-MORTGAGED BUILDING

An alternative investment with your $100,000 is to buy and pay cash for a building. You might then lease that building for $12,000, or 12 percent per year, under an agreement that is called a triple-net lease or a net-net lease. With a triple-net lease, you would be a non-operating owner, and the leaseholder would be the operator and would pay all variable costs such as taxes, insurance, and maintenance (whence comes the triple name), as well as a lease rental each month.

The company doing the leasing may find this arrangement advantageous, for it frees capital for inventory, expansion, or other activities related to the company's business. You as the owner, on the other hand, may like the arrangement because you have no variable costs to surprise you and you can anticipate a predictable income stream from the lease for a period of years. If you have included the proper clauses in the lease, your rentals should also increase with inflation on the gross volume of your lessee.

As a direct investor, you are also eligible for depreciation deductions for income tax purposes, which are allowed as if the building was decreasing in value with use. This may or may not be true, but depreciation is a bookkeeping entry, no checks are sent, and it does not reduce the actual cash flow. There are varying kinds of depreciation schedules, but let's assume that you are using what is called straight-line depreciation over an 18-year period.* (You are not permitted to depreciate the land on which the building is built, just the building and depreciable items connected with it.) Let's see how allowable depreciation affects the taxation of your cash flow. Your mathematics might run something like this if you had purchased land and building for $100,000, with a cash flow of $12,000, or 12 percent, and your accountant had set a value of $75,000 on the building and $25,000 on the land. The example below is grossly oversimplified, but it should introduce to you the basic effects of depreciation on your taxable cash flow. In this example, I have assumed a tax bracket of 40 percent:

HYPOTHETICAL EXAMPLE OF A $100,000 NON-LEVERAGED BUILDING, TRIPLE-NET-LEASED

$100,000 at 12% cash flow	$12,000
Building at $75,000—annual depreciation for 18-year period	(4,167)
Taxable cash flow	7,833
Taxes at 40% ($7,833 × 40%)	(3,133)
Cash flow	$12,000
Minus taxes	(3,133)
Net after taxes	$ 8,867

* Refer to the Tax Addendum in the Appendix for possible tax changes.

Your current after-tax return is now 8.9 percent. As you can see, you have almost doubled your return with a direct rather than an indirect investment.

DIRECT INVESTMENT IN A MORTGAGED BUILDING

When Bernard Baruch was asked how he had become so rich, one of his answers was "OPM—Other People's Money." The use of OPM to invest is called leverage and permits you to benefit from the next major tax advantage of real estate—deductible interest.* Using the same example as before, let's now take only $25,000 of your $100,000, use it as a down payment on a $100,000 building, and then borrow $75,000 from a life insurance company or, as a second option, assume an already existing mortgage at a lower interest rate. (This leaves you funds to purchase three more buildings at the same price.) In this example, let's assume that the life insurance company will lend you the money at 13 percent interest and that you are in a 40 percent tax bracket:

HYPOTHETICAL EXAMPLE OF A **$100,000** LEVERAGED BUILDING,
TRIPLE-NET-LEASED

$100,000 at 12% cash flow	$12,000
$75,000 mortgage at 13% interest	(9,750)
Net cash flow after interest	2,250
Minus depreciation	(4,167)
Taxable income (loss)	(1,917)
Net after-tax cash flow	2,250
Tax savings from excess deductions	766
Net after-tax return	$ 3,016

As you will note, your interest is deductible. This, of course, reduces your net cash flow on the building, but you have only invested one-fourth of your money (four buildings would produce $9,000). You are still allowed to depreciate the total $75,000 allocated to the building, even though you only invested $25,000, which amounts to $4,167, just as it did when you paid all cash. This provides you with

* Refer to the Tax Addendum in the Appendix for possible tax changes.

a shelter for your $2,250 of income so it will not be currently taxable to you, plus you will have an excess deduction of $1,917 which you can use to shelter some of your other income. In a 40 percent tax bracket, this would save you $766 in taxes ($1,917 × .40), giving you an after-tax return of $3,016 ($2,250 + $766) on your $25,000 investment, or 12.1 percent after-tax current return.

Operating Partnerships

In the above examples, I have used non-operating triple-net-leased arrangements for simplicity to introduce allowable deductions to you. The same deductions are also allowable to the limited partnerships we have already discussed, both non-operating and operating. However, the partnerships you will most likely want to consider for investment are operating partnerships in which the general partner operates the property and is responsible for all the expenses. Operating partnerships most often invest in multifamily housing (garden-type apartment complexes), office buildings, shopping centers, miniwarehouses, and business parks. In some, a portion of the money may also be invested in mortgages which participate in the increased rents and appreciation that may occur.

An operating partnership may invest for all cash or it may be leveraged. The one you choose will depend upon your financial objective and your tolerance for risk. If your need is for tax-sheltered income now, you will want to consider a partnership that invests in properties by paying all cash.

ALL-CASH OPERATING REGISTERED
LIMITED PARTNERSHIPS

Let's assume that you need the maximum income now. In this case, you will want to invest in partnerships that pay all cash for their properties or combine these with very well collateralized mortgages on excellent properties. You will have a wide range of combinations to choose from, with some partnerships investing only in apartment complexes, some in a combination of mortgages and suburban office buildings, some in miniwarehouses and business parks, and some in a combination of apartment complexes, selected shopping centers, and office buildings.

To the partnership, and to you as an investor in that partnership, the major advantage of paying all cash for your real estate is that it can usually be purchased at a lower price because the seller does not have to wait for his money. He has his money now and can put it to use. Assuming that the partnership can buy for all cash at a 30 percent discount and then sells at market, you have made 42 percent on your money. Also since there are no interest payments on borrowed money, your break-even point is lower and more of the income derived from the property can be available for distribution. The disadvantage is, of course, that your growth is limited because you put up a dollar and only control one dollar of real estate.

Let's take as our hypothetical example an all-cash partnership which invests in a combination of apartments, selected shopping centers, and office buildings. Let's also assume that you are in a 30 percent tax bracket (look at Table 13 in the Appendix to determine your bracket), that you are investing $10,000, and that inflation and skill of management will bring about an 8 percent appreciation in the value of property per year:

HYPOTHETICAL $10,000 INVESTMENT IN A
REGISTERED LIMITED PARTNERSHIP PAYING ALL CASH

NOW	Cash flow from operations	$800
	Depreciation and expenses	(800)
	Taxable income (loss)	-0-
	Net cash flow after taxes	$800
LATER	Equity buildup	-0-
	Appreciation	$800

As you can see from this example, when you invest in real estate you may have NOW benefits and LATER benefits.

NOW BENEFITS

Your NOW benefits in the above example would be $800 or 8 percent on your investment. But because there is an $800 depreciation deduction, your $800 would be sheltered from taxes. In your 30 percent tax bracket, this is equivalent to your receiving $1,143 if it were taxable, or 11.43 percent. (In a 40 percent bracket, this would be equivalent to $1,333, or 13.3 percent, and equivalent to $1,600 in a 50 percent bracket, or 16 percent.) This is your NOW benefit.

LATER BENEFITS

Real estate can also provide LATER benefits when the property is sold. There will be no equity buildup on the property, because there were no mortgages and your appreciation will be limited to whatever occurs on your original investment. If your appreciation is $800 per year, when the property is sold, let's say in five years, you will receive your proportionate part of the proceeds. If during the partnership you have received $3,000 in cash flow non-taxable, your cost basis for this property has been decreased for tax purposes by that amount, or would be $7,000. If the property was sold at a price that netted your investment $13,000, your taxable gain would be $6,000 ($13,000 − $7,000). Forty percent of this would be taxable, or $2,400, and in your 30 percent bracket you would lose $720 to taxes, leaving you an after-tax return of $2,280 ($13,000 − $720 − $10,000). For the five-year life of this investment, you would have earned $456 per year from the sale of the property ($2,280 ÷ 5), plus $800 per year after-tax cash flow for a total of $1,256 per year on a $10,000 investment or 12.56 percent per year, which is equivalent to 17.9 percent per year if taxable in your 30 percent bracket. If you were in a 40 percent bracket, it would be equivalent to 20.9 percent, and in a 50 percent bracket to 25.12 percent.

Some partnerships, instead of selling their properties, will place mortgages on them if favorable interest rates should become available. In the above example, if the partnership had been able to obtain a mortgage for the amount of the original purchase price, you would then receive back your $10,000, which is not taxable, since it is borrowed money, and you would still own the property and have your $10,000 for a new investment.

Real Estate for Your Retirement Programs

In addition to choosing all-cash partnerships for your individual investments when you want lower risks and higher cash flow, you may also want to place real estate investments in your tax-deferred accounts such as IRA, Keogh, and pension and/or profit-sharing plans. All-cash limited partnerships offerings qualify as fiduciary investments under ERISA. Since the passage of this legislation, pension trustees have been required to diversify their holdings for greater safety and growth potential. Real estate can be an excellent choice for these goals, and a large number of the syndicators of limited partnerships have responded to this need by making a wide range of combinations available. All of these partnerships will pay cash for their properties, thus avoiding the taxation on "unrelated business income," and some will include participating mortgages. Here are a few of the combinations now available:

1. *Combination of secured mortgages and all-cash quality suburban office buildings*. This program is designed for safety and income, although there can also be growth. It is directed primarily to pension plans and also as a municipal bond alternative to individual investors. Fifty percent of the funds of the partnership are invested in mortgages, secured by buildings of the highest quality of construction in excellent locations, with high down payments of 35 to 40 percent, and leased to companies with substantial net worth. The other 50 percent are invested in quality suburban office buildings with low break-even points bought with all cash. The pension plan investors receive a priority return of their original investment plus 12 percent per annum before individual investors receive their original capital plus 10 percent per annum. Fifty percent of the units in the partnership are sold to the pension plan investors and 50 percent to individual investors, with all of the tax-shelter benefits allocated to the individual side, sheltering their income. Cash flow is projected to start at 7 percent and go up to 12 percent, with an average of 9 percent. Growth is anticipated to be another 5 to 8 percent, producing a total return of 14 to 17 percent.

2. *Participating mortgages*. This program is a participating mortgage limited partnership designed for the tax-exempt investor seeking income and growth potential, together with a limited holding period. Income is projected to be approximately 9 percent per annum cumulative, which accrues and bears interest. The investor should also receive additional interest of up to 75 percent of the appreciation of the properties. Participating mortgages are to be secured by 20 to 25 income properties throughout the country. The lending portion is like a bank would make, taking a note against the property for collateral; and the borrower, upon sale of the property, repays the bank with

interest. However, the bank does not participate in the appreciation, and in this partnership the lender receives a significant share of the appreciation.

3. *FHA guaranteed mortgages on multifamily housing.* The principal and interest on these mortgages are guaranteed by the FHA arm of the federal government. Cash flow is projected to start at 8½ percent and increase by ½ percent per year. The investor also participates in 25 percent of any increases in rents and 25 percent of the appreciation on sale. Liquidity is provided through depository receipts.

4. *All-cash commercial properties.* Commercial properties are bought for all cash. Beginning cash flow is projected to be 7½ percent and increasing by 1 percent per year. The investor receives 85 percent of the appreciation.

5. *Participating mortgages and land-sale leasebacks.* These are projected to have a cash flow beginning at 8 percent and increasing 1 percent per year. The limited partners also receive 25 percent of the increase in cash flow and 25 percent of the capital appreciation on sale.

6. *Miniwarehouses built for all cash.* Limited cash flow projected for the first two to three years, then going to 10 percent and rising 1 to 1½ percent per year. (Some of the older programs are cash flowing in excess of 30 percent.)

Leveraged Operating Registered Limited Partnerships

To get back to the individual investor, if your financial objective is capital appreciation with some tax advantages, you will want to consider investing in limited partnerships that employ leverage. You have an even wider range of partnerships to choose from in this category, with various combinations of properties. Your growth potential is greater than with the all-cash programs because you may control three or more dollars for each dollar you invest and you will be permitted to deduct depreciation and the interest expense.* This

* Refer to the Tax Addendum in the Appendix for possible tax changes.

will not only give you the opportunity for more growth but will afford you greater tax advantages during your holding period. In a typical program you could write off 100 percent of your investment over five years.

Let us again take a hypothetical $10,000 investment, a 30 percent tax bracket, and a five-year holding period. (You should allow from three to eight years.) In this example, I will reduce our appreciation to 6 percent and use a very conservative leverage of only $1.50 borrowed for each $1 invested:

HYPOTHETICAL $10,000 INVESTMENT IN A LEVERAGED REGISTERED LIMITED PARTNERSHIP

	Your Cash		Mortgage		Total
	$10,000	+	$15,000	=	$25,000

NOW	$	300	current cash flow tax sheltered
	$	510	excess deduction (20% − 3% = 17%)
	$	810	Total (equivalent to $1,157 if taxable in 30% bracket)
LATER	$	300	equity buildup
	$	1,500	appreciation (6% × 2.5)

Again you will have NOW benefits and LATER benefits.

NOW BENEFITS

For your NOW benefits in the above example, I have assumed your first year cash flow to be 3 percent (it could increase another 1 percent or more each year). I have also assumed that you will be able to write off your investment through depreciation and interest at the rate of 20 percent a year for a deduction of $2,000. You will use $300 of this to shelter your distribution from taxes, and this will leave you $1,700 in excess deductions, which will enable you to save taxes on your other income. In a 30 percent bracket, this would be like receiving a check for $510 or not having to send the IRS that amount, making your tax-sheltered cash flow plus your tax savings $810. In a 30 percent bracket, this is the equivalent to receiving $1,157 if it were taxable, or 11.57 percent; in a 40 percent tax bracket it is equivalent to receiving $1,350 or 13.5 percent; and in a 50 percent bracket it is equivalent to receiving 16.2 percent taxable. This is your NOW benefit from the investment. Even though you may be investing for future benefits, as you can see, the NOW benefits can be attractive. You may be tempted to say, "Three percent certainly isn't a very good return. I can do better than that in a certificate of deposit." However, you may not need income now, and even if you do, you need to calculate carefully just how much income you would need to receive to be equivalent to what you would be receiving here. Learn to think in tax equivalents. (Remember that when you receive write-offs, you do reduce your cost basis.)

LATER BENEFITS

Even though you may like your NOW benefits from a leveraged registered limited partnership, you may be investing for LATER benefits. In this example, your first LATER benefit is equity buildup in the properties, which amounts to an average of $300 per year. This is created by the general partners collecting rents and paying a portion of that income on the mortgage, thereby decreasing the debt and increasing your equity.

Another LATER benefit is appreciation from good value-added management and from inflation. In the example above, I have assumed a conservative 6 percent. However, you are leveraged, so it becomes 6 percent × 2.5, or 15 percent, or $1,500 per year. You receive the equity buildup and the appreciation when the properties are sold, and at that time you would adjust your cost basis to reflect the write-offs you have received; and the difference would, for the most part, be taxed as a capital gain.*

It might help in your understanding of this concept if I gave you the statistics on a partnership a large number of our clients invested in and which has now sold, for all cash, nine of the ten properties in the partnership. The properties consisted of apartment complexes, a shopping center, and an office building. One apartment complex is left in the partnership. One of the advantages of having been a financial planner for a long time is that I have had an opportunity to see many partnerships go full cycle.

* Refer to the Tax Addendum in the Appendix for possible tax changes.

A CASE HISTORY OF A REGISTERED PROGRAM

This partnership was formed in 1975, and nine of the ten properties it held were sold in 1984 after a holding period of 8.4 years. (Most partnerships today have shorter holding periods.) The results below have been adjusted for a 40 percent tax bracket and are per $1,000 of investment. (Minimum investment was $5,000.)

The investors received back $3.73 after taxes for every $1 invested, giving a per annum return of 44.5 percent.

ESTIMATED PARTNERSHIP RETURNS BEFORE TAXES ON DISPOSITION	LIMITED PARTNERS PER UNIT BENEFITS
Partnership Operations:	
Cumulative cash distributions through June 30, 1984	$ 764
Cumulative ordinary taxable income from operations through December 31, 1983	(60)
Estimated after-tax proceeds from partnership operations	704
Cash proceeds from disposition of properties (2) Year of Disposition	3,581
Estimated return before taxes on disposition	$4,285
Taxes on Disposition:	
Year of disposition ordinary income-recapture	$ (45)
Section 1231—capital gain	(506)
Total taxes on disposition	$ (551)
Estimated Cumulative After-Tax Proceeds to Limited Partners:	
Estimated return before taxes on disposition	$4,285
Total taxes on disposition	(551)
Estimated cumulative after-tax proceeds to limited partners	$3,734

(1) Computations based on average investor entering the partnership midway through the offering period.
(2) Excludes the apartment building still owned by the partnership.

It might also be helpful in your understanding of limited partnerships to get a better picture of the size of these offerings, so I have included the total figures on the partnership level:

PUBLIC REAL ESTATE LIMITED PARTNERSHIP
THE RESULTS: BENEFITS RECEIVED BY INVESTORS
AS OF JULY 12, 1984

Property Acquisitions and Resales:

Total purchase price of partnership property acquired	$ 60,000,000
Total money raised from investors	18,223,000
Total number of properties acquired	10
Total sales price of properties sold	103,539,000
Total number of properties sold	9

Investor Benefits from Properties Sold:

Partnership capital allocated to properties, including all investor costs and reserves	$ 16,408,000
Cash distributions to investors from sales and working capital reserves, net of all expenses and fees	$ 65,254,000
Annual cash distributions from operations	13,685,000
Annual ordinary income from operations assuming an investor tax bracket of 40%	(1,134,000)

Total Benefits Received by Investors: $ 77,805,000

Average holding period for all properties sold	8.4 Years
Average annual return	44.5%

If you were to invest today in a similar partnership, could you expect to do as well? I really don't know, but here are some current figures I have received from other syndicators whose programs we also recommend. These are the results from sales of two of their recent programs. Their average holding period has been 5.17 years, their benefits to investors before taxes have been 354 percent, and their after-tax benefits from the property sales, in a 40 percent bracket, have been 294 percent. Their average annual equity appreciation was 49.1 percent, and their after-tax internal rate of return was 23.2 percent. These figures can further be illustrated in the following graph. Their general policy is to sell their properties in five years, and if they take back any mortgages, to sell them in two years.

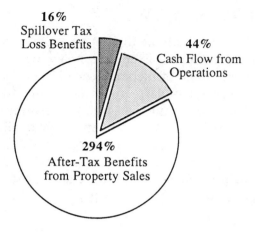

16%
Spillover Tax
Loss Benefits

44%
Cash Flow from
Operations

294%
After-Tax Benefits
from Property Sales

Figure 6-1.

Opportunities in Multifamily Housing

If you were to ask me what should definitely be in your investment portfolio to provide you with the opportunity for excellent growth, tax advantages, and downside protection over the next five to six years, my answer would be participation in limited partnerships holding multifamily housing. If your need is for tax-sheltered income now, then choose the programs that pay all cash. If you truly do not need income now, choose the leveraged programs. They offer you much greater potential for profits and have greater tax advantages. Choose programs offered by syndicators who have a long and successful track record and whose management team is still the same as when that successful record was achieved.

Why am I so enthusiastic about multifamily housing (garden-type apartment complexes)? The strongest land use in America today is rental housing, and this trend will grow even stronger as we move further into the New Economy. Given the demographic profile of current and future households in this country, and given the ongoing affordability problems of home ownership, demand for rental units will remain high for many years.

HOUSING AFFORDABILITY

Many Americans who would like to own a home today cannot afford to do so. Lack of sufficient fixed-rate financing, rising prices of homes, and the percentage of income needed to support home ownership have discouraged buyers, thus increasing the demand for rental housing. The average median priced conventionally financed home today costs $100,000. A 90 percent 30-year mortgage at 9.75 percent interest would require annual payments of $9,278, or $773.24 per month. Statistics show that only 20.1 percent of American families are able to afford a new home today, and those who do own a home are spending, on the average, 31 percent of their income to do so.

DEMAND FOR MULTIFAMILY HOUSING

As we have already determined, in the New Economy you want to invest your money where demand is greater than supply. Demand for rental units is increasing as our population is getting older. In 1970, 23 percent of our population was between 25 and 45 years of age. By 1980, the percentage had increased to 32 percent, and by 1990 it is projected that this group will grow to 43 percent. The trend is significant because this is the group that creates new households; from age 25 to 45 they get married, have children, and raise families. And since most of them cannot qualify for a home loan, many developers are building rental housing with the amenities to satisfy their needs.

Also in the New Economy we are experiencing a new era of the dynamic elderly. The number of single-family households, as well as two-family households, of those over age 65 is increasing. This group no longer wants the responsibility of home ownership, and many of them also face the affordability problem. Adults over the age of 65 now outnumber teenagers and are increasing in number faster than the population as a whole.

A less quantifiable factor today is the reluctance many people have toward home ownership. We have a very mobile society. If a home is now owned for five years or more, the high cost of purchase and sale makes it too costly, together with the limited appreciation potential. In addition, unlike the 1970s, owners are now buying for shelter instead of appreciation and are, therefore, buying smaller and less expensive houses. Another factor is that our population is putting a higher priority on freedom from household and home ownership chores and more emphasis on recreation and travel. Renting frees them from yard work, house maintenance, and other chores while bringing them more security and amenities.

THE "OPPORTUNITY SPREAD"

All of these factors have created a demand for rental housing that is far greater than the present supply. Supply remains short because of the relationship between present rental rates and what they will have to be to support new construction, known as "replacement rents." In 1974, market rents were 20 cents per square foot per month, which is equivalent to $160 per month for an 800-square-foot apartment unit. The replacement rent necessary to prompt builders to build was 28 cents, or a per-apartment discrepancy of $64 per month, or 40 percent between market rents and replacement rents. As long as this disparity existed, apartment projects were protected from competition. Only as rents rose to 28 cents did it make sense for builders to start new construction.

By 1985, rents averaged 40 to 45 cents a square foot, but replacement costs were 55 to 60 cents, which meant that rents would have to go up 15 cents or 45 percent over the current market price before new construction would occur. In 1974, we saw that the difference between market rents and replacement rents was 40 percent, and property prices since then have doubled. Today this figure is 45 percent. Rents will have to increase before new construction will occur, and no new construction should translate into sharply increased rent and increased value for owners of existing properties.

THE ECONOMICS OF RENTING VERSUS OWNING

The average new home with approximately 1,600 square feet costs in excess of $100,000 today. After making all the appropriate adjustments for interest deductions, equity buildup, potential appreciation, loss of use of money from both the down payment and larger monthly outflow, garden-style rental apartments represent one of the "best buys" still left.

Vacancy rates in the U.S. average around 5 percent. In such areas as San Francisco and Mobile, Alabama, the rate is around 1 percent; in New York City, Chicago, Washington, Boston, and Los Angeles, it is from 1 to 3 percent; and in Houston (the mecca that builders flocked to and built in just before energy prices declined) the vacancy rate is 19 percent. In many areas today there are real rental shortages and the syndication you will want to choose will seek out these areas for investing.

For all of the above reasons, I believe that one of your most profitable investments over the next five to eight years could be in a well-managed program investing chiefly in multifamily housing.

Miniwarehouse Limited Partnerships

If our homes and living accommodations are getting smaller, our need for space to store our unused possessions has grown larger. This need has made another area of real estate investing attractive—registered limited partnerships which invest in miniwarehouses.

As office space has become more expensive, businesses have also sought out economical storage space. And manufacturers' representatives and others have turned to this type of storage as conventional warehouse space has become more costly and often nonexistent. We have found that the miniwarehouse business succeeds under conditions of increased social and economic activity. This includes people moving into, out of, and within a metropolitan area; businesses moving in and out of an area; marriage and/or divorce; children moving back to and away from home; temporary or permanent job assignments; smaller living space with less storage capacity; death; inheritance; and positive and negative surges in the economy affecting individuals and businesses. Most of the miniwarehouse locations will have about 100,000 persons living within a five-mile marketing area. Since the average city dweller moves once every 7½ years, around 13,000 of these 100,000 people would have a potential need for temporary storage.

Miniwarehouses are relatively inexpensive to build in comparison to apartment complexes. They can be built for about one-half the cost per square foot and can be rented for a comparable amount per square foot with lower operating costs. In a typical situation, the warehouse manager lives in an apartment on-site, thus providing added security and management capabilities.

The average 10-by-10-foot cubicle rents for around $58 per month or 58¢ per square foot. A 10 percent increase in rent would mean an increase of only $5.80 per month, hardly enough to cause the renter to move his "treasures." Since a 10 percent increase in rent will flow down to a 1 to 2 percent increase in cash flow to the investor, this investment becomes a potentially good inflation hedge.

Miniwarehouses are usually built in areas of high traffic flow on what could be considered potentially prime land. The warehouses thus permit investors to warehouse the land while waiting for a more profitable use and support it with income while waiting.

There are several types of miniwarehouse partnerships available. The ones available since 1976 are those that buy the land and then build the warehouses for all cash. It normally takes 12 to 14 months to construct the complex and 12 months to complete the leasing, during which time your cash flow will be minimal. But after leasing is completed, cash flow should then move to around 10 percent and increase from 1 to 1½ percent per year thereafter. The elimination of interim financing costs and mortgage payments can make it possible for miniwarehouses to produce a positive cash flow with only a 28 percent occupancy rate. And in a good location, this level is often reached within 90 days of completion of the facility.

At 95 percent occupancy, miniwarehouses should begin producing a cash flow of 12 percent or more, and some of the programs already have a 32 percent cash flow. As an owner, you receive your proportionate part of the depreciation that is allowed on the warehouses, which could shelter 35 to 40 percent of your cash flow from taxes.

These partnerships are designed with the arrangement that when you have received your original investment back, the general partner can mortgage the building, and if a mortgage is obtained, you will receive your proportionate part of these borrowed funds. These funds will not be taxable to you, since they are borrowed and you will still own your proportionate part of the warehouses, less the mortgages, so you should continue to receive some cash flow after mortgage payments.

One such partnership has already made cash distributions of 153 percent of their original investment, and the financing will pay out to the investors another 240 percent from proceeds of the financing, which is tax deferred, and the investors will still retain a meaningful ownership of the properties in the partnership.

LEVERAGED EXISTING MINIWAREHOUSES

If you are interested in tax-sheltered cash flow from the beginning of your investment, rather than waiting for it to start in two or more years, you may want to consider a registered limited partnership that buys already existing miniwarehouses with financing on the properties. These usually begin with a 7 percent tax-sheltered cash flow, increasing 1 to 1½ percent per year, 7 percent of which continues to be tax sheltered, plus the hope of receiving back 2 to 2½ times your original investment in eight to ten years. If you have been considering investing in municipal bonds, you may want to compare this alternative. The municipality would only return to you the face amount of your investment at maturity. In a miniwarehouse partnership you have the potential for growth of your original investment. Also, if you are receiving Social Security benefits, you should be aware that you could be taxed on a portion of these benefits if you receive municipal bond income and your adjusted gross income, plus your tax-exempt income, plus one-half of your Social Security exceeds $32,000 annually on a joint return. Income that is tax sheltered as in the above miniwarehouse program or in the other all-cash partnerships would not be included.

Venture Registered Limited Partnerships

If you are in a higher tax bracket and want to assume more risk, there is at least one offering that gives you the opportunity to take an equity position. These are limited partnerships investing primarily in apartment complexes in selected distressed markets or from distressed sellers, often with substantial leverage, that can offer you greater growth potential. Suitability requirements for investors are increased to $50,000 of income and $50,000 of net worth or $100,000 of net worth, and you should be able to write off your investment in five years.

Possible Disadvantages of Registered Real Estate Limited Partnerships

What are some of the risks and disadvantages of investing in registered real estate limited partnerships?

First, there can be delays between the time you make your investment and the time the money is actually invested in the properties. During that time, you will probably receive interest comparable to the rate you would have been receiving in a money market mutual fund, but you will not be receiving tax-sheltered cash flow from real estate.

Second, partnership units can only be transferred with the consent of the general partner. (In the past, this has not been withheld unreasonably.) Therefore, there will usually be no public market for the units; however, some syndicators are now beginning to make a market for their units. There are also groups that offer to buy existing partnership units, but I have found that they usually offer substantially less than the investor would have received if he had held his units until the properties were sold.

Third, as a limited partner, you cannot participate in the selection and management of the properties without losing your limited partnership status.

Fourth, if you invest during the earlier months of the partnership, you usually will not know which properties will be placed in the partnership. As I mentioned before, this is referred to as a "blind pool," but to me this is not a disadvantage. I prefer a blind pool, because the general partner has much more bargaining power with the money in hand when going in to negotiate a purchase. So when you are investing with a general partner with an excellent past performance record, I believe it will be to your advantage to choose a blind pool offering, despite the "high risk" caption the SEC may require on the front cover of the prospectus.

Private Placements

Up until now we have been discussing registered limited partnerships. However, one of the disadvantages of registered offerings is that payments cannot be staged in over several years, so the offering cannot be structured for the maximum tax advantage. In public offerings your write-off may be 100 percent over five years, while with private placements they may range from 90 to 200 percent each year as you invest, plus additional write-offs in the following years. Also, there are times when syndicators will find a property that may not be suitable for a public program but has considerable economic merit, so they will buy the property and place it in a private offering.

If you have some of your income that will be taxed at 42 percent or above and you will continue to be in that bracket for several years, you may want to take a look at private placements. I usually prefer those that are offered by companies that also offer public registered programs.

With a private placement, you will not have the diversification that you have in the registered program, and, as a matter of fact, there will usually be only one property. You will, however, know in advance which property it will be and have an opportunity to study the economics. Perhaps the easiest way for you to understand how a private placement works is to give you a case history of a program I invested in a few years ago. The property has now been sold, so we can take a look at the numbers going in, during, and after the sale.

CASE HISTORY OF A PRIVATE PLACEMENT

The first year I invested $13,062.50, writing off 55.4 percent of the investment. The second year I invested $13,433.33, writing off 99.7 percent; and the third year $14,473.33, writing off 64.5 percent, for a total investment of $40,000 plus $969.16 of interest. Write-offs were projected to continue over another six years and to be 122 percent of the amount I invested. This made my average investment approximately $13,670 per year over the three-year period. My cash flow the second year was projected to be 3.2 percent tax sheltered (in reality it was over 5 percent, since this was 3.2 percent on the total three-year investment and I did not make the third-year investment until the third year and was actually earning on the funds in another investment), with equity buildup at 4.2 percent. By the fourth year, tax-sheltered cash flow was projected to move up to 8 percent, and the equity buildup to 4.9 percent. By the end of the third year, I calculated that my benefits in a 50 percent tax bracket would be:

	YEAR	CASH DISTRIBUTION TAX SHELTERED	TAX SAVINGS FROM EXCESS DEDUCTIONS
NOW	1	Minimal	$ 3,637
	2	$1,262	6,480
	3	2,614	4,190
		$3,876	$14,307

	YEAR	EQUITY BUILDUP	APPRECIATION
LATER	1	$ 48	
	2	155	?
	3	169	

My first three years:

$ 3,876	Cash distributions received
14,307	Tax savings from Write-offs
372	Equity buildup
$18,555	Total (average benefits of $6,185 per year)

The average benefits per year, $6,185, divided by $13,670, the average investment per year, gave me a 45 percent average after-tax benefit per year. To obtain the same current equivalent net after-tax benefit on a taxable cash flow, I would have had to earn 90 percent annually on a certificate of deposit in a 50 percent tax bracket. In addition, I anticipated six more years of tax write-offs without any additional investment and tax-sheltered cash distributions of 8 percent or more plus capital appreciation.

The property was sold on May 4, 1983. When I calculated my results, I had received $12,877 of write-off (saving me $6,438 in taxes) and I had received $34,000 of tax-sheltered cash flow. Sales results for my one unit were:

Cash distribution from sale proceeds	$ 68,813
Cash from principal payment on the second promissory note	81,375
Total—cash at sale and principal payment on the promissory note	$150,188
Estimated interest through maturity on the promissory note	54,500
Total estimated cash benefits from sale	$204,688

When I finished calculating my total investment return, I calculated it to be a 30.8 percent annual after-tax internal rate of return.

SELECTING A PRIVATE PLACEMENT

First, take a good look at what your annual tax situation will be early in the year. If you see that you will need to shelter some of your income, determine how much you want to shelter and then look for the private placement or placements that best fit your needs this year and for the years that you will be investing in them. Depreciation can only be taken for the number of days you are an investor that year, so as each day passes, your potential tax savings are reduced. Work with your financial planner to determine what best fits your tax picture and your temperament. Do not place the burden of determining the economic merits of the investment on your CPA, because this is not the role that he should be playing in your life. You should only have him determine if the investment will benefit your tax situation.

You will have a large number of private placements to choose from. For most of them, however, you will have to decide in a relatively short period of time whether or not to invest. Since many offerings are placed in just a few days, you will not have the luxury of a long study period as you will usually have with a registered offering.

Real Estate Investment Trusts (REIT's)

The many types of participation in commercial income-producing real estate we have discussed so far may appeal to you, but at this point in your financial life you may not meet all the suitability requirements, or you may not choose to invest this amount of money in a less liquid limited partnership. By suitability, I mean that the regulatory agencies may require that investors in limited partnership offerings have a certain income level and/or net worth in order to participate.

Are there ways you can participate with smaller amounts of money? Yes, you can, through what are known as "real estate investment trusts." This type of real estate investment was developed in response to the needs of those who wanted to invest small amounts of money in the profit potentials that real estate investing had to offer, but who wanted at the same time to maintain the liquidity of a stock. To fulfill this desire, the modern equity trust was created to acquire and hold income properties of all types, yet have the shares publicly traded.

REIT's may fit your needs, since their shares can be freely traded, in contrast to limited partnership interests. The trust must, by regulation, be a passive entity and must employ outside agents to perform required services. So long as it meets certain asset and income tests and distributes at least 95 percent of its net taxable income each year, it will not be separately taxed. However, distributions may be partially or wholly tax sheltered, but net operating losses cannot be passed through to you as an investor to be used to shelter income from other sources, as can occur under the limited partnership agreement.

You may find the operation of a REIT very much like that of a limited partnership, except that more emphasis will be placed on cash flow and equity buildup, because of its inability to pass through excess tax losses. However, the increased liquidity of shares and the restrictions on resale of properties may encourage REIT's to periodically refinance their properties, which in turn could allow current realization of some of the equity buildup.

A REIT that I use with many clients who want income and liquidity, while still having some growth potential, invests in a combination of: 1) all-cash joint-venture developments; 2) short-term loans on existing income property with some equity or income participation; and 3) acquisition of low-leveraged existing properties. Cash flow begins at 7 percent paid monthly and partially sheltered, increasing each year with the option to reinvest dividends. Shares and warrants are traded in the over-the-counter market at the conclusion of each offering, and the portfolio is self-liquidating. Warrants are issued at no extra cost and can be exercised at the original offering price of $20 between 1989 and 1990.

Raw Land as an Investment

Another area of real estate you may want to consider is raw land. Sometimes a young couple who have attended one of my seminars will come to our offices for counseling, as each person who attends is entitled to do, and say, "We want to buy land. They're not making any more of it, you know." Yes, I know they're not making any more of it, with perhaps the exception of the Dutch reclamation from the sea, but that does not mean that raw land is a valid investment consideration for them. Their finances, most often, are far too limited to take a meaningful position in a tract of land large enough to offer good profit potential.

Your financial situation may be quite different. You may possess sufficient liquid assets and have a high enough cash flow from other sources to allow you to service the interest on any funds you may borrow to finance your purchase of land and also to pay the taxes on the land while you are waiting for the opportunity for a profitable sale. If so, your next consideration should be whether to invest on an individual basis, to join others in a land syndication, or to invest in a private purchase limited partnership.

TIMING OF YOUR PURCHASE

Is this a good time to consider investing in raw land? I believe it could be for several fundamental reasons:

1. *Strong economic demand.* The link between economic growth and land values is straightforward. As real economic growth occurs, demand for land increases because it is needed for apartments, office buildings, single-family houses, commercial space, and so forth. And since there is a finite supply, the price tends to climb much more rapidly during periods of growth.

2. *Developers cannot afford to inventory land.* Until the early 1970s, land was a relatively insignificant cost of development, so developers could afford to acquire land inexpensively in the path of

growth and inventory it until they were ready to build. Today, however, with much higher costs and the difficulty of obtaining financing, this course is impossible for the majority of developers.

3. *Need for a "land bank."* Current conditions have created an opportunity for those with expertise to become a "land bank" to replace the developer as the interim landowner.

4. *Decentralization.* Many urban centers are becoming increasingly decentralized and land that was once unsuitable for commercial development is now being utilized. It is anticipated that the revolution in computer and communications technology in the New Economy will enable more people and businesses to move further from city centers; and as this sprawl occurs, it will require more and more land.

PROFIT POTENTIAL OF LAND

Land does not appreciate in a straight line, but rather it has a tendency to appreciate at a relatively moderate pace until development begins to take place in close proximity. Then the value soars. If, for example, land appreciates 400 percent over 20 years, 300 percent of that appreciation may occur in the last five years. Figure 6-2 illustrates this fact, as well as timing as a key factor in the purchase of undeveloped land—of buying just a few years before its potential is recognized by others.

PRIVATE PLACEMENT LIMITED PARTNERSHIP

If you are interested in the purchase of land, one possibility you will want to consider is an investment in a private placement limited partnership offered by a financially strong syndicator with years of experience and an outstanding past performance record in real estate.

Why a limited partnership? Because it can provide you with a number of specific advantages, such as:

1. *Buying power.* By pooling your funds with others you can have the potential of appreciation on a well-located, well-managed sizable parcel of land. Sizable parcels offer the most value per dollar and are less expensive per unit.

2. *Local specialists.* Specialized knowledge, timing, and management are the key ingredients. A partnership with a large amount of capital can afford to have specialists located in the area.

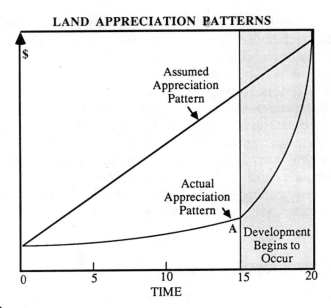

LAND APPRECIATION PATTERNS

Figure 6-2.

3. *Limited liability*. Your liability would be limited to the amount of your investment and there could be no capital calls.

4. *Geographical diversification*. Individual land buyers tend to invest in their own area and are not knowledgeable about other markets. The partnership can enable you to have access to the right markets at the right time over a wide geographic area.

5. *Freedom from management responsibilities*. To generate profits from raw land requires both skill and experience. The general partner can solve the complex management problems associated with maximizing the value of undeveloped land.

A team of specialists whose programs we use have acquired over $3 billion in commercial real estate throughout the country. They have in the past established a record for identifying and executing the right real estate strategy at the right time, and they have the financial strength to act quickly and a reputation for negotiating excellent acquisitions. They maintain twelve land acquisition centers, and this continuous presence should enable them to be aware of acquisition opportunities as they become available. And with this number of offices, they can keep in regular contact with landowners in "targeted" areas. They place heavy emphasis on research, with the goal of finding markets that offer the best potential, and they have established an excellent past record for being able to apply successfully a value-added strategy. This strategy applied to land could optimize future development and prepare the land for its "highest and best use." Their emphasis is on buying land at a price that does not require a speculative boom to be profitable, and they plan to limit their acquisitions to those tracts of land that they feel will be attractive for development in three to five years.

In summary, the private placement limited partnership is an approach to land acquisition that could provide you with 1) superior growth potential, 2) good tax benefits, 3) asset diversification, 4) inflation protection, and 5) professional selection and management.

FARMLANDS

Should you consider investing in farmlands? Your answer probably depends upon the amount of money you have to invest, your tax bracket, your temperament, and what you enjoy doing. Farmland property bought and financed in the right location during the late '70s and early '80s enjoyed excellent price appreciation. Unfortunately, the reverse has been true in recent years, and this trend could continue for several years. If you should decide to invest in farmland, you must be sure that you have a good knowledge about farming (or you can lease your land to an experienced farmer), have time to wait for your investment to mature, can emotionally and financially weather bad crop years (should you decide to put it into production), and have sufficient diversification elsewhere in your investment portfolio.

RECREATION LOTS

Should you invest in recreation lots? Most of the time the answer is no. Some work out well, but the vast majority are marked up so much before being offered to the public in tiny lots that the opportunity to sell at a profit is truly minimal. Once the aggressive sales force moves off the tracts, there is no one to sell your lot for you and you are left with a non-liquid, usually overpriced piece of property.

Home Ownership in the New Economy

The question of whether to rent or buy became considerably more difficult with the advent of higher mortgage rates and a decline in inflation rates. For a number of years in the 1970s, the cost of mortgage money was actually negative since it was below the inflation rate and soaring inflation and appreciation made home buying a profitable thing to do. But in the mid-1980s, this decision became less automatic. The same house could be rented in many areas for a smaller monthly payment than would be required to buy it, and the mortgage interest deduction might not have been enough to offset this expense, particularly in the lower tax brackets.

If there is an investment payoff to home ownership, it will have to come from appreciation, which takes time. A study done at the University of California found that on a present value basis the owner of a $120,000 house would be only 14.6 percent better off, including equity buildup, than a renter after ten years. *Questor Strategic Real Estate Letter* concluded, "Since 1979, many individuals would be better off had they chosen to invest in apartment syndications and rent rather than own the residence in which they live."

And as most homeowners know, monthly house payments have little to do with the real cost of owning a home. The real cost includes repairs, fire and homeowner insurance, property taxes, equity investment, and depreciation (value loss). Much has been said about the tax advantages of home ownership, and there can be advantages in the higher tax brackets, but the landlord gets these tax advantages too. He is also allowed to deduct interest payments and taxes,* plus he is allowed to depreciate the building over an 18-year-period* and deduct maintenance, landscaping, repair, and refurbishing.

You may be thinking if you owned a home you would be building up equity in return for your payments instead of tax receipts, but the proper investment of your savings from renting can also increase your net worth. There are many ways to build net worth other than paying on a mortgage.

If you do make a decision to become a homeowner, make the smallest down payment you are allowed, since inflation rewards

* Refer to the Tax Addendum in the Appendix for possible tax changes.

those who owe money, and interest is deductible. Shop for the best terms, buy a conventional home if you may need to sell, and buy the least expensive house in the best neighborhood you can afford. See Chapter 7 for a detailed discussion of home ownership.

The Ideal Investment?

I have never found an ideal investment. If you do, please let me know about it. However, I have found that the right kind of commercial income-producing real estate limited partnerships under the guidance and management of the right general partners have in the past contained some of the characteristics of an ideal investment. These are:

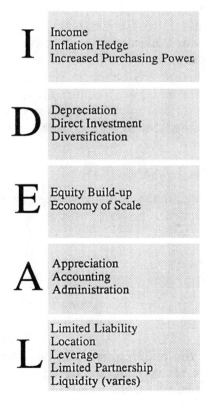

I — Income
Inflation Hedge
Increased Purchasing Power

D — Depreciation
Direct Investment
Diversification

E — Equity Build-up
Economy of Scale

A — Appreciation
Accounting
Administration

L — Limited Liability
Location
Leverage
Limited Partnership
Liquidity (varies)

Let's consider each in summary.

INCOME WITH A TAX SHELTER

The only money you will ever spend at the grocery store is what the IRS lets you keep. Income-producing real estate limited partnerships investing for all cash have in the past paid out cash flow quarterly with the major portion sheltered. This is because they are allowed to pass through to the limited partners the depreciation on the properties. Those investing in multiple-tenant properties using leverage have been able not only to shelter the cash distributions paid quarterly, but find that they also provide excess deductions that save taxes on income from other sources, since they also have deductible interest expense.

INFLATION HEDGE

If you have received no other message from this book, I do hope the one you have not missed is the absolute reality that inflation came thundering in with our government's dedication to full employment and "entitlement programs," and that it will never completely go away until this philosophy is changed. My advice to you is to quit worrying about inflation and get on the right side of it, because inflation can make you a lot of money if you place your funds intelligently in those areas where demand is greater than supply.

INCREASED PURCHASING POWER

By pooling the funds of many investors, the partnership can purchase more and larger properties on more attractive terms than most individuals.

DEPRECIATION

The limited partnership form of investing permits the pass-through of the depreciation expense deduction allowed by the IRS. Another important characteristic of real estate is that depreciation is allowed on the total cost of the building, not just on your investment.* You may have only put in $10,000 and the mortgage company $30,000, but your depreciation is based on the total $40,000. And you are allowed

* Refer to the Tax Addendum in the Appendix for possible tax changes.

a deduction for depreciation even when your asset is actually growing in value.

DIRECT INVESTING

A large percentage of money placed in savings institutions is invested in real estate. If you are a depositor, you are an indirect investor in real estate. If you invest in a limited partnership, the partnership may borrow the money for a mortgage from savings institutions, but you have a direct investment in the real estate and are in a position to receive your money's full earning power (but you also give up the fixed dollar guarantees). In my opinion, your only hope of staying even after inflation and taxes is to be a direct investor. Remember, you have to own the thing that owns the thing.

DIVERSIFICATION OF RISKS

One of the first rules of successful investing you learned in this book was diversification. Never put all your eggs in the proverbial one basket, but rather spread your precious eggs out in several baskets of various kinds of real estate and in various locations. Ten properties located in ten locations should offer more safety than one property in one location.

EQUITY BUILDUP

If you own your home on which you have a mortgage, you are already familiar with equity buildup (mortgage paydown). The difference between the equity buildup of your home and the equity buildup in the commercial properties of the limited partnerships is that you had to build up the equity in your home by your monthly mortgage payments, but in the limited partnerships the tenants build up your equity through a portion of their monthly rent payments. Equity also builds up without taxes until the property is sold.

ECONOMY OF SCALE

I can't emphasize enough how important economy of scale can be in the purchase, management, and sale of commercial real estate. Most of the truly significant profits are made on the very large real estate properties. There are fewer buyers to compete and they can also buy the carpeting, paint, refrigerators, stoves, and so on directly from the factory. And as a limited partner, you have the opportunity to participate in a proportionate part of larger properties than you may be able to do on an individual basis.

APPRECIATION

"Capital gains" have always been and still remain the golden words of the investment world. No federal income taxes are paid on the appreciation of real estate until the properties are sold. The properties can just sit there and grow in value without taxes. (They can go down in value, too.) Appreciation is realized when and if the properties are sold for a larger amount than was paid for the purchase. If the properties have been held for over six months, the profit on the sale is considered a capital gain and only 40 percent of it is taxable, with a maximum tax of 20 percent.* As inflation pushes up replacement costs, appreciation in real estate has a good likelihood of occurring.

ACCOUNTING

You may especially enjoy the accounting done for you by the general partners. You are sent a completed Schedule K-1 (schedule used for limited partnerships), plus a guide with red lines and arrows showing you where to enter the information on your tax return. By following the detailed instructions, you can complete your own returns if you so desire. (However, I find that truly competent and creative CPA's can be worth much more than they cost.)

ADMINISTRATION

Professional management frees you from the task of acquisition and day-to-day management, plus it handles the details involved in selling the property at the proper time.

LEVERAGE

Again, remember Bernard Baruch's answer to the question of how he became so rich: "OPM—Other People's Money." Let other peo-

* Refer to the Tax Addendum in the Appendix for possible tax changes.

ple's money work for you. Remember, inflation rewards those who owe money, not those who pay cash. (I am talking about long-term real estate mortgages, not revolving charge accounts.) When and if appreciation occurs, the total value of the building appreciates, including the borrowed portion. Leverage can work for you if properly used, but it can spell disaster if it is abused or if the economy of the area turns against you.

LIMITED LIABILITY

As a limited partner, you could not be called upon for additional funds. You have limited liability to your investment.

LIQUIDITY

Real estate investment trusts provide you with liquidity, but many other forms of investing in real estate curtail liquidity. Do not place funds into real estate limited partnerships that you want to grab back on very short notice. However, some syndicators are now making markets in their units and others are providing depository receipts that are tradable on the stock exchange.

LOCATION

The three most important rules in selecting the right piece of real estate are location, location, location (and when we have periods of tight money I would add terms, terms, terms). Your objective should be to become a proportionate owner of a diversified portfolio of properties selected and managed by top professionals who have established a long record of success and who have large pools of money for investing. This enables them to purchase properties that have the necessary characteristics of good location and the right terms.

Summary

If you are willing to give up instant liquidity, are in a 25 percent tax bracket or above, and can forgo the pleasure of looking up the market value of your properties in the newspaper each day, then you may find that the limited partnership is a good way to prevent double taxation and to allow you to participate in investments that, if made individually, would require large amounts of capital.

Investing in real estate should be considered in any program designed to build financial independence. In my opinion, the opportunity for relatively high leverage with relatively low risk makes it a viable inflation hedge. Unusual tax benefits can also enhance its attractiveness, but they should not be your principal motivation. Invest for economic reasons, not tax reasons.

Current tax-sheltered cash distributions can also be attractive. If your income stream needs to be higher and steady, then be prepared to sacrifice some of the growth potential. If current income is not your chief objective, then look at the operating leveraged partnerships where income may fluctuate but where the potential for appreciation is greater.

My formula for financial independence should now add real estate and might read thus:

Time + Money + Real Estate =
Opportunity for Financial Independence

APPLICATION

1. Which areas of real estate investing best fit your tax bracket and your temperament?_____

2. List the steps you will take to become better informed about investment alternatives:

    1)_____

    2)_____

    3)_____

3. Make a list of all your alternative investment possibilities. Calculate your expected rate of return, your loss to taxes, your keepable funds after taxes, your potential to hedge against inflation, and your potential for equity buildup and growth of capital.

YOUR WORKSHEET FOR COMPARING REAL ESTATE INVESTING WITH OTHER TYPES

$_____investment, _____% tax bracket

INDIRECT INVESTING

	Income	Taxes	Keepable	Inflation Hedge	Equity Buildup	Appreci- ation
Savings & loan						
Corporate bonds						
Municipal bonds						
Single-premium deferred annuity						

DIRECT INVESTING

	Income	Taxes	Keepable	Inflation Hedge	Equity Buildup	Appreci- ation
Multitenant leveraged						
Multitenant non-leveraged						
REIT						
Miniwarehouses leveraged						
Miniwarehouses non-leveraged						

4. List here the areas of our economy where you think demand will be greater than supply over the next three years:

1) _____

2) _____

3) _____

4) _____

5. List here the course of action you plan to take to profit from these shortages:

   1) _____

   2) _____

   3) _____

   4) _____

Chapter 7

Home Sweet Home—
To Rent or Buy?

There is one kind of real estate about which you have no option; you must have a place to live during every period of your life. You do, however, have a number of choices about how you allocate your funds to meet this and other needs.

Food, clothing, shelter—the three essentials of life! That's what you learned in grade school, and as an adult you probably do not question these necessities. Since shelter is a necessity, but only one of your necessities, it behooves you to approach its provision as coolly and economically as possible, for you will want to have funds left over for a few of the other goodies that put a bit of frosting on the cake of life.

There is much fuzzy thinking about the best way to provide shelter. Many couples, particularly young ones, hate to rent even for a short period of time. They are convinced that rent receipts are pure waste, not realizing that rent money is no more wasted than the money spent for food or medicine. Many view house payments as almost pure ''savings'' and rent money in terms of a leaky faucet.

You may be one of those who are deliberately closing their minds to economic realities in order to own their own home.

Single-Family Dwelling—Hobby or Investment?

A single-family dwelling may not be a good investment, in the real sense of the word, for either the landlord or the homeowner who is in the lower income tax bracket. Homes often are more of a hobby than an investment unless you have chosen a home in what later becomes a growth area where land values accelerate rapidly. This could then be an excellent investment. However, don't go overboard; inflation or a shift in location desirability may not bail you out of a costly real estate purchase. While you are waiting for the property to inflate in value, taxes and interest can put a very bad dent in your family budget.

THE REAL COST

The real cost of home ownership includes upkeep and repair, fire and homeowner insurance, property taxes, equity investment, and depreciation (value loss). These expenses are just as real for a homeowner as they are for a landlord. The big difference lies in the fact that a landlord usually recognizes them and includes them in the price he charges for the use of his property, whereas you may be tempted as a homeowner to pretend that these expenses do not exist.

The landlord knows that he must get over 10 percent per year in rent on his property to cover his expenses and net him a profit. You, as a potential or present homeowner, would be wise to think as he does.

If you have been living in an apartment, feeling you just must buy your own home and save all that rent money, do slow down and take heart. The drain on your solvency may not be as bad as you have been thinking.

AVOID THE APPLES AND ORANGES COMPARISON

The rather unemotional approach I have given home ownership should do one thing for you, and that is to make you aware that the monthly payments have little to do with the real cost of owning a home.

How do you go about comparing the cost of renting an apartment with the cost of buying a home? One way is to compare the annual rental for an apartment with 10 percent of the value of the home you are thinking of purchasing. If you foolishly compare the monthly payments on the house with the monthly payments on the apartment, you are, in effect, comparing apples and oranges. There is no comparative relationship. Mortgage payments have nothing to do with the cost of home ownership. Mortgage payments only relate to debt reduction.

Buy or Rent?

Should you buy or rent your shelter? Your answer should be determined by a number of factors. Chief among these would be: your tax bracket, need for space, temperament, lifestyle, savings in the bank, investment possibilities, familiarity with the various neighborhoods, current home prices, availability of financing, and likelihood of being transferred.

TAX ADVANTAGE

Much has been said about the tax advantages of home ownership and there are some excellent ones, but these advantages are not as clear-cut as they may appear at first. Interest and property taxes have both soared the past few years. Because these are allowable deductions on your tax return, they can be important to you if you are in a sufficiently high tax bracket. If you are in a 30 percent bracket, you are able to shift $30 out of every $100 you pay in interest and property taxes back to the IRS. In a 50 percent bracket, it's $50. As you can see, the higher your bracket, the greater the "subsidy" from the government.

This does not mean, however, that renters do not get tax breaks, too. The landlord is permitted to deduct interest and property taxes also. In addition, he is allowed to deduct two other important items the homeowner is not allowed. He can deduct depreciation on an 18-year basis on the total cost of the property and also operating expenses.

We have just learned how important depreciation deductions can be. If landlords were required to pay these bills without treating them as expenses, rents would have to be higher. By permitting treatment of these items as operating expenses, renters pay lower rents and find more apartments available.

In the lower tax bracket, the tax relief may be just an illusion. If your income is $20,000 per year, you may not get much of a tax break from the extra deductions. Even if you are in the middle income bracket, you will probably save no more than 20 percent of the net cost of your interest and property taxes by deducting them from gross income.

The IRS allows each family a standard deduction anyway, and unless you have enough deductions to itemize, including interest and property taxes, these last two costs become pure expenses.

If you have ever had a really aggressive real estate agent pull out his form entitled "Analysis of Home Ownership Costs," he may endeavor to persuade you that owning your own house will cost practically nothing, since the monthly charges consist almost entirely of tax-deductible interest and property taxes, and the remainder is your contribution to your equity, which will, of course, increase. He may then proceed to tell you that all you need is a down payment, which will be the best investment you have ever made. He will attempt to persuade you that you should be a wise house hunter and buy, and not a foolish house hunter and rent, with nothing to show for it but rent receipts.

But this arithmetic omits two crucial elements. One of these is the loss of income that the down payment might produce if invested elsewhere. Another is the transfer costs, the expense of buying and selling a house, which can amount to over 8 percent of its value. When these costs are put into your analysis, they can turn the calculations around in favor of renting.

However, our whole U.S. housing system encourages buying, not renting. Spouses, children, pets, neighbors, politicians, and bankers all argue for home ownership. It has become one of those fundamentals we look to as securing the nation. Our tax laws favor ownership. The Brookings Institution estimates that homeowners get $7 billion worth of federal tax breaks annually.

The IRS also exempts you from the capital gains tax when you sell your house, as long as you buy another house that is as expensive within a year or build another within twenty-four months. This all encourages home ownership to become a habit. With exceptions, these rules also apply to a condominium and stock in a cooperative.

Gains that are not taxed reduce the basis on your new home. (Losses are not deductible.)

MOBILITY—THE AMERICAN WAY

Another consideration that may recommend renting is that we are a very mobile society. Renting allows you to move more easily without the worry and delay of selling a home and the expense of sales commissions and horrendous closing costs.

At this point you may be thinking that if you owned a home, you would be building an equity in return for your payments as the years go by, whereas now you have nothing but rent receipts.

But remember, I have been comparing the cost of renting with the cost of owning. You can save money and acquire net worth in other ways than by paying on a mortgage. You can open a money market mutual fund or start a monthly investment program with the difference.

The Case of Mrs. Bailey. An elderly widow client of mine lives in a house that is debt-free and has a market value of $100,000. She asked if she should sell her house and rent an apartment. I told her that if she would bring me a list of her expenditures for the past year, I would be happy to advise her from a financial point of view. She gave me a list of her utilities, yard-work expenses, house repairs, insurance, and taxes. I then added a 6 percent "guaranteed" return she could obtain on the $100,000 that would be available for investment after the sale of the house, even though we should certainly do better than 6 percent on her money. When we added all of these together, we found that she could live in a $1,000-per-month apartment more cheaply than she could live in her own home. In addition, she did not have to worry about watering her yard or possible vandalism during trips out of town.

I advised her, however, not to rush into selling her home. Answering a question on a financial basis is one thing and answering it on an emotional basis is quite another matter. Sometimes you need to consider that some expenditures are an investment in living.

YOUR TEMPERAMENT

Home ownership may have great psychological benefits for you. Pride, a sense of belonging, having a place to put down roots—all of these can be very important. You may change, improve, and convert your home and grounds as you wish.

However, you now have an asset that may demand much from you. It will take your or someone's time, energy, and money. Home repairs and upkeep can be costly. You have now become your own landlord, garbage man, and repairman. Yards will probably have to be mowed and shrubbery planted, watered, and trimmed. This may take away some of your freedom to play golf or tennis or to travel.

Is your income variable? Could it drop by a large amount? Are you subject to transfer? If so, you could have difficulty selling your home if this happened in a recession or a period when mortgage money had either dried up or had become very expensive. When you rent, your commitment lasts only as long as your lease.

YOUR NEED FOR SPACE

If you have a growing family, they may need more space than renting would provide. Small children will need a place to play. The number of apartments that accept children or provide them with sufficient large play areas may be limited. Schools may be better and not as crowded in the suburbs. Investigate thoroughly the schools and recreational and cultural facilities.

What Price Home Can You Afford?

If you decide to purchase a home, it may be the largest single investment that you will make in your whole lifetime; therefore, invest carefully and within your budget.

There is no magic rule as to what percentage of your income should be spent for a roof over your head; however, I have found that usually this expenditure should not exceed 30 to 35 percent of your income. We have already concluded that there are other things that are important in life. You may desire good clothing, nutritional and tasty food, excellent medical care, a sporty or at least an adequate automobile, and an annual vacation. This makes it necessary to apportion your income.

There are certain guidelines lenders will use in determining the maximum mortgage they will grant. A rule of thumb used by many lenders is one-fourth of total income after long-term debt (any debt over ten months). For example, if you were purchasing a $100,000 home, and applying for an 80 percent loan of $80,000, at 10 percent for a 30-year mortgage to balloon in 15 years, your payments would be $702 per month and you would need an income of $2,808 per month after long-term debt, or an annual income of around $33,696. If your earnings are higher, you may want to consider spending less. After all, there are other things you'll want. A large home may not be as important to you as other pleasures and comforts.

These figures only take into consideration the principal and interest mortgage payments, and do not include other housing costs such as insurance, taxes, utilities, maintenance, and repair. Inclusion of these, of course, would mean that you would be required to have a higher annual income to qualify for a loan.

Should You Buy a New or Old Home?

ADVANTAGES OF THE OLD

New and used homes, if they appreciate, do so about the same rate if the neighborhoods are comparable. The possibility of your buying a used home is greater because more of them are available.

Also, you may be able to buy the older one for less. The rooms may be more spacious. The construction may be of higher quality. It may be nearer shops, schools, churches, and transportation. The neighborhood will be established, and the landscaping has probably been done. Taxes tend to rise less for older homes, and you may avoid assessments for such things as utilities and water systems. There has been increased interest in older, close-in homes in recent years as the cost of gasoline has increased and traffic congestion has become a greater problem.

DISADVANTAGES OF BUYING AN OLDER HOME

It may be more difficult when purchasing an older home to obtain the maximum mortgage, and the duration of the mortgage could be less.

Repairs and remodeling can be expensive. Upkeep can be greater. The older home may lack central air-conditioning and new built-in appliances; adding them now may be costly.

Where to Buy?

I once interviewed the head of the real estate department for Prudential Life Insurance company. When I asked him what the most important considerations in choosing real estate were, he drew himself up to his quite considerable height and said that there are three requirements you must never forget. They are "location, location, location!" (At another time when I asked a very successful real estate investor this same question, his answer was "Terms, terms, terms.")

The same is true in selecting your home. The three requirements you should never forget are neighborhood, neighborhood, neighborhood. The homes and people around you not only affect the resale value of your home but also your enjoyment of it.

THE LEAST EXPENSIVE IN THE NEIGHBORHOOD

Resist the temptation to buy the most expensive home in the neighborhood. It is much wiser to own a modest home in an expensive neighborhood. Your modest home may gain in value by being surrounded by more expensive homes, but an expensive home in a less expensive neighborhood will probably suffer because the mortgage obtainable may be limited in amount to the price of the least expensive home.

DISTANCE FROM WORK

Distance from work should also be seriously considered. Before you yield to the temptation to move far out from town to escape high land and tax costs, consider the cost of driving long distances to work. This cost can easily wipe out any savings. Savings of $4,500 on the price of a home 30 miles from work could be used up in a few years if it was necessary to drive an extra 1,500 miles a year.

The time required to drive the extra distance should also be of prime consideration. Time is money. Extra time spent in driving may subtract from your earning power and sap your energy.

If you find, after considering all of these factors, that you still want to live farther out, may I suggest that you utilize your commuting time by installing a tape cassette in your automobile. There are excellent educational and motivational tapes on almost any subject, including my own cassette album on investing.

PREMANUFACTURED HOUSING— THE "MOBILE HOME"

The conventional new or pre-owned home may no longer be a reality moneywise for you, or you may find that there are added amenities and more favorable locations available in a mobile home. I use the term "mobile home" because it is the term most used and understood. However, only 2 percent of such homes are ever moved, so mobility is no longer their major characteristic.

As you begin to study the pros and cons of whether you should consider premanufactured homes, you may discover there are a lot of myths surrounding this increasingly popular form of housing. One that has been prevalent for years is that only senior citizens live in them, but statistics show that half of the buyers are couples under 35 years of age.

Another myth is that they are shoddily built. However, a recent study showed that more than 60 percent of mobile homes built 20 or more years ago are still in use today. Still another myth is that the parks are overcrowded, are filled with noisy children, and are distant from shopping centers. Some of them are, but more and more of them are in beautiful surroundings and are near shopping areas, schools, and medical facilities.

You may be tired of city life and want to move to the country because you enjoy the fresh air and space and have the option of keeping horses or raising cattle, dogs, or other animals. The premanufactured homes may make this choice available to you.

Current surveys show that many individuals and couples with excellent salaries are preferring the economy and ease of maintenance of this type of housing. Also the first-time buyers are finding that the down payment and monthly payments can fit into their budgets more readily than the conventional home.

Since 1976 the federal government has set standards for construction and safety of these homes. This code sets standards higher than those established for conventional housing in many communities.

Housing and Urban Development's National Manufactured Housing Code holds all mobile homes in the United States to a single standard. In the area of energy efficiency, the code specifies standards for heat loss and gain, efficiency of appliances, and minimum-level insulation protection; for fire safety, it requires smoke alarms and pop-out windows in sleeping areas, two exits, plus certain flame-spread standards in walls, ceilings, and cooking areas. Incidence of fire in mobile homes is now slightly less than in site-built homes.

Today's manufactured housing bears practically no resemblance to the old-time trailer. The homes come with peaked and slate roofs, cathedral ceilings, skylights, storm windows, microwaves, sewing areas, wood siding, wet bars, sunken bathtubs, and fireplaces. And they feature shelves and cupboards.

PRICE OF PREMANUFACTURED HOMES

While the cost of the average conventional home has passed $100,000 nationally, that same home made in a factory would cost $40,000 to $50,000. The reason for the price break is the efficiency of the assembly line. To build 1,000 square feet of housing the conventional way requires around 600 man-hours. To factory-build this same space takes around 250 man-hours. When you add to this the more efficient quality control and no interruptions for bad weather or shortages of materials, the savings can add up.

In the past there have been restrictions on financing, locating, zoning, and licensing this type of housing; but these restrictions and hindrances are gradually being removed.

In Houston, for example, one of this country's largest builders of single-family, site-built homes has opened housing developments made up entirely of premanufactured housing. Another builder in California has developed posh double-wide premanufactured homes beginning around $90,000. Many Florida communities feature retirement divisions on lakes and canals or in beautifully wooded and landscaped areas.

The only obstacle that seems to remain in this type of housing is the public image. But, bit by bit, with changes in legislation and zoning and with increased quality of development, this type of housing is moving closer to the mainstream of acceptable housing and may be an option you will want to consider.

Large or Small Down Payment?

If you decide after looking at all the facts that buying a home of your own is best for you economically and emotionally, then should you make a small down payment or a large down payment?

From the point of view of a financial planner, there is no doubt that the down payment should be as low as you possibly can arrange in the money market you find yourself in. There are a number of reasons you should make this choice.

1. Any money tied up in a mortgage is a dead asset. The house doesn't know whether or not it has a high or low down payment on it. It will increase or decrease in value just the same. This is especially true in a state that has a homestead law like Texas. Once you've moved in, you cannot refinance this home and get that equity out. It is locked in until you sell. It's almost like that much money sitting in a checking account not drawing interest.

2. Interest is deductible. As you've seen, you don't want to miss this subsidy.

3. Inflation rewards those who owe money, not those who pay cash. You can pay off the mortgage with cheaper and cheaper dollars as inflation continues.

4. If you need to sell, it's easier to find someone with a small down payment than a large one unless you have a due-on-sale clause when an assumption is made.

5. You have additional funds to invest in other ways and so gain added diversification.

The Allens and the Bakers

To help you make your comparison, let's look at two families. Both found just the right home, and each home cost $96,300. Both families, fortunately, had an income of $70,000 a year, and two healthy children of approximately the same ages.

THE ALLENS

The Allens were reared by parents who programmed them with such admonitions as "Always pay cash"; "Never owe money"; "You might come upon hard times, so have your house paid for so you'll have a roof over your head"—the Poor Richard guidelines.

When it was time to close on their home, the Allens believed that the most prudent way was to pay cash, which they did. They then complimented themselves on saving "all that interest" and not having to make house payments each month.

THE BAKERS

The Bakers were reared by parents who were business oriented and held earning power of a dollar in high respect. They had taught their children to use or rent each dollar they could and to put it to work at its maximum potential. So when it came time to close on their home, they thought that the prudent course for their family was to move in with the minimum down payment and to obtain the best mortgage available.

Then they began shopping for terms and rates. First they went to a life insurance company—choosing the kind that has enticed its policyholders to do their "banking" with the company in the form of cash surrender value. These companies, consequently, have large sums to lend if they choose to lend them for home mortgages. In the past, they have been the largest single underwriters of real estate mortgage money. During the past few years, however, they have been demanding and obtaining a sizable portion of the equity in the commercial buildings they are financing.

The Bakers also went to the savings and loan associations. They found that the rates and terms varied from one savings association to another, depending on the amount of lendable money each had at the particular time and the value judgment of each of their loan officers as to the Bakers' ability to pay. They also looked at mortgage companies and found that the rates varied by the same criteria as did those of the savings and loans.

The Bakers decided on a financing plan that would allow them to make a $19,200 down payment, with a $77,040 mortgage for 30 years at 9.75 percent from a life insurance company, with monthly payments of $662 principal and interest. (Their taxes were estimated to be around $178 per month and the insurance around $50. This made a total of $890.)

ASSUMING A MORTGAGE

Since the homes were new, it was necessary for the Allens and Bakers either to buy with cash or obtain a mortgage. Had the homes been "used," a third option might have been available and desirable. This is to "assume" a mortgage—that is, to take over responsibility for the mortgage that the seller has on the house. Older mortgages usually carry a lower interest rate than new mortgages, and the closing costs are considerably less if the home is in a community in which banks charge "points" for a loan (a "point" is 1 percent of the amount of the loan). The purchaser pays the seller for his "equity" (the difference between the sale price and the mortgage) and then assumes the monthly payments. Ultimate legal responsibility for the mortgage, however, lies with the original buyer, so it is important for the seller to check the buyer carefully. At present, some lenders are requiring that they approve of new buyers and are escalating the interest rate and placing a due-on-sale provision in the deed of trust. If these changes are made, then the original buyer is relieved of the legal responsibility of the loan. If the owner's equity is high, it will usually be advisable to obtain a new loan commitment in order to avoid a high down payment.

WHICH COUPLE MADE THE RIGHT DECISION?

Let's look at the Allens. They will not have a monthly house payment, and they will not have to pay interest on $77,400. They felt smugly proud of their decision.

The Bakers, on the other hand, felt that they had made the right decision.

Which do you think made the right choice? Measure your value system against each of theirs to see where you feel you will be the most comfortable. This will help you to decide which course would be best for you.

But do remember what I said about inflation rewarding those who owe money, not those who pay cash. I realize that this is a sad commentary on life, but it is a fact you must learn to accept. You must learn to be a realist. Look at life the way it truly is, rather than the way you wish it were.

If the government is successful in keeping the rate of inflation to 4 percent (do you really think it will?), you would be paying off your "loaned" dollars in ten years with 60-cent dollars, in fifteen years with 40-cent dollars, and in 20 years with 20-cent dollars.

Think how long your dad had to work for a dollar 30 years ago, and then compare it with the minutes of work you have to do today. Any time you can postpone paying back a dollar that you have obtained on a long-term basis at a reasonable rate, always avail yourself of the opportunity. You must, of course, invest the money you have not paid down on the house in such a way as to earn more than the after-tax cost of renting it.

MAKING HOUSE PAYMENTS

The Allens do not have to concern themselves with paying monthly house payments; the Bakers do. The Bakers also have the responsibility of investing $77,100. How should the Bakers invest these funds to provide the extra $662 needed monthly for house payments?

There are various investment possibilities that they should consider. By the time you have completed this book you will know they have a wide choice of viable investment alternatives. Mutual funds with a systematic withdrawal program would be my favorite approach. A 10.3 percent withdrawal would make the payment and I hope still provide some growth. Other investments they may want to consider—although they would not provide this orderly use of dividends, growth, or possible capital appreciation—could be made in limited partnerships in oil and gas income programs, all-cash real estate programs, miniwarehouses, leasing, and other possibilities.

MEETING AN EMERGENCY

The Allens paid cash for their home, remembering their parents' warning about possible hard times. However, if the Allens have an emergency, they will not be able to redeem a few square feet of their house. If they live in a state with a homestead law, they can't even pledge it as collateral for a loan. The loan-free home may have given them joy at the time of purchase, but if they should have a real emergency, they may find that their home is a dead asset that does not offer liquidity.

The Bakers, on the other hand, could redeem a few shares of their stock or take their shares to the bank and use them for collateral to borrow any needed funds. Their limited partnership units could also be listed on their financial statement to qualify them for a loan.

Availing Yourself of an Opportunity

In money management, always put yourself in the driver's seat. Leave options open to yourself. Using your stock as collateral at the bank does not necessarily require an emergency. A good business opportunity may present itself. You'll have to pass it up if you don't have available funds. With collateral you can obtain these funds.

INTEREST IS DEDUCTIBLE

To give you an idea of how much of the Bakers' monthly payment is interest, which is deductible, the percentage schedule for the first five years of their loan was: 99.85 percent, 99.67 percent, 99.47 percent, 99.23 percent, and 98.96 percent. For the first year, $.998 \times \$661 \times 12 = \$7,916$ interest out of a yearly payment of $7,944.

The IRS lets the Bakers deduct interest payments, so if they are in a 40 percent tax bracket, Uncle Sam bears 40 percent of their interest cost. Thus, of the 9.75 percent interest they are paying, their net cost is 5.85 percent.

SALABILITY

As we mentioned earlier, one of the reasons you should consider renting is the fact that Americans are a mobile lot. Recent studies show the average family moves every seven years. The letters IBM in our neighborhood stand for "I've Been Moved." If moving is necessary, you may find it easier to find a buyer with $19,200 for a down payment than one with $93,000. Of course, the house can be refinanced, but this might cause your buyer to pay points on a new mortgage, which could run several hundred dollars; or refinancing may not be available.

There are reasons other than transfers for moving. If the children have grown and left the nest, a large home may be a burden rather than a necessity. The desirability of the neighborhood may have changed, or your company offices may have moved to another section of town. The reasons for moving can make a lengthy list.

RATE OF GAIN ON INVESTED CAPITAL

Let's assume homes escalate in value 5 percent a year for the next ten years. The Allens have $93,000 invested in their home. Five percent appreciation would increase their net worth by $4,650 per year, or $46,000 in ten years.

The Bakers' $96,300 home has also appreciated the same 5 percent, or to $144,450, but they have had only $19,200 invested. An increase of 250 percent on their invested capital, as compared to the Allens' 50 percent. (The figure for the Bakers must be adjusted for their interest deductions and taxes on their dividends and capital gains on their investments.)

Shopping for Terms

Money is a commodity. It is a commodity like peanuts, warehouses, and even houses. Never be emotional about money. If you do, you won't make rational decisions about it. Put it in its proper commodity status. Therefore, go in a businesslike manner to secure your mortgage.

If you have a contact at a lending institution, be sure to avail yourself of any help this person can give you; it does make a difference whom you know. Do not accept the first loan offered to you. Shop for rates and terms. Each institution's circumstances vary from time to time, so its lending conditions and rates will vary accordingly.

Rates are important, but the down payment and length of payment period far outweigh a slight differential in rates.

WHAT TO DO WHEN MORTGAGE MONEY IS TIGHT

In the latter part of 1981, several things happened virtually to dry up mortgage funds. The Federal Reserve Board tightened the money supply to such an extent that almost all mortgage money was dried up. This in turn forced up the rates for borrowing and the cost of money to the savings and loans that had been a large supplier of mortgage money. All this occurred at a time when a large number of our citizens became more savvy about money and moved their money out of 5½ percent passbook savings accounts and lower-interest-paying certificates into money market mutual funds.

Another source of funds had been life insurance companies that sold policies with savings programs in them. But these funds began to decrease as more and more people became knowledgeable after reading my books and others and began cashing in their cash surrender value whole-life policies. Also, insurance companies that already had large pools of money found themselves in a very enviable position. Developers of office buildings were in such need of permanent financing that insurance companies found they could demand and obtain 50 percent or more equity in the buildings they were financing. This was more profitable than making home loans.

Residential real estate sales consequently slowed to a trickle. Real estate salesmen, being the creative souls that they are (with the extra nudge of survival), came up with many "creative financing" plans. Most of these plans greatly favor the buyer (it became a buyers' market) and are to the disadvantage of the seller. You may find it necessary to buy or sell during such periods of tight money or chaos in the money markets, so let me introduce you to a few of the terms you'll be coming across.

GRADUATED PAYMENT MORTGAGES (GPM)

This type of loan will permit you to pay lower monthly payments in the early years of your mortgage, with payments rising in later years to a level sufficient to amortize your entire loan over the term of the loan. With lower initial payments, you may be able to qualify for a home loan with a lower income base or, conversely, buy a more expensive house with the same income. In most instances, your lender will require some good evidence that your future income will increase along with the increasing payments that will be due.

This type of loan will require you to pay more interest over the life of the mortgage, because in the early years with your lower payments, very little of your payments are being used to reduce your principal. In fact, in some instances your early payments are so low that they do not cover the interest, so the accumulated and unpaid interest is added to your principal balance for payment in later years. In this arrangement your principal amount at the end of your first few years will be greater than when you first obtained the loan.

If you decide to use the GPM, run the numbers out for the entire term of the loan to ascertain both the payments you'll need to make and the actual increase of your principal. Only then can you make an intelligent decision.

If you are a young, fresh-out-of-college professional with a long-term increased earning potential, this type of loan may be a viable consideration.

ADJUSTABLE RATE MORTGAGE (ARM)

Adjustable rate mortgages (also called variable rate mortgages or VRM's) have interest rates that move in tandem with agreed-upon economic indices. In general, you agree to make payments in one of two ways: monthly payments become larger/smaller, or payments remain equal but differing amounts are allocated to principal and interest, with the possible modification of the term of the loan.

There are some restrictions on the lender: The variation in interest rates must be based on an index over which the lender exerts no control, and the indicator must be readily identifiable by the borrower (such as the six-month Treasury bill rate).

Shop carefully if you're considering an ARM or VRM vehicle. Look particularly for: 1) the index used (don't accept the "cost of funds" index from the Federal Home Loan Bank Board, which has a tendency NOT to fall in tandem with other economic indices); 2) the initial payment amount; 3) how often the payment rate can be changed; and 4) a limit, if possible, on the extent of increase permitted.

BALLOON OR SHORT-TERM MORTGAGES

These mortgages usually require monthly payments just as if you were going to amortize your loan over a 30-year period, but they balloon in three to five years and the balance becomes due in full at that time. The thing you don't know with this type of loan is what the going interest rates will be when it balloons or if loans will even be available at all.

In some real estate circles these are now being called "bullet loans," meaning someone has a gun to your head on maturity. I heard a new name the other day—"neutron loans." They leave the building standing, but kill the owner.

ASSUMABLE MORTGAGES

In this type of mortgage, as the name implies, you would assume the payment schedule of the original mortgager, which in all probability would be at a lower rate than is available today. If you can find an assumable loan, this may be worthy of your consideration. However, it may require more cash than you have available or that you want to have tied up in equity. Funds unnecessarily tied up in down payments are really dead assets that could usually be working harder for you in a different position.

VA and FHA loans are assumable if the borrower is creditworthy. Other lenders may put a due-on-sale clause in the mortgage terms calling for the full payment of the balance in the event of a transfer of title. Make sure the lender agrees to an assumption in writing.

BLEND

Sometimes you may find that the lender will not allow you to assume the balance due at the original low interest rate, but will allow it at a higher rate that is still lower than the prevailing rate—hence the term "blend" to indicate the blending of the new and old interest rates.

In some instances the lender may even advance funds to make a larger mortgage, thereby reducing the amount of funds needed for a down payment.

Builder financing at lower than the going rates may also surface in times of tight money. Check these carefully, for the builder may be adding this lost interest into the purchase price of the home in order to make the financing package more attractive.

In any event, if you find yourself shopping for a mortgage at such times, do just that—shop, shop, shop. I know it adds another burden to the already heavy burden of making a buying decision on a home or an investment property, but it can greatly affect your standard of living or profit potential for many years to come.

IF YOU ARE SELLING

If you are selling a home today, you may find your realtor encouraging you to furnish financing in the form of a second mortgage. While this creative financing helps their salespeople preserve their commissions in times of high interest and tight money, it may cause you some serious problems. This form of financing may be based on the selling price of your home, not on the soundness and profitability of the financing arrangement, and may be at low market rates. Interest rates may rise considerably above the rate on the mortgage you are carrying, making you very sorry to be missing these higher rates. If you need to use some of the money tied up in the mortgage, you may not be able to find a buyer, and even if you do, you may have to discount the mortgage by a substantial amount.

Balloon mortgages are also common. This means that in three to five years the total second mortgage becomes due. But when the payment is due, the financial market could be very tight and the courts could rule due-on sale clauses unenforceable.

Deregulation of financial institutions allows the money market to control the level of interest rates, so the cost of financing may become greater than the rate of inflation. You may have no other choice if you must sell, but if you can avoid seller financing, it is more prudent to do so.

Timing Your Purchase

No doubt, some years are better than others for buying a home. If you buy your home when money is more abundant, your interest costs will be lower, which will result in lower monthly payments for you. The quantity of money, which influences the cost, is regulated by action of the Federal Reserve Board, which in turn is based on consumer borrowing demands and whether the current objective is to try to slow inflation or to increase employment. If the main thrust is to slow inflation, money will be tighter and interest rates higher. If the latter, credit will be more available and will cost less.

But what if you decide that you've reached that period in your family's life when you should buy a home, and it turns out that this is the time the Federal Reserve Board's money policies are restrictive and have driven money rates to a high level? Should you postpone your purchase?

The answer is probably no. Such Federal Reserve Board action is usually taken with the hope of slowing down inflation.

This means that you are looking for a house during a period of rising building costs. If you wait until interest rates are lower, the price of the house will by then have inflated, and your monthly payments will be just as great or greater. Since the part that is interest is tax deductible and the part that is principal is not, you may be better off with the combination of lower price and slightly higher interest. So if you feel you must buy a home, go ahead regardless of present interest rates.

The Hybrid Homeowner

If you want the advantages of owning your home and the advantages of an apartment, perhaps you should consider owning your own apartment.

This can be done either in a cooperative apartment or townhouse, or a condominium. What's the difference?

In a co-op you buy "shares" in the building and facilities, including recreational facilities. When shares are sold in co-ops, it must be by vote of the majority of the shareholders. You become both landlord and tenant, which means that you take your share of both economic and managerial responsibilities.

Co-op ownership does give the tax advantages of home ownership together with recreational facilities and maintenance at a lower cost than an individual family dwelling.

In a condominium, you own your own apartment and a pro rata share of the facilities rather than stock in the building. This means that you have the same responsibility for common areas, but you may sell your apartment to whomever you wish within the rules you accepted when you made your purchase. The tax and facilities cost advantages are identical to those in the co-op.

The methods of financing for both are similar to financing a one-family home.

What are some of the problems with these forms of home ownership? First, in co-op apartments, owners have occasionally had problems with a co-owner vetoing the sale of their shares, which means, effectively, they could not sell their home. More important, poor maintenance of an apartment complex seriously lowers the value and salability of your apartment, so it is imperative to buy in a well-located, well-maintained building, just as you should buy a home in a well-located and well-maintained neighborhood.

You may need to have an income above $20,000 to approach any meaningful break on your tax return through home ownership.

There are many legitimate reasons for buying a home. You may feel that it is a better place to raise your children. It may give you a sense of security, of belonging, or of status. A lovely home can be a true joy and a prestige symbol that adds to your self-confidence.

However, don't plunge into home ownership only because others are doing it—a kind of follow-the-follower pattern of thinking—without truly weighing the pros and cons. Even though there are a number of valid reasons for home ownership, I find that most of them are sociologic and very few are based on genuine economic facts. Houses should not be bought as investments per se but as places in which to live. Today 66 percent of U.S. families live in houses that they own. This still leaves a substantial minority who rent.

If you truly believe that owning your own home will bring you greater enjoyment of life, will make you a more respectable citizen, and will offer you that additional privacy that may be important to you, then consider buying a home. But if your reasons are to boast about all the money you are saving, be careful not to boast to an economist.

SHOULD YOU PREPAY YOUR MORTGAGE?

If the mortgage on your home carries a rate lower than the going rate, you may receive an offer from your mortgage company to give you a substantial discount for early prepayment of your balance. Should you consider such an offer? If you are looking at your decision from a business point of view, and I'm hoping you do treat your money in that way, your answer in most instances will be no. The companies don't give money away. They know it will be more profitable to them to get rid of your low-interest mortgage. This is the same reason you should keep it. You can usually obtain a better return on your money invested in another way. You also give up your liquidity. If you have an emergency, you can redeem a few shares of your stock, cash in your money market mutual fund or other investments, but you cannot redeem a few square feet of your home. As we have seen, in states like Texas, which have a homestead law, equity in a home is a dead asset. There are also tax reasons. Mortgage discounts are considered capital gains, taxable at a maximum rate of 20 percent.

The only time to accept such an offer is if you must sell your home soon and live in a state where due-on-sale clauses are enforced and you would have to pay it off anyway. If you intend to keep living in your home, do keep your valuable mortgage.

Mortgage Refinancing

Before we summarize some of the highlights regarding home ownership, let's discuss whether you should ever refinance your home. The answer may very well be yes, when mortgage funds are available at the right rate.

Your home could be an excellent source of capital. With your equity increasing each year because of inflation and brisk demand, you may be living in a giant savings account. If you want money to pay for college costs or medical bills or to invest, one way would be to refinance your mortgage. This approach not only frees capital but it gives you the advantage of paying off your new mortgage with a new level of inflated dollars.

Your home doesn't know whether it has a mortgage on it or not. It will inflate just as much with a small equity or a large, and if you use the funds obtained from refinancing (homestead law prevents this in Texas), you could have two assets escalating with inflation, rather than just one. Always look at the reverse possibility, too.

1. It can be less or more expensive to rent a multifamily dwelling than to own a single-family dwelling. Rental frees down-payment money for other investments and also allows you mobility to move to larger or smaller quarters or another location quickly and easily.

2. Calculate your true housing costs unemotionally, remembering that the mortgage payment is only one of several major items in your housing costs.

3. Monthly house payments should not exceed one week's earnings.

4. If you anticipate moving, buy a home similar in style to that of your neighbors. This does not do much for your sense of creativity, but it may help you avoid taking a shellacking on resale. A good rule to remember when making an investment in any asset of considerable value is "Be a conformist." The more conventional you are, the better your chances are of increasing the value of your assets. Preserve some of your individuality, but don't go overboard. You may find it quite expensive if you do.

5. Avoid paying too much for gimmicks. The builder may have spent an extra $1,000 on gadgets for flashy first-impression eye appeal and be able to sell you the house for an extra $3,000. As the years go by, you will want to build in your own charm, and the "gook" the builder originally added may turn out to be a hindrance rather than an enchantment.

6. Avoid paying too much for a view. Surroundings are important, but after a year you'll probably take the view for granted and wish that this extra expenditure had been avoided.

7. Keep your down payment as low as possible; inflation lets you repay with cheaper dollars; resale should be easier; return on invested capital can be higher; and liquidity or pledgeability can be available in times of emergency or investment opportunity.

Your home can be your castle, or under unfortunate circumstances, your prison, so use both your heart and your head in choosing how you'll provide that roof over your head.

APPLICATION

1. Should you rent or buy?_____

2. How long do you plan to live there?_____

3. If you decide to buy, should it be a house, a cluster home, a condominium, or a townhouse?_____

4. How much is available for a down payment?_____

5. Emotionally do you identify with the Allens or the Bakers in this
   chapter?_____

6. Whom do you know, or what contacts can you make, to obtain favorable financing?_____

7. Is the prime interest rate rising or dropping at this time?_____

8. If you have chosen to make a low down payment, how will you employ the remaining funds?_____

9. Items to include in your housing checklist:

   a. Location?_____

   b. Accessibility to work?_____

   c. Accessibility to schools?_____

   d. Accessibility to shopping facilities?_____

   e. Accessibility to recreational facilities?_____

   f. Neighbors?_____

   g. Traffic patterns?_____

   h. Noise?_____

   i. Smells?_____

   j. How does the cost of the home that you are considering compare
      with recent sales in the neighborhood?_____

   k. Conditions of the maintenance fund for upkeep of the neighborhood?
      _____

l. Is it located within the bounds of the 100-year flood plain as determined by the National Flood Insurance Program. (If it is, to obtain a loan you must buy flood insurance for the term of the loan.)_____

m. Towns grow and values tend to increase west, north, uphill, and away from rivers. Where is the house in relation to these?

_____

n. How old is the home?_____

o. If the home is ten years old or more, are you a good handyman on repairs?_____

p. Does the home fit your style? Yard work? Entertaining?_____

_____

Chapter 8

Energy Dynamics

We have already concluded that a major requirement for successful investing in the New Economy is to place some of your funds where demand is greater than supply. One commodity that is already in great demand, and most certainly will increase, is energy. Energy is a universal commodity as the developed nations of the world continue to increase their demands while the emerging Third World nations are rapidly joining the throng. The New Economy may indeed be based on advanced semiconductor technology, but it still runs on energy.

There are three viable areas for your investment consideration in the field of energy: 1) individual stocks of oil and gas companies, 2) oil and gas income limited partnerships, and 3) development and exploratory drilling limited partnerships.

Energy Stocks

There are a wide range of national and international oil company stocks from which to choose, and you will want to use the same basic criteria for stock selection outlined earlier. Some of the older, more heavily capitalized companies should fit the income category, if that is your financial objective. The smaller, aggressive companies are involved in adventuresome exploration and research and development activities that place them in the growth and perhaps more speculative categories.

The major advantages of investing in energy through the stock market are:

1. *Liquidity.* You can sell all or part of your stocks any time you choose or you can pledge them at the bank as collateral for a loan.

2. *Market value.* You can get daily quotes of the market value of your stocks, even though the value may fluctuate.

3. *Limited liability.* Your liability is limited to the amount of your investment.

The major disadvantage of investing in energy through the stock market is the tax treatment of your income. You suffer from double taxation and do not receive the full benefit of depletion, depreciation, and deductible drilling costs. For example, let's assume that you invested in a share of an international oil company and the numbers ran as follows:

$22.39	Earnings before depreciation and taxes
(4.72)	Depletion and depreciation
17.67	Pretax earnings
(10.83)	Corporate taxes (including minority interest expenses and excise taxes)
6.84	After-tax earnings
3.80	Dividend (taxable to the shareholder, thus double taxation)
$ 3.04	Retained earnings (corporation decides how they will be used)

As you can see, the dividend on your share of that corporation was only a very small portion of the amount of money that share actually earned.

Is there a way that you can avoid some of the double taxation, obtain the benefits of the depreciation and depletion allowance, avoid the worry of market fluctuation, and have limited liability by accepting limited liquidity? Yes, through the investment medium of oil and gas income limited partnerships.

Oil and Gas Income Limited Partnerships

In making any investment decision, you should attempt to find a vehicle that will supply a product that everyone wants, that everyone needs, and that you feel is now or will be in the future in short supply. As we have learned, there is no such thing as an ideal investment, but oil and gas income limited partnerships may fit a number of the criteria that you will want to have in your investment portfolio.

Oil and gas drilling programs have been offered to high-tax-bracket investors for many years, but it has only been since 1970 that you have had the opportunity to invest in production without the risks of drilling. This is accomplished through a program designed for both the smaller, lower-tax-bracket investor as well as the higher-tax-bracket investor. The concept of owning oil and natural gas reserves is more than a hundred years old, but before the advent of oil and gas income limited partnerships, ownership in production was limited almost entirely to oil companies, wealthy individuals, and institutional investors.

These oil and gas income partnerships are based upon a simple concept. A series of limited partnerships acquire existing, producing oil and gas properties for the income that they generate. The production from these wells is sold, and the income flows back to the limited partners and to the managing general partner. They offer good income potential, which is substantially tax sheltered in the early years, and a continuing partial shelter in the later years.

As in real estate limited partnerships, you, the limited partner, have limited your liability to the amount of the investment. The general partner who possesses the management expertise has unlimited liability. He secures the proper producing properties, has the responsibility of operating them on a profitable basis, and for doing so he usually shares from 10 to 15 percent of the costs and the revenues.

Despite the oil business's reputation for risk, a well-managed oil income program can have less risk than many investments. Furthermore, oil income programs are not particularly subject to short-term market fluctuations, since the value of the programs is based upon the value of their reserves and the level of income they produce. The true income partnership actually does no drilling. If an opportunity exists for in-field drilling, such drilling is contracted for by the general partner on a farmout basis. Some programs, however, do provide for limited drilling offsetting present production.

The structure of this type of partnership is similar to the diversified concept of a mutual fund, for the oil and gas income programs acquire a variety of already producing oil and natural gas wells for the income or profit they can generate as the natural resource is produced over the economic life of the properties. The properties acquired by the general partner for these programs have generally experienced several years of production. This is desirable because after sufficient time has passed, oil reservoirs have enough production history and reservoir data to allow reasonably accurate estimates on reserves. Such producing properties can be evaluated within an acceptable margin for error, usually in the 10 percent range. It is at that stage that oil income programs become buyers of producing properties.

If you become an investor in oil and gas income limited partnerships, the major portion of the revenues will flow directly to you on a quarterly basis. You will receive the depletion and depreciation allowance that will shelter a part of your cash flow, and you will pay taxes only once on the remainder that is not sheltered.

CASH FLOW EXPECTATIONS

What would you anticipate in the way of cash flow if you should invest in an oil and gas program? Programs vary, but here are some possibilities:

	CASH FLOW TO INVESTOR	TAX SHELTER
Year 1	10 to 15%	Sufficient to shelter 50% of cash flow
Year 2 on	15 to 20%	Sufficient to shelter 60% of cash flow after year 2

As in the case of the real estate programs in Chapter 6, any income you receive tax sheltered does reduce your cost basis.

Below is a record of past distributions and projections of future distributions made by the general partner of a 1982 program we have used. The cash flow projections are based on what they anticipate the price of oil and gas will be in those future years. Their projections may or may not be on target. The first three years are actual.

Year	Amount
1982	$ 1,490
1983	1,715
1984	1,705
1985	1,650
1986	1,633
1987	1,779
1988	1,937
1989	1,918
1990	2,184
1991	2,488
1992	2,463
1993	2,483
1994	2,458
1995	2,323
1996	2,195
—	—
—	—
—	—
—	—
Remaining	12,891
Total	$43,312

You will generally experience a gradual increase in your distributions over the first two or three years of a partnership's life. This is due primarily to the amount of time required to invest the partnership's funds in producing properties plus the need to dedicate a part of the cash flow to repay loans made by the partnership to acquire their properties if the management uses leverage in the programs in which that is permitted. Since each partnership is a depleting entity, once it has reached its maximum distribution level you see a gradual decline in your distributable cash flow over its remaining economic life. You have two choices regarding distributions in most programs: you may reinvest or take your distributions in cash. If you reinvest, you have the opportunity to increase your capital base. (The bookkeeping of these reinvestment programs has become so expensive that many partnerships no longer offer reinvestment privileges.)

Following are the projections of this same general partner on a $10,000 investment made in 1982. Of course, you may do better than or not as well as the projections.

		After 10 Years	After 15 Years
Option I:	All Distributions in Cash		
	Distributions in cash	$18,499	$ 30,421
	Purchase price	9,755	5,916
Option II:	All Distributions Reinvested		
	Distributions reinvested	$42,999	$122,123
	Purchase price	51,008	121,911

RESTORED LIQUIDITY

How long will it take for your cash flow to total your original investment? This concept is called "restored liquidity." Below is the general partner's projection of how quickly this might occur:

PROJECTIONS BASED ON HYPOTHETICAL $10,000 INVESTMENT

Year	Annual Cash Flow	Cumulative Cash Flow	Restored Liquidity
2	$1,490	$ 1,490	14.90%
3	1,715	3,205	32.05
4	1,705	4,910	49.10
5	1,650	6,560	65.60
6	1,633	8,193	81.93
7	1,779	9,972	99.72
8	1,937	11,909	119.09
9	1,918	13,827	138.27
10	2,184	16,011	160.11
11	$2,488	$18,499	184.99

DISCOUNTING FOR TIME

How does the general partner determine how much to pay for oil and gas properties? Since oil and natural gas are found in sand and rock formations, the resource cannot be extracted from beneath the earth's surface in a matter of days, months, or for that matter, sometimes many years. Because of this natural delay, the expected revenue to be returned over time is discounted to present worth when petroleum engineers are determining the price that should be paid for an acquisition.

The first thing the enginers determine is the amount of oil or gas a reservoir will produce annually and the estimated cost of producing it. They must then determine what price they expect to receive per barrel, which allows them to calculate the gross revenues to be realized over the property's economic life. By subtracting the operating costs from the gross revenues, the operating profits may be determined for each year of the well's economic production.

You wouldn't invest a dollar today for a dollar to be paid back to you at a date many years later, and neither would a managing general partner. Consequently, after the general partner has determined his objective rate of return for the partnership, he must discount each year's revenue by that factor to a present worth figure. The total value of each revenue year's net worth becomes the price that may be paid to achieve the target result. This is called the "time use of money" concept.

Discounting is nothing more than compounding in reverse. When you learned the "Rule of 72" earlier, you learned that money that is invested and compounded at 12 percent per year will double every six years. Conversely, if we wish to see our money compound at 12 percent per year, we would pay only half today what we would expect to realize in six years. With this in mind, we would be willing to pay only 50 cents for a dollar of net revenue to be realized in six years. If a dollar of revenue would not be realized for 12 years, we would be willing to pay only 25 cents today for that future dollar of revenue. If the dollar of revenue is not to be realized for 18 years, we would pay only 12½ cents today for that future dollar of revenue. With this formula, we would be willing to pay only 87½ cents for $3 of future revenue that would be realized, $1 in each of the sixth, twelfth, and eighteenth years as detailed in Table 7-1.

DISCOUNTING FOR RISK

For your added protection, the discounting does not stop there. The general partner who is acquiring the production of a property on your behalf then begins what is called "haircutting," which is applying a discount for an unspecified risk factor. The general partners do this

TABLE 7-1. PURCHASE PRICE PER $1

YEARS BEFORE RECOVERY	AMOUNT YOU WOULD PAY	RESERVES
1		
2		
3		
4		
5		
6	$ .50	$1.00
7		
8		
9		
10		
11		
12	.25	1.00
13		
14		
15		
16		
17		
18	.125	1.00
	$0.875 for	$3.00

because they know that engineering of reserves is more a scientific art than an exact science, so they want to build in protection for what they will pay for reserves. This discounting of future net reserves and "haircutting" the resulting figures provide a substantial degree of protection to an investor acquiring producing oil and gas properties. The actual risks hinge on two elements: 1) Is the engineering accurate? and 2) will the energy be sold for the prices anticipated? However, an error in either of these areas would probably have to be extremely large for an investor not to realize a return of his capital over the partnership's life. Therefore, if you are considering this as a viable investment, the real risk is whether the profitability will be as large as anticipated and at what rate you will get your money back.

Companies offering oil and gas income programs attempt to minimize errors in engineering by using various experts to estimate reserves. If multiple evaluations arrive at comparable results, then the risk of surprises should be minimized. First, they look at the history of the wells they are considering for purchase for the program. If this looks promising, their in-house engineering staff does an in-depth study; and if that looks good, they submit it to one or more independent engineering firms for study and calculation of reserves. If they also think that the properties are attractive, the general partner submits the properties for study to the oil and gas department of the bank that will be doing the matching financing, if leverage is to be used. If all of these areas agree, then an offer is made at a price that they think will allow them to fulfill their financial objective for their investors. All of these studies do not guarantee that errors in judgment will not be made, but I do know from discussing this matter with independent oil and gas consultants that they make very conservative estimates for banks and then discount these estimates sometimes as much as 30 percent.

The general partners spread the partnerships' investments into a number of different acquisitions. Wells may be selected to maximize diversification numerically as well as geographically and geologically. The wells in each partnership are selected for a broad blend of payouts. Some wells may have a high cash flow and deplete more rapidly, while others may deplete over a much longer period of time. The operators work continuously to increase production, since the general partners' interests in these programs parallel those of the limited partners. So as they increase productivity for you, they increase their own revenues.

In analyzing the risks you may be taking in any investment, always look at potential supply and demand. From all the oil and gas projections I have so diligently studied, I am convinced that long-term demand should exceed supply, although there may be temporary periods of oversupply, which in turn should be translated into buying opportunities for ultimately realizing higher oil and gas prices. We appear to have gone through one of these periods in the mid-'80s.

DEPRECIATION AND DEPLETION

Depreciation in an oil and gas program is similar to that obtained in real estate investment. The depreciation schedule for each piece of equipment depends upon the depreciation schedule allowed by the IRS.

Depletion allowances, on the other hand, are unique to natural resources and have been permitted because the resource is being used up and, therefore, a portion is considered to be a return of capital. As you are probably aware, percentage (statutory) depletion has been under attack by Congress constantly for several years. With the Tax Reduction Act of 1978, percentage depletion is no longer allowed for those buying already producing oil and gas properties. However, investors are allowed cost depletion. Since the oil and gas income partnerships now use cost depletion instead of statutory or percentage depletion, their tax-shelter benefits should not be greatly affected, particularly in the earlier years. Furthermore, tax reforms being discussed do not appear to create substantial adverse tax results for oil and gas income properties.

LEVERAGED AND NON-LEVERAGED PROGRAMS

Oil and gas income programs can be of two types: leveraged and non-leveraged. Leveraged programs use bank production loans to finance a portion of the purchase price. In the first example in this chapter, leverage was used and it works something like this. For every $1 that you invest, about 87 cents remains after start-up costs for doing the research on production and general expenses. Many of the start-up costs are fixed dollar items, so if the general partner can generate sizable subscriptions, the start-up costs as a percentage of the investor's dollar are lowered. This 87 cents may be supplemented by borrowing up to 17.4 cents to provide total purchasing power of about $1.044 for each gross dollar invested. The bank loans allow the general partner to purchase larger reserves from which to obtain cash flow. The loans are usually paid back to the banks over a period of years, dedicating less than 50 percent of the cash flow from the properties for debt service. For a well-managed program, this should still allow ample cash flow to insure good distributions to the limited partners, while you also have the potential for an increase in cash flow after the bank borrowings are repaid.

Non-leveraged programs usually provide a higher cash flow at the beginning than do leveraged programs, and they do not have the potential of repayment problems to the bank. If your objective is maximum cash flow now, you should choose the non-leveraged program. However, if your objective is cash flow later and you can accept higher risk, then you may want to consider the leveraged programs where profits could have more of an opportunity to grow.

INVESTMENT UNITS

Most states require a minimum investment of $2,500 ($2,000 for IRA accounts). New partnerships are available for investment monthly, quarterly, or yearly, depending on the programs selected. Some states require that the minimum be invested in each new partnership one wishes to invest in, while some states let you add as little as $50 into new partnerships as you go along, once you have met the original minimum in at least one offering. Recently the SEC added a suitability test for reinvestments, but if your tax bracket or net worth has not dropped appreciably, there would not be a restriction on reinvesting.

DISADVANTAGES OF OIL AND GAS INCOME PROGRAMS

There are three disadvantages to oil and gas income programs of which you should be aware. These are: 1) investment time lag, 2) limited liquidity, and 3) the aforementioned control of borrowing.

Oil and gas income programs may raise all of their money before they identify the properties that they intend to buy. (They may also have properties inventoried and ready for placement.) If they do not have the property available, the funds raised are usually invested in Treasury bills, certificates of deposit, or money market mutual funds while the program management searches for suitable purchases. They may be able to find the right properties immediately, or it may take as long as a year to do so. During that time, you would not be receiving oil or gas income, although you would be receiving interest on your funds.

A more important disadvantage of some oil income programs is their limited liquidity, since there is no ready market for the limited partnership interests in the absence of a "buyout" provision by the general partner. You should always view your investment as a long-term one; but, of course, you never know when you might need to convert your investment into cash. The general partners of most of these programs are obligated, as provided in the prospectus, to repurchase your program after one full year of operation, subject to their financial ability to do so, at their determined purchase price.

Oil and Gas Drilling Limited Partnerships

Another way that you may want to consider investing in energy is through drilling programs. There are basically two types: development programs and exploratory programs. If some of your taxable income is above the 45 percent tax bracket and you have sufficient net worth, you may want to consider investing some of your "soft" dollars in drilling programs. By "soft" dollars, I mean those you would be losing to taxes if you did not make a tax-deductible investment. "Hard" dollars, on the other hand, are your after-tax dollars and are the kind you might consider investing in the income partnerships.

TAX ADVANTAGES

In a development drilling program you can write off during the first year from 65 percent to 75 percent of your original investment and approximately 95 percent in an exploratory program. This write-off may be increased over the first five years by depreciation.

You can also receive a deduction against the income you receive from the programs through a depletion allowance, which helps compensate for the decline in oil and gas reserves as underground resources are depleted. You have the potential for partial long-term capital gains treatment upon the sale of your investment, and your program may also be structured in a way that will provide you with additional tax benefits through investment tax credits and depreciation of capital equipment.

DEVELOPMENT DRILLING

I have found that most of my clients have been happier with development drilling programs than with exploratory programs because of lower risk and earlier cash flow. In development drilling, you already know that production is nearby and it is just a matter of the economics of the program. Drilling is done only in proven areas where there is a vast amount of geological data. Cash flow usually begins within twelve months, and the success rate often exceeds 80 percent; and some areas, such as the Appalachian Basin, have exceeded 95 percent. Drilling is done near established markets, and transportation facilities are in the vicinity of the producing wells. Usually more than one potential pay zone is present.

The goals of these programs are to:

1) Provide you with the lowest possible risk in a drilling program.

2) Send you production income within twelve months.

3) Return your investment dollars in approximately five years.

4) Reduce your risk by geological and geographical diversification.

5) Return approximately 200 percent-plus of your investment over the life of the program.

The 2-to-1 return on most development programs assumes oil and gas prices will appreciate 5 percent per year. However, if inflation and scarcity values increase prices more than 5 percent per year, the 2-to-1 return could be greater. If not, it will be lower. What does doubling your money mean in after-tax dollars in a development drilling program? Your results on a $10,000 investment might be:

Cash investment	$10,000
Taxes saved over 6 years @ 40% on $8,500 write-off	(3,400)
Net after-tax on cash paid in	$ 6,600

Analysis

1) It costs you $6,600 to buy a $10,000 interest in the program.

2) If you receive $20,000 back (2-to-1 return), you will be tripling your $6,600 hard-dollar investment.

3) The $20,000 is subject to taxation, however, roughly 25% is tax sheltered by the percentage depletion allowance.*

Tax sheltered by depletion allowance	$ 5,000
$15,000 taxable income—net of 40% tax	9,000
Total return after taxes	$14,000
Investment cost	$ 6,600

Analysis

On an after-tax basis, 2.12 times your hard-dollar investment is received.

---

* Percentage depletion is 15 percent; however, it is taken on gross revenues before expenses and therefore results in approximately 25 percent tax-free income to the limited partners.

INVESTING YOUR TAX SAVINGS

You should remember that the IRS rarely forgives a tax but does let you defer a tax. You should therefore seriously consider reinvesting your tax savings.

Let's assume that on the above $10,000 investment you wrote off $5,500 the first year and that you are in a 40 percent tax bracket. This means you would save $2,200. If you invested this amount in a tax-exempt municipal bond paying 10 percent, your $2,200 would grow to $8,800 in 14 years. If you add this amount to your $14,000 net after-tax return, your total would be $22,800, which is more than triple your hard-dollar investment of $6,600.

IMPORTANCE OF EARLY CASH FLOW

Let's make some assumptions so that you can get a picture of how important early cash flow can be to your financial future. Let's assume that you were in a 50 percent tax bracket in 1979; that you invested in a drilling program with write-offs of 80 percent in 1979, 10 percent in 1980, and 10 percent in 1981; that your investment would return 2.15 times to 1 over the life of the program; that your cash flow comes in over a ten-year well life declining curve of 10, 15, 20, 15, 10, 8, 7, 6, 5, and 4 percent respectively over the ten years; and that we continue with our present depletion allowances.

Figure 7-1 gives you a picture of the time value concept of money. A well that starts a cash return in the first year would yield a 25 percent after-tax return, whereas the same program starting a cash return in the fourth year would yield only a 12.36 percent after-tax return.

TIME VALUE OF MONEY

The time value of money is a critical factor in computing the return from an investment. The time value of money simply recognizes that a dollar received immediately is preferable to a dollar received at

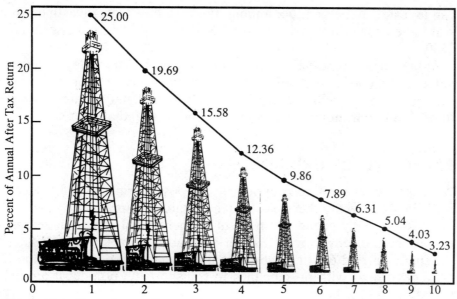

Figure 7-1. *Year that well starts providing a cash return to investors.*

some later date. To illustrate, consider two $1,000 investments, X and Y, each having the following cash flows:

YEAR	X	Y
1	$100	
2	150	
3	50	
4		
5		$600
	$500	$600

On the surface, in terms of total cash flow, investment Y appears to be preferable by $100 to investment X. However when the time values of the cash flows from investments X and Y are considered, the total return from X is actually greater. To explain: when discussing money, "now" is better than "later" for only one reason, the existence of interest. The receipt of $500 from investment X in the first three years of the investment period is preferable to the receipt of $600 from investment Y four years hence. This is because if you can invest at 10 percent per annum, the cash flow from investment X will have grown in five years to $733.51; and $733.51 is better than $600.

Money has a time value, and a dollar paid to you today is more valuable to you than a dollar that you will receive tomorrow. You can put today's dollar to work for you immediately, thus earning interest on your money and eventually interest on that interest.

EXPLORATORY DRILLING

An exploratory drilling program is composed primarily of wildcat wells in areas where there has been no established production. These programs usually spend 100 percent of their initial capital in search of new field discoveries in frontier wildcatting. Exploratory drilling is usually carried out in locations that are unexplored, often remote, very deep, and with no pipelines to transport the product if any is found.

A well is also considered exploratory if it is drilled in an area where production has been established at, say, 5,000 feet and the geologist thinks there might be additional production at 20,000 feet below that level and drills to either prove or disprove his theory. In exploratory drilling, your chances of finding anything commercially profitable are 1 in 20. These programs obviously involve the highest risks, but they may also return the greatest rewards.

STRUCTURING DRILLING PROGRAMS

There are many ways to structure a drilling program in terms of who bears the cost, who receives the tax advantages, and who receives the income. The structure of your program is important, but it may not be as important as the strength and technical qualifications of the general partner and the partner's ability to find and develop profitable reserves. The most frequently used sharing arrangements you will encounter are:

Functional Allocations. In this structure, all items that are immediately deductible for income tax purposes are paid out of investor funds, and the general partner pays for all non-deductible (capital) items. Oil and gas revenues are usually shared 60 percent to investors and 40 percent to the general partner. Because investor funds are used only for deductible items, this structure results in the highest deductibility, using 100 percent of the initial investment. Deductible items are primarily intangible drilling costs, including dry holes and abandoned acreage. This structure transfers all of the deductibility, and a disproportionately large share of risks, to the investor. Therefore, it is important that the general partner be required to make some minimum risk investment. Usually this minimum risk is set at 15 percent of the investor subscriptions if the general partner is to earn 40 percent of the oil and gas revenues.

Reversionary Interest. In this structure, investor subscriptions are used to pay for all costs. The general partner pays for a small portion of the program, usually 1 percent. Investors receive a high percentage of oil and gas revenues (usually 99 percent) until they have recovered their investment on some basis, at which time the investors' share of revenues decreases and the general partner's share increases. The key to this structure is the basis on which investors achieve payout before the sharing of revenues changes. The most desirable basis from the investors' point of view is for the interest to change only after the investors have recovered their entire investment in the program. From the general partner's point of view, the interest reversion should occur as the investors are paid out on each well. As a compromise, most programs are written so that the interest reversion occurs on the payout of each prospect. The difficulty with this is that the general partner decides what constitutes a prospect and will generally lean toward defining each well as a separate prospect. If you are interested in a reversionary interest program, be sure that the payout point is on a prospect or program basis and that the definition of "prospect" is clearly set out.

Promoted Interest. With this type of structure, investors and the general partner each pay a share of the cost and risk of drilling and acreage, and share oil and gas revenues on a disproportionate basis. Typically, investors pay for 75 percent of all initial drilling and acreage costs to earn 50 percent of the revenues, while the general partner pays for 25 percent to earn 50 percent. The general partner is more at risk in this type of program, and in return earns more equity.

Table 7-2 summarizes some of the significant characteristics of these three drilling structures.

TABLE 7-2. **THREE TYPES OF DRILLING PROGRAMS**

TYPE OF STRUCTURE	DEDUCTIBILITY % OF INVESTMENT	GENERAL PARTNER AT RISK	% INVESTOR EQUITY	REMARKS
Functional allocation	90–100	Moderate	50–60	Frequently used by established program sponsors for exploratory or balanced programs.
Reversionary interest	50–80	Low	99 before payout	Used mostly by new or financially weak program sponsors for developmental programs.
Promoted interest	50–80	High	50	Frequently used by established program sponsors for exploratory or balanced programs.

OTHER FEATURES YOU SHOULD KNOW

Three technical features of drilling program agreements that you should be aware of are:

Assessments. Drilling programs can be written so that you may or may not be assessed by the general partner for additional funds beyond your initial investment. If the program is assessable, assessments are typically limited to completion and development costs and are typically limited to 20 to 50 percent of the initial investment. There is no clear answer as to whether a program should be assessable or non-assessable, and there are many programs in each category.

Liquidity. The liquidity of all drilling program investments is generally poor, and these investments must be made with a long-term perspective. On the other hand, most drilling programs require the general partner to make one or more offers to purchase the limited partner units. Such repurchase offers usually begin two years after the formation of the partnership and are based on independent engineering appraisals of the revenues and cash flow of the partnership at that time. The evaluation formulas used for these repurchase offers are fairly standard within the industry, and they allow for profit to the general partner from the purchase. Many investors decline the repurchase offers and elect to retain their partnership units for future cash flow and potential appreciation in oil and gas prices. Most partnerships allow for limited transfer of ownership in events such as death and gifting with approval of the general partner.

Conflicts of Interest. All program structures and agreements contain the potential for conflicts of interest between the general partner and investors. Many of these potential conflicts are inherent in each structure and cannot be avoided. You should, therefore, select management on whose integrity you can rely to exercise fiduciary responsibility to the limited partners. However, two major conflict areas to look for and avoid are "marking up" and "proving up." "Marking up" means that the general partner provides acreage, materials, or services to the partnership at a marked-up basis above cost. Unless you are very sophisticated and knowledgeable in the oil business, you should invest only in programs that prohibit marking up of all types. "Proving up" means that the general partner assigns a small amount of acreage to be drilled by the drilling program while he retains substantial adjacent acreage for his own account. Program funds are thus used to prove up the acreage retained by the general partner. To avoid this potential conflict, be certain that the partnership agreement specifically prohibits proving up.

As you can see, you and your financial planner or broker will need to do some in-depth "due diligence" to determine which program best fits your needs and temperament. Choose a program offered by general partners who have good past records or, if no past records exist, become familiar with the expertise of their geological staffs, the net worth of the general partners, and the fairness of the "payouts." Determine whether you can make money with the compensation schedule if the drilling programs are successful.

REGISTERED PROGRAMS VERSUS PRIVATE PLACEMENTS

Should you invest in a registered program or in a private placement? By a registered program, you will remember, we mean that it is registered with the SEC and cleared by the state securities board of the state in which you are making the investment. The advantage of registered programs is that they usually raise larger amounts of capital, since they can offer smaller units and have more investors. Their greatest disadvantage is that all the investment has to be made in one payment, which may reduce their flexibility and tax advantages.

The private placement program, on the other hand, is exempt from registration by the SEC, but its prospectus will most likely contain as much information as the registered program. The disadvantages of these programs are: 1) the amount of capital to be raised will usually be less, therefore you will participate in fewer wells, and 2) the programs are open for relatively short periods of time, which may not fit your investment schedule. The chief advantage of private placements (I always use those offered by general partners who also offer registered programs) is that investments can be staged in over several years and can often be structured for greater tax advantage. If borrowing is used, a write-off of 200 percent of your first-year investment may be possible. However, you should be aware that you will be obligated to make additional investments over the prescribed period with only small write-offs. It is possible that proceeds from production will cover all or a portion of your payments after the first few years, but you cannot be sure this will happen.

Summary

An intelligent approach to financial planning cannot ignore the potential rewards from investing in energy. Ask yourself this question: "Will oil and gas prices be higher in five years than they are now, the same, or lower?" Many experts think they will be higher, and America's energy concerns are as real today as they were in the 1970s. Far from fading away, oil and natural gas continue to dominate our lives, playing a vitally important role in the economic well-being of our country. The nation sits perched on a fragile line between energy supply and energy demand. We still consume far more energy than we produce domestically.

If you are in the 25 to 44 percent tax bracket, the oil and gas income programs may best fit your investment needs. Even if you are in a 50 percent bracket, you will still have some "hard" after-tax dollars that you may want to put to work in the income programs.

If you are in the 45 percent bracket or above and have "soft" dollars to invest, you may want to consider investing some of those dollars in development and exploratory drilling programs. Oil and gas account for three-fourths of all the energy we consume, and the demand is growing, both here and in foreign countries. It is estimated that on a worldwide basis, there will be more oil consumed during the decade of the 1980s than has been consumed since petroleum was discovered.

Do your tax planning early, as this gives you an opportunity to look over the many viable possibilities. It also gives the companies time to do the drilling before year-end and possibly provide you with a larger write-off for the year. It also gives you the additional benefit of having your annual investment deductible in advance against your estimated quarterly tax liability. Be sure to complete your W-4 form at the beginning of the year claiming all the deductions you will be entitled to, since money has earning power and it should be in your account and not the IRS's. And you should consider investing smaller amounts in several partnerships rather than all of your funds in one, since this allows you to spread your risk over a large number of wells.

APPLICATION

1. Should some of your "hard" dollars be invested in oil and gas income-producing programs? _____ If so, why? _____

2. What other investments compare favorably for after-tax return and potential for appreciation? _____

3. What dollar amount should you invest in energy this year? _____

   What percentage is this of your total dollars available to invest? _____

4. Should you invest in energy stocks? _____ If so, which four stocks do you feel offer the greatest potential for price appreciation?

Stock	Market Price	Yield	Price/Earnings Ratio
_____	$_____	____%	_____
_____	_____	____	_____

_____   _____   ____   _____

_____   _____   ____   _____

5. If you have some income that will be taxed at 45 percent or above, how much of it should be invested in drilling programs? _____

Chapter 9

The World of Equipment Leasing, Cable Television, and Cellular Telephones

The New Economy has been called the Information Age, the Telecommunications Era, and the Silicon Age. No matter what it is called, American businesses are performing more services for more people today than at any time in our history, and most of them are being undertaken with the help of efficient, innovative, and improved types of equipment. This equipment can be either bought outright or leased, and in this chapter we will learn why equipment leasing has become one of the fastest growing forms of capital investment in the country today.

In addition to equipment leasing, the telecommunications explosion in the New Economy has created two other new forms of capital investment that are attracting considerable attention today: cable television and cellular telephones. Cable television is currently our most spectacular high-capacity information delivery system, and it appears that what we are looking at in cable is a transformation of our world similar to the one brought about by the printing press. The exciting reality of the home becoming once again a center of activity for entertainment, information, education, and work is due in increasing measure to the choices offered by cable television.

The other exciting new area of capital investment that is blossoming in the New Economy is the world of cellular telephones. In this chapter we will also explore the cellular telephone industry and learn how it is providing lucrative investment opportunities.

Equipment Leasing

While the use of sophisticated high-tech pieces of equipment is bolstering the progress of American business in the New Economy, obtaining that equipment usually involves a substantial outlay of capital, which these same companies do not have readily available or which they can employ more productively in other areas of their business. This need has spawned a gigantic new industry with approximately $225 billion of equipment on lease to American businesses. Because all parties can benefit from the equipment lease transaction, equipment leasing is one of the fastest growing forms of capital investment in the country today.

THE EQUIPMENT LEASE

An equipment lease is a contract whereby the owner of a piece of equipment makes that equipment available for use by another party for a specified period of time at a specified rental amount. At the end of the contract period, the user usually has the option of renewing the lease, purchasing the equipment for a specified amount, or returning the equipment to the owner.

Before the advent of our old friend the limited partnership, the only way you could invest in equipment leasing was to purchase the equipment, find a lessee, monitor the equipment, and collect the payments. But now, with a relatively small amount of money, you can choose from a wide variety of equipment leasing combinations. The type of program you choose will depend upon your financial objective.

Equipment Leasing Limited Partnerships

Basically, equipment leasing partnerships buy a diversified portfolio of equipment, ranging from airplanes and office furniture to railroad cars and computers, and lease the equipment to corporate users. The investors (limited partners) provide the capital and assume the risks of ownership. In exchange, the limited partners reap the tax benefits from depreciation and investment tax credits and receive cash flow from the rental income. The partnership can pay cash for the equipment (an unleveraged partnership) or go to the bank and borrow the money for the equipment (a leveraged partnership). There is also the potential for profits for the limited partners at the end of the lease when the equipment is either sold or re-leased. These benefits would also flow through the partnership to you as a limited partner.

THE PLAYERS IN A LEASING TRANSACTION

In order to help you understand the roles of the various parties in an equipment lease transaction, study the diagram on page 226.

In the diagram, the general partner buys for the partnership the equipment from the manufacturer, using the limited partners' capital and borrowed money. The equipment is then leased to the user (lessee). The lender or bank receives interest on the loan to the lessor, using the underlying lease as collateral, and the manufacturer uses the cash he receives for his profits and to produce more equipment. The limited partners in this type of partnership would participate in the benefits of the owner/lessor.

Different companies specialize in leasing certain types of equipment. For example, various equipment leasing partnerships currently lease computers, airplanes, trailers, railroad cars, marine cargo containers, oil and gas drilling equipment, mining equipment, and office furniture. Others will only lease equipment that is essential to the ongoing business of a particular firm, such as leasing a printing press to a printer. Others are primarily interested in equipment that has a long and useful life and the potential for a higher re-lease or resale value than comparable equipment with a shorter useful life. Many also prefer equipment that is bolted down so they know its location

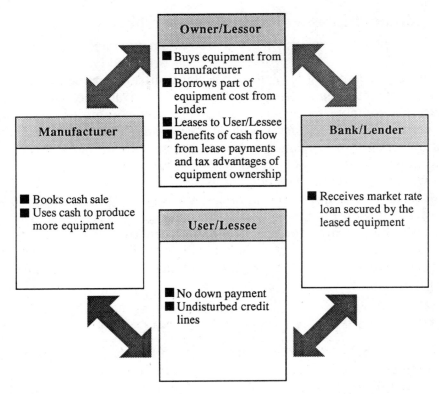

Owner/Lessor

- Buys equipment from manufacturer
- Borrows part of equipment cost from lender
- Leases to User/Lessee
- Benefits of cash flow from lease payments and tax advantages of equipment ownership

Manufacturer

- Books cash sale
- Uses cash to produce more equipment

Bank/Lender

- Receives market rate loan secured by the leased equipment

User/Lessee

- No down payment
- Undisturbed credit lines

at all times and can inspect it to see that proper care and maintenance are being performed.

TYPES OF REGISTERED LIMITED PARTNERSHIPS

In equipment leasing there is a wide range of partnerships available for your consideration. You should study them and choose the one or ones that best fit your financial objectives and temperament. Some will emphasize early cash flow, some will offer tax advantages at the beginning and heavier cash flow later, and still others will give a rapid payout and also provide you with the opportunity to participate in the future destinies of the companies leasing the equipment. Some will be leveraged, others will not. Let's examine some of these that you may want to consider.

TAX BENEFITS NOW, CASH FLOW LATER

A program we have used has 50 to 60 percent leverage and invests in such things as airplanes, boats, tractor-trailers, and large laser printers. With this program your write-off in the first four years should be from 90 to 100 percent, which comes from the Investment Tax Credit (I will discuss this in the next chapter), depreciation, and interest expenses. Your cash flow in year one is projected to be 1 to 2 percent; years two through four, 5 percent (all tax sheltered the first four years); years five through seven, 15 to 20 percent (taxed as ordinary income); and in the eighth year the assets will be liquidated and you are projected to receive 120 to 130 percent of your original investment.

Who should consider investing in this type of program?

Retirement Planning. If you plan to retire in five years, equipment leasing partnerships are worthy of your consideration. You should be permitted to write off your investment while you are still working and in a higher tax bracket. When you do retire, your cash flow from the investment should be excellent, and even though it is taxable, you will probably be in a lower tax bracket.

Educational Fund. Let's say that you have a child or grandchild who will be going to college in five years. With this type of program you could use the tax benefits in your high-tax bracket and after four or five years give the investment to the child when the cash flow starts. Your child can then use the income to pay for his education and either pay no tax if all sources of income are low or be taxed at a much lower rate.

Reverse Gifting. Let's assume you are a young professional earning good money and would like to do something for your parents to repay them for the money they spent on your college education. You would take the tax advantage from the investment in the earlier years of the program and then gift it to your parents in the later years. This could help them meet their cash flow needs during their retirement years.

Two Earners Now, One Later. Perhaps you are a young professional couple planning to have a family later. You might enjoy the tax benefits now and the cash flow later to compensate for the loss of income when the family is begun.

LEVERAGED OR NON-LEVERAGED PROGRAMS

You will need to make a decision on whether to choose a program that is leveraged (adds borrowed money to yours to buy more equipment) or is non-leveraged. If your need is for cash flow now, you will want to consider a non-leveraged leasing partnership. These programs usually purchase smaller pieces of equipment and have shorter-term leases of from one to four years. Short-term leases earn more (the equipment in one program we use is projected to produce a 26 percent cash flow), but the equipment may have a shorter useful life. In this example, the general partner plans to pay out to you around 13 percent and reinvest the other 13 percent in additional equipment for the first 7½ years. Because of this constant reinvestment during that period, your portfolio of equipment could double by the end of the partnership. This brings greater diversification to your partnership, hence lowering your risk and also adding a steady stream of new equipment. Around 80 percent of your cash flow should be tax sheltered during the first five years, and it is projected that through years eight, nine, and ten, your cumulative cash flow should be another 100 to 115 percent; and 40 percent of all distributions should be tax sheltered over the life of the partnership.

If you don't need liquidity, this type of partnership could be an alternative to certificates of deposit, municipal bonds, and could also be considered for pension plans. There will be some "unrelated business income" for the latter, but this should not be a problem if your investment is under $100,000.

Venture Leasing

The New Economy has spawned a cadre of entrepreneurs who are creating companies that will produce the products of the future, such as systems for disseminating information, telecommunications, biomedical research, and technology, to name a few. These dynamic new companies are creating a fantastic array of state-of-the-art products in their laboratories. And two of the fastest growing markets today involve equipment leasing and new ventures backed by venture capital companies. There are non-leveraged registered limited partnerships available now that combine these two areas.

Venture capital firms make capital available for selected start-up or new growth companies by infusing capital over a three- to five-year period as the companies meet their business plan objectives. They are actively involved in day-to-day management of these companies and often have a majority ownership position. However, this infusion of capital will most often be insufficient to cover the equipment that the companies need, and these companies will often lack the required collateral to borrow the funds to buy this equipment, and they have no established credit. Even if they do have credit, traditional lenders such as banks may require letters of credit or cash deposits before they will lend the funds. Hence the need for another source of capital for obtaining the equipment—the equipment leasing partnership.

Registered non-leveraged equipment leasing partnerships will buy that equipment and lease it to such start-up companies. They are very selective of the companies to which they will lease and of the kinds of equipment they will buy to lease. The equipment they choose is the kind that the company will need to use daily on the premises to stay in business, such as a "widget-making machine" for a company that manufactures "widgets." They prefer the equipment to be bulky, heavy, and bolted to the floor, making it easier to keep up with and inspect frequently to insure proper maintenance and care. The leases used in this case are called "master" leases, meaning that there is a signed binding lease in hand before the equipment is bought. The partnership will pay all cash, and the leases will be for a much shorter and higher payout period than usual—three years full payout.

In addition to having that equipment lease fully paid out in three years, the partnership requires and receives warrants for the developing company's stock. As you learned in an earlier chapter, a warrant is an option to buy a company's stock at a specified price within a specified time period. For example, let's say that the partnership had a warrant to buy the stock at $8 per share and the stock "goes public" at $14. The partnership would then realize a $6 gain per share on exercising the option. If, however, the stock goes public at below

$8, there would be no profit and the partnership sells the warrants rather than exercising them.

Many of the start-up or new-growth companies have been extremely successful; others have failed. What are the leasing partnership's chances of hitting a future Apple or Genenteck? I do not know, but from the projections I have seen, it would only take one moderate success to make the partnership profitable. From studies that have been made it has been determined that out of a hundred of these types of companies over a three- to five-year period of operation, five will be outstandingly successful, 75 will be moderately successful, and 20 will fail.

WHAT SHOULD YOU ANTICIPATE?

Even though venture leases are designed to be three-year payouts, the first year you are in the partnership could be a time of still raising the money and placing the leases, so your cash flow may only be at the rate of money market funds, or it could be higher, depending on the rapidity with which the leases are placed. If you have invested $10,000, for example, you also receive a $400 investment tax credit and $800 in deductions from depreciation. The second twelve months of operation, you could see an increase in your cash flow to $2,500 to $3,000, an investment tax credit of $400, and depreciation of $2,100, with a full payout over the next two years. The partnership is structured so that if there are changes in the tax laws, the lease rates are increased accordingly and the investor should not be affected.

The value of the warrants and the timing of the exercise of those warrants cannot be predicted, since the economy and investment markets will play a major role in determining when a company goes public. However, start-up firms with venture capital financing tend to go public within four to seven years. And even if the warrants have no value, you should receive a return of your capital plus a nominal return from the lease payments and still benefit from any residual value of the equipment.

WHO SHOULD INVEST IN VENTURE LEASING?

This type of program is a hybrid. The partnership will own short-term, high-payout leases, so there should be high cash flow—in fact, so high that it cannot all be sheltered, so there will be taxable income.

If there is a resale or re-lease, additional equity will be present, and if any of these companies become successful, there may be some additional equity there, too.

This type of partnership is designed to give you a return of your initial investment, plus a nominal return at the conclusion of the initial lease period. It is anticipated this will take place four to four and a half years after the close of the program; and at that time, the partnership will still own the equipment, plus any warrants it has received from the lessee. Profits, if any, from the warrants are not anticipated until five to seven years after signing the contract with the lessee.

Investment units in this type of partnership are $500 each, with a minimum of six or $3,000, required. Suitability is $30,000 annual income plus $30,000 net worth (exclusive of home, furnishings, and automobiles) or $75,000 of net worth regardless of income. You should find this an interesting opportunity to participate in the venture capital business with fairly low risk by virtue of having the equipment collateralize the investment and having a rapid payout.

Private Placement Leasing Programs

If you have some of your income that will be taxed in a 50 percent bracket this year and for the next four years, you may want to consider the tax-deferral and profit potential of a private placement leasing program. These programs involve leveraged lease transactions, and a major portion of the cost of the equipment will be financed by a loan secured by the equipment and the subsequent rental income from a lease. The benefit of such financing is that it reduces the cash investment required to purchase the equipment and leverages the tax benefits of each of your invested dollars. As a result of taking depreciation on the equipment, you have the use of these tax dollars, which can result in a positive cash flow for you in excess of the amount you have invested and represents, in part, an interest-free loan from the IRS.

As an owner, you will be entitled to depreciation deductions and can expect to earn a profit from your investment in the equipment from guaranteed rentals that should fully service your debt, from bonus rentals derived after the period of the initial lease, and from any residual value of the equipment.

As in the registered program, a leveraged equipment leasing program usually involves five major parties that stand to benefit from the arrangement: the equipment manufacturer, who sells the equipment to the leasing company, which finds a reliable user for the equipment and contracts for a long-term lease and arranges financing; you, as an investor who buys an interest in the equipment and expects to receive a profit from the sale or refinancing of the equipment as well as the tax savings and the capital for other investments; the mortgagee bank,. which provides most of the new money to purchase the equipment and earns interest by financing the transaction; and lastly, the equipment user, who has the immediate use of the equipment with no cash outlay, preserving capital for other business purposes. In addition, lease rates are often more favorable than the costs of borrowing for the purchase of the equipment. The blending of these five parties can offer timely benefits to you.

In a typical leveraged lease transaction, the user borrows a portion of the purchase price from a third-party lender. It should be noted that the typical equipment transaction is structured so that the investor and the lender rely primarily on the credit of the equipment user (lessee), rather than on the credit of the leasing company. A major benefit is that you provide only the cash balance of the purchase price in excess of the funds provided by the lender, yet you own the equipment outright and you hold title to the equipment.

WRAPAROUND LEASES

A popular extension of the leveraged equipment lease transaction is the leveraged wraparound lease. This transaction differs only slightly from those discussed but provides additional benefits.

Essentially, the original lessor or owner transfers the existing lease, subject to the third-party lender's debt, to the investor. The transaction then normally includes a leaseback of the equipment to the original user (lessee), which in effect keeps the existing lease intact. This transaction is illustrated on the next page.

FULL PAYOUT LEASES

A leveraged wraparound lease can offer significant advantages to you as the investor from what is termed a "full payout" lease. Under a

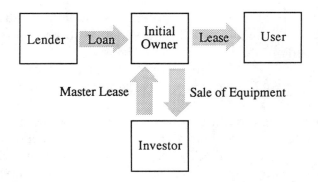

full payout arrangement, your income under the master lease is sufficient to cover your debt-related purchase obligations to the lender. Thus, with a full payout lease, you are not exposed to the risk of the rental rate being unable to service the debt. Obviously, full payout is an important feature to look for when selecting a transaction.

TAX CONSIDERATIONS

The tax losses generated through a leveraged equipment leasing transaction have two primary sources. The Economic Recovery Tax Act of 1981 enacted the Accelerated Cost Recovery System, or ACRS. Under this act, ACRS allows you, as the owner of the equipment, to recover your cost over a predetermined period which, in general, is less than the economic life of the asset. Property acquired in an equipment leasing transaction is usually depreciated over a five-year period under ACRS, which creates substantial depreciation deductions in the early years of the lease.

The other tax benefits are the interest deductions generated by the leveraged structure. By netting both the accelerated depreciation under ACRS and the interest deductions against lease rental income in the early years, significant reductions in your personal income tax liabilities can result.

OTHER FACTORS

It should be noted that any sale of equipment by you or your partnership that results in a taxable gain would be taxed as ordinary income, taking into consideration previously allowed depreciation. But in general, the cash savings realized from tax benefits in the early years of the lease more than offset any potential tax liability resulting from sale of partnership equipment. (You should also be investing these savings in a side fund.)

It should also be noted that you are prohibited from deducting losses in any taxable year beyond the amount you are "at risk" in the lease transaction.

On the next page is a fairly typical example of possible tax benefits and profit potential on a leveraged lease private placement limited partnership. As you can readily see from the chart, you will need to be in a high tax bracket for five years to receive the maximum tax benefit from this private placement partnership.

In summary, one of the major economic benefits of investing in equipment leasing is deferring taxes, and this deferral is generated mainly through depreciating the equipment. As depreciation deductions are taken, rental income is "sheltered" and can be used for cash contributions or debt repayment. As depreciation deductions decrease, taxable income increases. The amount of shelter in early years matches the amount of tax liability in later years—hence tax liability is only deferred. Unlike the sale of real estate (where depreciation is generally "recaptured" at capital gains rates), cumulative depreciation for equipment is taxed at ordinary income rates to the extent of sales proceeds.

Because of tax deferral, equipment leasing is best used if your marginal tax bracket does not increase over the life of the partnership, even better if you defer taxes until retirement or until you are in a lower tax bracket.

Cash distributions are usually the main economic benefit of public equipment leasing partnerships, which come from rental payments. The partnership pays expenses, makes debt payments, and distributes any remaining cash. The rate of distributions will vary depending upon the amount of leverage in the partnership. Income (unleveraged) partnerships do not borrow and will generate a larger stream of distributions sooner.

When leases expire, the partnership sells the equipment and distributes cash to liquidate. Cash generated on sale varies depending upon the type of equipment. An airplane may retain 90 to 100 percent of its original value over ten years, while computer equipment may become obsolete in just a year or two. This residual value is an important element of your return.

COLUMN NO.	1	2	3	4	5	6	7	8	9	10
YEARS	TOTAL CAPITAL CONTRIBUTION INCLUDING INTEREST	TOTAL TAXABLE INC./LOSS INCLUDING INTEREST	TAX EFFECT AT 50% TAX BRACKET	CASH DISTRIBUTION	NET AFTER TAX CASH FLOW EXCL. CAPITAL CONTRIBUTION	BALANCE AT BEGINNING OF YEAR	BALANCE COMPOUNDED @ 9%	CUMULATIVE AFTER-TAX BENEFIT	WRITE OFF CURRENT (2/1)	RATIOS CUMULATIVE
1985	$ 2,826	($11,570)	$ 5,785	—	$ 5,785	$ 0	$ 0	$ 5,785	4.09	4.09
1986	4,615	(14,801)	7,400	—	7,400	5,785	854	14,039	3.21	3.54
1987	5,173	(13,237)	6,619	—	6,619	14,039	1,561	22,219	2.56	3.14
1988	5,731	(10,310)	5,155	—	5,155	22,219	2,232	29,606	1.80	2.72
1989	6,288	(9,216)	4,608	—	4,608	29,606	2,872	37,086	1.47	2.40
1990	—	20,747	(10,374)	7,998	(2,376)	37,086	3,231	37,941		1.56
1991	—	24,810	(12,405)	9,105	(3,301)	37,941	3,266	37,906		0.56
1992	—	18,681	(9,340)	11,041	1,701	37,906	3,488	43,095		
TOTALS	$24,634	$ 5,104	($ 2,552)	$28,144	$25,592	N/A	$17,504	$43,095		

Equipment Leasing, Cable Television, Cellular Telephones   235

Carefully study the available equipment partnership offerings to see if any meet your financial objectives. And if they do, then they are worthy of your serious consideration.

Cable Television

Fundamental to the information revolution in the New Economy is the communications maelstrom. At its core is the movement of information from one brain to another, or from a computer to a brain, or from a brain to a computer, or from a computer to another computer. Cable television will play a significant role in this maelstrom because it is currently our most spectacular high-capacity delivery system.

Cable has in excess of 30,000 times the capacity of the twisted-pair telephone line that comes into your home, and this alone brings many new and innovative possibilities for delivery. Cable television is in the electronic pipeline business, and you will want to consider positioning some of your assets so you will have an opportunity to participate.

Cable television (CATV) has been around for more than 30 years, getting its start in communities where no broadcast television was available. It works very simply. A cable TV system collects signals from a programming source, processes and amplifies them, and delivers programming to the consumer via a coaxial cable connection direct to the customer's TV set.

Two developments of the 1970s, however, transformed cable from an essentially rural enterprise to a dramatic growth industry. First, in 1972 the Federal Communications Commission allowed cable television systems to compete with over-air broadcasters. Then, beginning with Home Box Office in 1975 and the Turner Broadcasting superstation several months later, satellite technology was applied to cable television. Needless to say, the change was dramatic. In 1968, barely 6 percent of the nation's TV households were wired for cable. By the end of 1983, more than 34 percent were signed up, with projections for 1990 ranging between 50 and 60 percent.

In 1980 there were 20 million cable subscribers and revenues were $2.2 billion. In the recession year of 1982, rather than decreasing, the number increased to 27 million subscribers, with $4.7 billion in revenues. By 1990, it is projected there will be 60 million subscribers, with $20 billion in revenues.

ECONOMICS OF THE CABLE TV BUSINESS

From the cable operator's viewpoint, the business looks promising. Well-managed cable systems in medium-sized and small communities can produce a 40 percent-plus operating cash flow margin to the bottom line. Typically, the revenue stream from a cable system is derived from a basic cable charge averaging approximately $8.73 per month, plus premium charges for Home Box Office, Showtime, The Movie Channel, The Disney Channel, etc. The average system now obtains $16.80 per month per subscriber; and it is projected that by 1990, dollar-a-day cable ($30 per month per subscriber) will be the industry average. Even relatively mature systems can experience 15 to 20 percent annual growth rates in net operating cash flow before debt service.

In addition, there are no inventory problems, and generally the system is operated by right of franchise, making it the "only store in town." It has a broad base of revenues, and as long as it is responsive to the needs of the community in which it is located, it should continue to increase its base. It appears to be recession proof, since it seems to appeal to the desire for low-cost home-based entertainment regardless of economic cycles.

As far as future revenues are concerned, most cable system operators make economic projections almost exclusively on basic subscription revenues, plus some premium movie services. However, at least three other areas are expected to produce significant additional revenues for cable television systems by the 1990s. These revenue sources are pay-per-view programs, advertising, and interactive services.

"Pay-per-view" means the ability to watch an event on a one-time basis for a fixed fee, such as a prizefight, a ballet, or a blockbuster movie. More and more television sets are being equipped with an addressable converter or decoder to provide this service.

The future for advertising revenues looks especially bright. Madison Avenue is now beginning to pay more attention to cable since the magic penetration figure of 30 percent of all households has been reached. The CATV industry can deliver audiences with specific interests at a very low cost compared to the mass-market network TV approach. A garden tool manufacturer, for example, can target his marketing efforts by advertising on a gardening show not popular enough to be carried by a network.

Interactive service revenues are longer-range possibilities. "Interactive" means the ability to communicate two ways, and at this time there are at least 20 interactive services on the drawing boards for cable. Some industry observers believe that with the popularization of the home computer, cable could become a communications center for the home of the future, offering such services as in-home shopping, banking, travel services, home security devices, meter reading, opinion polling, and voting. The future of interactive services can be compared to the growth of programming services. The future looks excellent, but no one knows which services will prove to be popular with the public and which will not. It seems certain that at least a portion of those services currently on the drawing board will succeed. Larger cable companies with marketing budgets can afford to test-market the new services and assess their profitability, while smaller systems will await the results without risking loss.

TAX ADVANTAGES OF CABLE INVESTMENTS

The tax treatment of investment in a cable system takes a profitable proposition and improves upon it. (If you are not familiar with some of these tax terms, they will be covered in the next chapter.) The most significant tax aspects of a cable investment are:

1. *ACRS deductions.* Most of the tangible assets making up a cable system will be considered "five-year property"—property the cost of which (reduced by half the investment tax credits claimed) can be written off on an accelerated basis over five years.

2. *Investment tax credits.* Five-year property will qualify for the 10 percent investment tax credit (the ITC on three-year property is available at the rate of 6 percent). Because a partnership can take ITC on only $125,000 of used property placed in service in any year, there will be more ITC available in a rebuild than in a straight acquisition of similar cost.

3. *Amortization of franchise costs.* A cable system will generally amortize the cost of its franchise (or franchises) over the life of the franchise (often 15 years).

4. *Recourse debt.* As an investor in many private cable offerings,

you can assume liability for a portion of the debt to finance the system, thereby obtaining basis and at-risk amounts in excess of the actual cash invested. You can then claim deductions from the system's "losses" up to the total of the cash invested and the additional debt for which you are liable. This option is generally available only in private partnership offerings, not in public offerings.

5. *Leveraging an investment*. If you invest in private placement offerings, you will usually pay in over three to five years; and most of them use leverage. This usually makes it possible to match your payments to the tax benefits, thereby reducing your net out-of-pocket investment and the cash needed to invest. Public offerings require and private placements can permit an all-cash purchase.

6. *Capital gain of sale*. Most of the gain realized on the sale of a cable system (other than the "recapture" as ordinary income ACRS deductions taken on three-year and five-year property) will be taxed at long-term capital gains rates. Moreover, this gain often can be expected after an intermediate term holding period of approximately five years, compared to the longer holding periods typical of many other tax-advantaged investments. Because of the cash flow generated by cable systems, you should not be taxed on phantom income (income you do not receive but for which you are taxed) even if the system is held beyond the five-year period during which most of the tax benefits are realized.

7. *Few preference items*. Cable investments can be especially attractive if you are concerned about the alternative minimum tax, because the ACRS and amortization deductions that produce most of the tax shelter in a cable system are not preference items.

LOCATION OF SYSTEMS

If the cable television industry has all of these positive characteristics going for it, why have there been so many negative reports? Most of these reports have centered around major city systems with politics rampant and many of the operators making the mistake of overbidding for franchises, promising too much for too little, and letting building costs get out of control. For those reasons, your investment considerations should be concentrated on medium- to small-sized communities and suburbs of major cities, because of the ability to control costs and to avoid overbidding. Building costs can accelerate to $250,000 per mile in urban locations where underground cable is required, compared to about $10,000 per mile for above-ground wiring in suburban locations.

HOW CAN YOU PARTICIPATE?

If you have funds you can put to work for five to seven years, you probably should consider positioning some of them so that you can participate in the future growth potential of cable television. For your after-tax dollars, you may want to consider registered limited partnerships. In addition, if you have some before-tax dollars in the 42 percent tax bracket or above, you may want to consider private placements.

Registered Limited Partnerships

Public limited partnership programs in cable television have been offered since 1972 and have established a performance record that qualifies them for consideration as a sound investment medium. As you have seen, they offer the potential for both capital appreciation and tax benefits. By pooling your capital with other investors, you can participate in larger projects, usually on more attractive terms, and have the management responsibilities handled by experts.

The concept of the cable television limited partnerships is similar to that of real estate partnerships. A series of cable television partnerships will acquire existing cable systems or build new ones with the objective being to develop these systems over a period of four to seven years and to increase their operating income and value. You will want to select a general partner with a good track record and recognized expertise in purchasing cable systems and in building new ones. Through skillful management the general partner can increase the system's cash flow by adding new subscribers, tending the system, offering new programming, selling advertising, and increasing rates.

What are some reasonable expectations if you invested in a registered limited partnership today? I don't know, but the following diagram illustrates some expected results of a syndicator whose programs we use:

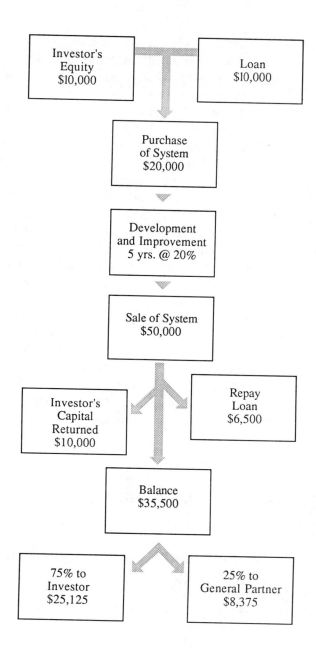

Total Return to You: $35,125

In the above example, you would have invested $10,000, and the general partner would have matched it by borrowing another $10,000 from the bank, making it possible for you to have a $20,000 proportionate participation in a several-million-dollar offering invested in several cable systems. Through saturation of the present market, extension of the systems, rate increases, and new services, the general partner hopes to increase the value of the systems by 20 percent a year over a five-year period. At that time, the systems would be sold, possibly for $50,000 in cash. The general partner would return to you your original $10,000, pay back the $6,500 still owed to the bank (he had been paying on the principal over the past five years), and the balance of $33,500 that should be left would be split 75 percent to you ($25,125) as the limited partner and 25 percent ($8,375) to the general partner, for a total return to you of $35,125 ($25,125 plus $10,000). During the five-year holding period, it is projected that you would write off 15 percent of your investment the first year and 25 to 35 percent in subsequent years, with 100 percent written off during the total five-year holding period.

Will the partnership accomplish its projection in the above example? I don't know, but to date this group has had four registered partnerships go full cycle (meaning that they have bought and sold all the systems in the partnerships). Their results on a $10,000 investment have ranged from a net to investors of $14,040 to $74,720 after holding periods for one system of six months, another for 2½ years, and another for four years and four months.

Private Placement Limited Partnerships

If you also have some soft before-tax dollars, you may want to consider a private placement partnership where the payments can be staged in over several years and leverage can be structured for tax advantage. In this case, there will usually be only one system in the partnership.

Though a great deal of capital is required to construct a cable system, leverage can be obtained by using institutional lenders specializing in making first-lien mortgage loans of 90 percent or more for the acquisition of high-quality cable systems. Commercial bankers who understand the cable industry like it because it acts like an annuity and also has the unusual aspect of being countercyclical. A high-growth industry that is countercyclical is an unusual combination. When high unemployment hit the lumbering industry in the Northwest in 1981 and 1982, cable subscribership increased, probably because people are reluctant to give up an inexpensive form of entertainment.

In a leveraged situation, the collateral for the loan is the system itself. A good way to limit the risk is to be sure the general partner limits the total borrowing on the system to no more than ten times cash flow. This financing is normally the responsibility of the general partner, who will have it in place when the partnership is presented to potential investors. You can usually write off more than you invest, usually somewhere between 125 percent and 200 percent of your investment. Most partnerships provide that your capital can be paid in over four or five years so that your write-offs can coincide with your payments. This is particularly true of new systems that are being constructed. (Urban new-build systems are not my preferred form of cable investing. I prefer the acquisition of systems in small- to medium-sized communities where the returns have proven to be superior.)

Typically, cable partnerships are structured in two ways. Growth partnerships feature up to 200 percent write-offs, few (if any) cash distributions (because the cash flow goes to retire the mortgage on the system), and a sale for all cash in as little as five years. Income partnerships, on the other hand, feature lower tax write-offs during the two- to five-year pay-in period with cash flow starting anywhere from the first to the third year of the partnership. A total cash return of 200 to 250 percent of the invested money may occur over a five- to ten-year period, not counting tax benefits.

Even with lower inflation rates, the value of cable TV systems has continued to rise because of increased cash flow. Experienced operators are increasing the cash flow of older systems through improved programming, better marketing, community relations, and tighter controls over who receives cable signals.

How might a private placement offering be structured? The following chart and figures are for a system we used recently for some of our higher-tax-bracket clients. It is a leveraged program with the assumed rate of interest being 14.25 percent for 1985 and 13.25 percent for each year thereafter. These figures assume that the investor is in a 50 percent tax bracket.

	1985	1986	1987	1988	1989	1990	TOTALS FOR 5 YEARS
Investment	$10,541	$14,394	$12,290	$10,463	$12,950	$14,890	$75,528
Deductions	(15,813)	(21,590)	(18,436)	(15,695)	(12,352)		(83,885)
Ratio of tax deductions to investment	1.50	1.50	1.50	1.50	0.95		
After-tax benefits	7,907	10,795	9,218	7,848	6,176		41,943

Projected Results: **Sale at 9% cash flow 1/1/90**

Sales proceeds	$112,850
Ordinary income tax from sale	(21,117)
Capital gains tax from sale	(14,943)
ITC recapture from sale	(916)
	$ 75,872
After-tax benefit during holding period	41,943
Total estimated after-tax benefit	$117,815
Estimated after-tax annual internal rate of return on leveraged investment	47%

Will our clients receive the benefits projected above? I do not know, but I am convinced that such a program should definitely be considered if you want to attempt to turn some of your tax liabilities into assets.

Cellular Telephones

Another exciting opportunity in the New Economy that should become a viable investment alternative for you is in the area of cellular telephones. Cellular telephones and their operations are new, but they have the potential for a burgeoning industry.

Radiotelephones have been around for over forty years but they have had severe limitations and therefore have not enjoyed universal popularity. If you have ever tried to use one, you may remember that it was nearly impossible to obtain a channel when you wanted to make a call. The old urban systems could handle a maximum of only fifty calls at one time. Bell Laboratories invented the cellular idea in 1947, but it took the computer technology of today to make cellular telephones fully operational.

How does a cellular telephone system work? The technology provides for a number of "cells" which cover an entire metropolitan area. Each cell has a low-power UHF television transmitter which broadcasts within that cell. A number of these cells combined together allow for approximately 300,000 simultaneous calls to take place in that metropolitan service area. Each cell has an operating radius of from three to twelve miles and can broadcast on the same frequency as an adjacent cell, because the frequencies are of a low-power nature and do not interfere with one another. In addition to the 300,000 simultaneous calls, a further division of cells is possible, which makes the potential number of subscribers unlimited.

Using San Francisco as an example, it is estimated that it will require sixteen cells to cover the entire Bay Area. The system computer enables callers to be "handed off" to the nearest cell transmitter as the individual drives his car from cell to cell. This transfer occurs by computer without the callers being aware of it.

It is predicted that one-third of all telephones in the United States will be cellular by the end of this century. It appears that the Dick Tracy wrist radio-telephone is finally happening, since these phones operate attached in your car or on a totally portable basis. When your voice is picked up within a cell, it is then transferred from the cell receiver to the telephone wires like a normal call. The only place you are in the cellular system is from your phone to the local cell and then you go into the regular telephone system. The United States is now gradually becoming covered with these cellular systems on a population size basis, with major cities being provided with service first. Consequently, rural areas will be the last to have systems.

The FCC began granting cellular licenses in 1982. They grant the license to operate the cells to only two companies in each metropolitan area, one wireline (the regular phone company in the area) and one non-wireline company. These companies actually operate the cells and earn the fees for each call being made in that area. They compete for subscribers in their given area. The really big profits in cellular telephone systems will come from operating these cells.

When the hearing process began, the FCC allowed for filings for the first thirty U.S. markets by non-wireline companies, and there were only five filers. Population centers ranked from thirty-first to sixtieth were next opened to filers, and there were ten filers for this group. In markets ranked sixty-first to ninetieth, the FCC set up a lottery system, and there were 125 entrants; but before the lottery could be held a settling process occurred, thus eliminating the need for the lottery in that group. Currently, the FCC has provided for a lottery for markets ninety-first to one-hundred twentieth, and there are apparently over 5,000 applicants so far for this group. There are some investment offerings that have been devised for filing on these lotteries, but these appear to be a pure gamble and should be avoided.

HOW TO PARTICIPATE IN CELLULAR TELEPHONE SYSTEMS

What is the best way for you to participate in this segment of the communications revolution? There are really no pure stock plays on cellular activities, whether they involve investing in the manufacture of the equipment or in the ownership of the cellular franchises. Typically, cellular systems are an adjunct to other corporate activities.

If you can invest in an actual franchise, this could be the best way to get involved. I have seen the preliminary projections for a major metropolitan area with a population of five million. It takes about fourteen cells to cover the service area at a cost of approximately $14 million to build. With only 1 percent penetration, it is projected that this system could produce a gross income of $28 million per year and be totally paid off and produce a bottom-line profit of 50 percent per year within two years. Time will tell if this actually occurs.

As more cities are hooked up for cellular systems, the price for equipment and time charges should fall, which in turn should bring in more subscribers and increase the revenue to those owning the franchises.

This is a new area of potential investment for all of us. The business history of cellular systems is very short and not too informative, because of brevity of operation and higher initial costs to consumers. However, it is easy to see the potential of buying into a partnership that has a franchise. As with cable television, the value of the franchises is substantial and creates a solid base for investment. Additionally, since it will take hundreds of millions of dollars to build all-cellular systems in America, I expect to see non-specified blind pools of money put together in partnership form in order to allow investors to buy parts of existing cellular franchises as they become available on the market. In cases where the general partnership is a strong and well-established company, I believe that these partnerships could merit your consideration.

Summary

To make an intelligent decision as to whether you should invest in a leasing or a cable television offering, you must first determine what your financial objectives are, then determine which, if any, of these offerings would most likely accomplish them.

If you have need for tax-sheltered cash flow now, you will want to consider investing some of your after-tax dollars in registered limited partnerships that, in turn, invest in lease equipment for which they paid all cash and then lease to several established companies. If you have a slightly higher risk tolerance, you would again choose one that pays all cash but leases to less well established companies.

If your need is for tax advantage now, maximum cash flow later, with appreciation potential, you would want to choose leveraged registered limited partnerships in either leasing or cable television.

If your tax bracket is high and you have before-tax dollars you are about to lose to the IRS, you may want to consider either or both highly leveraged leasing or cable television private placement limited partnerships. In this way, you may be able to turn a known tax loss into a possible gain later.

APPLICATION

1. Your financial objective is: Income now_____

   Income later _____

   Tax deferral_____

   Maximum tax advantage_____

2. What special needs do you have? Now_____

                                                In 5 years_____

                                                In 10 years_____

3. Will equipment leasing fulfill this need? _____

4. What type of program is best designed to fill this need? _____

5. Is cable television a viable option for some of your after-tax dollars?

_____

6. Do you have before-tax dollars that should be sheltered? _____

7. Look in the Appendix and copy the worksheet. Apply some possible figures to your tax situation. Does a private placement make sense in your situation? _____

8. What steps will you take to keep abreast of investment opportunities in cellular telephones? _____

Chapter 10

Tax-Saving Opportunities in the New Economy

Keeping your hard-earned dollars from taking a one-way trip to Washington is indeed a challenge in the New Economy and one worthy of your most careful attention. Few other endeavors will add more to your net worth, since the only money you will ever have for investing and spending is what the government lets you keep. I am absolutely dedicated to helping my clients and readers reduce their taxes. I truly believe that it is much better stewardship of money to invest these dollars in housing, energy, food, real estate, research and development, medical needs, security, entertainment, and transportation than it is to send them through a wasteful bureaucracy with the hope that someday some of the money may filter down into these areas of great need.

Why pay the IRS money you are allowed to keep? In this country you do have a choice as to whether you pay a smaller or a larger amount of income tax, but you must learn the rules each year and abide by them strictly. You will find them always changing, often contradictory, rarely simple, always difficult to understand and challenging to apply. Winning the money and tax game—and win you must—will require the maximum dedication of you and your financial planner, a great amount of knowledge aggressively applied, agility, and constant vigilance. The job of the IRS is to thwart your every effort. Tax reduction is the enemy of the IRS, which refers to deductions as "costing" the Treasury.

Perhaps you have previously shied away from tax-advantaged investments because you have considered them vaguely immoral. If so, you may be confusing tax evasion with tax avoidance. Tax avoidance is using your intelligence, whereas tax evasion is illegal and severely punishable. But tax avoidance is not only legal, it is also quite proper.

Congress has enacted laws periodically to encourage the shift of funds from taxable sectors of our economy to areas of public need or good by creating tax-free, tax-sheltered, or tax-deferred investments. There are those who delight in referring to these incentives as loopholes, implying that Congress is not intelligent enough to design a proper tax bill. They fail to recognize that without the incentive of potential gain, no funds would be risked in areas where money is much needed for the welfare of our citizens.

Judge Learned Hand, the famous New York State jurist, once said: "Anyone may so arrange his affairs that his taxes shall be as low as possible. He is not bound to choose that pattern which best pays the Treasury. Everyone does it, rich and poor alike, and all do right; for nobody owes any public duty to pay more than the law demands." Senator Byron P. Harrison of Mississippi, former chairman of the Senate Finance Committee, expressed the matter this way: "There's nothing that says a man has to take a toll bridge across a river when there is a free bridge nearby."

Unfortunately, over the years our tax laws have become so complicated that it now takes a great deal of study to avail yourself of some of their benefits.

Tax Reform

Since the mid-1970s, tax shelters have survived the Tax Reform Act of 1976, the Revenue Act of 1978, ERTA in 1981, TEFRA in 1982, and the Deficit Reduction Act of 1984. All indications are that, once again, there will be a change in tax laws coming soon. However, as long as projects such as restoring our inner cities, providing housing for the disadvantaged and elderly, and developing natural resources are deemed to be socially desirable, then public policy will encourage investment in these areas by offering tax incentives. Furthermore, as long as citizens of the United States must continue to pay taxes, they will seek investments which have tax incentives.

The D.C. Game

The tragedy of your paying a dollar in taxes is that not only do you lose that dollar, but you also lose what that dollar would earn for you if you were allowed to keep it. It is therefore imperative that you learn to play what I call the "D.C. Game." This means that you will either be sending your money to Washington, *D.C.,* or you will learn to *D*efer and *C*onvert these payments. I like to think of tax reduction as a game that I must win, because it makes the endeavor less grim, more fun, and often profitable. And even if it is not profitable, I will at least have had the satisfaction of knowing I tried.

Now let's take a look at some of the legitimate ways you can use in your endeavor to turn your tax liabilities into assets. Technically, the IRS, with but a few exceptions, does not forgive a tax, but our tax laws do allow you to defer a tax until a later date. If you have chosen certain investments, perhaps you can also convert ordinary income into capital gains, currently taxed at a maximum of 20 percent.* You may be tempted to say, "If I'm going to have to pay the tax someday, why don't I just pay it now, and that way I won't have to worry about it in the future?"

There are four reasons why you should always defer paying a tax:

1. *Inflation.* Every year that you postpone paying a tax, you not only continue to receive earnings on that money, but when and if you ever have to pay the tax, if we continue to have inflation, you can pay it with cheaper dollars for which you have had to work fewer hours. If you have $1 of taxable income today in a 40 percent bracket, you lose 40 cents of purchasing or earning power if you pay the tax. But if you can postpone the tax for 12 years, and if by some miracle

---

* Refer to the Tax Addendum in the Appendix for possible tax changes.

the government does change its printing press mentality and inflation averages only 6 percent, you can pay the tax with one-half of the purchasing power that you would have had to use if you had paid it today.

2. *Convert to capital gains*. Often over this period of time you can convert ordinary income into capital gains. If you can make this conversion, you can reduce your tax liability to 8 cents of purchasing power in 12 years; that is, if you decide to quit playing the money and tax game and pay it at that time. You may, however, want to start the D.C. game all over and again postpone the tax.

3. *Time value of money*. Money has tremendous earning power, so strive to keep it working for you. For example, let's assume that you can postpone paying $10 of tax for five years and that you can invest it at 10 percent (and surely we can do better than that). Your results would be as follows:

		BEFORE 50% TAX	AFTER 50% TAX
After year 1	$10 =	$11.00	$10.50
After year 2	$10 =	12.10	11.03
After year 3	$10 =	13.31	11.58
After year 4	$10 =	14.64	12.16
After year 5	$10 =	16.11	12.77
Pay tax	$10 =	$ 3.05	$ 2.77

4. *Stepped-up basis*. If your goal is to build an estate for your heirs, upon death there is a step-up in your basis and there is a strong possibility that the tax can be completely avoided. Then we have a whole new game for your heirs.

So, never "bite the bullet" until it is absolutely necessary, and put your tax dollars to work as long as you can. Learn to play the D.C. Game well; and if you work with a knowledgeable financial planner, perhaps it can be turned into the D.C.E. Game—*D*efer, *C*onvert, and *E*liminate!

A POSITIVE MENTAL ATTITUDE

The first essential for winning the money game, as we have already seen, is a positive mental attitude. This is especially true for winning the tax game. If you are again getting little twinges of doubt that you can ever understand our tax laws, repeat the affirmation you made in the real estate chapter and again raise your right hand and repeat after me: "I can understand what Venita is going to tell me!" Of course you can develop the right mental attitude! William James, the great psychologist, once said, "The greatest revolution in our generation is the discovery that human beings, by changing the inner attitudes of their minds, can change the outer aspects of their lives!" Go to work right now on developing a winning mental attitude. Now, let's get ready to meet the challenge.

Meeting the Tax Challenge

First, you must look at the various kinds of income that you may receive or could receive and how this income is taxed. There are basically four kinds of income from a tax point of view: taxable, tax free, tax deferred, and tax sheltered.

TAXABLE INCOME

This is the income you receive from salary, commissions, royalties, bonuses, ordinary business profits, interest on savings accounts, mortgages, corporate bonds, 40 percent* of your capital gains, and so forth. The total, less permissable deductions, will be taxed by the IRS at different percentages at different levels or brackets. That is the percentage of your income you will lose to the IRS if you do not take steps to shelter it.

TAX-FREE INCOME

You may receive tax-free income from municipal bonds, municipal bond funds, and municipal bond trusts. Income from these is not taxable (unless you are receiving Social Security and your adjusted gross income, plus your tax-free income, plus one-half of your Social Security, is above $32,000 on a joint return. I cover this in more detail in Chapter 11). Other income that is tax free is your first $200 of dividends from American corporations on a joint return, or $100 on a single return. Also, 60 percent of your capital gains are not taxable.

* Refer to the Tax Addendum in the Appendix for possible tax changes.

TAX-DEFERRED INCOME

This is income earned now but on which you are allowed to defer the taxes to a later date. An example of this type of income is the single premium deferred annuity. In this type of investment, an insurance company guarantees your principal plus a minimum interest rate, and your tax on the interest is deferred until you withdraw it. The chief advantage of tax-deferred annuities is that your interest is compounding tax deferred; and because there is no immediate loss to taxes, you are compounding dollars that would not have been in your account had they been siphoned off by taxes. Again, the tragedy of paying taxes is not only that you lose the dollars but you lose what the dollars would earn if they were still in your possession.

TAX-SHELTERED INCOME

You may receive tax-sheltered income from various limited partnership investments and certain individual investments. This type of income, though probably incidental to the reason you made the investment, will most likely become your favorite type. In these investments, your cash distributions are sheltered by write-offs from depreciation, interest expense, and other allowable expenses. Not only can your deductions shelter all or part of your income from these sources, but there may also be excess deductions that will shelter taxable income you are receiving from other sources. You have already seen how this works in the chapters on real estate, energy, and equipment leasing. When you receive tax-sheltered income, however, you do reduce the cost basis of your investment. Therefore you have larger taxable capital gains when the properties are sold. The tax deferral should still be beneficial to you, because you have had the earning power of that money during the deferral period.

Your First Step to Tax Planning

Where do you begin your program of intelligent tax planning? First, do it early in the year. This gives you more time to plan your strategy and more days to qualify for depreciation, etc. The quality of the tax-advantaged investments that are available is usually much higher in the earlier part of the year than in the latter part; and you have time to investigate and judge the quality and potential profitability of each investment without the threat of an immediate deadline, which could force you into a poor decision. In other words, don't find yourself desperately looking for a shelter on December 28.

Taxable income is that portion of your income that is left after you have made all of your permissible deductions. Perhaps one of the best ways to calculate this number is to take the government's tax form itself and fill in the blanks. If this seems too painful, at least list all the income you anticipate this year on one sheet of paper, and on another sheet list all of your allowable deductions and compute the difference. This will give you an idea of the extent of your problem and where we need to start to solve it. Even if you don't take any constructive steps to shelter income—and surely you will—the work you have done gathering this information should greatly reduce the number of hours for which your CPA will bill you when he prepares your tax return.

Now that you have tallied your income and your deductions and have a figure for your taxable income, look at Table 13 in the Appendix to obtain an indication of your tax bracket and the taxes that will be due if you take no action to reduce this loss.

Up to this point, with the exception of private placements in real estate, oil and gas drilling, equipment leasing, and cable television, we have been mainly discussing how to invest your after-tax hard dollars. In this chapter, our chief emphasis will be on how to invest your before-tax "soft" dollars.

Investing Before-Tax "Soft" Dollars

If you are in a 50 percent tax bracket, you could lose $5,000 of the last $10,000 you earned to taxes, which would only leave you $5,000 to invest. But there are a number of options you may want to consider that could allow you also to invest all or a portion of the $5,000 you have been losing to taxes.

HIGH RISK

Before I cover deductibility and investing tax dollars, let's discuss risk. Tax-favored investments do involve high risk, and I will never promise any client who makes a tax-favored investment with me that he will ever get one penny back. But I am also quick to point out that paying taxes is high risk, too. The return on a tax receipt is zero, and the risk is 100 percent! The choice is yours. You can invest these funds with me or another financial planner, or you can send them to Washington. All I ever hope to do for you or any client is to help you attempt to improve your odds. Risks are the very reason that Congress has provided the tax incentives. They want to encourage you to invest in high-risk areas that provide for the social good of our country.

A number of pitfalls can be found in tax-sheltered investments, such as economic risks, recessions, overbuilding and poor management of real estate, dry holes when drilling, cattle deaths, fluctuating markets, unsuccessful research and development projects, lack of sales, and changes in government regulations. There is also the risk of being a passive investor; as a limited partner, you cannot participate in the management of a partnership without losing your limited liability status. That is why it is so important to evaluate management carefully. Because of the risks involved, you should never invest more than you think you are emotionally prepared to lose. You should always analyze the economics of the investment carefully and you should not be tempted by a tax overkill at the price of eventual returns.

You also have tax risks. There are degrees of certainty that deductions will be sustained. Certain areas are probable; others are gray. You also run the risk of constant changes in the tax law, and you always face the risk of an audit by the IRS.

WHOSE MONEY IS IT?

There was a period when there seemed to be more prospective clients than usual coming to my office and saying, "My CPA says I'm paying too much in taxes, so I should buy some municipal bonds." After a few months of this, I decided to conduct a seminar for both CPA's and clients on the subject of "Whose Money Is It?" I continue to conduct this type of seminar each year, and at the seminar I hand out the chart shown below when we are discussing tax-favored investments.

As you can see from the circle, a portion of your income belongs to the IRS and will be catapulted on its one-way trip to Washington if you don't take some action to prevent it. We call these your "soft" dollars—the dollars you will lose to taxes. The ones left are your "hard" dollars. (When I was giving this explanation to a very hard-working builder the other day, he protested, "But they're all hard dollars. I've worked so hard for every one of them.") Regardless of how hard he had worked for them, he was not going to get to keep those dollars unless he made some tax-favored investments. I find that this concept of "hard" and "soft" dollars is a difficult one for clients to comprehend. You must learn to do different things with your soft dollars than you do with your hard dollars. Even after I have carefully explained all this, time and time again a prospective

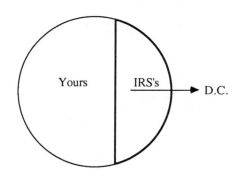

| | Deductibility | Approx. 50% Bracket | |
		Your Money	IRS's Money
1.	0%	100%	0%
2.	50%	75%	25%
3.	100%	50%	50%
4.	200%	0%	100%
5.	Over 200 %	0% + investable funds	100%+

2 Choices:
D.C.—Washington
or
D.C.—Defer & Convert

Figure 9-1. *Whose Money Is It?*

client will tell me, "Oh, I'm a very conservative person who never takes risks, and this sounds like a risky investment." Again, I have to ask them, "How risky is it to send your money to Washington? What rate of return are you expecting from your tax receipt? How much will your tax receipt increase your net worth?" Yes, I know you may have to pay the piper someday, but with time and inflation you may be able to improve your odds.

DEDUCTIBILITY

Now look again at our diagram and let's discuss deductibility and its effect in a 50 percent tax bracket:

1. *0 percent deductible.* All of the investment was made with your money; none of it was the IRS's. A good example of this would be a municipal bond or a stock investment.

2. *50 percent deductible.* If an investment is 50 percent deductible, 75 percent is your money and 25 percent is the IRS's. Examples of this would be certain agriculture, marine container, and leasing programs.

3. *100 percent deductible.* If it is 100 percent deductible, 50 percent is your money and 50 percent is the IRS's. Good examples of this would be programs of oil and gas drilling, cattle feeding, certain real estate programs, and combination cattle feeding and embryo transfer programs discussed in the latter part of this chapter.

4. *200 percent deductible.* In this instance, none of the investment is your money; all of it is the IRS's. Some leveraged cable television programs and certain two-tiered real estate programs would be good examples.

5. *Over 200 percent deductible.* In this investment, not only have you not used your money, but you have actually been paid not to do so. Examples of this are certain leveraged programs entered into early in the year in such areas as cattle breeding, feeding, and embryo transfer programs; agriculture programs; oil and gas drilling programs (first year, but not over the pay-in period); and equipment leasing.

Do these examples give you a better idea of whose money we are talking about?

Progressive Federal Income Tax Rates

You will note from Table 13 in the Appendix that taxes begin at the 11 percent level on your first dollar of taxable income above the "zero bracket amount" and run up to a maximum of 50 percent. (The zero bracket amount replaced the old standard deduction. It is the amount of taxable income on which no tax is levied, and it is built into the tax tables. This figure is currently $2,300 for single taxpayers and $3,400 for married individuals filing jointly.)

As we have previously seen, we all have some hard dollars and some soft dollars. However, most of the tax-favored investments discussed in this chapter require that some portion of your income be in the 42 to 50 percent bracket and that you have varying amounts of net worth for investment to be "suitable" in the eyes of the regulatory agencies. I know that if you are in, say, the 30 percent bracket, you don't like paying taxes any more than the person in the 50 percent bracket, but your broker and financial planner's hands will usually be tied by the regulatory agencies because of suitability requirements. But do read on and take hope, for there are more and more tax-favored investments becoming available to the lower-bracket investor with lower net worth requirements.

Deductions and How You Qualify

Many investors do not understand why or how deductions (write-offs) are allowed against taxable income or against their tax liability. Since this may be true of you also, let's look at some of the characteristics of deductions. These cannot be treated comprehensively in just one chapter, so you will need to do some in-depth study on your own. I especially recommend that you obtain and read booklets on current tax provisions available upon request from most large national CPA firms.

First of all, you need to understand how limited partnerships and, in some respects, subchapter S corporations are treated for tax purposes. As you will remember, limited partnership investors are treated as individuals, so that all of the tax deductions flow through to the limited partners. The most common sources of these deductions are depreciation, interest expense, investment tax credit, cost depletion, royalty and lease payments, and losses due to various causes. You've already become familiar with most of these deductions, but let's briefly review them here, since it is essential to your understanding of tax-advantaged investments to know how they work. And be sure to look at the Tax Addendum in the Appendix as the footnotes in this section suggest.

DEPRECIATION

You were introduced to this deduction in the real estate chapter. You will remember that depreciation is a bookkeeping entry, no checks are sent, and you are permitted to depreciate the cost of the depreciable asset, including the amount you have borrowed to pay for it if you are liable for the debt, which is called being "at risk." Real estate is the exception to the "at risk" rule.* You can still depreciate the building (not the land on which it is built) even if the lender can only look to the value of the property for the repayment of the mortgage.

Depreciation is allowed because buildings, materials, equipment, and so on, have a limited useful life and must be replaced. Depreciation allows you to set up a reserve to replace the asset. Be sure you avoid accelerated depreciation on commercial non-residential properties, or your gains upon sale will be taxed at ordinary income rates rather than at capital gains rates. You can avoid this by using straight-line depreciation over a period of 18 years.* Straight-line depreciation will enable you to get back the depreciation as long-term capital gains with a maximum effective tax rate of 20 percent.*

When considering an investment, be sure to read the portion of the offering memorandum that deals with the method of depreciation to determine if it meets your objective. All depreciation on commercial property is subject to recapture at ordinary rates if the Accelerated Cost Recovery System (ACRS) is used (explained below). Only the amount of depreciation in excess of straight-line depreciation is subject to the recapture rules if ACRS is used for residential property, and that property you have not taken accelerated depreciation on comes back as capital gains. (Subsidized housing and certified his-

* Refer to the Tax Addendum in the Appendix for possible tax changes.

toric rehabilitations have their own set of special rules.) Also, be sure to see if preference items are produced which will affect your Alternative Minimum Tax calculation.

ACCELERATED COST RECOVERY SYSTEM*

The Economic Recovery Tax Act of 1981 (ERTA) attempted to make socially desirable or economic investments more appealing through quicker depreciation or write-offs. ERTA greatly liberalized depreciation schedules by introducing a new system of depreciation called the Accelerated Cost Recovery System (ACRS). In general, you are allowed to recover your costs on the basis of statutory periods of time that are shorter than the useful life of the asset, or the period for which it is used to produce income. The cost of eligible property is recovered over a three-year, five-year, ten- or fifteen-year period, depending on the classification of the property.

If you acquire property for use in your trade or business or for the production of income and the property does not fall within one of the enumerated ACRS classes, you may deduct the entire cost of the property in the year of purchase. However, the cost of machinery, equipment, buildings, or other similar items that do fall within an ACRS class must be deducted over the period of time and in the manner specified by the code and regulations. I won't go into further details, for there are a number of booklets that will give you the various depreciation schedules. Especially note the provisions regarding real property.

INTEREST EXPENSE

You were introduced to this deductible expense in the real estate chapter. If you are an investor in a limited partnership, sole proprietorship, or partnership, you may be allowed to deduct your proportionate part of the interest expenses incurred for the investment. Prepaid interest is not deductible. Interest expense occurs anytime leverage is used by borrowing funds. (Your deduction for investment interest is limited to your net investment income plus $10,000 if it is not incurred in a business. This limitation may seem grossly unfair to you, as it does to me, since my father didn't set up a multimillion-

* Refer to the Tax Addendum in the Appendix for possible tax changes.

dollar trust from which I could receive investment income, as is the case of a particular senator who pushed for this limitation. What about the hardworking entrepreneur who is still trying to make it?)*

Let's take a moment to talk about leverage, for the use of leverage generates interest expense and larger depreciation than other deductions per dollar invested. There are a number of advantages to leverage. Leverage can entitle you to tax deductions in excess of your cash contributions, but as you have seen under the depreciation heading, you must be "at risk" (except for real estate),* meaning that you must pay on the due date if the cash flow from the investment has not paid off the indebtedness or if the due date is not extended. Your basis in your investment determines the amount of the deductions that you may take and includes your equity investment, your undistributed revenues, and the proportionate part of any partnership debts for which you are personally liable.

There are also some pitfalls of leveraging, as leverage can be a two-edged sword. Your debt must be serviced, meaning that interest must be paid, so there will be less cash flow available to pay out to you if you are an investor. Also, payment must be paid on the principal from these revenues, which is not deductible. If payment on the principal is made on your behalf on debt other than real estate, it will produce phantom income—dollars that are not paid to you but are taxable to you.

If you have taken deductions in excess of your "at risk" investment, you cannot avoid the day of reckoning by making a gift of the property or permitting the loan to be foreclosed. For tax purposes, this is treated as a sale. This is the reason you should also invest the funds you would have sent to Washington. Do not treat these as spendable dollars, but only as assets to build your net worth and to pay a tax when it becomes due.

INVESTMENT TAX CREDIT (ITC)

We have already mentioned investment tax credit, but let's now discuss it in detail. The investment tax credit is a credit against your tax liabilities that is allowed on qualified investments on certain depreciable tangible personal property used in a trade or business or for the production of income in the first year the taxpayer places the prop-

* Refer to the Tax Addendum in the Appendix for possible tax changes.

erty in service. Most deductions you will receive are deferrals, meaning that your tax has not been forgiven but has been deferred until a later date. With the investment tax credit, if you hold the property the required length of time before selling it, your tax is permanently forgiven.

A tax deduction is applied against your gross income and lowers your taxable income, whereas an investment tax credit is a credit against the tax itself, so you are allowed to subtract it after you determine the amount of tax due on your taxable income. In a 50 percent tax bracket, ITC has twice the value of a write-off. In lower brackets, it may be worth three times a write-off.

If you dispose of property on which you have taken ITC prior to the close of the recapture period (generally the first full year after the property is placed in service and the succeeding four years, except for three-year property, in which the period is reduced by two years), your tax liability will be increased.

The Economic Recovery Tax Act of 1981 liberalized incentives to encourage investment in both new and used property (with limitations) by establishing new investment credit rules. A 6 percent credit applies to qualified property in the three-year depreciation class and 10 percent applies to all other qualified property. If you cannot use the credit this year because of lack of taxable income, you may carry it back three years or carry it forward for fifteen years for credits arising in taxable years ending after 1973.

You should become familiar with the various at-risk limitations and recapture provisions.

DEPLETION

You were introduced to depletion in the energy chapter. In addition to oil and gas, other natural resources qualify for statutory depletion, such as timber, coal, minerals, and metals.

OPERATING LOSSES

Losses that occur in a business or investment that you invested in to make a profit are deductible, although there are certain limitations on the timing if they are capital losses. The purpose of investing is not to obtain real losses. The tax laws are structured to give you the incentive to invest in areas of need that may show losses at the beginning but that have hopes of gains at a later date. Real losses are to be avoided whenever possible.

Deferral vs. Permanent Shelter

PERMANENT SHELTER

Certain forms of tax-sheltered investments generate deductions that are "permanent" in nature. These are: investment tax credit (if the equipment is held for the required time), energy tax credit, research and development credit, and rehabilitation credits.*

DEFERRAL

Such items as depreciation, interest, and certain losses merely defer your taxes, but as we have seen, deferral can be very important. It may permit you to shift a tax to another year and allow you to pay with a cheaper dollar, and it may also give you added time to do tax planning. Deferrals reduce your cost basis, and when the property is sold, your taxable gain will be based on the difference between your sale price and your adjusted cost. If you are an investor in a partnership, the general partner will provide you with a K-1 form to be used for your tax return and from which you can calculate your cost basis.

Diversification

A vital requirement for any succesful investment program you ever undertake should be diversification—the not-all-your-eggs-in-one-basket rule. This rule applies especially to tax-favored investments, since most of them are definitely higher risks than investments without tax advantage. It is prudent to spread this risk within the investment area itself as well as among various areas. For example, if you have chosen a general partner who offers a number of oil and gas

* Refer to the Tax Addendum in the Appendix for possible tax changes.

exploration programs throughout the year, spread your investment throughout several of his programs. Also, spread your tax-favored investments into as wide a variety of industries as is practical.

Spreading your dollars into several offerings allows you to lower your risks and increase your potential for profit. If one tax-favored investment goes sour—and you should go into each of them with the full knowledge that this could and probably will happen sooner or later—don't spend your time crying and moaning and saying, "I'll never try another tax-advantaged investment." You really will lose if you do that. You have been smart enough to earn the money that put you in a higher tax bracket, so do as you have been doing in your business—dust yourself off and go out and try again. If you do your homework, you will win most of the time. You *know* you are going to lose if you capitulate to the IRS.

Most tax shelters you will be considering will be structured as limited partnerships, either registered or private placements. Under the limited partnership arrangement, the pooling of funds by a large number of investors provides more funds and thus more diversification. The advantage of the limited partnership arrangement is that all the tax benefits and revenues flow through the partnership to the individual limited partners. This makes it possible for a person who has investable funds but little or no expertise and who wants to avoid liability beyond his investment to put to work a general partner with expertise who is willing to take liability.

Types of Tax-Favored Investments

In order to solve your tax problem, you must make a tax-favored investment. This must be a business that is "engaged in for profit" to pass the IRS "nose test." Large volumes have been written on the various tax-favored programs available in the marketplace, but here I will cover a few of the ones you are most likely to encounter. The fact that I have not covered a particular shelter does not mean that the one you are offered is not a viable one, nor does the fact that I have covered it relieve you of the responsibility to do your "due diligence," which means trying to become as informed about a particular investment as you can.

REAL ESTATE

In the real estate chapter you became familiar with the part that properly structured, economically sound real estate programs can play in your goal to build your net worth while avoiding having your funds take that one-way trip to Washington. Real estate has in the past been favored by our tax laws, and its economic performance has made it an attractive investment. This does not mean that every real estate tax shelter is a good investment, but rather that the right ones can provide the best combination of economic benefits and tax advantages. From an economic perspective, when measured against the long-term performance of other investment areas, real estate has typically outperformed most of them in terms of consistency of return, hedging against inflation, and asset appreciation.

In the real estate chapter, I discussed private placement limited partnerships involving apartment complexes, office buildings, shopping centers, etc., but there are two types of real estate programs I did not cover. My reason for not including them there is that, in my opinion, without the tax incentives, they do not make sound economic sense. These two are subsidized housing and certified historic rehabilitation.

SUBSIDIZED HOUSING

If you are considering investing in a subsidized housing program, be sure to be relatively certain that you will be in a high tax bracket for a period of many years. Most programs require long pay-in periods, have long holding periods, have limited capital gains potential, and have limited cash flow.

Most of these programs do, however, permit you to write off from 225 percent to 230 percent of your investment each year, so in reality you are being paid to make the investment. If you do choose to invest in subsidized housing, choose projects that rent to the elderly or the handicapped and are located in our smaller cities. Also use the following checklist:

1) Is the developer selling the property to the syndication at cost or at a substantial premium?

2) What depreciation schedule is being used?

3) What occupancy rate must the property have to break even?

4) Check out the area. Is it declining or growing?

5) Find out what other subsidized housing already exists in the area.

6) What are the recapture problems on sale?

CERTIFIED HISTORIC REHABILITATION

Congress has determined that the preservation and rehabilitation of certain historic buildings are socially desirable, and to encourage developers to modernize and rehabilitate these structures, they wrote into our tax laws certain tax incentives. In addition to the usual deductions for mortgage interest and depreciation, there is a 25 percent tax credit for rehabilitation costs, as well as an immediate charitable contribution deduction for the donation of the façade easement if that arrangement is used. The entire renovation cost qualifies for a one-time 25 percent rehabilitation tax credit when the structure is placed in service, provided that the applicable rules and regulations are followed. For example, if you invested in a limited partnership that spends $10 million over the next twelve months to rehabilitate completely a certified historic building, this would create a tax credit of $2.5 million when the building is placed in service. In most cases, your share of the available credit would represent a dollar-for-dollar reduction of your tax bill, since this is credited directly against your tax. This is significantly different from most other tax benefits, the values of which are dependent on your tax bracket (i.e., the higher the bracket, the more tax savings per dollar of deduction).

The rules governing most tax credits require that 100 percent of the credit be deducted from your cost basis before applying depreciation. However, the value of the historic rehabilitation credit is enhanced even more by the requirement that only 50 percent of the credit be deducted from the depreciable basis of the building, and there is no recapture if the property is retained for at least five years.

There is also a provision whereby the exterior shell of the building can be donated to the community, in perpetuity, in exchange for a charitable contribution deduction equal to the value of the donation. The community receives a perpetual benefit from a building that will retain its historical appearance while providing commercially desirable modern space. The donation of the façade easement prohibits the replacement of the building by any other structure, and since the owner of the building has fewer future options for the building, its current value is diminished. The amount of that reduction in value, as determined by an appraisal, is generally used to determine the value of the façade easement. The façade easement contribution creates a charitable deduction in the year it is contributed, even though the rehabilitated building is completed and placed in service the following year.

The net result is that a historical rehabilitation project creates tax benefits, the bulk of which are realized during the year of investment and the year of rehabilitation, which may or may not be the same year. Normally this involves two calendar years. In contrast, the bulk of the tax benefits from other real estate projects must be realized over a longer period of time. To qualify for these benefits, a rehabilitation project could be structured as follows:

YEAR	INVESTMENT	WRITE-OFF	CREDIT	TAX SAVINGS	AFTER-TAX INVESTMENT
1986	$ 50,000	$100,000	-0-	$ 50,000	-0-
1987	50,000	20,000	$40,000	50,000	-0-
	$100,000	$120,000	$40,000	$100,000	

(Assumes a 50% tax bracket.)

As you can see, the positive tax impact from this type of project is immediate. A traditional real estate tax shelter may yield tax savings in an amount roughly equivalent to the above, but it would take longer to do so.

The experience of the general partner is always an important consideration when analyzing any limited partnership, and an experienced and capable general partner is absolutely essential in a partnership which is going to rehabilitate a historical structure. In addition to the normal considerations and requirements of a real estate development, the general partner of a rehabilitation project must be thoroughly familiar with all governmental processes affecting the project.

OIL AND GAS DRILLING PROGRAMS

Another tax-favored investment you will want to consider, which was covered earlier, is oil and gas drilling programs. The registered programs should allow you to make a smaller investment and should give you more diversification, whereas the private offerings usually require larger minimum investments but can also be structured to provide larger first-year write-offs using leverage. Determine if there are programs available that fit your tax needs and your temperament.

In choosing a program for your investment dollars, select one that has a general partner who is well capitalized, has considerable expertise, and has a successful track record. His track record does not guarantee that your program will be successful, but I do like to place my money with people who have a record of being winners. Go into programs at the beginning of the year to obtain a larger write-off for the year and give the general partners time for orderly and efficient drilling throughout the year. Drilling rigs and crews may also be more readily obtainable at a lower cost earlier rather than at the end of the year, when there are likely to be many operators scrambling for equipment.

EQUIPMENT LEASING

You have already become familiar with the tax implications of equipment leasing, and as you have seen, your potential benefits come from tax savings, cash flow, and ending value. Tax benefits come through investment tax credits, depreciation of the equipment, and interest deductions on loans, while gains come from rental payments during the term of the lease. In addition, you may receive residual values when the equipment is sold.

This type of investment is mainly a deferral and should allow you to move some of your income and tax problems from a year of high tax liability to one that is not as high, perhaps after retirement, or this investment may buy you the time to carry out additional tax planning. If the program you choose flows through the investment tax credit, this credit is deductible in the year in which you make the investment and brings a permanent elimination of the tax if held for the required time. Some equipment leasing programs can offer the dual advantage of tax deferral and tax elimination.

MOVIES

Another area that can offer you tax advantage and profit potential, together with high risks, is the production, acquisition, and distribution of motion pictures. The movie industry is growing, as evidenced by box office receipts reaching new highs last year for the fourth consecutive year. The number of movie screens is rapidly increasing, the foreign market for American movies is growing, and technological advances are bringing more movies into the home via pay TV, cable TV, and VCR.

Most of the offerings you will see in this area will be private placements with high leverage for maximum write-off during the first years of the investment and high risks. On the other hand, the growth potential for movie production and distribution is also attracting well-known and well-financed syndicators offering registered limited partnerships. One that you may want to study plans to raise in excess of $50 million to produce eight to twelve low-budget films averaging in cost from $3 to $4 million per picture. This partnership may also co-finance the production of additional pictures and acquire the rights to distribute others. It also has another profit opportunity in that the partnership will own notes and stock in the company that will be producing and distributing the films. It is projected that you will be eligible to write off 35 to 50 percent of your investment in the first two years, plus receive cash distributions greater than your original investment. As a limited partner you would receive 99 percent of these distributions until you have received 100 percent of your original capital; 90 percent of the partnership's revenues between 101 and 150 percent; 85 percent between 151 and 200 percent and 80 percent of revenues thereafter. Dividends on the stock and principal and interest payments on the note will be distributed 100 percent to the limited partners. It is projected that your original capital will be returned to you in three to five years and the life of the partnership will be five to six years. The production company plans to reduce risks by producing modest-budget movies targeted at the 13- to 25-year-old market, which is the largest segment of American moviegoers, and preselling rights to auxiliary markets such as foreign countries and syndicated television.

If the partnership has a modest success, it is projected that your write-offs on a $10,000 investment would be $3,500 to $5,000 during the first two years and your pretax return would amount to $20,000 in six years. With a large success, it is projected that your write-offs would be from $1,000 to $2,000 and your pretax return would be $35,000 in six years. The value of the stock would be in addition to these returns. If the earnings of the company were $10 million and the stock sold at ten times earnings, the value of the stock would be around $2,100, and at 20 times earnings around $4,300. With earnings of $20 million, the value of the stock would be around $4,300 and $8,600 respectively.

CATTLE FEEDING PROGRAMS

You can use a cattle feeding program to defer income from the current year to the following year. These programs can be structured as registered limited partnerships, private placement limited partnerships, or you can invest as an individual. In these programs, cattle are purchased and placed in a feedlot for fattening. In four to six months, the cattle are sold for slaughter. The cost to purchase the cattle is not deductible, but all of the cost for feed and maintenance is. With cattle feeding programs, you should either invest early in the year, or in the third quarter of the year so you can deduct your cost in the current year and defer your income to the following year. These programs could be especially useful if you are retiring, receiving a large bonus, exercising a stock option, or receiving an unusual income the current year that you do not anticipate receiving the following year. They can also buy you time to plan other possible tax-advantaged investments the following year.

Cattle feeding programs are usually leveraged, and you will have a choice of being "at risk" for additional deductions or not. If you choose not to be "at risk," your deduction will usually be around 100 percent. If you choose to be "at risk" through signing a note, your deductions can be 200 percent or greater if investment is made in the earlier part of the year.

The risks associated with cattle feeding programs are disease, bad weather, fluctuating grain costs, and declines in beef prices. Some ways to lower these risks are to maintain cattle in different geographic locations, thereby lowering the risk of bad weather and disease; hedging in the futures market to lock in grain prices and sale prices of the finished cattle; and the use of cost-plus contracts. With cost-plus contracts you presell your cattle through an arrangement whereby the sale price of the cattle includes all costs to feed and maintain the cattle plus a margin of profit on your cost for the cattle.

CATTLE BREEDING PROGRAMS

Breeding programs can be structured separately or in combination with a feeding program. The goal here, however, is usually to improve the purebred herds to convert feed more efficiently into beef production or dairy production. The tax advantages of a breeding program come from your being allowed to depreciate the cattle over a five-year basis, deduct feed and maintenance, receive an investment tax credit of 10 percent in the year the cattle are purchased, and receive long-term capital gains treatment upon sale if the cattle have been held for two years for breeding purposes.

EMBRYO TRANSFER

Investing in an embryo transfer program is another way you can obtain tax benefits from cattle. Embryo transfer is the process by which a genetically superior cow becomes, in effect, a bank of genetically superior eggs. Using superovulation, a cow of outstanding performance can produce an unlimited number of superior calves in her lifetime compared to nine or so under natural conditions. The donor cow and the inseminating bull provide all of the genetic material for each calf, and the recipient cows merely serve as incubators for the embryos until birth and as a milk source until weaning.

All the costs to collect embryos from the superior cattle and then transfer them to recipient cows are tax deductible. Also, feed and maintenance for both the recipient cows and the calves after they are born are deductible expenses. If you hold the calves for two years, they receive long-term capital gains treatment when they are sold. This method can provide tax deferral for several years and then allow you to convert to long-term capital gains.

The risks in both the cattle breeding and embryo transfer programs are the quality of the cattle produced and the sex of the cattle produced. The females are the most desirable because of a larger market. (One program I am familiar with is now working on the technology to sex the embryos.)

COMBINING FEEDING, BREEDING, AND EMBRYO TRANSFERS

My favorite way of using cattle for tax advantage is to combine feeding, breeding, and embryo transfer into one program under the right management. The combined program allows you to lower your risk through diversification, defer your taxes, and convert any profits you may make into long-term capital gains. If you choose to be "at risk" in such a program, you can write off up to 250 percent if you enter the program early in the year. (This drops to 200 percent later in the year.) If you do not choose to be "at risk," you can still deduct 100 percent. Programs such as these are available in registered offerings.

HORSE BREEDING

Another area of investing that can offer tax advantage, and may on rare occasions produce tremendous profits, is the breeding of thoroughbred and quarter horses for racing, standardbreds for trotting and pacing, and Arabian horses for their beauty and endurance. Of all the tax-advantaged investments that have high risk, this one should probably be at the top of the list.

Most of the horse offerings you will see will be private placement limited partnerships for breeding purposes. A typical breeding program will generate expenses for the first two years of the partnership, but no income; operate close to break-even in years three, four, and five; and seek to generate capital gains in year five and the first quarter of year six, when the partnership would probably be dissolved.

There are some registered limited partnerships that buy standardbreds for trotting and pacing for all cash. To reduce risk, the partnership will only participate in purchasing, breeding, and selling offspring of championship racehorses. It will not engage in racing. The mares will be bred and their offspring sold at annual auctions. It is anticipated that all horses will be sold in five years. The general partner's profits on most of these programs are subordinated to the limited partners, who receive back their original capital plus 12 percent.

HORSE RACING

Horse racing is the largest spectator sport in the United States and one of the leading sources of recreation in the entertainment industry. Approximately 95 million Americans go to horse races each year (32 million more than go to baseball games, the second-ranking spectator sport). Horse racing is larger than the motion picture and record industries on an annual revenue basis, and it seems to be truly unaffected by business cycles. In times of prosperity, people go to the races because they can enjoy themselves there, and when economic conditions take a nosedive, people still go in order to forget their worries. The industry is unaffected by price controls, and its marketability is enhanced by portability.

The average price for one-year-old thoroughbreds (yearlings) has increased steadily from $7,670 in 1968 to around $42,000 today. This growth has outstripped inflation and resisted recession. The supply of yearlings for sale has increased around 10 percent per annum, and the price has increased around 30 percent per annum. Well-bred colts, fillies, and mares are a highly economic international commodity whose prices have been escalating each year. The chief reason is that in the United States alone there are over a hundred racetracks open a total of 7,515 days a year. Last year more than 64,000 horses went to the post over 500,000 times to fill the cards of 68,236 races. England, France, Italy, Germany, Japan, Australia, South Africa, Argentina, Venezuela, Chile, and countries of the Far East also have racing programs.

Most of the programs offering ownership of racehorses will be private placements. A winning filly can, of course, earn large sums from racing and be worth millions on retirement as a broodmare. The same is true of the winnings of a stallion at the races and on retirement to the stud farm. Your potential from one of these offerings can be dramatic, but the probability of that happening is very slim. You should study each offering carefully and then decide.

A racehorse (over two years old) lends itself to the following tax treatment: 1) You are allowed a 25 percent depreciation write-off when you place the horse in service during the year, 38 percent depreciation write-off the next year, and 37 percent the next year. The rates are subject to certain short taxable year rules. 2) If you start breeding a racehorse that is over two years old before the three-year depreciation period is up, you do not have to change to the five-year depreciation period. 3) If horses are held for at least 24 months, some portion of the sales proceeds can be treated as long-term capital gains, except for sales of offspring. These will produce ordinary income unless they are held for 24 months and are used for either racing or breeding purposes. Breeding horses over twelve years old when placed in service are also included in the three-year class for depreciation. The younger ones can be depreciated over five years, and a two-year-old racehorse can be depreciated in three years.

The first-year depreciation rate applies regardless of when you place your horse into service during the first year, be it January or December (unless you have a short tax year). Salvage value is completely eliminated from any computation of depreciation, and you are allowed to depreciate horses to zero.

Additional incentives include the residual income provided through the state aid programs to thoroughbred breeders. California, Florida, Louisiana, New Jersey, and New York have state-wide organized programs. It is estimated that over $8 million will be available each year to breeders of horses racing in New York State.

ARABIAN HORSES

Investing in Egyptian and Polish Arabian horses can also provide you with tax advantages and an opportunity to build your net worth. Owning Arabian horses was once only for the very rich; but, again, through limited partnerships the units can be small enough so that even if you only have a relatively small amount and are only in the 45 percent bracket, you can participate in the fun and at the same time enjoy tax advantages.

As in the case of racehorses, you should choose a partnership that is managed by a general partner with a proven record in the selection, breeding, and training of Arabians. The partnership should have the facilities and personnel necessary to breed and raise a foal from a weanling to a yearling or two-year-old. Here, too, the business requires careful planning, diligent effort, and intelligence.

RESEARCH AND DEVELOPMENT (R & D)

Some R & D offerings involve the start-up of a new company with the possibility of developing a new product. As an investor, you could share in the proceeds, if there are any, from the new product under development and perhaps a piece of the start-up company itself. Another variation you may find is an existing company that needs funds for R & D. With proper structure, financing for the project can be kept off the books so earnings will not be depressed and the balance sheet won't be laden with debt. In this way, the company gets low-cost funds while the investor gets venture capital opportunities, partly subsidized by tax breaks.

However, the 1984 tax act put a serious crimp in the tax-shelter side of most R & D programs because it disallowed the deduction for prepaid expenses, and instead required that they must be deducted as incurred. You should examine R & D programs on a case-by-case basis, with special emphasis on potential economic results. Look at the track record of the management of the partnership. Also study what it takes to manufacture and market the product once the product is developed. Is the company well regarded in the industry? Ask what happens if the money runs out. Budget inadequacy is a major flaw of some R & D programs. Can you be assessed? Is other financing available? If so, how will your interest be diluted? Because of the inordinately high risk associated with such ventures, you should have the potential of receiving an inordinately high return to justify taking the risk. There is no question that R & D investments fall into the "long-shot" category, so if you do choose such a program, try to select one that is more "D" than "R."

RETIREMENT PROGRAMS

Other areas you will want to study carefully for tax savings are pension and profit-sharing programs, which I will cover in detail in the chapter on planning for a financially secure retirement. Also included in that chapter are self-employed retirement plans (Keogh plans), Individual Retirement Accounts, 401 (k) plans, and tax-sheltered annuities. We have already discussed the various other private placements and registered offerings you are likely to encounter that can provide tax advantage. And near the end of this chapter, I will show you how to calculate the effect on your taxes from using these programs.

Additional Tax-Saving Options

INCOME EARNED ABROAD

If you work for a multinational corporation abroad, you may qualify to exclude some of your foreign-earned income attributable to the period of your foreign residency or presence in the foreign country. The 1984–87 maximum foreign-earned income exclusion is $80,000 per year, increasing to $95,000 in 1990, for "qualifying individuals." Also, there is a deduction available for "excess" housing expenses, or an exclusion available for "excess" housing expenses paid by the employer.

TAX LOSSES

If you are approaching the end of the year and have losses in your stock or bond portfolio, you probably should establish the loss. You may charge off $1 of capital loss against $1 of capital gain. If you still have losses you have not used in this manner, you may charge off $2 loss against $1 of ordinary income up to a maximum of $6,000 of loss against $3,000 of ordinary income. Any excess you have may be carried forward to be used in future years.

MUNICIPAL BOND SWAPPING

If you own some municipal bonds and interest rates have risen since you made your purchase, but you still want to own municipals or corporates, you might consider swapping bonds. You must be sure that the bonds you repurchase are either from a different issuer or of a different issue date or coupon maturity.

The swap could work like this. You own bonds with a cost basis of $10,000, a coupon rate of 4 percent that is due in ten years, and a market value of $7,200. You sell these bonds and replace them with $10,000 par value bonds carrying a 6.5 percent coupon rate, due in 20 years at a discounted price of $7,200. Your net results would be: 1) your yearly income is increased $250 per year; 2) you have established a capital loss of $2,800; and 3) you will recoup your loss in 11.2 years by the increased income of $250 per year. If you have a long-term capital gain to charge your loss against, you will recoup it sooner. If you do not have a long-term capital gain or if your loss exceeds the gain, $6,000 of your excess can be applied against $3,000 of ordinary income. If your losses are greater than this, they can be carried forward indefinitely to be applied against future gains and/or applied against $3,000 per year ordinary income. If your capital loss is considered long term for each dollar of loss, only one-half can be offset against ordinary income, subject to the $3,000 limitation.

DISCOUNT CORPORATE BONDS*

Another way to realize capital gains is to buy discounted bonds, which are often available at the peak of high interest rates. For example, you could have bought:

AT&T: $5\frac{1}{8}$% of 2001 at 57 to yield 10.90%
Houston Lighting & Power: $7\frac{1}{4}$% of 2001 at $70\frac{5}{8}$ to yield 11.30%
New York Telephone: 6% of 2007 at $58\frac{3}{4}$ to yield 11%

All of these bonds are high grade and should pay $1,000 per bond at maturity, providing you with long-term capital gains. For example, par is $1,000 and let's assume the current price on American Telephone and Telegraph $5\frac{1}{8}$% is 57, therefore, in the year 2001 you would have a capital gain of $430. (This example also points out the risk of a "riskless" investment.)

An easier way that takes less expertise on your part and that should carry less risk because of their professional management and diversification is to invest in mutual funds investing in deeply discounted bonds. When interest rates go down, bond prices should go up, and the sale would produce a capital gain. Also, as the discounted bonds mature and par value is received, a capital gain would occur.

S CORPORATIONS

An S corporation is a small business corporation that has elected not to be taxed as a corporation. A shareholder of an S corporation must include in his income his pro rata share of the corporation's taxable income, whether the amount was actually distributed to him or not.

* Refer to the Tax Addendum in the Appendix for possible tax changes.

This can become a tax shelter when lower-income family members are given or sold stock in such a corporation.

Another use may occur when you have a good bankable idea for a new business that will by its very nature probably be operating in the red for its first few years. By setting up the company as an S corporation, the losses can flow directly to you, and you can charge them off against your ordinary income. Later, when the business becomes profitable, you may or may not want to convert it to a regular corporation. The validity of converting was lessened with the reduction in maximum rates for individuals from 70 percent to 50 percent.* The maximum number of shareholders permissible in an S corporation is 35, with certain qualifications. A qualified trust is now allowed to be a shareholder.

HOME OWNERSHIP

If you are in a tax bracket of 40 percent or above, you may want to consider owning your own home, even though today it is cheaper to rent than to own. You should obtain the maximum mortgage you are allowed, for the interest is deductible, and your interest cost is therefore subsidized by the amount of your tax bracket. If your interest is 13 percent and you are in a 40 percent bracket, your net interest cost is 7.8 percent. If your bracket is 50 percent, your net interest cost is 6.5 percent.

PRIVATE ANNUITIES

A tool that may fit your financial objective is the private annuity. This type of annuity involves the transfer of your property to a transferee —an individual, a partnership, or a corporation—in exchange for an unsecured promise to make periodic payments to you in fixed amounts for a designated period of time. In most cases, this will be for your lifetime. The assets you may use for this are real property, stocks, bonds, mutual funds, limited partnerships, and so forth. The advantage to you is that this method can usually increase your cash flow from your assets without substantially increasing your income tax liability. Capital gains taxation will be spread over the life of your agreement and, as a result, may be reduced in amount.

* Refer to the Tax Addendum in the Appendix for possible tax changes.

Since these assets are generally not includable for estate tax purposes, there could be a savings on estate taxes in the event of your premature death. The private annuity can be partly taxable under certain conditions that your attorney can explain.

There are some disadvantages to the private annuity. Let's assume you transferred this property to your son and you died prior to the completion of the agreement. There is the possibility that your son may be subjected to an adjustment in the basis of that property. If your son held the property for at least six months before selling it, the gain would be treated as long-term capital gain. If he sold before six months and you died, it could be subject to short-term capital gains treatment. If you live longer than the life expectancy table indicates, the payments may be greater than the original value, but the tax savings and appreciation could more than make up for this. Also, there is no tax deduction accruing to your son for interest paid to you. Another disadvantage is the provision that you are unable to secure the annuity payments by collateralizing through a trust or by a mortgage.

To provide the necessary funds for the monthly payments the buyer will need to make, he could consider investing the proceeds from the sale of the assets in shares of a high-quality mutual fund that is within a family of funds and that also has a money market fund so he could superimpose a timing service to move in and out of the market as market conditions dictated. In this way diversification could be obtained in a quality cross section of securities that are professionally managed, and the custodian bank could send you a check each month. Other investments you may want to consider are oil and gas income limited partnerships, real estate income limited partnerships, and quality stocks that pay generous dividends.

In summary, the advantages of the private annuity are: 1) avoids all the costs of probate, 2) could save on federal estate taxes at death, 3) could save on state inheritance taxes, 4) could spread the long-term capital gains tax over a number of years, and 5) there is no future appreciation to increase estate valuation.

The Living Trust

The proper use of the living trust (also referred to as the revocable or the intervivos trust) can reduce the cost of passing your assets to your heirs. With the living trust, a pour-over will should be drawn to cover all assets you have not registered to the trust.

Your trust can be written so as to pass your assets as you would do in a will. You should have the trust drawn in the state in which you reside. Some states will allow you to be your own trustee, while others require co-trustees. You may also use a bank or a corporate trustee. All of the assets you want to place in the trust should be listed, and as changes are made, the list should be updated. The trust can offer the following benefits:

1. The cost of probate and administration fees are saved because the trust assets are not probated through the courts.

2. The prolonged probate time can be saved, as the assets can be passed immediately. All creditors must be paid, and the federal estate taxes and state taxes can be put into an escrow account with the trustee liable.

3. The problem of incapacity is lessened. Generally, under the will method the individual has no document while he is alive and, should incapacity occur, the court must be petitioned to declare him incapacitated in order to sell any property. The trust document can state that three doctors can declare the individual incapacitated and the co-trustees or successor trustee assume trustee role.

4. The trust can afford privacy in death as to the amount of assets held in the estate, since it does not go through the probate court. No listing of assets, which usually ends up in the local newspapers, is required.

5. A trust can keep the estate under family control. Since assets such as stock, property, or a closely held corporation or business are not under court control, these can be sold to raise cash for costs and fees and for state and federal estate taxes.

There are some assets that you should avoid placing in the living trust, such as automobiles, jewelry, furs, and home furnishings. Nor should you place in the trust professional corporation stock, since most states require that the stockholder be of the same profession as the original stockholder. The transfer of assets into a living trust is not of taxable consequences. (Gift taxes can occur when assets are placed into a short-term or irrevocable trust.)

Income Splitting

If you are in a high tax bracket and if you have dependents, you may want to consider income splitting. For example, the interest and dividends you are receiving are being taxed at your higher bracket. If they were shifted to your children, who may have low or nonexistent brackets, you could reduce the family's overall tax burden. To do this, you will have to transfer the income-producing assets to the children either temporarily or permanently.

How should income splitting be done? You probably want to avoid outright gifts or guardianships, since contracts of minors can be voided and guardianships are cumbersome. Ways you might consider are custodial accounts, special trusts for minors, Clifford trusts, and gifts.

Custodial Accounts. These will be discussed in more detail in the chapter on financing a college education. Briefly, you may set up an account with an adult as custodian for your child. You cannot use any of the income for the support of your child, but this income could be used, however, for such things as summer camp, riding lessons, or college expenses, since these are not legal obligations. You will still be entitled to the $1,040 exemption for your child (or for each child if you have more than one) as long as the child is either a student or under 19 years of age. Each child can receive $1,040 per year tax-free from his own additional exemption plus the $100 dividend exclusion of dividends from American corporations. Until income exceeds $3,430, there should be little or no taxes. You may apply the $10,000 annual gift exclusion for each child and do this each year. If your spouse joins with you, $20,000 each year can be gifted to each child without a gift tax. If you want to avoid having these gifts considered a part of your estate in the event of your death, you should not be the custodian, nor should your spouse if the spouse has joined in the gift.

Special Trust for Minors. Perhaps you think it prudent that your child or children not have access to the principal until age 21. Under the Section 2503 (c) Trust, you may use your $10,000 per child annual gift exclusion ($20,000 if joined by your spouse). These assets and income can be used for the child before age 21 and if the trust's assets have not been spent by then, the principal must be paid to the child at age 21.

Clifford Trust. Income can also be split through the use of the Clifford Trust, which will also be discussed in a later chapter. This is a short-term living trust created for a period of the lesser of ten years and a day or the life of the beneficiary. At the end of this period, the trust terminates and your property is returned to you. This type of trust may be used for your dependent children, dependent parents, or others for whom you want to provide income for a period of ten years. Its chief advantage is that it permits you to split income without giving up your asset permanently.

Making Gifts. You may give $10,000 each year to as many people as you desire without a gift tax. If you and your spouse join in the giving, this amount can be $20,000. Any amount you give above this amount counts against your tax credit and can be taxable. This can have the effect of your prepaying your estate taxes. However, if you are gifting an income property to a person in a low tax bracket, it could be a reason for gifting above this amount. Another reason might be that the gift is an appreciating asset and therefore the appreciation can then take place outside of the estate.

EMPLOYING FAMILY MEMBERS IN YOUR BUSINESS

If you own your own business, you should thoroughly investigate the tax advantages that may be derived from employing your spouse and/ or your children. The same federal income tax will usually be paid whether or not your spouse is paid a salary for work performed. However, by paying the salary you could decrease payroll taxes, qualify the family for the marriage tax deduction, reduce the family's state income taxes, qualify the spouse for retirement benefits, qualify the spouse for certain tax-free fringe benefits, and increase the allowable business deductions.

In addition to many non-tax benefits, you may also be able to enjoy some tax advantages by providing bona fide employment for your children. The first most significant tax advantage is the ability to shift income among family members to reduce your overall tax burden. Payments made for bona fide business services are deductible and shifted to the child for tax purposes. These must be reported as income by your child, but as we have already mentioned, no federal income taxes are usually incurred until the child's earned income exceeds $3,430. You may also avoid or reduce your payroll taxes, and your child may be able to enjoy tax-free fringe benefits provided by you to your other employees.

Charitable Giving

Charitable giving is much too complex a subject to cover completely in this book, but if you have a fairly large estate and have charitable inclinations, you should thoroughly investigate the tax savings potential in this area.

Briefly, for federal income tax purposes, you may claim an itemized deduction from your adjusted gross income for contributions made to or for the use of religious, educational, public, or scientific organizations, or of the states, the United States government, an Indian tribal government, or other governmental units. No matter how needy a group, however, it might not qualify as an eligible donee. The Internal Revenue Service publishes a listing of eligible donees in IRS Publication 78, which also indicates what category the organization falls into for purposes of percentage limitations for itemized deductions. These limitations are based on the percentage of adjusted gross income that can be given in one year, on a tax-deductible basis, to various types of organizations.

There are many charitable plans which you may want to consider and these should be discussed with a qualified financial planner and/ or an estate planning attorney. The options they will discuss with you will probably include charitable remainder annuity trusts, charitable remainder trusts, gift annuities, pooled income funds, life estate plans, bargain-sale agreements, charitable lead trusts, and others.

Capital Gains and Losses on Stocks

Your chief incentive for investing in stocks should be to make a profit; and when you can't make a profit in the market, get out. You should sell when you anticipate that market conditions may become unfavorable or that your stock may have topped out for what appears to be a prolonged period of time. If you sell for more than you paid for the stock and you have held it for over six months, you will trigger a capital gain, 40 percent* of which will be taxable unless you have offsetting losses.

For example, let's assume that you bought 1,000 shares of a stock at $5 and that you sold it more than six months later at $10. You now have a $5,000 long-term capital gain, of which 40 percent is taxable. This $2,000 will be added to your taxable income and will be taxed at your top rate.

If you have realized capital gains and it is toward the end of the year and you have losses in some of your other stocks, bonds, or other assets, you should consider selling them, establishing your loss, and charging it against your capital gains. Be sure to wait 31 days before buying the same asset back, or it will be considered a "wash sale" and the loss will be disallowed. Also, don't let the fact that you will pay a capital gains tax keep you from selling stock that has matured and seemingly reached a plateau. Often I see people plant good fruit trees and let the fruit rot on the trees. Of course, they can avoid the capital gains if they hold a stock until it goes back to what they paid for it, but this hardly seems like brilliant financial planning.

These are some of the ways that you can lower your taxable income. Now we'll explore the effect of using certain tax-advantaged investments to continue reducing taxable income.

Calculating the Effect of Using Various Tax Shelters

Appendix Figure 3 is a sample tax-saving worksheet. Make several copies for yourself and make calculations for each tax-advantaged

* Refer to the Tax Addendum in the Appendix for possible tax changes.

investment you are considering. You can also calculate various combinations because you will want to diversify in your efforts to lower risks. After each calculation you can see your net cost after tax savings for the year.

In addition to doing these calculations, if you have had large capital gains and other tax preference items, which are listed below, you will need to calculate your Alternative Minimum Tax. This is an insidious tax that can devastatingly slip up on you if you are unaware.

Alternative Minimum Tax

The reduction of the taxable portion of a long-term capital gain from 50 to 40 percent was a step in the right direction by Congress. But there was a blockbuster in this legislation if your tax liability was reduced because of proper deduction of items deemed to be "tax preferences" in the eyes of the legislators. One of the preference items is the 60 percent capital gains deduction. Others include the dividend exclusion, excess depreciation and accelerated cost recovery deductions, excess intangible drilling costs, and incentive stock options.

This law introduced a new idea of taxable income—Alternative Minimum Taxable Income (AMTI)—with computation of a "flat" tax, currently computed at 20 percent of AMTI. If the resulting tax exceeds tax computed in the usual way, then the excess is added to your tax bill.

A worksheet is included in the Appendix (Figure 4) for use in making preliminary calculations, and I strongly suggest that you consult your tax adviser if you have received substantial capital gains or have incurred significant other items of tax preference. If, for example, you have realized long-term capital gains of $70,000, then the 60 percent capital gains deduction of $42,000 exceeds the exemption of $40,000 for a married couple, and you may be headed for the new tax-shelter status symbol—Alternative Minimum Tax.

Benefits Derived from a Creative, Knowledgeable CPA

Do find yourself a creative, knowledgeable CPA who is truly dedicated to helping you reduce your taxes. If all your CPA does for you is tally up how much in taxes you owe on April 15, the IRS will do this without sending you a bill. You don't want a tax tallier. You want a person who conscientiously works for you to lower your tax liability, since your greatest single expense each year is probably your tax bill. An excellent CPA is invaluable, and his fees are deductible. Don't, however, shift to him the burden of deciding on the economics of a particular tax-favored investment, because that is not his role. I repeat, that is not his function in life. Your financial planner or broker has that obligation. Your CPA should only be concerned with the tax aspects of the investment to determine if it fits your needs and if he agrees with the tax opinion in the offering memorandum.

If you mistakenly place on your CPA the burden of determining the investment merits of a proposal, he may be tempted to say no, for he may feel that he is in a no-win position. If the investment turns out well, you will congratulate yourself, and if it does not, you may blame him; and he runs the risk of losing you as a client, which he does not want to do. If he says no, he will never be wrong. Of course, he will never be right either, and you will have condemned yourself to sending your dollars on that famous one-way trip to Washington. Start paying your CPA for helping you reduce your taxes by devoting time to your cause, and don't expect him to take the place of an experienced financial planner.

Summary

For that portion of your income that will be taxed in a 22 to 28 percent tax bracket, you should consider making investments that give you tax-sheltered income, such as registered limited partnerships that pay all cash for real estate, oil and gas, equipment to be leased, real estate investment trusts and mortgages.

If you are in the 28 to 42 percent bracket, you may want to consider registered limited partnerships that use leverage and invest in multi-family housing, office buildings, shopping centers, miniwarehouses, equipment for lease, and oil and gas income-producing properties.

If you are in the 42 percent bracket and above, you will have a wide variety of both registered and private placement instruments to choose from. You hit that level on a joint return at $62,450.* If you are not earning that amount at present, look around you diligently, as there are many exciting career opportunities that will bring you that amount of income and much more. You will find that if you search with an open mind, it is not hard to succeed, because there are so few people out there trying. As you will remember, we have learned that it is not how hard you work or how many hours, but that your rewards in life will always be in direct proportion to what you do, your ability to do it, and the difficulty of replacing you. And when you have reached those loftier income levels and are searching for the best tax-favored investment, seek out areas in which demand exceeds supply. Then look for investment packages that have been fairly structured so that if the investment is profitable you will make money. Seek out investments with general partners of unquestioned expertise, high integrity, substantial net worth, and an excellent past performance record. The latter may not always be possible, since the area of investment may be a new one. But if you persist in a spirit of serendipity, you should reap great rewards.

As you look for better ways to lower your tax burden, do not be foolhardy, but neither should you be obsessed by a fear of risk. Tax-advantaged investments will probably never be classified as "safe" investments, but a tax receipt is not a "safe" investment either. The probability of your receiving any income from your tax receipt is quite remote. Payment of taxes means a guaranteed loss, and investing in tax-favored investments and tax-sheltered investments does contain risk, but at least you have a fighting chance of turning some of your tax liabilities into assets.

Not only were tax-favored investments put on our law books by Congress to fill a social need, but by your reduction in the amount of taxes you send to Washington, you can hope to force the government to curtail some of its wasteful spending and leave more investment

* Refer to the Tax Addendum in the Appendix for possible tax changes.

dollars in the private sector to be used to create much-needed jobs and consumer products.

Tax-sheltered investments are not gimmicks or loopholes, as some politicians are fond of calling them at election time. The beneficiaries of these investments are you and me and your fellow Americans. You are financing areas of public need much more efficiently than can be done by the federal government. The performance record of free enterprise is far superior. Just look around you at government's dismal failures in public housing, energy, postal service, and Amtrak, to name only a few. Congress made conscious decisions to grant tax incentives for investments in key industries rather than through government subsidies or government-owned-and-operated companies. Tax incentives serve the nation's needs as well as your needs. Congress did not enact tax incentives for the benevolent purpose of reducing your tax bill. So when you invest in areas of great social need, you should feel patriotic, because you are providing venture capital that benefits the country and that you hope will increase your spendable income and your estate.

You should always keep in mind that, even though the characteristics of the various shelters vary greatly, they are all complex, involve risk, and are usually non-liquid. Even with the tax benefits you may receive, you can lose money as well as make it. Most tax shelters are far removed from the traditional investments such as stocks and bonds, and even if you are an experienced investor, you may find it hard to determine what is glitter and what is gold.

Search for the right tax-favored investment. Work with the knowledgeable pros with the hope of keeping some of your hard-earned dollars from taking that long one-way trip to Washington!

APPLICATION

1. Calculate your anticipated taxable income for this year. The amount is: _____

2. What is your tax bracket before shelter? _____

3. Do you have a knowledgeable and concerned financial planner or broker who can help you build a living estate? If your answer is no, what steps are you going to take to find one? _____

4. Do you have a creative, knowledgeable, and competent CPA who cares about your financial future? If not, what steps will you take this week to find one?_____

5. Would you be happier paying the taxes and not worrying about tax shelters? If your answer is no, what constructive steps will you take this year to reduce your taxes?

   1) _____

   2) _____

   3) _____

   4) _____

Chapter 11

Investing in Hard Cash and Hard Assets

There is no investment for all seasons, but there is an investment for every season. When inflation is increasing at an increasing rate, you may want to consider shifting some of your assets into tangibles and investment-quality collectibles. On the other hand, when inflation is increasing at a decreasing rate, some thought should be given to shifting more of your assets into cash and cash equivalents.

Regardless of where we are on the inflation cycle, you will need to have some of your funds in cash reserves for convenience, liquidity, staying power, and as an interest-earning storage place while you are waiting for the right investment opportunities. Where should these dollars that you want to hold in a "guaranteed" position be placed?

In an earlier chapter, you learned that there are only three things that you can do with a dollar—spend, loan, or own. You will always need to have some of your funds in a "loaned" position, but exactly how much should this be? There was a time when I taught that you should keep three months' expenses in cash reserves, but now I suggest that you should keep as much of your funds in a guaranteed position as it takes to give you peace of mind, for peace of mind is a good investment. Your peace of mind may require that you keep idle a certain amount of what I call "patting money," money that you can mull over and pat like a security blanket. If that is the case, by all means keep it there, for I will never try to disturb your peace of mind. I must warn you, however, that I will try to educate you to such a point that you won't have any peace of mind if you leave too much of your money idle. Determine how much you need to give you peace of mind and place those funds into a "loaned" position, knowing full well that they may be working for someone else harder than they do for you and that they are "guaranteed" to lose some of their value to inflation and taxation. In this chapter we will cover the various ways that you may want to consider "loaning" your money.

But again let me remind you not to confuse two very similar-sounding words that have vastly different meanings: "stability" and "safety." Stability is the return of the same number of dollars plus interest at a point of time in the future. Safety is the return of the same amount of food, clothing, shelter, etc., at a point of time in the future. You can be stable but not be safe if your after-tax return does not keep up with inflation and your principal has less purchasing power when it is returned to you than when you placed it in the stable condition.

Investment Options for Your "Guaranteed" Dollars

In my opinion, there are only three basic choices for the placement of most of your "guaranteed" dollars. However, we will also examine a number of other choices that are available to you. The three that should take care of most of your needs for liquidity and staying power are checking accounts, money market mutual funds, and money market accounts at your financial institution.

BANK AND SAVINGS AND LOAN
CHECKING ACCOUNTS

A very important consideration in your plan to become financially independent is the selection of the right banker, for he can play a vital role in the accomplishment of your plan. Take the time and effort to select and establish a close relationship with a banker who is knowledgeable and creative and whose institution has sufficient assets to finance any bankable project you may want to undertake. Then open your checking account with him. As your net worth grows, you may also want to establish a close relationship with another bank, as this will give you two sources for bank loans if necessary.

You will always need to have one or more checking accounts at a bank or savings and loan to be used for convenience and for ease of recordkeeping. Keep a sufficient amount on deposit to enable you to write a check whenever you choose, since feeling "poor" is not emotionally satisfying and does not contribute to the necessary positive mental attitude that you must have to win the money game. However, do not keep your balance too large. I remember one woman who came to my office for counseling who had $159,000 in her checking account. When I asked her if she had a reason for keeping this amount there, she said, "Well, I've been thinking of taking a little trip." I suppressed the desire to ask her which planet was her desired destination!

As financial institutions have become more and more deregulated, various types of checking accounts that pay interest have also become available. The one you should choose will depend upon the amount you have to place into the account and the number of checks you will need to write on that account on a monthly basis.

MONEY MARKET MUTUAL FUNDS

You have already been introduced to money market mutual funds in Chapter 5. Briefly, these funds are invested in cash and cash equivalents. There is no cost to put money into these accounts, it compounds daily, your rate of return will usually be comparable to that on a million-dollar certificate of deposit, you can write a check for $500 or more (some funds less), and you draw interest while your check is clearing. Regular money market funds are invested in large-denomination short-term money market instruments issued by the Treasury, government agencies, banks, and corporations. There are also some money market mutual funds that invest 100 percent of their assets in Treasury, federal agency obligations, or repurchase agreements backed by them. Their yield is generally ½ to 1 percent less, and some are exempt from state and local taxes.

You will probably need at least two money market mutual fund accounts. One should be used as a depository for the liquid funds you need or the funds you are waiting to invest. You should also have another one that is part of a family of mutual funds that has an aggressive growth stock fund that you would like to have some of your funds invested in when the market timing is right. You may also want to have others for your bookkeeping convenience.

MONEY MARKET CHECKING ACCOUNTS

If having the gold seal of the Federal Deposit Insurance Corporation or Federal Savings and Loan Insurance Corporation is important to you, you may want to consider money market accounts at your bank or savings and loan institution. These usually pay you a slightly smaller rate of return than money market mutual funds, but your peace of mind may be worth the difference. Most of these accounts offer unrestricted check-writing privileges.

JUMBO CERTIFICATES OF DEPOSIT
($100,000 AND UP)

Offered by most banks and savings and loans, these certificates are negotiable paper specifying a fixed rate of interest for a fixed number of days, usually seven days to one year. Your funds are tied up for the term of the certificate and cannot be withdrawn early without payment of a penalty.

INVESTMENT CERTIFICATES OF DEPOSIT
($500 OR MORE)

The term of these certificates range from 32 days to five years or more, and they carry the same restrictions as the larger certificates above.

MONEY MARKET SAVINGS ACCOUNTS

Checks are issued on this type of savings account, but debit activity is limited. My bank allows up to four debits per month; and because of this restriction, the rate is 1 percent greater than for a money market checking account that offers unrestricted check-writing privileges.

COMMERCIAL PAPER ($50,000 AND UP)

These are unsecured promissory notes issued by large corporations to help finance current operations and maintain liquidity levels. These have maturity dates of 30 to 270 days and offer rates today from ¾ to ⅘ percent higher than the money market savings accounts.

BANKERS ACCEPTANCES

These are bills of exchange or time drafts drawn on and accepted by a commercial bank. They are used internationally and within the U.S. to finance the shipment and storage of goods. These vary in maturities up to 180 days. Interest is received at maturity and reflects the difference between the discounted price and the face amount. They are backed by the bank.

REPURCHASE AGREEMENTS (REPOS)

The purchaser of a repo has an interest in a specific U.S. government security held by the bank, with an obligation by the bank to repay the amount invested plus interest. The units are $100,000, with increments of $1,000 thereafter, and maturities are from one to 90 days. Payment of interest is at maturity, and they are backed by U.S. government securities held by the bank.

In addition to all of the above, my bank also offers U.S. Treasury bills, U.S. Treasury notes and bonds, federal agency securities, tax-exempt notes, bonds and bond funds, and they handle buying and selling of foreign currency.

Federal Government Obligations

The federal government also offers you numerous possibilities for your "guaranteed" dollars, including savings bonds, Treasury bills, Treasury notes, Treasury bonds, and various federal agency obligations. All of these (with the exception of some federal agency obligations) are guaranteed by the federal government.

TREASURY BILLS

Treasury bills have either three-or six-month maturities, and the minimum denomination is $10,000, with $5,000 increments thereafter. Bills are issued in original maturities of 13, 26, and 52 weeks. The first two are auctioned weekly, while the 52-week bill is auctioned every 28 days. A simple way to purchase them, for a small fee, is through a stockbroker or a bank. They are issued on a discount basis under competitive bidding, with the face amount payable at maturity. The investment return on bills is the difference between the cost and the face amount. Bills may be sold prior to maturity at a competitive market rate, which can result in a yield greater or less than the original acquisition rate. The yield on bills, like other short-term money market instruments, can fluctuate greatly.

TREASURY NOTES

Treasury notes have a fixed maturity from one to ten years and bear interest payable semiannually at fixed rates. They are available in minimum amounts of $1,000 if the maturities are four years or longer and $5,000 if the original maturity is shorter than four years. Selected notes are auctioned competitively through the Federal Reserve System on a periodic basis. Buyers can subscribe through a commercial bank or broker, and yields are determined by the acquisition price. These notes may be sold prior to maturity at the current market rate and may result in a yield greater or less than the original acquisition rate. Yields on Treasury notes generally are lower than their corporate counterparts because of the excellent marketability and credit rating of government securities.

TREASURY BONDS

Treasury bonds have a fixed maturity of ten to thirty years and are the long-term counterpart of Treasury notes. Yields on Treasury bonds, because they are of longer maturity, are sometimes higher than on Treasury notes, if we assume a "normal" positively sloped yield curve.

FEDERAL AGENCY SECURITIES

These are obligations of various U.S. government agencies such as the Federal Farm Credit Bank (FFCB), the Federal Home Loan Bank (FHLB), the Government National Mortgage Association (GNMA), and others. The Federal National Mortgage Association (FNMA), which also issues obligations, is a private corporation. FHLB's and FNMA's have minimums of $10,000, with increments of $5,000 thereafter, whereas FFCB's have a minimum of $5,000 with increments of $5,000 thereafter. Their maturities vary, and interest is paid semi-annually or at maturity, depending on the issue.

You are probably most familiar with the term "Ginnie Mae." These are mortgage-backed securities guaranteed by the Government National Mortgage Association. Ginnie Maes offer a number of special attractions, but one in particular is that they pay a fixed return that is often higher than the return paid on a long-term government bond.

Probably the main reason Ginnie Maes aren't better known is that when the certificates first appeared in 1970, the minimum unit that you could buy from most brokers was $100,000. Consequently, the buyers were banks, insurance companies, pension funds, and other institutions. Soon thereafter, the minimum purchase was cut back to $25,000. Since then, at least one brokerage firm has created a unit trust that allows individuals to invest in Ginnie Maes for as little as $10,000.

Ginnie Mae pass-throughs were hatched during the credit crunch of 1969–70, when mortgage money was tight. The Government National Mortgage Association (GNMA), established by an act of Congress, said, in effect, to savings and loan associations, banks, and mortgage bankers, "When you have closed enough mortgages, collect them into a pool, then issue certificates backed by the mortgages to raise cash so you can loan out more mortgage money. We'll guarantee the pool, so investors will buy the certificates without worry." The packager of the mortgage pool then "passes through" the mortgage payments he receives to certificate holders.

Why should you buy a Ginnie Mae pass-through instead of a corporate bond? Well, it does give you a way of spreading a portion of your money into mortgages without any of the worries of collecting payments, defaults, or bookkeeping. Full payments, on time, are "backed by the full faith and credit of the United States Government," and no corporate bond can make that statement. Bonds can be called back by the issuer, some within five years of issue date, and you would lose the high interest return you were counting on. Ginnie Mae certificates usually assure their rates for twelve years.

But perhaps most important, you are buying a mortgage, and the pool sponsor sends you a monthly check. Part of the payment represents interest and part return of your principal. (The principal portion, since it is a return of your capital, is not taxed as income.) Of course, you have to wait until a bond matures before your principal is returned. This feature may be of special value to you if you are retired and need a monthly check. If you do not need to use the earnings for monthly expenses, you can reinvest them. The effect of monthly compounding is a return higher than that of a bond that pays the same return but sends you interest checks only twice a year.

A number of firms make a secondary market in Ginnie Maes to avoid liquidity problems. There is the risk, however, that interest rates may go up. Therefore, since a prospective buyer can get a higher return if he buys a new pass-through instead of yours, your certificate will bring a lower figure than you paid for it. If the interest rate goes down, the reverse occurs and your pass-through can probably be sold for more than you paid for it.

MUTUAL FUNDS INVESTING IN GOVERNMENT SECURITIES

If you are interested in having some of your funds invested in federal government obligations, the best way to do so, in my opinion, is to use a mutual fund that invests in these instruments. In this way, through pooling of your funds with others, you obtain professional management, diversification, increased return through the fund's sale of call options, greater stability through hedging by sales of financial futures and purchases of options on financial futures. In addition, though most government securities pay interest semiannually, by using the funds you may receive your distributions on a monthly basis. You also have greater liquidity, for you can easily redeem your shares at current net asset value through your broker or directly from the fund. You will also find the funds to be more convenient, since you won't need to travel or write to a Federal Reserve Bank to buy or redeem your government securities. You also do not have to take your government securities certificates to your safe-deposit box to store them for security or maintain records of their maturity dates. If you would like to have checks of a specified amount sent to you monthly or quarterly, you may arrange for a systematic withdrawal program. If the amount of the withdrawal is higher than the interest the securities are earning, you will be using some of your principal and if it is less, you will be reinvesting for compounding. If your government securities fund is part of a family of mutual funds, you also have the privilege of exchanging your shares for shares of other funds in the family. And if you want to add to your shares systematically, you can establish a bank draft so that money is withdrawn automatically from your checking account and invested in the fund. With a mutual fund, almost any combination of financial objectives can be conveniently accomplished without the necessity of your becoming a specialist in government securities.

SERIES EE BONDS

In addition to the above, if you desire to have the interest you receive deferred, or would like to make small gifts of government bonds with interest deferred, you may want to look at Series EE bonds. These bonds are issued on a discount basis, which of course means that you pay less than their face value, and their value gradually increases with time. The difference between what you paid and what you receive at maturity or redemption is your interest.

Some of the characteristics of these bonds are: 1) If you hold them for five years or longer you earn market-based interest with a guaranteed minimum; 2) interest is exempt from state and local income and personal property taxes; 3) taxes are deferred until you cash them in; 4) they can be exchanged for current-income HH bonds with continuation of tax deferral on accrued interest; 5) they range in denomination from $50 up to $10,000 and in purchase price from $25 up to $5,000; 6) they cannot be transferred, sold, or used for collateral; 7) the annual limitation is $30,000 face amount ($15,000 issue price); 8) if cashed before being held five years, EE bonds earn 5.5 percent, compounded semiannually, after one year, rising 0.25 percent each six months to the minimum guaranteed five-year yield of 7.5 percent; 9) they are eligible for exchange to Series HH bonds six months after issue, though the current redemption value must be $500 or more. Owners who have deferred reporting, for federal tax purposes, the interest as it accrued on the securities exchanged, can defer reporting to the tax year in which the HH bonds received in exchange are redeemed, or reach maturity.

SERIES HH BONDS

If you have held Series EE bonds for a long time, have deferred the payment of taxes on the interest but now want current income, you may want to consider exchanging them for Series HH bonds. The payment of taxes on the accrued interest will still be deferred; however, current interest on HH bonds is taxable as it is paid. HH bonds are issued in denominations of $500, $1,000, $5,000, and $10,000; and interest is paid every six months.

Some other characteristics of the HH bonds are: 1) Even though interest is subject to federal income tax, it will not be subject to state and local income tax; 2) in addition to the EE bonds, E bonds and savings notes can also be exchanged for HH bonds. Series H bonds cannot be exchanged and should be redeemed as they reach final maturity; 3) interest on HH bonds issued on or after November 1, 1982, is paid semiannually by Treasury check at a rate of 7.5 percent per annum, and they mature ten years after purchase; 4) most of the other characteristics that are true of the Series EE bonds also apply to Series HH bonds.

SHOULD YOU INVEST IN
FEDERAL GOVERNMENT INSTRUMENTS?

Will you win the money game by buying any of the government credit instruments that we have just discussed? Analyze the possibilities rationally and then formulate your answer. Inflation, which reduces the purchasing power of your money, has the effect of lessening the repayment of your loan. Would you seriously protest if you loaned the government $10,000 and it returned $5,000 to you? That is exactly what will happen to you if the rate of inflation is 7 percent over any ten-year period that you hold a government bond.

Beginning with the Roosevelt administration, the federal policy has been to manipulate interest rates in favor of the borrower; and the federal government, of course, has been chief among the borrowers. If you analyze the relation of interest rates to inflation, you will find that since 1940 the investor in Treasury bills and long-term government bonds in most of those years has lost purchasing power. Losses by investors in government securities constitute direct gains for

Washington, and as the purchasing power of your dollar declines, the government can pay you back in cheaper dollars.

Since 1940, the Federal Reserve has acquired billions of government obligations, paying for them with checks drawn on itself, thereby converting paper into primary reserve assets of our banking system. As the assets pass through our banking system, which operates on a fractional reserve basis, they are converted into money and credit.

When you lend money to the government, if your after-tax rate of return is less than the rate of inflation, you have set yourself up for the confiscation of your property. If your after-tax return is greater, you win.

Local Government Obligations—Municipal Bonds

Municipal bonds are issued by various local governments such as states, cities, various districts, and political subdivisions. Usually, municipal bonds have lower yields than government bonds because of one special feature: the interest paid on these municipal obligations is exempt from federal income tax and usually from state income tax if the owner of the bond is a taxpayer in the state that issued the bond.

Yields on municipal issues are determined by the current level of interest rates, the credit rating of the issuer, and the tax laws. Most municipal bonds are issued in serial form, some maturing each year for several years, with maturities as long as thirty years. Interest is usually paid semiannually; and municipals, like other bonds, can be sold prior to maturity in the secondary market at prevailing market rates.

There has been talk from time to time about Congress eliminating the tax-exempt privilege inherent in municipal bonds, but if such a change were legislated, it should not affect those bonds issued prior to the legislation, and their scarcity could easily enhance their value. Since federal taxation of state and municipal bonds does require an amendment to the Constitution ratified by two-thirds of the states, heavily indebted states are not likely to look favorably on such an amendment.

Another important feature of municipal bonds has been their relative stability. Next to U.S. government bonds, municipal bonds have been the "safest" of all such securities, with the exception of some cities that did not practice prudent fiscal policies and some utility districts of Washington Public Power.

TYPES OF MUNICIPAL BONDS

There are three main types of municipal bonds:

1. *Full faith and credit bonds* of a state or political subdivision of the state have the full taxing power of the issuing local government available to pay both the principal and interest.

2. *Special tax bonds* have a designated tax (gasoline, liquor, cigarettes, etc.) specifically pledged to pay the principal and interest.

3. *Revenue bonds* are backed by the earnings generated in a particular facility and do not have the taxing power of a local government upon which to draw. Many of these bonds are of a very high quality and are often rated equal to or higher than some bonds backed by taxes.

HOW BONDS ARE RATED

If you are going to purchase bonds yourself, it is essential that you learn about the quality ratings assigned to the bond issuers. If you are letting professionals select the bonds for you, this knowledge will still be helpful as you study their portfolios.

Bonds are rated by both Moody's Investor Service and Standard & Poor's on the basis of their relative investment qualities. The following definitions for the major rating of municipal bonds are provided by Standard & Poor's (similar definitions apply to corporate bond ratings):

AAA. Prime or highest-grade obligations, possessing the ultimate degree of protection of principal and interest.

AA. High-grade obligations, differing from AAA issues only to a small degree.

A. Upper-medium-grade bonds with considerable investment strength, but not entirely free from adverse effects of changes in economic conditions.

BBB. Medium-grade category bonds on the borderline between definitely sound obligations and those in which the speculative element begins to predominate. These bonds have adequate asset coverage and normally are protected by satisfactory revenues. This category is the lowest that qualifies for commercial bank investment.

BB. Lower-medium-grade, possessing only minor investment characteristics.

B. Speculative, with payment of interest not assured under difficult economic conditions.

HOW TO BUY MUNICIPAL BONDS

If tax-free income fits your financial plans, you can select the bonds yourself. You will find a wide variety of them are available for your consideration. However, if you do not have the required expertise, do not have the time to supervise and watch maturity dates, or sufficient funds to diversify, you may want to consider investing in a municipal bond trust or a municipal bond fund.

MUNICIPAL BOND TRUSTS

Under this arrangement, professionals would select the bonds and place them in a bond trust. You can choose trusts that invest in short-term, intermediate, or long-term maturities. You can also select trusts where all the bonds are insured, which guarantees that you will receive on-time payments of your interest and your principal upon maturity. The bonds in the trust may have staggered maturity dates, so that you will receive returns of principal over a span of years. Since the portfolio is not managed once the bonds are purchased and placed in the trust, there will be no management fee. The trust will be self-liquidating as the bonds mature. However, the sponsor usually makes a market for the trust units in the event you desire to redeem your units before the bonds mature.

MUNICIPAL BOND FUNDS

A municipal bond fund functions like a stock mutual fund except it is invested in municipal bonds. Again, you have professional management that selects your bonds, but in these funds you do have a management fee because the management does buy and sell the bonds in an effort to give you a greater yield or greater safety of your principal. As with a regular mutual fund, you may redeem your shares at net asset value, reinvest your distributions, or accept them in cash.

MUNICIPAL BONDS AND TAX EQUIVALENTS

In evaluating whether or not you should invest in municipal bonds, you will find it helpful to consider what another investment with a taxable yield would have to yield to be equivalent to the tax-free yield on the municipal bond. The equivalent yield table on p. 305 illustrates the benefits of tax-exempt income versus taxable income. Locate your income tax bracket (after deductions and after exemptions) and read across to see the taxable yield needed to match the tax-free return.

As you will note from the above table, in a 45 percent tax bracket a yield of 7 percent would be equivalent to receiving 12.73 percent if it were taxable, and in a 50 percent bracket it would of course be equivalent to 14 percent.

SHOULD YOU INVEST IN MUNICIPAL BONDS?

When I am asked this question, my answer is "It depends on what you are going to do with the money if you do not invest in municipal bonds and what the rate of inflation will be in the future." If you are planning to put your funds into a savings account or a certificate of deposit and you are in a relatively high tax bracket, then the tax-free feature of municipal bonds may provide you with a higher after-tax yield. But you must consider whether you can make other investments with higher current yields plus higher total return in the future that will leave you with more keepable income after taxes. It is not how much taxes you don't pay but how much you have left after taxes over a period of time that will determine what was the best investment. You can also receive tax-sheltered income from all-cash real estate limited partnerships, plus have the potential for appreciation, which could bring you a higher total after-tax return.

I should warn you that you should be careful about borrowing money if you own or are planning to buy municipal bonds. The interest you pay on money borrowed to make investments that pay you tax-free income is not deductible. If your investment in tax-exempt bonds is substantial (more than 2 percent of your portfolio), the IRS may examine all of your investments to determine whether there is "sufficient direct relationship" between your other borrowing and your investment in tax-exempt bonds.

1985 TAXABLE EQUIVALENT YIELD TABLE

| Taxable Income | | FEDERAL TAX BRACKET | Tax-Exempt Yield Equivalents | | | | | | | | |
SINGLE RETURN	JOINT RETURN		7.00%	7.25%	7.50%	7.75%	8.00%	8.25%	8.50%	8.75%	9.00%
$24,460–29,970	$ 31,120–36,630	28%	9.72	10.07	10.42	10.76	11.11	11.46	11.81	12.16	12.50
		30	10.00	10.36	10.71	11.07	11.43	11.79	12.14	12.50	12.86
	36,630–47,670	33	10.45	10.82	11.19	11.57	11.94	12.31	12.69	13.06	13.43
29,970–35,490		34	10.61	10.98	11.36	11.74	12.12	12.50	12.88	13.26	13.64
35,490–43,190	47,670–62,450	38	11.29	11.69	12.10	12.50	12.90	13.31	13.71	14.11	14.52
43,190–57,550	62,450–89,090	42	12.07	12.50	12.93	13.36	13.79	14.22	14.66	15.09	15.52
	89,090–113,860	45	12.73	13.18	13.64	14.09	14.55	15.00	15.45	15.91	16.36
57,550–85,130		48	13.46	13.94	14.42	14.90	15.38	15.87	16.35	16.83	17.31
	113,860–169,020	49	13.73	14.22	14.71	15.20	15.69	16.18	16.67	17.16	17.65
Over $85,130	Over $169,020	50	14.00	14.50	15.00	15.50	16.00	16.50	17.00	17.50	18.00

Corporate Bonds

Another way you can lend your money is through the purchase of corporate bonds. Until recently, there have been only two main categories of bonds: straight bonds (or debentures) and convertible bonds. Straight corporate bonds, like most government and municipal bonds, pay semiannual interest to maturity, whereupon you receive the principal amount. Convertible bonds offer one additional feature. They can be exchanged, at any time you wish, for a fixed number of shares of the issuing company's common stock. Therefore, convertibles have dual characteristics of fixed-income securities (like any other bonds) and equity securities that may appreciate (or depreciate) in accordance with the price movement of the company's common stock. If a convertible bond trades at a higher price than it would as a straight bond for the same company, the same maturity, and so on, it is usually considered an equity security rather than a bond.

Corporate bonds are usually sold in minimum amounts of $1,000, although there are some $500 bonds. The yield is subject to the current level of interest rates, the maturity, and the credit standing of the issuer. Because no corporation is considered to be as creditworthy as the federal government, corporate bonds generally pay a slightly higher return (usually ½ percent to 2 percent higher) than comparable government bonds. Obviously, when any two corporations are compared, one will be riskier and therefore will have to pay more to borrow money.

Bonds are issued in registered form with "interest mailed to holder." Some older bonds may be in a bearer form with coupons to be clipped and mailed to a paying agent through the bearer's bank. Many bonds permit the issuing corporation to redeem them early, usually for a price slightly higher than the maturity value. This call privilege gives the borrower an element of protection, in that he can call in his bonds and issue new ones at a lower interest rate if rates have declined since the time the original bonds were issued. Actually, only bonds trading at a premium over par (indicating that interest yields are now lower than they were at time of issue) are likely to be called. Like other bonds, corporates can be sold prior to maturity at prevailing market rates. Bear in mind, however, that if they have a call privilege, this privilege lies only with the issuer and not with you.

Because bonds represent a fixed stream of income, their market value will fall when the general interest rate rises, and their market value will rise when the interest falls. Although most bonds are issued at par of $1,000 and may sell there or at a premium or discount on the day they are issued and will be redeemed at par on the day of maturity, their market value wanders considerably during the interim.

CORPORATE BOND FUNDS

If you have limited funds, it will be difficult for you to buy and sell small quantities of bonds because of the spread between "bid" and "asked" prices in these small purchases. It is also difficult to diversify adequately. For this reason, if you are considering investing in bonds, you may want to use professionally managed corporate bond funds. They offer a savings in the time and talent required to judge the merits of individual issues, their ratings, their maturities, their coupon rates, and to determine how much to invest in each issue. They also assist in clipping coupons, watching for called bonds, safekeeping securities, and year-end accounting. You have a wide variety of corporate bond funds from which to choose, and many of them are a part of a family of mutual funds, making it possible for you to move from the bond fund to the equity funds and back without commission.

ZERO-COUPON CORPORATE BONDS

Zero-coupon bonds have attracted attention for the past few years. One of the reasons is because certain brokerage houses have given them such cute names as Tigers, which stands for Treasury Interest Guaranteed Receipt, and CATS, which stands for Certificate Accrual Treasury Securities.

What is a zero-coupon corporate bond? It is a bond issued at a discount, just like the Series EE bonds we discussed earlier. However, instead of the interest compounding tax-deferred, it is taxable in the year it is credited to the bond. With zeros you will obtain a specified investment rate over the life of the bond and you will know exactly the amount that will be available at maturity. The prices you receive for a zero if you need to cash it in early are very volatile because of their unique mathematics where the entire income is discounted from a future date. They are typically sold in denominations of $5,000 (maturity value) or integral multiples thereof.

An example of a "zero" would be as follows:

MATURITY DATE	MATURITY VALUE	PRICE (AS A % OF MATURITY VALUE)	DOLLAR PRICE	INTEREST RATE
1998	$100,000	26.132	$26,132	10%

Though I believe there are much better ways to finance college costs, one way that you can consider is using zero-coupon bonds. If you want to accumulate $20,000 for the future education of, say, your six-year-old child, you might buy about $6,000 worth of zeros and stagger their maturity dates so they will mature when the child is age 18, 19, 20, etc. The bonds could be bought in your child's name, and each year the child would report the interest income; but, in most cases, his or her personal exemption should eliminate or lower any tax. If your child has more than the personal exemption allowed, taxes may be due, but probably at relatively low rates. Not only can such a purchase be an income-shifting device, but it can also remove property from your estate. If you purchase the bonds in custodian form, you should not name yourself as custodian. If you die while your child is a minor, the value of the bond would be included in your estate. Also, if income from the bond is used to satisfy your obligation as a parent to support your child, the income will be taxed to you.

Should you invest in zero-coupon corporate bonds or those that are composed of stripped treasuries? Probably not. They are fully taxable, volatile, and in the corporates you have a situation where present management is, in reality, postponing some of its present burdens to future management. You also have the risk that the corporation may fall on hard times before the maturity date.

Zero-coupon municipal bonds have all the same characteristics of zero-coupon corporate bonds but have the advantage of the accrued interest not being taxable. Of course, they have a lower yield. Some of them accrue interest for a certain number of years and then start paying interest for a number of years before maturing, while others just accrue interest until maturity.

BOND RATINGS

Moody's and Standard & Poor's rate corporate bonds as well as municipal bonds. Their ratings indicate their opinion of the company's ability to meet its principal and interest payments under adverse economic conditions. Two measures of this ability are 1) the amount by which earnings exceed interest payments over a period of years and 2) the amount of stock equity in a corporation in relation to borrowed funds.

If these rating services rate a bond in one of the top four categories, the bond is considered to be of investment-grade quality. Bonds that merit the top rating have a very low speculative element. By the fifth rating, it is significant, and by the seventh, it predominates.

SHOULD YOU BUY BONDS?

You can make as much money trading bonds as trading stocks, but in my opinion you have to be more agile and more knowledgeable. Buying a particular bond, throwing it into a drawer, and forgetting about it has not over the past thirty years been considered brilliant investing. In fact, it has been a very risky thing to do. You must watch your bonds as closely, or maybe more so, as your stock investments.

Because a bond has a guaranteed interest rate and a guarantee to return your principal at a point of time in the future, do not make the mistake of thinking that it is a riskless investment. There is nothing that is a riskless investment—and certainly not bonds. Your two chief risks are rising interest rates and rising inflation rates. If you own a bond that pays 8 percent and rates go to 16 percent, the amount someone will pay you for your bond, if the maturity date is many years away, can be cut in half. Of course, the opposite is true if you have a bond with a rate of 16 percent and interest rates go to 8 percent.

The devastation that inflation can bring to the purchasing power of your interest, to say nothing of what it can do to the purchasing power of your principal, is also a very real risk. As a general rule, long-term fixed-rate investments are not advisable as long as the economy is inflationary; and as we have seen in an earlier chapter, inflation shows no signs of ever going away. In the long run, your chances are usually greater "owning the thing that owns the thing," rather than being a lender. In the short run, on the other hand, excellent profits can be made trading bonds, and during periods of falling interest rates, holding bonds can be quite profitable. During the three-year period 1982 through 1984, high-grade corporate bonds increased in value 73 percent, S&P long-term government bonds increased in value by 71 percent, and S&P municipal bonds increased by 77 percent. However, during the ten-year period 1974 through 1983, S&P high-grade corporate bonds decreased in value by 39 percent. In fact, a loss would have been suffered in all of the thirty ten-year periods previous to 1983 going back to 1945. The average loss for all these periods was 24.94 percent.

Traveler's Checks

How would you like to lend a large, well-known company $2,000 for two months, earn no interest on the loan, and in addition pay the company $40 for the privilege of lending it your money? No? This is what happens every time you buy traveler's checks. If you don't use all your checks, you have extended the loan, as you are encouraged to do. My purpose in pointing this out is not to discourage you from using traveler's checks when you go on a trip. I just want you to be constantly aware of the time use of your money.

Cash Surrender Value Life Insurance

Many people do not realize it, but when they purchase cash surrender value traditional whole-life insurance, they are really lending their money to the insurance company. They are, in effect, banking with a life insurance company by buying protection that contains a savings program. Of all the ways that you can "lend" money, this is perhaps the least rewarding. Although the policy may indicate earnings of 2½ percent or above on the cash reserve, if the policyholder dies, his family receives only the face amount of the policy, not the face amount plus the cash reserves, regardless of the amount of savings in the policy. Many people are under the impression that the face amount plus their "savings account" goes to their beneficiary. We will discuss this more fully in Chapter 13.

Single-Premium Deferred Annuities

If you were to say to me, "Venita, I have to have my money 'guaranteed,' yet I'm in a high tax bracket and don't want to pay taxes. Is there anything you can do for me?" I would tell you that perhaps you should take a look at a single-premium deferred annuity.

Single-premium deferred annuities are a different breed entirely from the old annuity contracts, and they can play a part in your "guaranteed" dollar investment program. With these annuities, income is accrued to your account tax deferred. For example, if you invest $10,000 in a single-premium deferred annuity that is earning 10 percent, at the end of the year your account will equal $11,000. Until you make a withdrawal from your account, no tax is due, and it compounds tax sheltered.

Single-premium deferred annuities offer 1) guaranteed principal; 2) interest guarantees; 3) tax deferral; 4) special tax treatment at retirement if annuitized (I do not recommend annuitizing); 5) tax-free exchange from one custodian to another; and 6) avoidance of probate, with its publicity, delays, and costs, with proceeds being paid to the beneficiary.

What is meant by annuitizing? It means that the insurance company with a fixed annuity enters into an agreement with you to guarantee to pay you a fixed monthly amount for the remainder of your life. If you are willing to accept a smaller monthly payout, another option you have is to provide for a joint beneficiary who will continue to receive a monthly income for the rest of his or her life in the event of your death. Another option is that a monthly check would be paid to your named beneficiary for a specific period of time, say ten years.

Some of these annuities charge an acquisition fee but make no charges for early withdrawals. Others do not charge an acquisition fee, but if you withdraw more than 10 percent in any one year during the first five years, they charge you a percentage on the amount exceeding the 10 percent. If you are considering lending your money to an insurance company through a single-premium deferred annuity, you will need to determine which type of investment program the company has and which will best fit your needs.

Equity-Based Variable Annuities

Instead of placing your funds in an annuity with guaranteed rates of return for fixed periods of time, you may want to consider variable annuities, where you can choose fixed dollars or equity dollar investments. This discussion could have also been placed in Chapter 5, since the choice you will most likely want to consider for your investment is an equity mutual fund.

Variable annuity funds are issued and backed by an insurance company, and most variable annuities will allow you to invest as small an amount as $1,500 initially, and $300 a year or $25 per investment thereafter ($300 in IRA's and $25 in 401 (k)'s or 403 (b)'s). The maximum age for starting a program is usually 85. The rates at which a program grows and the income it pays after annuitization depend on the investment results achieved by the underlying portfolios. But because the investing is being done by professional money managers, you have the opportunity for above average return during the accumulation period and rising monthly income payments after you annuitize, if you choose to do so.

One equity-based variable annuity program that we offer to our clients contains the following features: 1) you pay no sales charge; 2) four different investment choices plus a fixed account, so that you can create a portfolio to match your financial objective; 3) you can make a single purchase or invest on a periodic basis; 4) no current taxes are payable on the earnings, thus giving your account an opportunity to grow faster than if earnings were taxed each year; 5) you can alter the mix of your investments without charge and without tax consequences; 6) your account is liquid if you need your funds (may be penalties); 7) if you should die during your accumulation phase, your beneficiary will receive the total amount of your contributions, less any withdrawals you have made or the value of your account, whichever is greater; and 8) your beneficiaries receive death benefits free of probate costs and delays.

Tax deferral can make an enormous difference in your net results. Below is a table comparing a $50,000 investment yielding 8 percent, 10 percent, and 12 percent compounded quarterly for a person in a 50 percent marginal tax bracket with and without tax deferral:

$50,000 INVESTMENT	TERM	TAX STATUS	8%	10%	12%
(50% bracket)	5 years	Taxed	$ 61,101	$ 64,101	$67,343
		Tax-deferred	74,297	81,931	90,306
	10 years	Taxed	74,443	82,181	90,701
		Tax-deferred	110,402	134,253	163,102
	15 years	Taxed	90,835	105,359	122,161
		Tax-deferred	164,052	219,989	294,580
	20 years	Taxed	110,836	135,074	164,533
		Tax-deferred	243,772	360,478	532,045

As you can see, in five years a tax-deferred investment compounding at 10 percent would be worth $81,931, nearly $18,000 more than the $64,101 value of the same investment whose earnings were taxed. At the end of ten years, the difference is more than $52,000, and after twenty years it is over $225,000.

If you should decide to annuitize, you have your choice of a fixed annuity or a variable annuity based on the value of your underlying investments. Of course you will have to pay some taxes, but at that time you may be in a lower tax bracket. The smallest amount you can annuitize is $5,000, or $50 monthly. If your investment is worth under $5,000, a lump-sum payment will be made to settle the contract. Once you have annuitized, the taxes you pay will depend on the kind of contract you have. If it is a qualified contract—an IRA or other retirement plan—you will pay ordinary income taxes on the money you receive each year. If it is an individual contract, a certain percentage of every annuity payment will be a non-taxable return of principal. You will pay ordinary income taxes on the balance.

If you withdraw any money during the accumulation period, taxes will depend on when and how much you withdraw, on whether or not the money you deposited was originally tax deferred (as in an IRA or other retirement program), and on your tax bracket. If you take a lump sum distribution, you may be eligible for ten-year forward averaging to minimize taxes. All withdrawals from qualified retirement plans are generally taxed as ordinary income. For non-qualified individual programs, the IRS considers that withdrawals prior to annuitization come first from earnings, then from principal. Earnings are taxed as ordinary income, and principal (if any is withdrawn) is not taxed.

You may make withdrawals prior to annuitizing and are allowed to withdraw up to 10 percent of your investment that has been in your account for longer than one year without a redemption charge. If you withdraw more than 10 percent in a single year, you must pay a 5 percent charge on the amount that exceeds 10 percent. Any amount that has been in your account more than seven years can be withdrawn whenever you choose without charge by the insurance company. Your withdrawal must be at least $500 and you must still have a balance in the account of at least $500. There is also an additional penalty of 5 percent imposed by the IRS for any withdrawals before age 59½, which is to prevent you from using an annuity merely to defer taxable income from the IRS instead of using the annuity as a true retirement vehicle.

SHOULD YOU EVER ANNUITIZE A FIXED ANNUITY?

In my opinion, the answer is no. Once you annuitize an annuity, you are locked in to that monthly amount from that time on, so that if inflation continues and you are dependent on this annuity for your essentials, you will have to lower your standard of living every day for as long as you live. If you must have your money guaranteed for your peace of mind, and you don't want to pay taxes as you go along, then go ahead and use a deferred annuity, but don't annuitize it.

Don't accept an annuity if you are retiring from your company, if it can possibly be avoided, for the same reasons I have given above. Petition your company for a lump sum and do an IRA rollover or ten-year forward averaging.

Mortgages as an Investment

In recent years, especially as mortgage interest rates have escalated, many people have been lending their money by carrying part or all of the mortgage when they sell their homes or other real estate. For some people, such "creative financing" has been the only way they could sell their homes. So-called creative financing, as we discussed earlier, may be great if you are the borrower, but usually that is not the case if you are the lender. The rates are frozen throughout the life of the mortgage, and the mortgage is a non-liquid instrument except when sold at a considerable discount. If during a period of inflation you carry the mortgage after selling your real estate, your wealth may be transferred to the person who bought your real estate.

If you are selling a piece of property and are convinced that the only way you can get the extra few thousand you desire for it is to take a second lien for that amount, go ahead and do so. If you collect on the loan, fine. If you do not, don't worry, for you could not have sold it for the full amount you desired anyway. I have done this when selling my home on two occasions and have received payment on both the second liens ahead of schedule and for the full amount.

Should You Ever Borrow Money?

Should you ever consider reversing the "lending" process and become instead a borrower? Of course you should, if you can put the money to work so that your after-tax cost is less than the amount you will earn on the investment you made with the loan. Never borrow for essentials or luxuries. Borrow money only to invest or to leave in place an investment you already have that is doing a good job for you. In fact, in these days of high taxes, it is difficult to accumulate a large estate without borrowing money. Remember Bernard Baruch's "OPM"—other people's money? Another well-known real estate tycoon said the three most important factors in his real estate acquisitions were "terms, terms, terms." Terms in real estate purchases usually mean little or no down payment and a big, big mortgage—borrowing from those who want "guarantees" and are willing to lend.

Where, when, and how should you borrow money? If you have collateral in the form of publicly traded stocks, your least expensive source of loans in normal times will usually be your own bank. You should go to the collateral loan department (never to the consumer loan department unless you lack collateral).

Assume that you want to buy an automobile. You own 100 shares of an excellent stock for which you paid $50 a share, and it is now trading at $100 with excellent growth potential for the future. Why kill the goose that is laying the golden egg, and why realize a $5,000 capital gain, 40 percent of which will be taxable?* Take your stock to your banker and pledge it as collateral. You will be required to leave the stock certificate with him and sign a stock power that allows him to sell the stock and keep the amount you owe to him if you do not repay or renew the loan when it becomes due. Collateral loans are usually made for 90 days or 180 days, and you may pay on the principal in the interim, but you are not usually required to do so.

SAVINGS ACCOUNTS AND CERTIFICATES OF DEPOSIT AS COLLATERAL

I often find that a person I am counseling proudly tells me that he has found an inexpensive source for a loan by pledging his savings account as collateral. If you need funds and have them in a savings account, go ahead and draw them out and use them. The savings institution is probably paying you 2 percent less than it is charging you; therefore you are 2 percent in the hole by borrowing your own money.

If your funds are in a certificate of deposit and you are near its maturity date, it may very well pay you to use it for collateral and borrow the money until the maturity date. Calculate your cost both ways and choose the one that works to your advantage. If your certificate of deposit or savings account is at a bank, you can usually borrow up to 100 percent. If it is in a savings and loan, you can usually borrow up to 90 percent.

BORROWING FROM CREDIT UNIONS

Many people who belong to credit unions through their employers think that their credit union offers the least expensive way to borrow money. You should not automatically assume that this is so, because if you have acceptable collateral, you may be able to borrow at a lower cost from your banker. Whenever you borrow money, always check all possible sources and compare the cost of borrowing.

* Refer to the Tax Addendum in the Appendix for possible tax changes.

Build up your collateral and you will always have the wherewithal for borrowing money that you can put to work. You may want to consider, if you have the temperament for it, putting your dollars to work 1.7 times, since 70 percent is what your banker will usually lend you if you have publicly held stock for collateral.

INTEREST IS DEDUCTIBLE

As we have already learned, interest is deductible on your income tax return with certain limitations. Assume you borrow at 12 percent and you are in the 42 percent tax bracket; your net costs after taxes will be 6.96 percent. If you are in the 50 percent bracket, your net cost is 6 percent. Can you invest this money so that your after-tax return will be greater than your after-tax cost? If so, rent the money. If not, your answer is obvious.

SERVICING THE LOAN

You will need sufficient funds or income to pay the interest on your loan when due. There are some investments that have a high after-tax yield that you can use to service your loan while you are enjoying equity buildup and appreciation.

BORROWING AGAINST CASH VALUE
OF AN INSURANCE POLICY

Many consider borrowing against insurance policies a low-cost source of loans. In my opinion, the only time you should borrow on your cash surrender value is when your health is so poor that you cannot pass a physical for a new policy. If you can pass a physical and obtain pure protection at a lower cost, do so, and when you have the new coverage, redeem the old policy. You will then have the cash you need without paying the insurance company to borrow "your own" money.

If your health is such that you cannot pass a physical, borrow the money out each year from your policy and put it to work advantageously. Let's assume that you can borrow the cash surrender value for 5½ percent. Technically, at the same time, the insurance company may be building cash reserves at 2½ percent. This is only a 3 percent spread; and, in addition, the interest can be deductible if you send a check for the interest to the insurance company each year.

In summary, should you ever put your dollars in a "loaned" position? Yes, for staying power, for a temporary place for your investment dollars, and when interest rates reach attractive heights. But you should rarely do so on a long-term basis. You should use fixed-income instruments when it is to your advantage to be out of equities, but do not complacently overstay.

What is your financial objective? To be able to retire in financial dignity? To have funds for your children's college education? Never send a fixed dollar to do a variable-dollar job.

On the other hand, should you ever do the reverse and borrow money? The answer is yes, if your return is greater than your after-tax cost and if you can sell your investment for more than you owe. Always be solvent. That means you own more than you owe.

When inflation is increasing at a decreasing rate, you will want to shift the emphasis of some of your investments to the guaranteed fixed return we have been discussing. But what if inflation is increasing at an increasing rate? Where should your emphasis be? You may want to look at the opposite end of the spectrum and consider investing some of your funds into hard assets.

Investing in Tangible Hard Assets and Collectibles

Hard assets and collectibles represent a very ancient form of investment. They can offer protection against the ravages of high inflation, economic uncertainty, and political unrest. There are a number of hard tangible assets that you should know about, the most important being rare silver and gold coins, uncirculated silver dollars, junk silver coins, gold and silver bullion, gold and silver bullion coins, diamonds, gemstones, rare stamps, and various "collectibles." In addition, there are mutual funds that invest in gold stocks and stocks of gold mining companies here and abroad.

What has been the past performance of these tangible assets in comparison to other financial assets over the past one-, five-, ten-, and fifteen-year periods? As you will note from the Salomon Brothers study on page 320, their rankings vary depending on which periods you are studying.

RARE NUMISMATIC COINS

Rare U.S. coins can be a way to preserve capital. They date back to 1793, were coined in gold and silver, and are in low supply, owing to the small number originally produced and the subsequent melting that has occurred. All U.S. coins minted from 1793 through 1964 are considered to be collectibles, since after 1964 the government significantly lowered the silver content in its minted coins. Before that time we had coins that were equal to their intrinsic bullion content, so the coins could be melted and the metal retrieved and sold on the open market.

Rare coins are a highly concentrated, portable store of wealth and are not subject to governmental regulation or exchange controls, and in the past they have been excluded when government confiscation of gold and silver has occurred. Over 75 percent of U.S. rare coins are held by long-term investors, a factor that should give underlying price stability. As you will note from the above table, U.S. rare coins have shown a 17.7 percent compounded growth rate over the past 15 years and they ranked second highest in performance of the 14 investment categories. Over the past ten years they have outperformed all the other investments listed above, appreciating by 20.4 percent. However, for the five-year period, which includes the market peak of 1980 and bottom of 1982, they appreciated only 0.1 percent.

A number of factors determine the value of a coin, including age, condition, date, type, metal content, its rarity,and its supply and demand. There are approximately 15 grades of excellence recognized by the American Numismatic Association, ranging from Proof, the mirrorlike finish of a coin that was manufactured by the mint and then carefully preserved from any nicks or scratches, all the way to the fifteenth grade, Good, which actually means "Very heavily worn with portions of lettering, date, and legends worn smooth. The date may be barely readable."

Rare coins are graded on a scale of MS-0 to MS-70, with the most active markets existing in the coins that are graded between MS-60 and MS-65. The higher a coin's grade, the more money a dealer can sell it for. As a result, dealers can be tempted to overgrade the coins they are trying to sell.

COMPOUNDED ANNUAL RATES OF RETURN

	15 YEARS	RANK	10 YEARS	RANK	5 YEARS	RANK	1 YEAR	RANK
Oil[a]	19.7%	1	8.0%	9	(5.4)%	12	(4.5)%	10
U.S Coins	17.7	2	20.4	1	0.1	9	11.5	4
Gold	15.5	3	6.9	13	(11.0)	14	(20.3)	14
Chinese Ceramics[b]	14.3	4	17.1	2	1.0	8	5.9	6
Stamps	14.1	5	14.5	3	0.1	10	(9.6)	11
Diamonds	10.4	6	9.5	7	1.2	7	0.0	9
Old Masters[b]	9.1	7	10.7	4	1.5	6	13.6	3
Treasury Bills	9.1	8	10.0	6	12.0	3	9.5	5
Bonds	8.7	9	9.3	8	13.2	2	42.9	1
Silver	8.7	10	3.5	14	(15.9)	15	(34.3)	15
Stocks	8.5	11	10.4	5	15.2	1	28.7	2
U.S. Farmland	8.5	12	6.9	12	(1.7)	11	(10.0)	12
Housing	8.2	13	7.9	10	4.3	5	2.5	8
CPI	7.1	14	7.3	11	6.7	4	3.7	7
Foreign Exchange	2.0	15	(0.6)	15	(7.9)	13	(11.3)	13

Inflation Scorecard (Number of Assets That Outperformed Inflation)

	15 YEARS	10 YEARS	5 YEARS	1 YEAR
Tangibles	10 out of 10	7 out of 10	0 out of 10	3 out of 10
● Collectibles	4 out of 4	4 out of 4	0 out of 4	3 out of 4
● Commodities	4 out of 4	2 out of 4	0 out of 4	0 out of 4
● Real Estate	2 out of 2	1 out of 2	0 out of 2	0 out of 2
Financials	3 out of 4	3 out of 4	3 out of 4	3 out of 4

[a] Reflects revision in oil index.
[b] Source: Sotheby's.
Note: All returns are for the period ended June 1, 1985, based on latest available data.
(Reprinted with permission from Salomon Brothers Inc.)

To make sure you are buying coins that are accurately graded, take a close look at the dealer's buy-back guarantee. Not only should the dealer guarantee that he will buy the coin back, but he should offer to buy it back at the same grade at which it was purchased. Furthermore, he should guarantee that he will buy the coin back at his own published prices—that he will make a market for the coin. If you have such a guarantee, you will know exactly where you stand on a daily basis and that you can pick up the phone, send in your coins, and know the price you will get.

In addition to getting a dealer's guarantee, you should make sure that the grades and types of coins that he deals with are compatible with your investment goals. If you want to buy a few expensive coins and put them away for your descendants, you might choose to consider coins graded MS-65. On the other hand, if you are planning to invest in coins with a short-term goal in mind, you may want to consider a larger quantity of lesser-quality coins by buying rolls of 20 MS-63 coins or BU rolls—brilliant uncirculated rolls that typically contain MS-60s and MS-63s.

Here are some of the features and potential benefits that well-selected numismatic coins can offer:

FEATURE	POSSIBLE BENEFIT
1) Potential Appreciation	Growth, assets increase
2) Diversification	Risk-spreading can lower losses, allow appreciation in other areas.
3) Inexpensive Entry	Small amount of money needed initially to establish an account.
4) Anonymity	Maximum protection and discretion
5) Long-Term Capital Gains	Gains on coins held over six months qualify for long-term capital gains treatment.
6) Tax-Free Exchange	When coins are exchanged rather than sold, tax payment is deferred until finally sold for cash.
7) Durability	No special handling or environmental considerations necessary. Careless handling can be avoided by special coin holders.

8) Insurable	If lost or stolen, the entire investment is not lost.
9) Easy Maintenance	Cost to maintain is no more than a safe-deposit box.
10) Relatively High Liquidity	Coins may be tendered to a coin dealer at wholesale, or consigned to a commissioned auctioneer.

RARE STAMPS

Another area you may want to familiarize yourself with is rare stamp collecting. It is one of the most popular hobbies in our nation, with over 20 million collectors here and 50 million around the world. Most people who collect rare stamps consider it a hobby, but there are growing numbers of persons who are buying stamps as an investment and are finding it very profitable.

As you will note from the Salomon study, rare stamp investing has yielded a 14.1 percent compounded annual rate of return for the past 15 years. However, over the past five years it showed only a 1 percent increase and the past one year a 9.6 percent loss. Philately, as stamp collecting is referred to in trade circles, is a fairly big business. Around a billion dollars in sales occurs each year, and there appears to be no scarcity of willing investors, although dealers are beginning to complain that they cannot obtain enough quality stamps to sell—again a situation where demand exceeds supply.

Some rules you may want to follow when investing in rare stamps are: 1) Begin as a collector, and work into becoming an investor; 2) diversify in stamps; 3) choose only top-quality stamps; and 4) look for stamps that are old, clean, undamaged, and, of course, rare. If you do not have the inclination or time to do this on your own, work with a financial planner who is knowledgeable in this area.

Why have rare stamps performed so well? Some characteristics that they possess that may be of interest to you are:

1. *Price appreciation*. Stamps have outdistanced the rate of inflation, and their prices are maintained over the long term because of the unflagging interest of 50 million collectors throughout the world.

2. *Safety*. Prices have a tendency to rise in both good and bad times. Stamps are portable and can be used as a shield against political or economic unrest.

3. *Tax advantage*. An investment in stamps is taxed only when you sell, and then at the lower capital gains rates. You are also allowed to take deductions for any expenses incurred in connection with your investment, such as a safe-deposit box, insurance, and so on.

4. *High liquidity*. There is a steady, active market for quality stamps. New collectors and investors are constantly entering the market. It may actually be easier to sell rare stamps than to buy them.

5. *Ease of maintenance*. Stamps can be easily protected, transported, and insured. When stamps are kept in a safe-deposit box, insurance rates are extremely low.

GOLD

Gold should be looked at as a store of value, not as a medium of speculation. In the past people accumulated gold not because they thought it would bring them wealth but because it was a means of representing and preserving the wealth they already had.

The Salomon Brothers study shows that the 15-year compounded rate of return for gold has been 15.5 percent (rating just behind rare U.S. coins). However, in the latest five-year time period it has shown a negative 11 percent return and in the last year a negative 20.3 percent return. What does the future hold for gold? I do not know, but you should have some knowledge of this hard asset.

Over the years, gold has held a special attraction. Charles de Gaulle spoke lovingly of "gold, which never changes, can be shaped into ingots, bars, coins, has no nationality, and is eternally and universally accepted as the unalterable fiduciary value." From biblical references to the gift of the Magi to the gold medals awarded at Olympic competitions, gold has been held in high esteem.

Should gold have a place in your total financial planning? Should you use it as your "fail-safe" plan in the event other more conventional approaches fail, or regard it as one of the items you should value for its investment merits alone? Should you treat gold as you do fire insurance on your home? If your home doesn't burn down, you probably won't cancel your fire insurance. Or should you treat it as a viable investment for profit? This you will need to answer for yourself.

Let's say you have determined that a portion of your assets should be in gold or gold-related investments. What approach should you take? Should you invest in gold bullion, gold coins, gold medallions, gold jewelry, gold mining stocks, or in mutual funds that invest in gold mining stocks?

There are five types of gold demands:

1. *The monetary demand.* Even though most politicians condemn the backing of gold or silver for paper currency in circulation as archaic, it does have the advantage of limiting the amount of currency and credit governments can create. Today, in spite of the often repeated U.S. position that gold is being demonetized, over 50 percent of the monetary reserves of the world's central banks are held in gold bullion.

2. *Industrial demand.* Industrial and jewelry demand for gold absorbs over one-half of the world's production, and this demand is growing.

3. *Political demand.* This factor could be the most important. Political demand for gold occurs when there is political turmoil in the world, as "smart money" of a particular region moves out of the currency of that region and into the world's most liquid and anonymous instrument, gold.

4. *Inflation hedge.* Over the years the gold coin has retained its purchasing power. When inflation is accelerating, or there is a threat that it will, the demand for gold increases. When the prospects for inflation decrease, the price of gold decreases. The correlation is obvious as the Reagan administration has been effective in slowing the inflation rate and the price of gold has dipped accordingly.

5. *Gold in times of depression.* What has been the record of gold-related investments during times of depression? There are two kinds of monetary turmoil. One is inflation, in which money becomes worth less every day, and which causes people to turn to gold to protect their purchasing power. A second kind of monetary turmoil is depression, in which money becomes worth more every day. In such circumstances people fear the loss of their money and can also turn to gold, which many consider the ultimate money. The result is that in a depression people have turned to gold and to gold mining shares as a mechanism for both income and appreciation.

Ways to Invest in Gold. There are five ways you may invest in gold: mutual funds investing in gold mining shares, gold bullion, gold coins, gold futures, and gold mining ventures.

1. *Mutual funds investing in gold mining shares.* I personally pre-

fer investing in gold mining shares through a well-managed mutual fund for a number of reasons. Usually the prices of the stocks lag behind the bullion itself, giving me an opportunity to see the direction gold prices are moving. Most of the time the shares outperform the bullion, and they also pay a dividend, which in the past has run as high as 10 percent. There is daily liquidity by wire or mail. Also, the government could ban the ownership of gold and could require that it be turned in for less than its market value.

2. *Gold bullion*. You probably should not consider buying gold bullion, since it would generally have to be assayed prior to resale. You could consider this method if you are buying a large amount of gold and plan to leave it on deposit at a bank and eventually sell it without ever taking possession.

3. *Gold coins*. One way you might consider, which is the most popular way, is buying low-premium bullion coins that trade within a few percent of their bullion content. These coins—such as the one-ounce Krugerrand, the one-ounce Canadian Maple Leaf, the 1.20-ounce Mexican 50 peso, and the .98-ounce Austrian 100 Corona— are very liquid, require no assay upon resale, and are concentrated forms of wealth in a convenient and anonymous bearer form. These can be purchased at a 3 to 7 percent premium above bullion price. A large network of gold coin dealers is spread across the country, and they make two-way markets in the popular bullion coins (as well as silver coins and bars). A typical commission is 2 to 3 percent, and most gold coins are delivered by the dealer directly to the investor, although larger dealers will store the coins for a nominal fee. Most investors keep their coins in a safe-deposit box.

4. *Gold commodity futures*. These are highly speculative and very difficult to trade successfully. Go this route only if you are willing to take heavy risks.

5. *Gold mining ventures*. This is also a high-risk approach and should be avoided by most investors.

SILVER

In the Salomon Brothers study, even though silver showed an 8.7 percent compounded rate over the past 15 years, it showed a negative 15.9 percent over the last five years; and during the past year it was the worst performer shown, with a negative 34.3 percent. What does the future hold for silver? I don't know, but to add to your store of knowledge about this metal, let's look at the three most popular silver investment vehicles in the United States:

1. *Junk silver coins*. These are bags of dimes, quarters, and 50-cent pieces minted prior to 1965, before the U.S. government replaced the silver with plastic and copper.

2. *Silver bars*. These bars come in sizes of 1, 10, 100, and 1,000-ounces, with the 100-ounce bar being by far the most popular. Only bars from well-known refiners, such as Englehard, Johnson Mathy, or Crédit Suisse, should be purchased. These well-known bars will not have to be assayed upon repurchase.

3. *Uncirculated silver dollars*. These dollars, minted in the late 1800s and early 1900s, were for the most part melted down over the years. The few that remained were held either by collectors or the Federal Reserve banks until the 1950s and 1960s. Morgan or Peace silver dollars have had very favorable price appreciation in recent years because of their silver content and their scarcity. They tend to be much less volatile in price than gold or silver.

DIAMONDS

"Diamonds are forever." "Diamonds are a girl's best friend." These are the ads most familiar to us, but are diamonds forever the best investment? The answer is no, not every year, and often not for several years; but over the long run in the past, the prices of high-quality investment-grade diamonds have kept ahead of inflation.

As you will note from the Salomon Brothers study, investment-grade diamonds have shown a compounded annual rate of return over the past 15 years of 10.4 percent, the past five years of only 1.2 percent, and no growth for the last year.

The brilliance and durability of diamonds have always fascinated humans, and the desire for them has not diminished over the years. However, during the high inflation years between 1965 and 1980, the beauty of diamonds became secondary and they began to be viewed more and more in terms of their investment potential. Diamonds have long been a haven for some of the assets of the very rich, and while worldwide affluence is a relatively recent phenomenon, Europeans have a much longer tradition of mistrust of governments and fiat currencies than do we Americans. Consequently, gemstone investing has a much older history in Europe.

Since investment-grade diamonds can be considered a viable part of a diversified portfolio, you should become more knowledgeable about this area of investing. The information I will present here will not make you an expert on the subject, but it should teach you a few do's and don't's.

All gems have three attributes in common: They are beautiful, they are durable, and they are rare. Beauty may be in color, iridescence (as in pearls or opals), or fire (as in diamonds). Durability is necessary for a valuable gem. Pearls are soft, yet durable. A diamond is the only colorless, transparent gemstone that has all three of these qualities; and it stands alone in its ranking of gemstones for its transparent, colorless beauty, as well as its rarity and durability.

Diamonds are costly to mine, and searching for the diamond of high value is not unlike looking for the proverbial needle in the haystack. It is estimated that current procedures may require mining from 45 to 200 tons of rock or sand to uncover one carat ($\frac{2}{10}$ of a gram or $\frac{1}{142}$ of an ounce) of quality diamond, an extremely costly and arduous process. Approximately 80 percent of all diamonds found are unsuitable for jewelry or investment and are used for industrial purposes. The industrial diamond, because of its color, structural defects, size, or shape, does not meet the high standards required for gemstones. Of the remaining 20 percent, only about 3 percent are considered to be of investment grade, and of this 3 percent, only 1 percent will yield a gemstone of at least one carat in size.

Today's diamonds are mined in South Africa, South-West Africa (Namibia), Angola, Australia, Russia (20 percent of the world's supply), Brazil, and India. U.S. production has been quite modest.

The major control for distribution of diamonds is by the De Beers Consolidated Mines of South Africa Ltd. Since the 1930s, De Beers has held an ironclad monopoly on the diamond industry that amounts to from 60 to 85 percent of the world's supply. The Central Selling Organization (CSO), the wholesaler arm of De Beers, purchases rough diamonds not only from De Beers mines but also from other producers. In the past, major producers and cutters have cooperated with De Beers because they have agreed that control and stability are as good for the industry as for De Beers. There are some indications now that this control is beginning to erode.

The Four C's in the diamond industry refer to cut, color, clarity, and carat. The "cut" of a diamond refers to its proportions and dimensions, based upon certain measurements. The brilliance of a diamond depends not only on the light reflected from the surface but also on the rays that have been partly absorbed before being refracted. The perfectly cut diamond maximizes the amount of light returned to the viewer; hence, the more finely proportioned the stone, the higher the value. The word "cut" is also used to mean the "shape" of the stone, or the design of its finished form.

Diamonds come in a full range of colors, including red, pink, blue, and yellow, with the highest grade of color for a diamond being the whitest possible, or colorless. As color is detected in a stone, its value decreases as the hue deepens. This is true until the diamond reaches the optimum point—when the shade is so rich that the value rises precipitously. This rare and quite valuable color is termed "fancy," and fancy diamonds are in great demand for investment stones as well as for jewelry.

The third C is for clarity, and the clarity of a stone is another factor that governs its price. Clarity is defined as the degree of internal perfection, or the degree to which the stone possesses inclusions, or irregularities, which may diffuse or scatter light. Undesirable reflections may be caused by the presence of foreign matter within the stone, surface defects, minute cracks, natural strains in the crystals, or certain other imperfections. The method of quantifying clarity is a point system generally based on the size of the inclusion, its position, and the extent to which it interrupts the optimum passage of light. For a diamond to be classified as "flawless," it must be free of external blemishes as well as being clean internally.

The fourth factor affecting value of diamonds is the carat weight. This is a familiar standard, but must not be confused with the "karat" used to describe the purity of gold. The international standard of the carat weight is .2 grams, while each carat is divided into 100 points. For example, a ¾-carat stone would weigh exactly 75 points, or 75 percent of the weight of one carat, or .15 grams. In determining carat weight, laboratories use extremely accurate caratronal electronic scales that weigh to one-thousandth part of a carat. This sophisticated equipment is believed essential to proper evaluation, since carat weight is a prime factor in assessing the value of the diamond.

Regarding your ability to turn your stones into cash should the need arise, the liquidity of diamonds falls somewhere between that of gold coins and real estate. They are more liquid than real estate but less liquid than gold coins. Diamonds are a relatively long-term investment and should not be purchased with a speculator's eye for quick overnight profit. On the other hand, diamonds do represent a tremendous opportunity for concentrated wealth that occupies a minimum amount of space.

After learning what you have thus far about diamonds, if you still feel that they are worthy of some of your investment dollars, there are certain criteria to follow and pitfalls to avoid.

First, deal only with reputable persons or firms. This is the first, primary, and essential criterion for choosing wisely; and care should be taken to get recommendations and to investigate past records. A gemstone of any kind, particularly a diamond, should not be bought from a person or firm without strong backing and a solid reputation. Also, as a general rule, one should not buy an investment stone from a jeweler, since the jeweler is at the end of the escalating price chain within the industry and seldom can give the best prices.

Second, the selection of a stone must be made with extreme care. This does not mean merely looking at the beauty of gems displayed on black velvet, but rather the selection of a stone that maximizes the qualities described above (color, clarity, cut, carat weight, and proportion) in line with the amount of money you have to invest. The best investment still seems to be the Round-Brilliant cut, H or better color, at least ½ and preferably one carat or more in weight. Once the parameters of the possible choice have been defined, it will be your pleasure to see a selection of stones within these guidelines and appreciate the beauty of the diamond chosen. This, however, is not completely necessary. More important is the transaction with the trusted broker, and the most important aspect, the certification of the stone by an independent laboratory such as the Gemological Institute of America. And if you have taken the first precaution (in choice of broker), certification will be an automatic procedure, with the cost probably absorbed by the company. You should be very careful in dealing with any sellers who claim to do their own certification. Certification of a polished diamond is one of the most important developments in the industry, since each diamond has its own "fingerprints" which make it unique.

Third, think of diamonds as a long-term investment, not a short speculative venture. Two years should be the minimum time for you to consider holding a stone, and much longer is better.

Fourth, in case it should become necessary to liquidate your investment in the future, check beforehand how to resell. Many companies make a resale-on-consignment service available to their diamond customers, although they will not guarantee a repurchase because of risk of having the sale classified as a security transaction by the SEC. Also, diamond marketing is carried on in the United States through computer listings, brokers, and companies that sell investment stones. Just as you should not purchase your investment diamonds from the typical jeweler, neither should you sell them through that avenue.

Fifth, plan to protect your investment through careful maintenance. Diamonds are the easiest of all hard assets to store and care for, vaults and safe-deposit boxes are readily available, and adequate insurance is easy to obtain.

COLLECTIBLES

What are collectibles and should you invest in them? I personally do not, but then I am not a collector and do not relate particularly to collections. But that does not mean that collectibles are not a viable alternative for you. I would recommend that you approach your collecting as something to be enjoyed. You will probably do a better job of learning about the subject, and even if you don't make money, you will have had some fun.

Collectibles include a broad range of tangible goods that usually have in common some degree of: 1) rarity, 2) scarcity, 3) demand, 4) popularity, 5) craftsmanship, 6) antiquity or age, 7) aesthetic qualities of beauty and taste, and 8) absolute or classical value to our society and culture. In addition to the rare coins and stamps already discussed, collectibles include Chinese ceramics, rare books, plates, antiques (furniture, dolls, classic cars, etc.), art (old masters, prints, and sculpture), and oriental rugs and carpets. On the other hand, collectibles also include the more faddish, and perhaps less prudent and yet irresistible, nostalgia items, such as toys, Mickey Mouse watches, beer cans, gum machines, comic books, baseball cards, stock certificates, record albums, patriotic items, cast-iron and tin toys, movie posters, and the list goes on and on.

The Salomon Brothers report shows the performance of only two collectibles: Chinese ceramics, which showed a 14.3 percent compounded annual rate of return over 15 years based on sales at Sotheby's, the last five-year period of 1 percent, and the last year of 5.9 percent; and old masters, which, on the other hand (also based on sales at Sotheby's), showed a 9.1 percent return for 15 years and an increase to 13.6 percent for the past year.

Of course, collecting for investment purposes is an entirely different game than collecting collectibles merely for the sake of collecting. The latter practice is considered more of an exhilarating hobby, a treasure hunt, and a means to exhibit a display case full of proud possessions. Investing in collectibles can be a method by which money is made and can be a calculated and serious business. Experts are available to advise their clients on how to make a prudent investment in a collectible specialty area, how to diversify, and how to make profits in collectibles both in the short term and over the long term.

The Fascination with Tangible Assets. The increased interest in investing in collectibles and tangibles can be attributed to several factors: affluence, nostalgia, inflation fears, confiscatory taxes, increased leisure time, disenchantment with other forms of investment, and well-publicized accounts of increased prices of collectibles. Much of the fascination with collectibles appears to be as related to stiff taxes as it is to inflation, for profits on them often elude the tax collector, unlike the gains on securities. The collectible marketplace operates in a free-market atmosphere with little or no regulation. There is a free wheeling-dealing atmosphere where markets are cornered to make a sale at a profit and where there is no SEC to interfere.

You will find that dealers in collectibles are similar to stockbrokers, except their credentials are not regulated in the conventional stock brokerage ways. You will find a significant number of excellent dealers who are totally honest, but you must be cautious, for any area as unregulated as this one will also attract the opposite type of dealer—one who is dishonest, who may even receive your payment without delivering your purchase to you, or who may sell forgeries and counterfeits as if they were the "real things."

Disadvantages vs. Advantages of Investing in Collectibles. In addition to the number of wheeler dealers in the marketplace, there are other disadvantages and pitfalls you will want to know about before making a commitment of any kind to this type of investing. Because the positives tend to outweigh the negatives, I will present the disadvantages first:

1. There is no spot price for collectibles. A collectible has a spread

between the bid and asked prices which can run as much as 30 percent per item.

2. There is a sales tax on the collectible item added to its price when you keep it in the state in which you purchased it, and this can turn out to be a sizable amount.

3. The extra money spent on the spread and the sales tax means that the collectible must be bought with the idea of holding it for at least eighteen months to two years, and selling it then only if the market is right.

4. Not all collectibles have kept pace with inflation. Generally speaking, high-grade coins, art, and antiques, when professionally selected, have done as well as some other kinds of investments.

5. Prices of collectibles can "skid."

6. The collectible market is fraught with fakes and flawed merchandise. When a collectible starts coming into demand, the forgers may grind out reproductions in massive quantities.

7. Many hundreds of get-rich-quick and other spurious investment schemes have occurred in the collectibles market. All are risky, some are rip-offs.

8. Collectibles do not pay interest or dividends, and they often entail such costs as insurance and storage. They may be difficult to sell within the timetable you have set.

9. Their profits may be a bit deceptive. For instance, the collector-investor may have bought a Victorian clock for $1,000 and sold it at an auction five years later for $1,500. On first blush, that may seem good, but after paying the auction house $300 he only has $1,200 left, and his net gain is only $200, or 4 percent a year. So he didn't win the money game.

None of these disadvantages should necessarily discourage you from becoming better informed about collectibles, since they can pay off, both in enjoyment as well as in financial rewards. Advantages of investing in collectibles include:

1. During inflationary periods, some collectibles have outperformed more conventional types of investments.

2. With the lifting of exchange controls in Britain, which enables British individual investors and pension funds to invest abroad, there should continue to be a larger number of potential buyers of American collectibles and antiquities.

3. The willingness on the part of some banks, investment firms,

and auction houses to inform and advise their clients about collectibles makes expert advice much more available to you and to others interested in collectibles as investments.

4. When you sell your collectibles, if you have held them for at least six months, your profits will be taxed at the more favorable capital gains rate. Another tax advantage that may fit your tax-planning needs and philanthropic nature is to give your collectibles to a museum or a university. This could entitle you to take deductions of as much as 30 percent of your adjusted gross income for up to five years.

5. Because the tangibles trading market has not been tapped yet by federal regulation, you have greater freedom.

Guidelines on Investing in Collectibles
1. Purchase only what you wish to specialize in, and if it is something you like, all the better, as it will maintain your high level of interest over the years.

2. Buy the best you can afford, even if you must accept limited quantities at first. If possible, purchase your collectibles from a dealer who will guarantee your purchase price back in the future if you trade in for a higher quality.

3. Confine your purchases to collectibles in excellent condition, as these will always enjoy outstanding resale value.

4. A collectible of any real value should carry a ticket guaranteeing its origin and, in the case of very fine items, its travels as well.

5. The authenticity of the collectible should be guaranteed against a full cash refund.

6. Read as much literature as you can on the subject. Study your line of collectibles for quality, art form, and all aspects of its category.

7. Buy only from reputable dealers or at reputable auctions.

8. Become attuned to holding your collectibles for long periods of time, since you must allow time for the markup to cover the difference between wholesale and retail prices.

9. If you are a novice, purchase and specialize in collectibles of known and proven work with a history of regular price appreciation.

10. Undergo a "comparison shopping" spree before you actually purchase your item. If you are considering a major purchase, call in a professional appraiser.

11. Be informed and up to date on all prevailing economic and

political trends that will influence the collectibles market. A rising stock market can result in extra discretionary income for investors and therefore a likelihood of surplus funds for items such as antiques. The reverse can have the opposite effect.

12. At auctions, try to spot the dealers in the crowd. It may pay to outbid the dealers, since they are planning to pay wholesale prices.

13. Regarding sealed bids, bid what you are ready to pay and don't expect to get the item at a lower price.

14. When bidding from the floor, start high, because continued bidding from a low level stirs up crowd interest. On the other hand, a high bid can knock competition out of the game before the crowd knows what is happening.

15. Don't be afraid to go to the top for advice, even if you are a small investor. Such establishments as Sotheby's and Christie's of New York have been known for their extreme courtesy to all clients.

16. Always arrange and investigate trucking arrangements, insurance, storage areas such as bank vaults or safe-deposit boxes, storage fees, pickup terms, burglar alarms, and other security precautions before buying the actual items.

17. When choosing the collectible you wish to invest in, apply the old truism "Follow the smart money." This means that one way to find a shrewd investment is to observe the actions of the wealthy, the sophisticated, and those who have demonstrated beyond question their acquisitive abilities.

Summary

We may have periods in the New Economy when the rate of inflation is less than the after-tax return you can obtain on a fixed or "guaranteed" dollar. During these periods you can obtain a "real return" on your money, meaning that after subtracting the rate of inflation and the tax bite, you actually have a real gain. It is during these periods that you may want to consider having some of your funds placed in cash and cash equivalents and in debt instruments. As you have seen, you have a wide variety of instruments and combinations from which to choose. Keep as much of your funds in this position as it takes to give you peace of mind, but stay always alert to the potential of making your money work harder for you by being an "owner" rather than a "lender."

On the opposite end of the scale are hard assets. As you have just seen, the world of hard assets is varied and complex and fraught with pitfalls. Prices are cyclical and are greatly influenced by the public's perception of what future inflation rates will be. It can be worth your time to become knowledgeable about this area so that you can properly hedge your positions against future eventualities. But if you do not want to invest considerable time and energy in this area in order to become a knowledgeable investor, my advice to you would be to stay away from investing in tangibles.

APPLICATION

HARD CASH

1. How much "patting money" do you need to give you peace of mind?

   _____

2. Where is the best place for your liquid assets? (1)_____

   (2)_____ (3)_____

3. Can you borrow money and still have peace of mind?_____
   If so, what steps will you take to make the right banking connections?

   _____

HARD ASSETS

1. What investment medium best fits your assets, temperament, and time

   frame?_____

2. Which hard asset areas do you plan to become more knowledgeable about?

   Rare coins_____

   Rare stamps_____

   Gold_____

   Silver_____

   Investment-grade diamonds_____

   Collectibles_____

3. What specific steps do you plan to take to become knowledgeable in the areas you have selected?_____

   _____

4. The next time you are in a large city, do you plan to visit Sotheby's or Christie's?

   _____ If so, what particular areas interest you?_____

   _____

Chapter 12

Attaining Millionaire Power

W. Clement Stone was once asked how he would describe the feeling of being so wealthy. His answer was ''power''—and then he added, ''the power to do good.''

Money does give you options in life that you would not have without it. It gives you the option of doing what you consider to be good. If you have a sufficient amount of money, you can greatly influence what books will be printed, what movies will be produced, what television programs will be shown, and what jobs will be created for others.

Do you really want to become a millionaire? If your answer is yes, your next question may be ''Is it still possible to do so today?'' The answer to your question is a resounding yes if you have enough time left, if you have a strong desire, and if you are willing to devote sufficient time and effort to pursuing this goal.

To begin, I think it is only fair to tell you I've never helped anyone become wealthy overnight. I've never helped someone with $10,000 turn it quickly into a million. The only people I've ever helped make a million dollars in a relatively brief period of time are those who brought me a million dollars to invest. Remember though, that it takes only an average return of 10 percent compounded to double your money in 7.2 years. At 12 percent it takes six years; at 18 percent, four years; and at 24 percent, three years. My minimum goal for my clients is in excess of 20 percent.

I remember calling the office of Percy Foreman, the nationally known and brilliant criminal lawyer, to invite him to appear on my weekly television program "Successful Texans." When I asked to speak to him, the receptionist blurted out, "He's in jail." After chuckling over this response, I left word for him to call me when he "got out of jail." Later that afternoon he called, and I invited him to be my guest. He accepted my invitation; and just as I was about to say my goodbye, he said, "Aren't you that lady stockbroker? Can you make me rich?" I answered, "Mr. Foreman, I understand you are already rich; but I believe I can make you richer."

Let's assume that you do not have the elusive million with which to start your high adventure. Is it still possible for you to become a millionaire? The answer is probably yes, if you have the discipline to save, the inclination to study, and a life span of sufficient length.

First, let me say that there are more desirable goals in life than becoming a millionaire. But if this is your desire, there are some very practical ways to approach your objective. To reach any goal, the first step is to divide it into its component parts so that it can be approached one step at a time.

Component Parts of a Million Dollars

What are the component parts of a million dollars? It's $1,000 multiplied by 1,000, isn't it? Trying to reach a million dollars in your lifetime may not be all that difficult to do.

How do you obtain the first $1,000? The most obvious beginning is to save from current income. If you save slightly under $20 per week, you should have your $1,000 in a year. Or if you do not want to wait until you have saved the $1,000, you can start investing as you earn on a weekly or monthly basis from your current income. Another possibility is to borrow the $1,000 from the bank at the beginning and pay the bank back on a monthly basis. This could give you a head start toward your goal.

Therefore, the first requirement for reaching your goal is the ability to set aside the relatively small amount of $20 per week.

Money, Yield, Time

The second requirement is to obtain a high return produced by adherence to aggressive but sound investment practices. These can be readily learned if your desire is strong enough.

The third requirement is a life span of sufficient length.

So you see, the two most important things are time and yield. If you set your sights on a million dollars, you must keep these two factors in mind. Time is something over which you have very little control. But yield is different. I believe that anyone of good intelligence has the potential to earn a high return on his investment, and high returns are absolute musts if you ever expect to become a millionaire.

When we speak of "yield," we ordinarily think of income (dividends or interest) as an annual return on the sum invested, expressed in the form of a percentage. For instance, if you receive $5 at the end of a year on a $100 investment, your yield is 5 percent. However, we shall broaden this definition for the purpose of this chapter and use "yield" to describe any distribution, plus any growth in market value. For example, if $100 grows to $318 in ten years, we would say its "yield" is 12 percent compounded.

One thing you must be fully aware of is the magic that comes from compounding the rate of return. This means that you are never to treat any income, capital appreciation, or equity buildup as spendable during the period you are building toward your million-dollar goal, but only as returns that are to be reinvested to increase your accumulation. In other words, don't eat your children. Let them produce more children, and before long you'll have a whole army of dollars working for you. Remember Benjamin Franklin's words, "Money is of a prolific, generating nature. Money can beget money, and its offspring can beget more."

For the purpose of our calculations, any taxes that you must pay on your investments are deemed to have come from another source.

One of the most important things you must remember is how important the rate of return you receive on your investment is to your compounding. For instance, if you can put to work $1,000 each year and can average a compound rate of 10 percent per annum, you will be able to reach your goal in 48.7 years.

However, if you can increase this compound rate to 20 percent per annum, you can reach your goal in 29.2 years. So you see, it does make a great deal of difference what return you obtain on your money.

Diversification—Based on Demand and Supply

Risk in investing can be reduced by following some basic investment principles. In this dynamic world in which we live, the two key concepts you must always keep in the forefront of your thinking are agility and diversification—that means spreading your risks.

In Basic Economics 101 you learned an economic law that you must never forget: the law of supply and demand. Regardless of how diligently governments and economists have tried to repeal it over the years, they have never been able to do so for any length of time. Russia has tried it and failed. England has attempted it and brought a once proud empire of plenty to its knees. Our own Congress continues to attempt to repeal this universal law. Its action has caused shortages and disruptions in energy, beef, housing, labor, utilities, and so on.

In making your determination of where the demand is greater than the supply, be an alert reader of the daily metropolitan newspaper; also read such papers and publications as the *Wall Street Journal, Time, Business Week, U.S. News & World Report, Fortune, Barron's,* the *Financial Planner* magazine, and *Money* magazine. Also begin to study the St. Louis Federal Reserve Board reports. You'll begin to develop an awareness of demands and shortages.

Avoid the Blue Chip Syndrome

There are those who have the mistaken idea that all one has to do to make money in the stock market is to buy "blue chips," throw them in the drawer, and forget about them. In my opinion, this can be riskier than buying more aggressive stocks and watching them like a hawk. As I've mentioned before, the "blue chips" of today may become the "red chips" or "white chips" of tomorrow. We live in a dynamic, throbbing, changing economy.

Just think back a few years. What car did the "man of distinction" drive? A Packard. I would have had difficulty convincing my father that only a few years later the manufacturers of the Packard automobile would be out of business. What was the chief family home entertainment medium before television? It was radio, wasn't it? And who was the chief manufacturer of that half-egg-shaped wooden box in every home? Atwater-Kent. As you know, the Atwater-Kent Company no longer exists. You live in a world of constant change, and you must always be alert and ahead of this change if you want to become a millionaire through your investment know-how. You must sharpen your talents to predict trends before they happen, and move out before they have run their course.

If the money supply is being greatly restrained in our country, as you've already learned, you will want to develop a more conservative approach to the stock market. As the supply becomes even more diminished, move into money market mutual funds so that you will have adequate liquidity to go back into the market as the money supply is accelerated and also to enjoy the higher yield that money will attract during this period of short supply.

This is not to say you should always avoid the Fortune 500 companies. If there has been an extended decline in the market, the larger, better-known companies are often the ones that respond first when the market begins to climb. As it reaches higher levels, you may then want to move out of them into other areas.

Aggressive Growth Mutual Funds with Timing

As discussed earlier, a well-managed family of funds that has an aggressive growth fund and a money market fund with a timing service superimposed on it can also perform very well. Using this system with the aggressive growth fund in the same family as the Seminar Fund, we have averaged 24 percent (doubling funds in three years) over the past four years.

Investment Advisory Services

I'm also aware of a group that have attained an average annual gain of 54 percent in their aggressive portfolio over the past seven years in an annual increase of 10 percent of the Standard & Poor's index. Their more conservative portfolio has posted a 27.5 percent annual increase. At 54 percent you would have doubled your investment in 1.33 years, and at 27.5 percent in 2.62 years.

Dollar-Cost-Averaging

As you've just seen, timing can be a problem, but dollar-cost-averaging in large or small amounts can greatly reduce the need for timing. Such an approach is useful for anyone who has a regular amount to invest over a period of years. Under this plan, you invest the same amount of money in the same security at the same interval. This will always buy you more shares at a low cost than a high cost and give you an average cost for your securities. If the market eventually goes up (so far, it always has), you should increase your capital.

The best way to accomplish this is to select a high-quality mutual fund that is a part of a well-managed family of funds that also has a money market fund. Establish a bank draft for the amount you can invest each month so the fund can draft your account. The advantage of this system is that the fund doesn't forget. I find that sometimes my clients do. Also, you don't have the temptation to skip a month or try to second-guess the market. There are certain decisions in life you need to make and move on—becoming financially independent is one of them.

When the value of your mutual fund reaches $10,000 you may also want to superimpose a timing service that can move it from the aggressive fund to the money market fund and back, as market timing dictates, while you continue your dollar-cost-averaging on the new money you are adding. (Most timing services require a minimum of $10,000.)

This system won't furnish you with fodder for excessive bragging over cocktails, but it has great potential for helping you reach your financial goals.

Capital Shortage

If shortage of capital exists you may have more opportunities for triple-net leases of real estate and equipment leasing. If money is tight, it is difficult even for major corporations to float bond issues at good rates, so they may sell their buildings and then lease them back. This gives them working capital. Triple-net leases of the buildings of major corporations, I believe, offer a much safer investment than their corporate bonds. Any court in the land will evict for non-payment of rent, but not for non-payment of interest on bonds. In addition to offering some tax shelter, leases provide equity buildup and appreciation.

Housing Shortage

Another investment potential occurs when housing is in short supply, as it is today.

For example, if you read that the average family income of the nation is $27,000 and the average home is $100,000, then you know that a large number of families will not be able to qualify for a home loan even if they could be granted interest-free mortgages.

I've already shared with you a comprehensive chapter on investing in real estate and you may want to go back and look at it again now. Suffice it to say here that a number of the registered real estate limited partnerships that we have used for our clients for a number of years invest in apartments, office buildings, and shopping centers and average a 24 to 62 percent gain per year on sale. These partnerships have averaged holding periods of 3.5 to 8.4 years. At 24 percent you've doubled your money in three years, and at 36 percent in two years.

The real estate private placements we have used have far exceeded this yield, so if you are a "suitable investor" and there is a private offering by one of the general partners with an excellent track record, you may want to consider this route. Your diversification and therefore your risk will be greater, but your potential for gain will be greater, too. Will the placements do as well if you invest in them today? I really don't know. However, with the housing shortage growing even more acute, and in view of the spread between what rents are today and what they must become before any new housing will be built, I believe your gain could exceed the gains of the past. As in the other investments, you would be following our guideline of seeing a need and filling it.

Historic Returns

What skillfully selected investments have offered compound growth rates in excess of 20 to 50 percent in the past? There is no guarantee the rates will be the same in the future, but a study of past rates can shed some light on areas for you to explore. Those you will want to study are:

1. Carefully managed family businesses or closely held corporations. I consider a profitable closely held corporation one of the best opportunities for tax shelter and creative financial planning that there is.

2. Well-located real estate—raw land, croplands, ranches, homes, residential and commercial income properties—using leverage when the timing is right. For every $1 you invest, consider borrowing at least another $2 to $3 to put with it through long-term mortgages when funds are available at the right price.

3. Carefully and aggressively selected and traded growth common stocks in emerging industries.

4. Selected growth mutual funds, using timing.

5. Antique furniture, art objects, and other collectibles, properly bought and sold.

6. Paintings and sculpture of gifted artists, properly bought and sold.

7. Rare stamps and coins carefully managed.

8. Commodities, if skillfully handled.

9. Entrepreneurial activities.

Reaching a Million Dollars

Let's assume that you are 25 years of age, have saved $1,000, can save $50 per month, can maintain an average of 15 percent performance on your investments, and can pay income taxes from another source. Your progress report over a 40-year period should then look something like this:

AGE 25	$1,000 + $50 PER MONTH
30	8,663
35	18,054
40	40,967
45	87,052
50	179,745
55	466,185
60	741,183
65	1,495,435

If you are 30 years of age and fortunate enough to be able to make a lump sum investment of $10,000 and can obtain an average return of 15 percent compounded annually, without adding new money to your investment but reinvesting all distributions and paying taxes from another source, your progress report should look something like this over a 35-year period:

AGE 30	$10,000
35	20,113
40	40,456
45	81,371
50	163,670
55	329,190
60	662,120
65	1,331,800

If you can move up the performance ladder to 30 percent and if you had started with $1,000 and added $50 per month for 40 years, your figures would be the following:

AGE 25	$1,000
30	17,326
35	36,108
40	81,934
45	174,104
50	359,490
55	932,370
60	1,482,366
65	2,964,732

As you can see, at 30 percent you accomplished your goal in 30 years. With a lump sum of $10,000 at 30 years of age and a 30 percent performance, your progress report would look like this:

AGE 30	$10,000
35	40,226
40	80,912
45	162,742
50	327,340
55	658,380
60	1,324,240
65	2,648,480

You've accomplished your goal here in less than 25 years.

Remember, we are not talking about "guarantees." All we are doing here is obtaining a visual picture of what compounding accomplishes over a period of years if you are able to maintain a 15 percent average and a 30 percent average.

We do not know what our future economy will be. Of one thing we can be certain, however: You will never reach your million-dollar goal with this amount of savings using "guaranteed" dollars. As a matter of fact, you may not keep even after inflation and taxes. If you hope to reach your goal, you must save and let your money grow. Investing your money aggressively and intelligently in well-managed and strategically located U.S. companies that are in the right industry at the right time, real estate expertly selected and intelligently leveraged, natural resources, leasing, cable television, etc., will not guarantee you growth of capital, but you will have provided your money with the opportunity to work as hard for you as you had to work to get it. The working dollar is an absolute necessity if your goal is to become a millionaire.

Sitting Tight

Do not be tempted to rationalize that because market conditions are unsettled now you should postpone starting your investment program or making investment decisions. When has the outlook been so obvious that you knew exactly what course to follow? If you take this attitude, you might as well dig a hole and bury your money. There is risk in any investment at any time. There is also a risk in a liquid position because of the steady erosion of fixed dollars due to inflation and taxation.

There are always good reasons for investment inactivity, but by sitting tight you may miss an entire lifetime of opportunities. Do the thing, and you will have the power!

Reread the first chapter of this book and recognize that to become a millionaire you will need to form the habit of doing things that failures do not like to do. Don't assume that you have certain dislikes peculiar to you and that successful people don't have these dislikes and do things you don't like to do. They don't like to do them anymore than you do. These successful people are doing things they do not like to do in order to accomplish the things they want to accomplish. Successful people are motivated by pleasing results. Failures search for pleasing experiences and are satisfied with the results that they can obtain by doing the things they like to do.

Let's assume that your purpose is to become a millionaire—that your purpose is strong enough to make you form the habit of doing things you don't like to do in order to attain this goal.

To have maximum creativity, your body needs to have pure air, wholesome food, aerobic exercise, and creative thoughts. When you get home from work, do you grab a can of beer, light up a cigar, and sit in front of the tube to watch a wrestling match or an actor solving one of the murders that occur on television? Or do you jog, ride a bicycle, exercise on a treadmill, walk a distance, eat a light nutritious dinner (sans large amounts of simple carbohydrates, sugar, salt, caf-

feine, saturated fats, and alcohol, but containing complex carbohydrates, vitamins, minerals, and sufficient proteins), and then read the
Financial Planner magazine, *U.S. News, U.S. Washington Letter,
Money* magazine, *Barron's, National Business & Financial Weekly,*
the *Wall Street Journal,* and *Business Week?* The successful investor
does these things not because he wants to but because he must in
order to accomplish his goals.

You must, too, if you desire to become knowledgeable. Then you
must learn to act upon that knowledge. Failures avoid decision making. Successful people know they must act. They have no other
choice if they want to reach their goal.

Time plus money plus American free enterprise may make you a
millionaire. If it does, fine. If it makes you financially independent,
that will be a major accomplishment of which you can be justly
proud.

APPLICATION

1. What metropolitan newspaper will you subscribe to immediately?

   _____

2. What current affairs magazines?

   (1) _____

   (2) _____

   (3) _____

3. What business publications and newsletter?

   (1) _____

   (2) _____

4. What period each week will you faithfully set aside to read and study
   financial publications?

5. What uninterrupted one-hour period will you set aside each week to
   contemplate where demand is greater than supply in our country?

   Day of week: _____

   Time of day: _____

6. What two-hour period will you spend driving around your city or a city
   nearby to observe building and land developments?

Week of the month: _____

7. What day each year will you take a financial inventory to see your progress dollarwise?

   Month: _____

   Date: _____

8. What self-improvement course will you take or what motivational tapes will you order to stimulate your thinking and improve your mental attitude?

   _____

   When? _____

9. Which books will you read to become better informed about nutrition?

   _____

10. What exercise program will you faithfully follow to become physically fit? (Dr. Kenneth Cooper's book *The Aerobics Program for Total Well-Being* is an excellent guide. I am on his aerobics program and heartily recommend it.)

11. What motivational books will you read to help you develop a positive mental attitude? I have found all of Dr. Robert H. Schuler's books and his cassette-tape package on "Possibility Thinking" of immense help. Also listen to his "Hour of Power" television program each Sunday, which is broadcast from the Crystal Cathedral in Garden Grove, California. Dr. Denis Waitley's cassette tapes "The Psychology of Winning" and his book by the same title are excellent. Also listen to Mike Vance's cassette album "Creative Thinking" and subscribe to his "Brain Exchange" cassettes. Earl Nightingale's tapes have been a part of my daily life for so many years that his thoughts have long ago been absorbed into mine. I especially like his "Direct Line" series. All of these can be ordered, including my cassette album "The Power of Money Dynamics," from Nightingale-Conant, 1-800-323-5552.

Life Insurance—Still the Great National Consumer Dilemma

I am tempted to start this chapter with the words of a familiar advertising campaign: "You've come a long way, baby." When I wrote my first book, *Money Dynamics,* in 1974, Chapter 13 of that book was titled "Life Insurance, The Great National Consumer Fraud?" Needless to say, it hit the life insurance industry like a megabomb; and those who espoused whole-life cash surrender value insurance attacked it with such unbelievable vigor that they were successful in getting it banned as sales literature in a number of states. But in spite of their untiring efforts, the chapter would not go away. It is estimated that over four million copies of the individual Chapter 13 have now been spread across the U.S. by those who believe as I do, plus over 950,000 of my books containing the chapter. Life insurance companies have, in the twelve years since its publication, been forced to make some revolutionary changes in the policies they offer, much to the benefit of the consumer. How much can actually be credited to Chapter 13 I do not know, but I have to smile when I think of the tremendous impact it has made in the boardrooms of the life insurance companies across the United States. I am equally convinced that thousands of widows and orphans owe their financial security to Chapter 13, together with my books, tapes, speeches, seminars, and radio and television series. Just perhaps that is the reason I was allowed to pass this way.

The great mystery of life is the length of it, and you should have a plan with the hope that you will live a normal lifetime. But you should also have a plan in the event that you die before you have had time to accumulate a living estate. Since you do not know which will occur, you should prepare for either event. We have learned that in the New Economy it will be quite possible for you to become financially independent if you have a reasonable ability to earn, the discipline to save, apply your talents, seek competent advice, and are granted sufficient time.

How can you be sure that you will have this time? You cannot. However, there is a way that you can "buy" time, and it is called "life insurance." This is a name that was given to it by the insurance companies that desire to sell it, but a better term would be "financial protection for dependents" or "death insurance." After all, there is nothing that can insure your life.

The Purpose of Life Insurance

Life insurance is a wonderful thing. There is no substitute for it until a sufficiently large estate has been acquired to protect those dependent upon you. It can provide you with a way to guarantee that your dependents will have the financial means to continue to maintain your targeted standard of living in the event that you should die prematurely. It can be an economic extension of yourself, and you should provide this protection for your dependents before you begin an investment program.

If you have dependents and you have not yet acquired a living estate, you need life insurance to cover the difference between what you have already acquired and what would be needed if you were not here to provide. For example, let's say that you have determined that your dependents would need an income of $3,000 per month to maintain them at their present standard of living. At a 6 percent return this would require $600,000 of invested capital; at 8 percent it would require $450,000; at 12 percent $300,000. Let's assume that you have already acquired a living estate of $50,000 and you believe that an 8 percent rate of return is reasonable. You would, therefore, need to provide a death estate of $400,000 (exclusive of Social Security) for a total estate of $450,000. As you increase your living estate, if your dependents' requirements have not increased, you can reduce your coverage, reduce the unnecessary expenditure of your money on premiums, and free dollars to be put to work more productively. You could picture your goal in this manner:

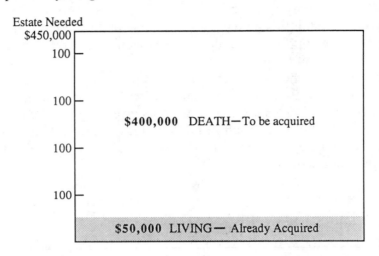

Your objective is to acquire a living estate—to substitute "living" for "death" until you become self-insured and no one has to die for the estate to be realized—and then you can all sit on the veranda and rock together. Your goal is to become self-insured as soon as you can, not to see how much life insurance you can carry. Life insurance premiums are an expense paid with after-tax dollars, and you will want to reduce and eliminate this expense as soon as possible.

The purpose of life insurance is to place over your family's head the umbrella of time—the time to accumulate a living estate. You obviously do not need to protect dependents whom you don't have. Yet, I am amazed at how many people burden themselves to pay life insurance premiums to protect nonexistent dependents. After all, they would not buy automobile insurance if they did not own an automobile, so they should apply the same common sense to the purchase of life insurance.

At the beginning of this book I stated that I have found through my many years of financial counseling six main reasons why most of our citizens reach the age of 65 flat broke: 1) procrastination, 2) failure to establish a goal, 3) ignorance of what money must do to attain that goal, 4) lack of a winning attitude, 5) failure to learn and apply our tax laws, and 6) being sold the wrong kind of life insurance. I say "sold" because I believe that had these people been better informed about life insurance, its purpose and cost, they would not have made the mistakes that I continue to see them making.

So that you and your family will not suffer from being sold the wrong kind of life insurance and so that you can change any program that does not make the best use of your money, let's now look at the various types of policies and the names given to them by the life insurance industry. Regardless of what these policies are called, they contain protection alone or protection plus cash surrender value, which is often illegally referred to as a "savings account." Premiums on policies that contain a "savings" element must of necessity be higher than those that do not. Since the number of dollars that you have in your budget for insurance is limited, the higher the premiums, the less coverage your dollars will buy. This in turn may cause you to be vastly underinsured, so that if death occurs before you have had time to accumulate a living estate, your family may not have sufficient funds to continue to live in financial dignity.

Names Given to Life Insurance Policies

There are six major names given to life insurance policies that have been or are being sold in the United States: term, ordinary or traditional whole life, limited payment life, universal life, universal variable life, and endowment. Each of these types can be participating or non-participating, which I will explain later. In addition, there are special policies that provide combinations of these six types. Regardless of what kind of life insurance policy you purchase or what it is called, the true cost of insurance goes up each year. Rates are based on likelihood of death which is reflected in a standard mortality table, and each year as you become older you are more apt to die.

TERM INSURANCE

There are three basic kinds of term protection: annual renewable term, decreasing term, and level term, plus some special kinds that contain the basic characteristics.

Annual Renewal Term. If you have an annual renewable term policy, the face amount of your insurance remains the same and the rate per thousand increases each year. You can obtain annual renewable term in most states to age 100. There are two rates quoted in most ART policies: the guaranteed rate and the current rate. The current rate will be lower than the guaranteed rate, and the insurance company has the right after a stated period, usually after three to five years, to charge the guaranteed rate if they have had adverse mortality experience. Another feature you may find is what is known as a "set back," meaning that the rate will be set back to a lower one if you take a physical and prove you are still healthy. If you do not do so, your rate will be raised to the guaranteed rate.

When choosing a policy, look at the rates over a ten-year period, because some companies may do what is termed "low ball" the rates for the first few years to entice you to take their policy and then increase the rates faster after a few years, making your total ten-year rate higher than comparable policies.

If you work for a company that has group life insurance for its employees, these policies will most likely be annual renewable term, and the amount is usually determined by your salary. The rates your company can obtain are usually cheaper, and it may pay all or part of the premium for you. However, a group policy is usually subject to your continuing to work for the company, and if you should leave its employ you usually lose the term protection and must convert to a higher-premium policy if you wish to retain your coverage.

Decreasing Term. Another type of term insurance is decreasing term. In decreasing term, the premium remains the same from year to year and the amount of insurance decreases. A special form of decreasing term is called mortgage insurance, where the rate of decrease matches mortgage amortization at a specified rate of interest. Other forms decrease at specified rates, such as equal percentage or equal amounts of the initial face value.

Decreasing term may serve your purpose very well, but the coverage does diminish each year automatically and does not provide you with the option of deciding if your coverage should decline. You can make your annual renewable term policy a decreasing term policy by just dropping the amount of coverage that your family no longer needs.

Level term. Level term means that the face amount of the policy remains level for the term of time chosen and the premium remains level. The most common periods are five, ten, fifteen, and twenty years, and level term to age 65. For example, if you choose a ten-year level term, in essence the insurance company is adding up the annual renewable term premiums for ten years and spreading the premiums so that you will pay the same premium each year for ten years. You would be overpaying in the early years and underpaying in the later years.

"Deposit" Term. In addition to the straight level term policies, you may want to consider those that require a first-year additional premium (referred to by many as a "deposit"). This concept was developed because of the high cancellation rate on conventional policies. Reportedly, one of every three new policies written is lapsed within two to three years. These lapsed policies are expensive to the insurance company because of the substantial costs to place the policies in force initially, since the company has paid for your physical examination, paid a sales commission to the agent, and paid numerous other charges in relation to the policy. Accordingly, it often charges a higher premium to all policyholders than would be necessary if there were no early lapses or if the company were given some protection against the cost of lapses. By requiring an additional first-year premium, the company obtains this protection, because if the policy is dropped before the end of the period, it is entitled to keep all or part of it. "Deposit" term policies usually require an additional first-year premium of $10 per $1,000 of coverage, and at the end of, say, a ten-year period, the amount returned to you is usually doubled, or would be $20. Under current tax laws, this additional $10 per $1,000 you receive is not taxable. If you should die during the ten-year period, the death proceeds plus the "deposit" will be paid in some policies. Others will double the deposit as if you had lived to the end of the ten-year period.

The most important thing for you always to remember is that all life insurance is pure term insurance. In some policies a "savings" portion has been added, and it is this "savings" feature that has caused a great amount of confusion. Let's now take a look at those policies that have a "savings" feature, commonly referred to as "cash surrender value."

WHOLE LIFE

A traditional whole-life policy, or ordinary life, as it is commonly called, is a policy where the face amount and the premiums remain the same for the whole life of the policyholder. In order to have a level premium, even though there is an increasing likelihood of death as the policyholder becomes older, the premium charged must be higher than would otherwise be necessary in the earlier periods of the policy so that the same premium can be charged when the policyholder is older.

In Figure 13-1 below, you will note that the cost-of-insurance line is below the level-premium line for many years and then crosses it around age 65. Assuming a life expectancy around age 78, you would have overpaid for 30 years (age 35 to 65) so that you could "underpay" for 13 years (age 65 to 78).

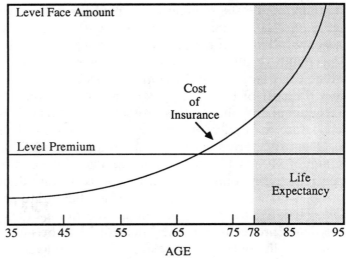

Figure 13-1. *Level premium method.*

A portion of these larger premiums that you would have paid go to build what is called the cash surrender value of the policy. The building of these values does not increase the amount that will be paid to your beneficiary in the event of your death. As the cash surrender value increases, the net amount at risk for the insurance company decreases. Therefore the policy, in reality, takes on the characteristics of a decreasing term policy. Ask yourself the commonsense question "Would I overpay my telephone bill for thirty years so that I could have the privilege of underpaying it for thirteen years?" If your answer is no, then use the same intelligence to protect your dependents.

Let's now examine the component parts of a whole-life policy by assuming that you bought a $10,000 whole-life policy a number of years ago, that your premium is $200 per year, and that the policy now has a cash surrender value of $4,000. We might diagram this policy in the following manner:

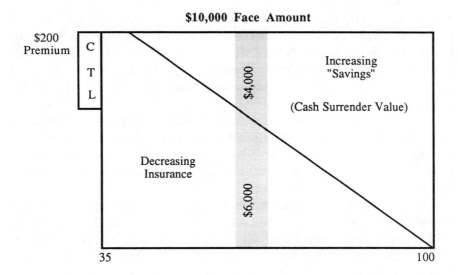

In the above example, the face amount of the policy would be $10,000 and the annual premium would be $200. This premium can be divided into "C," "T," and "L." "C" stands for cash, "T" for term insurance or mortality, and "L" for load or sales commission. When you originally took out the policy, your cost was $20 per thousand ($200 divided by 10). Now that your cash surrender value has built up to $4,000, what is your cost per thousand? If death occurs, your beneficiaries would receive only the $10,000 face amount. However, there was already $4,000 in cash in your policy. For your beneficiaries to have received the full death sum ($10,000), you would have had to pay a $200 premium. Therefore you have allocated to this policy $4,200 ($4,000 + $200). If you had invested this $4,200 at 6 percent net it would have grown to $4,452. Thus the benefit of your policy at death is $5,548 ($10,000 − $4,452). The extra sum you gave up to own the policy was $452, which yielded your beneficiaries an additional $5,548, making your cost per thousand $81.47 ($542 divided by $5,548). As you can see, your cost has increased from $20 per thousand to $81.47 per thousand. Costs per thousand increase because they are based on expectancy of death, which increases with age. (To calculate the cost of each of your policies, use Worksheet 1 at the end of the chapter.)

In short, dollars you might have thought you were "saving" have not produced for you their full earning potential. In addition, you have had to use after-tax dollars and have had to substitute them for insurance dollars that you could have bought for much less. Also, if you want to use any of these dollars, you must pay interest to do so, and if you die your beneficiary will receive only the face amount less any loans outstanding against the policy. Finally, if you refuse to pay interest to borrow the cash value and you withdraw it, you lose your coverage.

Contrary to what most policyholders (and a surprising number of agents) believe, the cash surrender value in most policies belongs to the insurance company, and it can only be obtained by the policyholder by borrowing against it at interest or by cancelling the policy and thereby losing the coverage.

Policies containing cash surrender value are often mistakenly referred to by some life insurance agents as "permanent" insurance. Webster defines "permanent" as "not subject to alteration; lasting, fixed, constant." Therefore, anything that is permanent does not disappear. In this policy the "insurance" portion, or net amount at risk, is decreasing or disappearing each year; therefore, it is not permanent. Only pure term protection kept in force until death is permanent insurance.

LIMITED PAYMENT LIFE

Another kind of cash value policy is one for which you pay premiums for a limited period of time. This type of coverage is called limited payment life. It provides lifetime coverage, with premiums payable for a specified period of time: 20 years, 30 years, or paid up at age 65 (which would be a variable number of years depending on your age). This type of policy has higher premiums and offers your family less coverage for the funds spent in the years when they will most likely need the most protection, so that you can pay little or no premiums when your need for protection has lessened and your ability to pay has probably increased. In addition, and especially with our pattern of continued inflation, you have used "expensive" dollars while you were young—meaning dollars for which you had to work many hours —so that you could save less expensive dollars later on—meaning dollars for which you had to work fewer hours.

ENDOWMENT

Another type of life insurance policy that you may have been sold is endowment. In this kind of policy, the face amount will be paid (endowed) to you if you are still living on a specified date or to your beneficiary should you die prior to that date. Some are designed to endow in 20 years, others endow at age 65; although I am amazed at the number of policies I come across that endow at age 80. Yes, 80! In reality, a whole-life policy is really an endowment policy that endows at age 100. You may not be too interested in fun and games at that age.

The premiums on an endowment policy, as you might expect, are very high in comparison with other types of policies, because you are funding for a specified amount over a specified period. Endowment policies have been sold as retirement programs or college education programs, but since these premiums are paid with after-tax dollars and the cash surrender values usually compound at a very low rate, they can make an endowment policy an expensive and often quite inadequate way to invest for retirement or for college.

In an endowment policy, as well as in other policies that accumulate cash surrender value, you may choose a lump sum payout or an annuity of a specified amount per month for as long as you live. If you make the latter choice, the monthly payments will cease upon your death. You may choose, however, to have your beneficiary continue to receive payments after your death for a set number of years. If you make this choice, you will receive smaller monthly payments.

UNIVERSAL LIFE

During the past few years you may have noticed a burst of advertising by a number of insurance companies and stock brokerage firms about a new concept in life insurance called "universal life." Its proponents present it as the answer to everyone's life insurance and savings problems, offering flexibility both in premiums paid and in death benefits to be received. Universal life begins with a specified premium and death benefit; but from that time on, the policyholder may exercise some flexibility as to premiums paid and death benefits.

Although the death benefit is specified at the time the policy is taken out, the policyholder may change the death benefit upward, subject to evidence of insurability requirements, or downward, subject to some minimum. This flexibility is referred to as "unbundling," meaning that the policy is broken down into three parts: the protection component, the savings component, and the expense component.

As the policyholder makes his payments, a portion of them goes into a savings fund to yield interest to pay the premium. In effect, the policy puts together term insurance and a tax-sheltered annuity with variable rates, rather than the fixed rates most annuities provide. Policies vary greatly. A policy for a male 40 years of age might have a first-year premium of $1,000 for a death benefit of $100,000. His combined fees and insurance cost that year could use $900 of that premium, with $100 left to be put into a savings fund to earn interest at 4 percent.

The advertising for such a policy may show higher interest rates on the savings, but the ad does not specify what portion goes into savings and what portion goes to fees and other charges. The policy may in reality have no net earnings at all the first several years, might break even in the fourth to fifth years, might get you ahead in the tenth year, and might go to the advertised rate by the twentieth year. If a loan is taken out against the policy, a lower rate may be paid on the cash that secures the loan. As you have looked at the rates some of these companies are advertising and then looked at how poorly these same companies have performed in the past with their own funds, do you begin to question if they can really deliver these projected rates for you? Also, do you really want your money to be a part of the insurance company's general account, where it must often choose the "guaranteed" side of the investment spectrum rather than the equity side of the free enterprise system?

If you have an extra $2,000, for example, you may want to establish an Individual Retirement Account or invest in a tax-deferred annuity directly yourself. This book contains many ways to increase your net worth more rapidly and safely than "bundling" living and dying.

UNIVERSAL VARIABLE LIFE

Recently some innovative companies have begun to develop universal variable life, which overcomes many of my objections to universal life. In these policies, the "cash value" is not placed into the general cash value account, but your money is segregated just as it is in a mutual fund. Your account is charged monthly for the mortality, so in many ways it is like buying monthly renewable term insurance and investing the difference.

Typically, you control the investing of your money into an equity, money market, or government bond portfolio, and the money can be invested in one or all three funds in any percentage you choose. You are able to take advantage of timing by moving the money at least once each year at no cost and at more frequent intervals at a nominal cost. Unfortunately, many companies that have begun to offer this product are trying to manage the portfolios themselves as opposed to finding good equity money managers. Should you choose this type of insurance, be sure that the life insurance company is not making the investment decisions. This will be fully disclosed in the prospectus.

Under current tax law, the accumulation within this policy is on a tax-deferred basis. That is to say, your money accumulates over the years without your paying current taxes, but you will pay taxes on the amount that you earn in excess of the premium payments at the time you liquidate your assets. Since this tax is at ordinary income rates, you need to weigh this against buying term insurance and investing the difference and taking advantage of the long-term capital gains and dividend exclusions.

MINIMUM DEPOSIT PLANS

Minimum deposit insurance plans, affectionately called "mini-dip" by the salesmen who sell them, are whole-life or limited-pay life policies that charge a very large premium to create artificially high early cash surrender values. If you have this type of insurance, it was your money that produced these high cash values. This type of policy is often presented to those in a 42 percent or above tax bracket, usually in the form of impressive computer printouts that show borrowing out most of the cash values as soon as possible and charging off the interest on their income tax returns.

The impression is often given that the IRS is the one actually financing the insurance program. Even if the interest could be deductible in this plan (and there does seem to be some doubt about the legality of deducting all of it), it is not brilliant economics to use after-tax dollars to substitute for insurance dollars that can be bought for a few pennies, pay a salesman to put those dollars into cash surrender value, and then pay an insurance company for the privilege of taking these dollars back out of the policy. No interest at all is better than tax-deductible interest. After all, none of us is in a 100 percent bracket.

When talking with insurance salesmen, you may be tempted from time to time with overly impressive computer printouts. If you will just remember the old warning regarding computer output—"Garbage in, garbage out"—perhaps you will have a better chance to survive in the true world of economic reality. Computers can manipulate numbers and can sometimes make even a very bad policy look great. While printouts can be helpful, be wary and truly analyze the calculations.

Only One Kind of Life Insurance

There is only one kind of life insurance, and that is pure protection based on a mortality table. All others are pure protection plus a cash value element that I call "funny" banking (with perhaps the exception of universal variable life). Term protection can be a wonderful bargain, and a real necessity for your family if you have not yet had time to acquire a sufficient living estate. Once this has been achieved, you no longer have any need for life insurance; your need to protect their financial livelihood has already been accomplished. Life insurance is to protect an economic potential, and you have either made it financially by age 65, or you will probably never make it.

After you have "made it," you have fulfilled your obligations to your family and yourself. However, at that point you may have another desire. You may want to pass on your estate intact, or at least partially so, to your heirs. You do not have this obligation, but if it is your desire, it is easy to calculate how much insurance will be needed to pay inheritance taxes and retain that amount.

"FUNNY" BANKING

What do I mean when I use the term "funny" banking in reference to cash value life insurance? Do I mean that a whole-life policy is similar to a savings account at a banking institution? Of course not! What I do mean is that the vast majority of people who buy and those who sell cash value life insurance do so because they believe (or are led to believe) that owning such a policy is a good way to save for the future.

To illustrate the differences between cash value life insurance policies and bank accounts, and why the former has always been such a dismal vehicle for any useful savings program—and is even more so with inflation—I invite you to imagine the following scenario. Suppose that you were to go to an institution named "The First Funny Bank of America" and told the polite man inside that you wanted to open a savings account. And suppose he said to you, "We're happy to have you, and here are our rules: First, you must buy term life insurance with us to open your account. Second, in addition to what you pay us for the insurance, you must deposit a certain number of dollars into your account for each unit of insurance that you buy. Third, we'll take everything that you deposit into the account the first year and keep it for ourselves. After that, we'll charge you to deposit money into your account. If you want to borrow from this account, we'll charge you 5½ percent to borrow this money. If you should die while this loan is outstanding, we'll subtract it from the amount that we'll pay your beneficiary. If you refuse to pay us for the privilege of borrowing from this account and withdraw from the account, we'll cancel your life insurance policy. If you do not borrow from this account and should die, we will not pay your beneficiary the face amount plus the accumulated deposits, but only the face amount.''

If the bank had said all of these things to you, would you have opened the account? Think carefully about your answer, because I have just described some of the end results of a traditional cash value policy!

The Sales Presentation

In an effort to increase your level of awareness, I feel that it would be helpful at this time if I were to pretend that I am a life insurance agent, which I am, who has come to sell you the life insurance policy that would best benefit my children. (Let me hasten to add that this is not by any means a blanket condemnation of all insurance agents. I firmly believe that most agents who sell the wrong kind of insurance do so out of ignorance and not out of malicious intent. This was also the conclusion reached by Senator Philip Hart's investigative committee on the life insurance industry.)

Okay, here I come. Are you ready? Let's say, for example, that you are a male, age 35, and I come to you and say, ''I can obtain for you a $10,000 level non-participating term to 65 policy for only $75 per year.'' You decide that the price fits within your budget and begin to say yes, but I interrupt you to say, ''But your insurance will be all gone at age 65, and you don't want that to happen, do you?''

At this point you stammer, ''Why, no, I wouldn't want to be without life insurance.'' (Analyze that statement. ''You've either made it financially by age 65, or you'll probably never make it.'') So I say, ''Well, now, here's a policy for only $150 a year that never runs out; it's called whole life.'' (I don't add that you must pay premiums your whole life and it endows at age 100.) Just as you are about to agree to this policy, I say, ''You don't want to pay premiums all your life, do you? Here is a policy for $250 on which you can quit paying premiums in 20 years. It's all paid up.''

Just before you sign, I say, ''But let me tell you about another policy. At the end of 20 years you've only put in $8,000, we will give you $10,000. You've had your insurance free for 20 years and made $2,000 profit. Isn't that great?''

But how great was it? Let's analyze the purpose of your life insurance. Its purpose was to protect those dependent upon you in the event that you do not live long enough to accumulate a living estate. Right?

Let's say that you actually did die in ten years. (Take a few minutes here for a thorough study of Figure 13-2.) In the first policy pictured, you would have spent $750 in ten years and your beneficiaries would have received $10,000. In the second, $1,500 would have been spent and they would have received $10,000. In the third, $2,500 would have been spent and they would have received $10,000. In the fourth policy, you had a first-class demise: $4,000 would have been spent and your beneficiaries would have received $10,000.

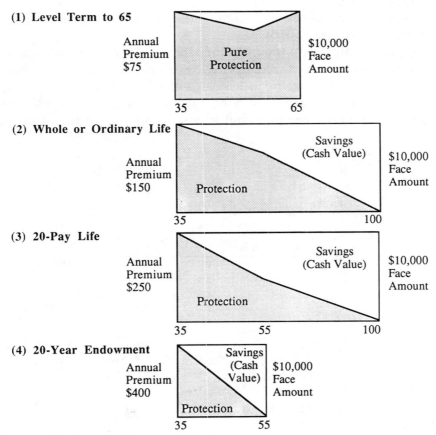

Figure 13-2. *Four basic types of level coverage.*

What if I told you that for $50 per year you could have bought a $10,000, 20-year decreasing term policy and that if you did nothing more constructive than take the $350 savings in premiums each year to your bank (Figure 13-3) and your banker paid you only 5 percent on your savings, in 20 years you would have $12,152 instead of just the $10,000 that you would have received from the endowment policy? If you obtained 8 percent from your banker, your $350 annual savings would have grown to $17,298 instead of $10,000. Your "free" insurance and $2,000 "profit" were indeed expensive. (Tax-free municipal bonds and municipal bond funds—providing you with the privilege of reinvesting so that you can have tax-free compounding if tax considerations are a factor—currently pay this amount or more.)

Again, never combine living and dying—unless you have learned to do both at the same time! "Banking" with an insurance company can prove to be very costly to you.

Remember that with life insurance the cost per thousand goes up each year. Because of the widespread misunderstanding of this basic fact of life, I reiterate, regardless of what kind of policy you buy, your cost per thousand dollars of coverage increases as you grow older because cost per thousand is based upon likelihood of death.

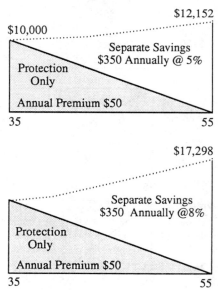

Figure 13-3. *Twenty-year decreasing term and bank account.*

There is an increasing cost to insure an increasing risk, and as you grow older you are more likely to die.

The true risk of a traditional whole-life policy is shifted from the insurance company over to the cash value portion of the policy a little more each year. This is how the insurance company can afford to provide you with the same death benefit coverage year after year without seeming to charge you any more for it.

MORTALITY TABLES

The mortality table is the initial base for calculating the cost per thousand dollars of coverage of your life insurance policy. Nothing can repeal the table, regardless of how many tantalizing names the advertising industry dreams up to call the various policies. The "insurance" factor is the likelihood of death and is listed by deaths per thousand.

The first table used by insurance companies was the American Experience Table. It was based on statistics gathered between 1843 and 1858. During that time, of 1,000 men aged 35, statistically 8.95 died during a given year. That was the death rate in the days of Abraham Lincoln. The next table used was the 1941 Standard Ordinary Table, based on death statistics gathered between 1930 and 1940 —before penicillin. During that period, the death rate had dropped to 4.59 per 1,000 men aged 35. On the 1958 Commissioners' Standard Ordinary Table, the death rate had dropped to 2.51 per 1,000. And on the most current table, the 1980 CSO Table, the death rate has dropped to 2.11 per 1,000. Insurance companies are not required to go back to old policyholders when a new mortality table becomes available. They, therefore, may continue year after year to charge rates based on the old table.

Table 13-1, following, is a combination of all four of the mentioned mortality tables, showing deaths per thousand at each age and life expectancy. Study it carefully.

TABLE 13-1. DEATHS PER 1,000 IN FOUR STATUTORY MORTALITY TABLES

AGE	AMERICAN EXPERIENCE TABLE	COMMIS-SIONERS' 1941 TABLE	COMMIS-SIONERS' 1958 TABLE	COMMIS-SIONERS' 1980 TABLE	LIFE EXPECTANCY 1980 TABLE IN YEARS
20	7.80	2.43	1.79	1.90	52.37
21	7.86	2.51	1.83	1.19	51.47
22	7.91	2.59	1.86	1.89	50.57
23	7.96	2.68	1.89	1.86	49.66
24	8.01	2.77	1.91	1.82	48.75
25	8.06	2.88	1.93	1.77	47.84
26	8.13	2.99	1.96	1.73	46.93
27	8.20	3.11	1.99	1.71	46.01
28	8.26	3.25	2.03	1.70	45.09
29	8.34	3.40	2.08	1.71	44.16
30	8.43	3.56	2.13	1.73	43.24
31	8.51	3.73	2.19	1.78	42.31
32	8.61	3.92	2.25	1.83	41.38
33	8.72	4.12	2.32	1.91	40.46
34	8.83	4.35	2.40	2.00	39.54
35	8.95	4.59	2.51	2.11	38.61
36	9.09	4.86	2.64	2.24	37.69
37	9.23	5.15	2.80	2.40	36.78
38	9.41	5.46	3.01	2.58	35.87
39	9.59	5.81	3.25	2.79	34.96
40	9.79	6.18	3.53	3.02	34.05
41	10.01	6.59	3.84	3.29	33.16
42	10.25	7.03	4.17	3.56	32.26
43	10.52	7.51	4.53	3.87	31.38
44	10.83	8.04	4.92	4.19	30.50
45	11.16	8.61	5.35	4.55	29.62
46	11.56	9.23	5.83	4.92	28.76
47	12.00	9.91	6.36	5.32	27.90
48	12.51	10.64	6.95	5.74	27.04
49	13.11	11.45	7.60	6.21	26.20
50	13.78	12.32	8.32	6.71	25.36
51	14.54	13.27	9.11	7.30	24.52
52	15.39	14.30	9.96	7.96	23.70
53	16.33	15.43	10.89	8.71	22.89
54	17.40	16.65	11.90	9.56	22.08
55	18.57	17.98	13.00	10.47	21.29
56	19.89	19.43	14.21	11.46	20.51
57	21.34	21.00	15.24	12.49	19.74
58	22.94	22.71	17.00	13.59	18.99
59	24.72	24.57	18.59	14.77	18.24
60	26.69	26.59	20.34	16.08	17.51

When Should You Buy Life Insurance?

Have you ever heard "Buy your insurance when you are young because it is cheaper?" Of course it is. A young man of 25, buying term protection on his life for his twenty-fifth year of life, will obviously pay substantially less than a man of 55 buying identical protection for his fifty-fifth year. But here is the distinction that many people miss: The fact that an individual has bought coverage early in life has no bearing whatever on what he will pay for that identical coverage when he is older. There are no special mortality tables for people who bought insurance when they were young. They are just as apt to live or die as those people who did not buy coverage at an early age. Those who bought insurance at age 25 will not have a lower cost per thousand at age 55 than those who did not buy at age 25. The same mortality tables apply to everyone, and all healthy 55-year-old policyholders should pay essentially the same cost per thousand for protection during their fifty-fifth year if they have the right policy.

Double and Triple Indemnities

The question often arises about the amount of accidental death insurance that a young family should carry. In our financial planning, we do not count accidental policies when calculating the family's need for protection. Even though most young fathers are convinced that if they die, that is the way they will go, it is not too likely—that is why the rates are low. It is more likely that they will die from a heart attack while mowing their lawns. It doesn't really matter how you die—you are just as dead, and your family's needs are just as real. Buy sufficient life insurance to cover their full needs and don't worry about how you may die.

TO PAR OR NOT TO PAR

A rose is a rose is a rose. But a life insurance dividend is not a dividend is not a dividend! It is a partial return of an overcharge. Those policies that pay "dividends" are often called "participating" policies and on the front lower left-hand side of the policy you may read "Par" or "Non-Par." The words "dividend" and "participating" have a nice ring to them. After all, you certainly enjoy your dividends from your 100 shares of General Motors or Exxon or from your Seminar Fund. But what is a "dividend" from an insurance policy? "Dividends" declared by participating insurance companies are not dividends in the commercial sense of the word but are simply refunds to the policyholder of a portion of the overcharge collected, which overcharge is merely held in trust by the company issuing the policy. Annually, or at stated periods, all, or a portion thereof, is returned to the person holding the policy.

To test whether a dividend is a dividend or a partial return of an overcharge, ask yourself if you have to pay taxes on it. The answer is no, and I am sure you will agree that the IRS is never charitable; and if it were truly a dividend, it would be taxable.

Participation—How Much Does It Cost?

Carefully study Table 13-2 and you will discover that your cost for "participating" depends on your age. Generally, the younger you are the more you will be overcharged. For example, if you purchased a participating policy at age 20 from one of the largest insurance companies, you would have paid $12.94 per thousand dollars of coverage that first year. If you had purchased a non-participating policy from another large company using the very same mortality table, you could have paid $8.98 that year. The amount of your overcharge was $3.96 per thousand, or 44 percent. At age 35, your overcharge was 33 percent, and at age 50 it was 19 percent.

As the years go by, the insurance company's board of directors can vote to return to you a portion of this overcharge. In fact, your net premium (premium less "dividend") in later years could even be less than for a non-participating policy taken out at the same time. Why do I object then to a participating policy? Because of the time use of money—your hard-earned money. Money has tremendous earning power, and you should put it to work for you and your family from day one. Don't prepay or overpay for anything with the hope that you may later get a portion of the overpayment back.

TABLE 13-2. COMPARATIVE ANNUAL WHOLE-LIFE PREMIUMS (PAR AND NON-PAR)

ISSUE AGE	WHOLE LIFE (PAR)	WHOLE LIFE (NON-PAR)	AMOUNT OF OVERCHARGE	PERCENTAGE OVERCHARGE
20	$12.94	$ 8.98	$3.96	44%
21	13.25	9.23	4.02	44%
22	13.57	9.49	4.08	43%
23	13.91	9.78	4.13	42%
24	14.27	10.08	4.19	42%
25	14.65	10.40	4.25	41%
26	15.05	10.73	4.32	40%
27	15.47	11.09	4.38	39%
28	15.91	11.48	4.43	39%
29	16.38	11.88	4.50	38%
30	16.87	12.31	4.56	37%
31	17.40	12.77	4.63	36%
32	17.95	13.25	4.70	35%
33	18.54	13.77	4.77	35%
34	19.16	14.32	4.84	34%
35	19.81	14.90	4.91	33%
36	20.51	15.56	4.95	32%
37	21.24	16.26	4.98	31%
38	22.02	16.98	5.04	30%
39	22.84	17.76	5.08	29%
40	23.71	18.58	5.13	28%
41	24.63	19.43	5.20	27%
42	25.59	20.34	5.25	27%
43	26.62	21.31	5.31	25%
44	27.70	22.32	5.38	24%
45	28.84	23.40	5.44	23%
46	30.04	24.53	5.51	22%
47	31.31	25.74	5.57	22%
48	32.65	27.01	5.64	21%
49	34.06	28.36	5.70	20%
50	35.56	29.78	5.78	19%
51	37.13	31.29	5.84	19%
52	38.80	32.89	5.91	18%
53	40.56	34.59	5.97	17%
54	42.43	36.39	6.04	17%
55	44.41	38.30	6.11	16%
56	46.51	40.35	6.16	15%
57	48.73	42.52	6.21	15%
58	51.11	44.83	6.28	14%
59	53.71	47.28	6.43	14%
60	56.32	49.88	6.44	13%

Calculating Your Cash Surrender Value

Let's now discuss how to take the first step in analyzing your own policies. First, you will need to get them out of the safe-deposit box or wherever you have them stored. Now read them. I will bet that you never have, even though you have been pouring some of your lifeblood into them for years. After you have finished, look at the front of each policy. There you will find the date the policy was acquired, or its birthdate. Take today's date, less the policy's birthdate, and this gives you the age of the policy. If you find that you bought your policy ten years ago, turn toward the back of the policy and, if you have the "cash surrender value" kind, find the cash surrender table and go down to the tenth year of the non-forfeiture section. Go across and you will find a "cash surrender" or "loan" value. This amount will be for either the face amount or per thousand dollars of coverage (it will state one or the other at the top of the chart). For example, if it is a $10,000 policy and your cash table shows $350 opposite ten years and the table shows "per $1,000," you would have a cash value of $3,500. So you know that the net amount or the true amount of your insurance is $6,500 ($10,000 minus $3,500).

How Much Life Insurance Should You Have?

How do you calculate the amount of life insurance that you should carry? There are a number of ways, but one of the simplest approaches is replacement of monthly salary. Let's assume that your monthly salary is $3,000. Multiply this amount by 70 to 75 percent, using 75 percent if you have three or more children. This is about what your family would need to maintain them at their present standard of living, with no provision for inflation, if you were not here to provide for them. At 70 percent, $2,100 would be needed. Let's assume that your family would be eligible for Social Security and that they will receive around $1,200 per month. $2,100 less $1,200 = $900. How much capital is required to produce $900 per month (given an annual net yield of 6 percent)? Just multiply by 200 (12 months divided by .06) to determine the principal, which in this case gives you $180,000. Let's also assume that you have accumulated $20,000 in liquid assets (exclusive of home furnishings and other non-liquid assets). Subtract this amount from $180,000, leaving $160,000 in capital needed.

Other financial planners use a formula of five times your current income before taxes, adding one more year's income for each child over two children plus the mortgage on the home and college costs. Others use ten times your current income.

For a more in-depth and comprehensive determination of your life insurance needs, you might want to answer the following questions:

1) What standard of living do you desire for your surviving spouse?
2) What indebtednesses are to be paid off at death?
3) What contingent liabilities or other cash commitments do you have?
4) What educational costs will need to be funded?
5) What earning capacity does your surviving spouse have? Should this be considered in the income-needs calculation?
6) What assets do you have that are currently producing income that can be used? What assets can be converted to income-producing assets? What other sources of income would there be (e.g., survivor pension benefits)?
7) What Social Security survivor benefits would your beneficiaries be entitled to, and how long would they continue? How long would the period be between the time Social Security survivor benefits stop (after all children are age 18 or out of college) and retirement benefits begin?
8) What rate of return can assets earn with your spouse's risk tolerance?
9) What do you anticipate the rate of inflation will be?

If it is your desire to pass on your estate intact to your heirs, you may also want additional coverage and you would need to answer these questions:

1) What deductible debts are in the estate?
2) What final expenses will there be?

3) What legal and administrative expenses will there be?
4) What bequests (charitable, children, former marriage, etc.) do you desire to make?
5) What non-deductible debts do you have?
6) What taxes will be due?

Regardless of which system you use for calculating your life insurance needs, determine if the premiums for this amount of coverage in term insurance will fit into your family's budget. If they can, fine. If they cannot, you must reduce the coverage to the amount that you can afford and still live comfortably today.

From Whom Should You Buy Your Protection?

Certainly one of the prerequisites for buying should be that the agent not be a member of a captive sales force, meaning that he can write a policy only for one company to which he is beholden. He cannot be impartial under these conditions, since circumstances will not allow him to be. Also, his company may not even have a policy that fits your needs, and if he does have one hidden away, the sales structure in which he works may discourage him from even mentioning it to you.

In my opinion, you should plan your life insurance needs with a financial planner who is dually licensed in life insurance and securities and is knowledgeable in investments to help you build a living estate and in life insurance to help you buy the time to acquire that estate. These two areas of financial planning are inseparable, since you don't know how long your life will be or how long it will take for you to acquire that estate.

I must warn you, however, that dual licensing alone does not insure that the advice you receive will be objective. Some dually licensed individuals maintain that it will not make any difference to them whether they sell you securities or insurance. Actually, it makes a great amount of difference in their compensation. If they sell you "term" and invest the balance for you in a mutual fund, they would receive only a small fraction of the amount they would if the total amount was placed inside of your insurance policy. Develop an ongoing relationship with a competent financial planner and keep your life insurance finely tuned to the rapid changes that are occurring in the New Economy.

Selecting a Life Insurance Company

Does it make a difference from which legal reserve life insurance company you buy pure protection? No, generally it does not, but you should seek the one that offers the best features at the best rates, designed to help you build a living estate (beyond the policy). It should offer policies that are renewable and convertible at your option to a variety of other policies, without evidence of insurability, to a ripe old age. This puts you in the driver's seat, and that's where you should be in designing and carrying out your financial plan.

Buying Life Insurance for Children

I am amazed at the amount of money spent each year on premiums for life insurance on children. If you have a policy on the life of your child, ask yourself, "Who is dependent on my child for a livelihood?" You should never make a practice of protecting your liabilities, but only of protecting your assets. As much as you love your child or children, they are financial liabilities until they are old enough and sufficiently prepared to leave your nest. If you desire some coverage on your children, you can place a rider on your policy. A common rate is $8 per unit, which provides $1,000 of coverage on each child until age 25, at which time it can be converted to $5,000 of coverage without evidence of insurability. From one to ten units can usually be obtained.

Buying Policies for College Expenses

I have seen many endowment policies taken out at the time of a child's birth for the purpose of providing for the expenses of four years of college that did not even cover the cost of the first semester. It makes me sad every time I see an advertisement portraying a beaming youth with a mortarboard jauntily atop his head, proclaiming that his college endowment policy brought him to this happy occasion. Although you certainly want to plan for your children's education, a college endowment policy is not an effective way to accomplish this worthwhile goal. Planning for this expense is covered in Chapter 15.

A Good "Compulsory" Savings Plan?

It should be clear to you by now that life insurance should never be used for putting to work your savings program. You may have been told that life insurance does provide a very convenient way to "set aside" a certain amount each month without the "bother" of setting up a separate savings and investment program. If you have the self-discipline to make premium payments over a period of several years, you can surely manage to invest money in ways that will achieve much more satisfactory results.

An Inexpensive Way to Borrow Money?

Sometimes people will proudly point out to me how very bright they have been to have figured out that they can borrow on their policy for 4½ percent to 8 percent instead of from a bank at a higher rate. If you are doing this, you are paying to borrow after-tax dollars that you placed there to begin with. Would you agree to the same arrangement with your bank? Also, you are reducing the amount of your life insurance coverage when you borrow against your policy, because the loan is subtracted from the face amount if it is outstanding at the time of your death. Borrowing against your policies serves only to increase your cost and reduce your coverage. If you are healthy enough to pass a physical, get pure protection. If you are not, by all means consider borrowing out the cash value and putting it to work in an investment that gives you a higher after-tax return than the interest you are paying. In most instances, the interest will also be tax deductible.

Do You Lose Anything When You Change Your Policies?

The belief that you will lose if you change your insurance policies may have scared you away from commonsense alternatives based on need. Your concern should not be how much you will lose by dropping an existing cash surrender value policy, but "How much more will my family and I have if I replace my policy and invest the difference?"

As more and more people have become better informed about the lower life insurance rates due to our increased longevity and competition among insurance companies, the potential earning power of their money, and also more aware of inflation's devastation to its purchasing power, they have been searching for more productive ways to put their dollars to work. After all, the life insurance industry is the only one I know that tries to keep people from trading in their old obsolete product for a new, improved version. And in an attempt to keep these changes from occurring, some companies have waged very successful campaigns to get regulations passed to require that agents complete and submit lengthy, detailed, and often difficult replacement forms if they recommend the replacement of any policy, regardless of the mortality table in use at the time the policy was sold. Replacement forms in some states have become so tedious and time-consuming that many a conscientious financial planner has left his client's present insurance program alone, even when it was grossly inadequate and unnecessarily expensive, rather than spend the many hours required to complete these forms.

My own state of Texas had such a form until recently. When it was first proposed, I testified before the state's insurance commission to encourage them not to enact this requirement. However, the whole-life insurance industry lobby was so strong that they were successful in getting it passed. They later found it not to their liking, for they also had to abide by the same rules when their own agents replaced policies. The requirement has since been removed.

Some cash value life insurance salesmen like to call financial planners who recommend the replacement of one of their policies "twisters." This implies that anyone who recommends changing your insurance program is a "twister." This is not true. A cash value salesperson, a term insurance salesperson, or a financial planner is said to be "twisting" if he uses misrepresentation or an incomplete comparison to induce you to replace a policy to your detriment. If he provides you with an honest, complete explanation and disclosure, he is not a "twister."

Some insurance companies, when they receive a notice that one of their cash surrender value policies is going to be replaced, send a dire warning letter and pamphlet to the policyholder, warning him of the serious mistake that he is about to make.

WHEN SHOULD YOU REPLACE A POLICY?

You should replace your policy any time you can qualify for a policy that will lower your cost per thousand. This cost can usually be reduced if you presently have any of the following in your life insurance program:

1. You have more than one policy. A policy fee is charged each year for each policy to pay for administration, in addition to the mortality cost. This fee averages from $10 to $30 per year, so if you are carrying six policies and you have an average $20 policy fee per policy, you are spending $100 per year unnecessarily. This extra amount could be used for investing or obtaining additional coverage.

2. You have cash surrender value in your policy. If your bank had the same requirements for your savings dollars as the insurance company, would you do business with them?

3. Your policies are not on the 1980 mortality table.

4. Your policies are participating.

WHEN SHOULD YOU NOT REPLACE A POLICY?

Under the following circumstances you should not replace one or more of your insurance policies:

1. You are uninsurable.

2. You cannot lower your cost per thousand by obtaining a new policy.

3. Any of the non-forfeiture provisions of your present policies are important to your current financial planning. These provisions may include paid-up additions and extended-term provisions. Extended term provides that if you quit paying premiums, the company uses the cash surrender values in the policies to extend the period of your coverage. There may be income options and annuity options in your present policies that you should examine. Determine if your financial planner can provide you with better alternatives.

4. You are planning to give false information on your new insurance application. There is a two-year contestability period that could result in your heirs receiving only the amount of coverage those premiums would have purchased had you given accurate information.

5. You bought your policies from a friend, and you feel that you would lose him as a friend if you replace them, and a friendship based on his economic benefit is more important to you than the economic future of your family.

6. You cannot withstand the pressure that may be brought to bear on you by your present insurance company or its agents if you attempt to replace.

7. You are planning to commit suicide within the next two years.

My Personal Insurance Testimony

From reading this chapter I want to be sure that you have not obtained the impression that I am anti–life insurance. All widows believe in life insurance and I was widowed only eleven months after a conscientious insurance agent had shown us how to obtain more coverage for the dollars that we were spending. Because of the life insurance proceeds I received and my ability to make them grow, I am now financially independent and am writing this book, presenting investment seminars, and counseling because I want to, and not from economic necessity. I am proud to say that I am a life insurance agent and I receive immense satisfaction from helping families properly buy the time to accumulate a living estate.

Life Insurance—A Very Personal Matter

Your life insurance program should be designed to fit your needs at this particular time. Your needs will change from year to year and, therefore, your policies should be reviewed constantly. Your need for protection may be less, the same, or more each year. Have the effects of inflation made your present coverage inadequate? Is there a new mortality table available? If so, you will want to apply for a new policy, if you can lower your rate per thousand. Work with a creative financial planner to keep your insurance program finely tuned to your changing needs. A good insurance program should not be expensive, if properly designed, and should be well within your family's budget.

In summary, let me reemphasize that life insurance is a necessary umbrella until you have had the time to accumulate a living estate. It should be purchased with these nine points in mind:

1. Life insurance is for dying. Investments are for living. Rarely combine the two unless you have learned to do both at the same time.

2. All life insurance is pure term insurance, but some policies have an added "savings" factor.

3. The purpose of life insurance is to provide your dependents with the means to continue to live at the level you want them to live in the event you die before accumulating a living estate. Year by year, you should be building your income-producing estate and decreasing your insurance coverage by the same amount if their needs have not changed. Your goal is to become self-insured, not to see how much life insurance you can carry.

4. Determine your life insurance needs as if you were going to die today, but also include an extra amount in your coverage to offset inflation.

5. Life insurance is based on a mortality table and it should cost more each year because you are more apt to die. Every time a new mortality table is written, apply for a new policy so you can lower your cost. Medical science is making great strides in enabling us to live longer, and this is reflected in the new tables.

6. No insurance policy is sacred. If yours is not right, you should obtain more efficient coverage and then redeem or cancel the old one. Have no more sentimental attachment to your life insurance policy than you would your automobile policy.

7. Don't do business with an insurance company under conditions that you wouldn't accept from your bank.

8. Be sure that your policy is renewable and convertible without evidence of insurability.

9. Avoid so-called participating dividend-paying policies. These "dividends" are a partial return of an overcharge.

My wish for you is that you will live a long, secure and happy life and that all the life insurance premiums you ever pay will be pure waste!

APPLICATION

1. Complete the Life Insurance Worksheet at the end of this chapter.

2. What is your current cost per thousand? $_____

3. At what cost per thousand can you currently obtain life insurance?

   $_____

4. How much will this reduce your expenditure for life insurance per

   year? $_____

5. How much cash will this change in premium release for you to put

   to work? $_____

6. The date you plan to take action to reduce your costs?_____

POSTSCRIPT

Now let's turn to another kind of death—economic death.

Guarding Against Economic Death

The purpose of life insurance, as you have just seen, is to protect those dependent upon you in the event you do not live long enough to accumulate a living estate. But what if you do not die physically but die economically? Under the age of 65, you are much more likely to be disabled for three months or longer than you are to die. Your disability could be caused by an accident, cancer, arthritis, or a heart attack; and it could interrupt your flow of income drastically enough to cause a financial disaster for your family. You need life insurance only if you have dependents to protect; you need disability income insurance if you do not presently have sufficient assets on which to live for the remainder of your life expectancy.

HOW LIKELY ARE YOU TO BE DISABLED?

The chart below shows the odds at various ages for disability versus death.

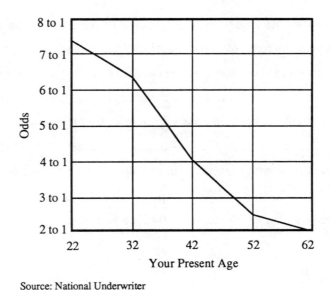

Source: National Underwriter

Figure 13-4. *Disability versus death.*

This graph shows the comparative odds of your suffering a disability (of three months or longer) this year rather than death. Go across the bottom of the chart to your age and then go up. If you are now 32, your odds are 6½ times greater that you will suffer a disability rather than death. At age 42, the odds are 4 to 1 and reduce as you get older.

THE DISABILITY INSURANCE CONTRACT

The value of a disability income policy lies in the insurance company's promise to cushion you against loss in income resulting from sickness or accident. You buy this promise with your premium. The value of a company's promise to pay you benefits is measured by the answers to several questions: How much? How soon? How long? And under what circumstances?

How Much Does Coverage Cost? You can't buy a disability policy that pays as much as or more than your gross income. If you could, you would have an incentive to become or remain disabled, so there is a maximum amount of coverage the insurance company will write—usually 30 to 60 percent of your gross income. A person of more modest income can usually obtain a higher percentage of income coverage than a person with a higher income. Also, the higher your liquid net worth, the lower the percentage of coverage you can obtain. You may not choose to buy the maximum, either because you don't need that much or because you can't afford it. At the end of this chapter you will find Worksheet 2, which you can use to calculate your disability insurance needs.

As with most types of insurance, the premium you pay is in direct proportion to the amount of the benefit yielded by the policy. It is usually expressed as a cost per $100 of monthly benefit. To determine the cost of a policy paying a $600 monthly benefit, for example, you would multiply the cost per $100 by 6.

Benefits you receive from disability insurance policies are normally not affected by any benefits you may receive from other private or public disability programs, such as Social Security. However, a few policies provide that you will receive a specified level of income from the policy and Social Security combined.

Premium scales are determined by your sex, age, and occupation. Since the Norris decision by the Supreme Court, more and more insurance companies are moving to unisex rates. Current statistics show that women's disabilities do not last, on average, any longer than men's, nor are they more severe. However, statistics do show that women are disabled much more often than men.

If you are female, you may want to choose a company that is using unisex rates, whereas if you are male, you may want to choose one that uses sexed rates for morbidity. For mortality, on the other hand, the reverse would be true. Since females live longer than men, if you are female you may want to choose a company that uses sexed rates, and if you are male use one that uses unisex rates.

The effect of age is straightforward. With each passing year, the chance of disability increases, so disability coverage costs roughly twice as much at age 50 as it does at age 30.

Your occupation is another factor the insurance company considers in your rate. Insurance companies seem to agree that a doctor is a better risk, for example, than a construction worker. Doctors, as a group, enjoy relatively good health and, when disabled, are generally quick to return to work. Construction workers, as a group, are sick or injured more often and, experience indicates, may be somewhat slower to return to work.

There is room for differences in judgment, however. Most insurance companies classify people into four or five underwriting categories, or risk groups. One company might put a construction worker in group three, another company might decide on group five, still another might refuse to insure the person altogether. When you are applying for disability income protection, therefore, it is important to find out how each company you are considering for coverage would classify you.

How Soon Should Coverage Begin? A policy that started paying benefits as soon as you missed one day of work would be unwieldy for a company to administer. Most companies give you a choice: Benefits can begin 30 days, 60 days, 90 days, 6 months, or 12 months after you are disabled. The more risk you retain—in other words, the longer you are willing to wait—the lower your premium will be.

The time you choose to wait between the beginning of a disability and the beginning of benefit payments is called the elimination period. I recommend that you select the longest elimination period your financial situation permits. That will help you lower your policy's cost per $100 of benefit, so you can buy enough benefits to have adequate coverage when you really need it. If you can manage financially, you should consider a policy with at least a 90-day elimination period.

For How Long a Period Should You Be Covered? The elimination period determines how soon you start to get benefits, while the benefit period determines how long the benefits will continue. You might consider selecting a policy that carries benefits to age 65. Selecting a shorter benefit period, such as one year, two years, or five years, would save money but would also leave you open to the devastating possibility of a long-term loss of income. On the other hand, having the benefits go beyond age 65 may make a policy prohibitively expensive.

Some policies have different benefit periods depending on whether a disability was caused by accident or sickness. I would not recommend such a policy, because if you need protection, you need it regardless of what causes a disability.

What Counts as Being Disabled? At first blush, that might seem a simple question, but upon examination, it becomes complex. Consider a waiter, earning $15,000 a year, who suffers a heart attack. He returns to work 40 days later but is now able to earn only $12,000. Is he disabled? Now take a surgeon, who normally earns more than $195,000 a year. If she has a stroke and can then earn only $30,000 in a hospital administrative office, is she disabled? And what about a man who now earns $40,000 as a talent scout who made $150,000 as an actor before his auto accident?

Several points are involved here. Is the person able to do any work at all? Is he able to work at his old job? Has he suffered a loss in income? And if so, how much? These are just some of the elements that go into a definition of disability. Every disability income policy contains its own definition. And it is the policy's written definition, not any phrasing of it by a salesperson, that determines what benefits will or won't be paid. You should insist on seeing a sample policy before purchase. Read it carefully, with a special eye to the way disability is defined. The longer disability is defined as your inability to do the material duties of your *own* occupation, the better.

Renewability. The conditions under which a policy can be renewed vary substantially from policy to policy, and the differences are highly important. There are three basic kinds of renewability provisions: class-cancellable, guaranteed renewable, and guaranteed renewable and non-cancellable.

Class-cancellable means that the insurance company can cancel all policies in a given class or group, such as all policies issued before 1970 or all policies in, say, the state of Oklahoma. If your policy is cancelled, you will have to go to the trouble of replacing it, and you will probably pay more for the replacement coverage, since you will be older than before. And if your health has deteriorated in the interim, you might be unable to obtain new coverage, or be able to get it only for a very high premium. Class-cancellable policies should be avoided.

If a policy can't be taken away from you so long as you pay the premiums on time, it is guaranteed renewable. However, the company may have the right to increase premiums on its existing policies. In recent years, most companies have not exercised this right, but some have.

The word "non-cancellable" is industry jargon meaning that the policy's premiums aren't subject to increase. Calling a policy "guaranteed renewable and non-cancellable" is not, therefore, a redundancy; it means you can keep the coverage and the premium won't go up.

Definition of Disability. A typical policy definition of disability might go something like this: "For the first two years after you are struck by sickness or accident, you are considered disabled if you are unable to do the main duties of your regular occupation. After that, you are considered disabled if you are unable to engage in any occupation for which you are reasonably suited by education and experience."

When you read a policy with that sort of definition, you should watch the nuances. Some policies consider you disabled only if you are unable to do *all* the duties of your regular job, not just the main duties. Instead of a two-year "own occupation" period, some policies use a one-year or five-year period. I prefer a policy that says quite simply that you are disabled if your income goes down as a result of sickness or accident. Since income loss is what you are insuring against, a pure income loss test of whether you are disabled makes the most sense.

If you disclose a health problem when you apply for insurance and the company issues you the policy anyway, most companies agree that you are then covered for any disabilities arising from that condition. Some do not, so be sure to check.

Quite a few companies use a loss-of-income test for *partial* disability benefits (also known as residual disability benefits). The catch is that in many cases you don't qualify for partial disability benefits unless the partial disability was preceded by a period of total disability. And those companies define total disability by some criterion other than loss of income. Thus, you might have a real and sustained loss in income without ever being totally disabled, or without being totally disabled long enough to trigger the partial disability provision.

Provisions covering rehabilitation also vary. A company will usually promise that if you enter a rehabilitation program, it won't count you as being recovered and cut off your benefits. In actual practice, some companies will even pay for rehabilitation sessions and equipment, but they won't promise to do so in the policy.

Along with your basic coverage, you can choose any of several riders, or optional provisions, although usually at extra cost. One rider that deserves consideration is the so-called social insurance substitute, a feature that replaces Social Security benefits in the event that you don't qualify for them under the Social Security Administration's strict definition of disability. Some companies offer the SIS benefit as part of the basic policy.

Another rider deserving consideration is the so-called option to purchase. As its name implies, it gives you the right (but not the obligation) to buy more insurance in the future, usually in specified amounts at specified intervals, regardless of changes in your health. The price is usually based on your age at the time of each additional purchase.

Cost-of-living riders may also have appeal for some buyers. These adjust your benefits according to some measure of inflation, often the consumer price index. There usually is a limit to the adjustments, both per year (such as 5 percent a year) and in total (such as a 100 percent maximum increase in coverage). Benefits may be adjusted automatically each year either from the time the policy is purchased or from the time you are disabled.

With life insurance you protect your dependents in the event you should die before having had the time to accumulate a living estate. Disability insurance protects you and your dependents against economic death. Your financial plan is incomplete if you have not prepared for either possibility.

APPLICATION

1. Complete the Disability Income Worksheet at the end of this chapter.

2. If you were ever disabled and could not work, what would be you and your family's income per month? $_____

3. How much monthly disability benefits do you need? $_____

4. If your disability coverage is deficient, what steps will you take to obtain this additional coverage?_____

WORKSHEET 1

COST OF LIFE INSURANCE WORKSHEET

1. Face amount of policy $_____
2. Cash surrender value $_____
3. Premium this year (less dividends) $_____
4. Total funds allocated $_____
5. If funds invested @ _____% $_____
6. Total funds allocated plus lost earnings $_____
7. Net benefit $_____
8. Lost earnings $_____ (line 5)
9. Premium costs $_____ (line 3)
10. Total $_____

    $_____ (10) buys net benefit $_____ (line 7)

Cost per thousand (10) ÷ (7) × 1000 $_____

    Available cost per thousand $_____

WORKSHEET 2

DISABILITY INCOME WORKSHEET

1. Current monthly take-home (after-tax) pay $_____

2. Existing disability benefits:

    a. Social Security benefits $_____

    b. Other government benefits $_____

    c. Company programs $_____

    d. Group disability policy benefits $_____

3. Total existing disability benefits $_____

4. Subtract existing benefits from current take-home pay to determine monthly disability benefits needed $_____

Chapter 14

Planning for Your
Golden Years

As we have learned, your financial life can be divided into three periods: your "Learning Period," your "Earning Period," and your "Yearning" or "Golden Period." Whether the third period of your life will be "golden" or "yearning" will, in all probability, be determined by the financial decisions you make during your "Earning Period." Unfortunately, a large number of your fellow citizens are making the wrong financial decisions. Presently, the annual income of 3.3 million of your fellow Americans over the age of 65 is under the poverty level ($4,979 for a single person over age 65). The median income for males over age 65, including Social Security, is $10,450, and the figure for females is only $6,020.

This is a tragedy—a tragedy that need not occur. And as medical science achieves more and more success in efforts to make us live even longer, the tragedy is compounded, since the number of years spent in any of these conditions could be extended for the vast majority of older citizens. Being broke is a devastating experience—especially so when you are old.

The likelihood of your living to an older age is increasing. A study made by the U.S. House of Representatives' Select Committee on

Aging revealed the following: In 1960, 9.2 percent of the population was age 65 or over. By 1990, it is projected that 12.7 percent of the total population in the U.S. will be in this group; by 2010, 13.8 percent; and by 2030, 21 percent. In absolute numbers this means that there will be 31.5 million elderly in 1990, 39 million in 2010, and 64.5 million in 2030.

The population of those 75 years of age and older is growing faster than any other age group, and this will continue as we move further into the New Economy. Between 1990 and 2010, the number of people age 75 and over is projected to go from 13.6 million to 18.8 million, and by 2030 to 30 million.

Raising the Consciousness Level

I have sincerely tried through my twenty years of seminars, financial counseling, my four books, and my national monthly *Money Dynamics Letter* to raise the level of comprehension of my fellow countrymen about these desperately important financial matters. I feel that I have made a tiny dent in Texas and in the surrounding states, as well as some impact on the nation as a whole because of my fellow financial planners and stockbrokers who have recommended my books in every state and abroad; the colleges and universities that are using my books as texts; and the nothing less then phenomenal enthusiasm for my two Public Television series, "The Money-Makers" and "Profiles of Success," which are being carried nationally by over 180 stations. I can assure you that I will continue to dedicate my time and talents to helping as many Americans as I can to retire in financial dignity.

It saddens me to see so many uninformed and frightened people trying to cope with a subject for which they are completely untrained. Our educational system continues to send forth our young with so little information about financial matters that they are like time bombs about to destroy their own and their families' economic futures. We equip them to earn good incomes and to live the good life, but we fail miserably as a nation to prepare them to know what to do with the money they earn. While there are a few progressive school systems and colleges that provide some basic money management courses, most young people venture forth into the most sophisticated money world ever known with little or no preparation.

Perhaps you, too, have been a victim of this void in our educational system. But the fact that you have reached this point in my book indicates that you want to fill the void that may be there. Congratulations! Please know that I am delighted to be the channel for your learning. And perhaps the most important lesson is to accept the reality of inflation and taxes and then resolve to learn to use the former to work for you and to reduce the latter. While they may ebb and swell, neither of these will go away, but you need not sit idly by and let them engulf you.

If you prepare well and develop a spirit of serendipity, opportunity invariably presents itself. Don't just sit and say, "God will provide." God gave you talents, a mind, energy, and a strong body. You have all the tools you need to till and cultivate the productive loam, but God will not take your spade in hand. Furthermore, don't sit and say, "The government will provide." The government's efforts to provide are what have brought destructive inflation and higher taxation.

I firmly believe that you owe it to yourself, to your family, and to your fellow taxpayers to accumulate the financial means to take care of yourself as long as you are on this earth. However, I personally feel that you and your spouse, if you are married, do not have an obligation to pass on an estate to your heirs if they are physically and mentally fit and you have provided them the opportunity for a good education.

I am also convinced that if you have a reasonable ability to earn and a little discipline to save a portion of what you earn, and if you apply average intelligence to investing these savings, you can acquire sufficient assets to retire in financial dignity. If you are male and retiring today at age 65, you probably have a life expectancy of another 15 to 17 years. If you are female, you have an average of another 18 to 20 years. So, the sooner you begin, the better your chances are for reaching your retirement years with financial independence.

As you learned at the beginning of this book, there will be only three sources of income at retirement: you at work, your money at work, or charity. Which source do you want to depend upon at age 65? Since you at work may not be an option open to you because the world may retire you, and charity will not be fun, that only leaves your money at work.

Building Your Net Worth for Retirement

Before we take a look at the various qualified retirement plans that our tax codes have provided to encourage you to prepare for your later years, let me reemphasize two areas that we have already explored that should play a vital role in your efforts to build your net worth.

MUTUAL FUNDS

This is my fifth comprehensive book detailing the many ways you can profitably invest your money, but the truth of the matter is that if you did nothing more than set up a bank draft for $300 a month so the custodian of a good growth mutual fund could draft your account and invest it in the fund, I am convinced you would become financially independent if you started early enough. Remember the Seminar Fund that we studied earlier? If you had invested $300 a month for the last 25 years, it would now have a value of $424,587. If you had invested $100 a month over the life of the fund, it would have grown to $3,371,100 today (exclusive of income taxes). I urge you to begin a systematic investment program as young as you possibly can and use this as a base for your retirement program.

REGISTERED LIMITED PARTNERSHIPS

We have discussed a variety of registered limited partnerships that can play a vital role in your being financially able to retire in dignity. These include those partnerships investing in apartment complexes, office buildings, shopping centers, mortgages, miniwarehouses, cable television, equipment leasing, and agriculture. These, properly chosen with adequate diversification, can add much to your net worth.

In these registered programs you had to use your after-tax dollars. Let's now examine some programs especially designed and blessed by Congress to let you use before-tax dollars.

INDIVIDUAL RETIREMENT ACCOUNTS

The Economic Recovery Tax Act of 1981 (ERTA) expanded both the amount and eligibility for Individual Retirement Accounts. Under this act, every person under the age of 70½ can contribute 100 percent of earned income up to $2,000, deduct that amount from taxable income, and let the amount compound tax deferred. If there is an unemployed spouse, $2,250 can be contributed if no more than $2,000 is placed into any one spouse's account. If both spouses are earning, each can have a $2,000 account. This applies even if the spouse only earns $2,000; the whole amount can be placed in an IRA. If the amount earned is less than $2,000, of course, the whole amount can be contributed.

The liberalization of IRA's can be considered an admission by the Congress that adequate Social Security may not be there when you are ready for it or that it may be in ailing health; but I hope you will have no complaint, since you have had an opportunity to provide for your own retirement outside of Social Security.

If you average 15 percent per year on your money (and shame on you if you don't), your results will be:

YEARS	$2,000	$4,000
10	$ 46,699	$ 93,398
20	235,620	471,240
30	999,914	1,999,828
40	$4,091,908	$8,183,816

In addition, your contribution will be deductible. In a 33 percent tax bracket ($36,630 joint taxable income), your tax savings will be $660 per year if $2,000 is contributed, and $1,320 if $4,000 is contributed. If you invest this tax savings at 10 percent net after taxes, your results will be as follows:

YEARS	$660	$1,320
10	$ 11,570	$ 23,140
20	41,582	83,164
30	119,423	238,846
40	$321,322	$642,644.

If, for example, a working couple age 35 establishes an IRA with the above averages, they will have $1,999,828 plus $238,846 or $2,238,674 in their retirement program at age 65. That amount should put a bit of nutritious food on the table and, if the Love Boat is still sailing by then, provide the opportunity for a bit of enjoyable diversion.

If you haven't made your IRA contribution for this year, do it today. Your funds should be compounding inside your tax-deferred IRA rather than be diluted by taxes outside the plan. You are allowed to make your contribution up to April 15 of the following year. However, the following chart shows the penalties of procrastinating on your yearly contributions to an IRA:

FUTURE VALUE OF ANNUAL $2,000 IRA INVESTMENT AT 10 PERCENT ANNUAL RETURN

| YEARS INVESTED | *Date of Contribution Each Year* | | | |
	JANUARY 1	JUNE 1	DECEMBER 1	APRIL 15 (NEXT YEAR)
10	$ 35,062	$ 33,467	$ 31,874	$ 29,195
20	126,005	120,271	114,550	109,989
30	$361,886	$345,429	$328,988	$319,548

As you can see, after 30 years, the January investor has $42,338 more than the April 15 investor. At just 10 percent per year, the additional $42,338 would continue to earn an additional $350 a month for the "early bird investor" during retirement.

Have you been reluctant to open an IRA account because there would be a penalty of 10 percent on the portion withdrawn before you reach 59½ years of age? If so, study the table on page 396—you may be surprised at how early in a program you can cross a break-even point.

In a 35 percent marginal bracket and a 15 percent rate of return, you reach a break-even at 3.6 years, and in a 50 percent bracket and 20 percent rate at 2.6 years. Everyone who has earned income and is under 70½ years of age should consider opening an IRA account. It may pay to open an account even if you are young and have taxable earned income you are saving for college. It may pay to take the deduction now, let your contributions compound tax deferred, and then pay the penalty as you withdraw it.

BREAK-EVEN POINTS IN YEARS FOR INVESTING IN AN IRA COMPARED TO A TAXABLE INVESTMENT AT THE SAME RATE OF RETURN

RATE OF RETURN	Tax Rates							
	15%	20%	25%	30%	35%	40%	45%	50%
5%	17.5	14.0	12.0	10.7	9.9	9.5	9.3	9.3
10%	9.1	7.3	6.2	5.6	5.2	4.9	4.8	4.8
15%	6.3	5.1	4.3	3.9	3.6	3.4	3.3	3.3
20%	4.9	3.9	3.4	3.0	2.8	2.6	2.6	2.6
25%	4.1	3.3	2.8	2.5	2.3	2.2	2.1	2.1

I am excited about what I think IRA's will do for America. To me they could become People's Capitalism and could very well be a major contributing factor for the preservation of the free enterprise system.

How Should You Invest Your IRA? We recommend that you begin your investment of IRA funds in a well-managed family of mutual funds that has in its stable an aggressive growth fund and a money market mutual fund. A mutual fund account can be opened with as little as $250 (even less in some funds), can be added to in amounts of $50 (less in some funds), and all dividends and capital gains are automatically reinvested. The custodian fee is usually modest, about $6 per year.

When the account grows to $10,000, we recommend that a timing service (discussed earlier) be superimposed on the fund so that the timing service can move the funds as market conditions indicate, from the growth fund to the money market fund or vice versa. There is no commission for switching and no tax consequences, since the funds are still under the tax-shelter umbrella of the IRA account.

After you have at least $10,000 in the mutual funds (and you should consider building up these accounts to $25,000), we recommend that you open a trust account and begin the use of various registered limited partnerships. These partnerships do not usually have reinvestment privileges, so the mutual fund will be a good depository for the partnership's cash distributions. In this way, we have all funds compounding without any dollars remaining idle.

Now let's examine some more formal retirement plans that require legal documents and yearly reporting to the IRS.

Qualified Retirement Plans

Since 1984 there has been parity between corporate and non-corporate plans (formerly known as Keogh plans for those who were self-employed). If you own a business, one of the best tax-sheltered ways to prepare for your financial needs at retirement is through either a profit-sharing or a pension plan, or a combination of the two. By utilizing these options, you can place before-tax dollars in the plan and then let them compound tax deferred. If this decision is your responsibility, you will find it most advantageous to have a comprehensive study made by a specialist in the field. Specialists can determine which type of plan is most advantageous to you while keeping within the IRS guidelines. If you are a lower-level employee, however, you may not be permitted to offer any input into that decision.

Technically, profit-sharing and pension plans are designed to attract and hold good employees, which they do if employees are kept adequately informed about their benefits. However, let's assume that you are either a chief operating officer or head of a closely held company. You probably receive higher pay than most of your employees, so the largest advantages will usually accrue to you. You may be able to receive an even greater advantage if you are older than your employees and you establish a defined benefit pension plan.

While I cannot make you a pension specialist in one chapter of this book, here are a few of the options you will want to know about.

DEFINED BENEFIT PENSION PLAN

If you own a business and are much older than your employees and you receive a relatively high compensation compared to theirs, you may want to have a defined benefit plan. A defined benefit plan is designed to provide a fixed benefit for the retiree. Several options are available:

1. *The percentage unit benefit formula.* This is the most widely used and usually provides a monthly pension benefit based on 1.5 percent of your earnings for each year of your service to the company.

2. *The flat amount unit benefit formula.* With this formula the employees are given a flat dollar amount per month for each year of service.

3. *The flat percentage formula.* With this formula the employee receives a percentage of annual compensation (usually with a minimum service requirement).

4. *The flat amount formula.* With this arrangement all employees receive the same amount as a retirement benefit.

A defined benefit plan can be designed by a specialist to allocate a higher percentage of the contribution to you, so that under certain circumstances it is possible to shelter in the plan more than you earn. The only limitation on the dollar amount that can be set as the annual deductible contribution is the amount required to fund the allowable intended annuity when you retire as determined by an actuary. If you have employees, however, the plan cannot discriminate in your favor. But, because your employees will generally be younger than you, the cost of funding the pension plan for them should be far lighter proportionately than for you without being discriminatory.

Your company may set aside and deduct sufficient money to fund a straight life or joint and survivor annuity on your retirement equal to the lesser of 1) $90,000 at a retirement age of at least 62, or 2) 100 percent of your compensation for your highest consecutive three years of service with the company.

At present, if your business is incorporated, there can also be provisions in the trust document to permit you to borrow from your own plan under IRS guidelines. This privilege continues to be debated in Congress, so you will need to check the status on any pending legislation regarding the ability to get a loan from the plan. At present, if you or your employees do borrow, the plan must utilize a legal note with a definite repayment schedule including the going interest rate. The loan must be repaid within five years unless it is for buying or adding to your principal residence, to avoid it being treated as a distribution. The amount must not exceed the lesser of $50,000 or one-half the present value of the non-forfeitable accrued benefit under the plan. Also one can borrow up to $10,000, notwithstanding the previously stated rule. The cost of the interest, with certain limitations, may also be deducted from your taxable income.

If you own a closely held business and all the conditions are right, probably no other vehicle will provide you with such good tax shelter without the IRS questioning your deductions. If you follow all the rules, it will give you the flexibility to play the game to your maximum tax advantage. You can balance the funds between your company, yourself, and the pension plan for maximum tax advantage, compatible with your needs for living expenses and what the IRS guidelines will allow.

DEFINED CONTRIBUTION PENSION PLAN

Another possibility for you to consider is the defined contribution plan with an individual account. Unlike the defined benefit plan, the balance in the account determines the benefit the retiree will ultimately receive. The amount contributed is not dependent upon funding a specific annuity amount but, subject to adjustments for vesting provisions, remains stable.

Defined contribution plans include profit-sharing, money-purchase, and target-benefit plans. The benefits are derived solely from the contributions made to the various individual accounts, and the amount of the contribution is generally based upon a percentage of the annual compensation of each participant or upon a specific dollar amount. The benefits are increased by the earnings attributable to investment of the account and by forfeitures from other participants. The benefits are decreased by the losses attributable to investment of the account.

Profit-Sharing Plan. This type of plan has a contribution formula that permits the employer to allocate a percentage of the corporation's profits to the plan. The actual contribution to the plan is then determined by the employer on the basis of the available profits. If there are no profits, no contribution can be made. However, if you do not make a contribution one year because of lack of profits, you may carry 10 percent of the 15 percent of covered payroll into the next year. If there are profits that year, you can make up to a 25 percent contribution so long as you do not exceed the lesser of 25 percent of covered compensation or $30,000 for any individual participant including forfeitures. The remaining 5 percent can be carried over to the next year and thus you could make a 20 percent contribution.

Most profit-sharing plans have discretionary formulas. A profit-sharing plan may specify, however, that a stated percentage of your company's profits will be contributed to the plan each year. Once the amount of the contribution is determined, the total contribution is then allocated to the individual account of each participant in the plan. There are a number of possible formulas for so doing. The simplest, and perhaps the most common, method is to allocate the contribution to the participants on the basis of compensation of each participant compared to the compensation of all participants.

Forfeitures are allocated to the accounts of each of the participants on the same pro rata basis on which contributions are allocated. The maximum amount that may be added to a participant's account in a profit-sharing plan is the lesser of 25 percent of each participant's annual compensation or $30,000. Cost-of-living adjustments are frozen until 1986. Included in the annual additions that are to be within this maximum amount are employer contributions, certain employee contributions, and forfeitures. The amount of contribution deductible may not exceed 15 percent of the total covered compensation of all participants in a profit-sharing plan.

Money-Purchase Pension Plan. Unlike the profit-sharing plan, the money-purchase pension plan always specifies the formula in the plan document. The formula cannot be discretionary and it is stated as a rate or percentage of compensation.

Like the profit-sharing plan, the money-purchase plan allocates the amounts contributed on a predetermined pro rata basis among the participants. But unlike the profit-sharing plan, the money-purchase plan allows all forfeitures to reduce your company's future contributions.

Generally, the amount deductible in a money-purchase plan is equal to the amount of the required contributions under the provisions of the plan. The annual amount that can be added to a participant's account is the lesser of 25 percent of the participant's compensation or $30,000 adjusted for the cost of living (frozen until 1986). Included in the annual additions that are to be within this limit are employer contributions and certain employee contributions. Forfeitures reduce your contributions rather than being reallocated as in a profit-sharing plan. The amount of deductible contribution cannot exceed 25 percent of the total covered compensation of all participants.

Target-Benefit Plan. The target-benefit plan is a combination of the defined benefit and the money-purchase pension plans. It targets a particular benefit for participants but does not promise to deliver it, as the defined benefit plan does. The company's contributions can remain level each year, regardless of the turnover of personnel and the performance of the portfolio.

SIMPLIFIED EMPLOYEE PENSION PLANS

Since 1979, employers have been permitted to establish Simplified Employee Pension (SEP) plans, utilizing Individual Retirement Accounts or annuities. Contributions to a SEP can be contributed or deducted up to the lesser of 15 percent of compensation or $30,000. These plans reduce some of the red tape and paperwork that Keogh and corporate pension plans require.

SELF-EMPLOYED PENSION PLAN

Are you self-employed as a professional person, a proprietor, or a partner of an unincorporated business? If so, you can set up what was formerly referred to as a Keogh Plan. While Keogh plans are still referred to by the congressman's name, the Tax Equity and Fiscal Responsibility Act of 1982 virtually wiped out any distinctions that existed between qualified plans of corporations and those of self-employed individuals.

How much can you contribute to such a plan and how much are you required to contribute for your employees and which ones are you required to include? You must include all full-time employees age 21 or older who have worked for you for three years (less if you had your business for fewer years). To determine the maximum amount of your contributions, let's assume that you earn $100,000 per year and are 50 years of age and have an employee 25 years of age to whom you pay $20,000 per year. If we fund your plan to a retirement age of 60 and assume a joint and survivor benefit, we can reduce your taxable income from $100,000 to $44,784 and make a tax-deductible pension contribution of $55,216. You and your employee's calculations would be as shown on page 402, based on a 5 percent performance on your funds.

As you will note, 94 percent of your contribution would have been on your behalf. In this example, it is assumed you make the same contributions each year and the performance you obtain is only 5 percent on your investment. The higher the performance, the lower the annual contribution required. The formula used here is funding

CURRENT AGE	RETIREMENT AGE	SALARY OR NET INCOME	MONTHLY BENEFIT	PENSION CONTRIBUTIONS	TOTAL CASH AT RETIREMENT
50	60	$44,784	$3,731.97	$51,983.36	$653,841
25	60	$30,000	$1,666.66	$ 3,232.94	$292,000

for 100 percent of compensation, but you may choose a lower target. The last column is your total benefit at retirement, which can be annuitized or received in a lump sum.

INTEGRATING PENSION PLANS WITH SOCIAL SECURITY

All of the plans I have discussed can be integrated with Social Security. This means that you can exclude from the plans all covered compensation up to the Social Security limit, and the exclusion may be set at a lower figure. This has the effect of favoring the company's more highly paid employees. With the passage of the Tax Equity and Fiscal Responsibility Act of 1982, Keogh plans are also permitted to integrate with Social Security.

THE 401 (k) PLAN

401 (k) refers to the section of the IRS code that permits these plans. These are qualified deferred compensation plans that allow employees to receive part of their compensation in cash or to defer it into a defined contribution plan. Currently, 401 (k) plans may only be a part of a profit-sharing or stock option plan, not a defined benefit, money-purchase, or target-benefit plan. Ordinarily, the 401 (k) is part of a profit-sharing or stock bonus plan that the employer already has set up. In a word, an adjunct. Although Section 401 (k) of the code was enacted in 1976, final regulations have never been issued, thus these plans are operating on proposed regulations.

The 401 (k) plan is unique in that it does not have to cost the employer any money. The employee can provide for his or her own retirement, although the employer *can* contribute to the plan. Like all qualified plans, before-tax dollars are contributed, they are deductible, and they grow, tax deferred, until distributed to the employee. All of the employees' contributions are immediately 100 percent vested.

The 401 (k) plan includes all the withdrawal restrictions of an IRA with one exception: hardship. Proposed IRS regulations allow financial hardship distributions without tax penalty for funds that are not reasonably available from other sources, in a situation where the employer has adopted and is practicing non-discriminatory standards for all employees in the plan.

Setting up the plan is the most complicated part. Under current laws, the participants are divided into two groups, the upper-paid one-third and the lower-paid two-thirds. The amounts that may be deferred by the upper one-third are dependent upon the amounts deferred by the lower two-thirds. In any event, the maximum annual addition to an individual's account can be no more than 25 percent of the post-deferred income. Also, no more than 15 percent of post-eligible payroll can be contributed by the company. Employers can also integrate with Social Security, but most do not.

If you are the employer, obtain the specific rules from a pension actuarial firm. If you are an employee, your employer will no doubt furnish you with a booklet describing your options.

TERMINATING A QUALIFIED PLAN

As you approach that day when you want to "hang it up" or you want to become an employee of another corporation, you will have only sixty days to decide on one of four options regarding the benefits that have accrued in your account, so before then, select a good reputable and knowledgeable financial planner to review these options with you.

To start your calculations, subtract any contributions you have made to the plan. You made these with after-tax dollars, and they can therefore be recovered without tax. For the balance you have the following options:

1. You can take your funds in an annuity or other installment payment method. Distributions will be taxed as ordinary income.

2. You may roll over the entire amount into an Individual Retirement Account. The entire sum, unreduced by taxes, continues to accumulate, tax deferred, until you begin withdrawals at retirement.

3. You may keep out a portion, pay taxes on it at regular income rates, and roll over the remainder, tax deferred, into your IRA rollover account. You might consider this approach if you need some funds to start a new business or other such purpose.

4. Take the entire balance as a lump sum distribution. This entitles you to use a special ten-year forward averaging.

IRA ROLLOVER ACCOUNTS

The IRA rollover was originally designed to give portability to employee pension plans; that is, if you had been working for a company with a retirement program and you decided to move to another company, you could take your vested interest with you and transfer it into an IRA rollover and not be currently taxed on the distribution. The people who have used it most, however, are those who are retiring but want to defer the taxes and let their funds continue to compound tax deferred. If you choose this option you are free to move your investments around for maximum gain without losing any of your funds currently to capital gains taxes and also have those funds compound tax deferred. You must wait until age 59½ to start your withdrawals without a penalty, and you must start a withdrawal program by April 15 of the year after you reach age 70½.

You will have a large number of investment choices, but regardless of which you make, you will be required to use a custodian or trustee that is acceptable to the government. You may use the custodian of a mutual fund; a custodial account with a trust company, a commercial bank, or a savings and loan; or a life insurance company, investing in one of their fixed or variable annuities.

Of these choices, I prefer the first and/or the second one. Let's consider the first option. If you choose a mutual fund that is part of a family of funds that has a money market fund, you always have the choice of being in stocks or in a cash equivalent position. You may divide your funds between their growth funds, middle-of-the-road funds, special situation funds, bond funds, and so on, and you can move from one to the other without commission and without tax.

If you choose the second option, you can use any investment that is acceptable to your trust company. This lends itself to a wide array of limited partnerships in oil and gas, real estate, individual stocks, bonds, or mutual funds. You may also direct a custodian to increase or decrease these areas as you see fit.

Your third option is a commercial bank or savings and loan association. If the only investment options they offer are fixed "guaranteed dollars," you should not choose this route. If they have an excellent investment department or if you are capable of self-directing your plan, then you can also consider this option.

The fourth option of using a fixed annuity of a life insurance company should be avoided. With any inflation, annuities will usually guarantee that you will have to reduce your standard of living each month you live.

TRANSFER OF ASSETS

If you have chosen a particular custodian and later decide to change to another, you may do so, with the exception of an annuity which you have annuitized, meaning that you have already accepted that first annuity check. This is called a "transfer of assets" from one custodian to another. It is not a taxable event, because no "constructive receipt" has occurred. For example, if you previously rolled over your pension plan assets into certificates of deposit at a bank or savings and loan, you do not have to leave them there. You need only have your financial planner or broker prepare a "transfer of assets" form for your signature. Such a transfer is easily accomplished if you provide your planner with a copy of one of your confirmation notices from your present custodian. You may also take receipt of your assets once a year and redeposit them within sixty days with another custodian without tax consequences (called a rollover). You may also use the same arrangement—a transfer of assets—if you have your regular IRA account at a bank, savings and loan, or an insurance company and want to transfer it to a mutual fund custodian or trust company custodian.

AN ACTUAL CASE STUDY OF AN IRA ROLLOVER

A couple who had attended one of my three-session financial planning seminars requested an appointment, as every attendee is entitled to do. When we sat down for our two-hour uninterrupted personal session in my office, I discovered that the husband had taken early retirement, had received his distribution fifty days previously, and was faced with a $14,056 tax bill on an $88,201 distribution. I quickly ordered two computer printouts, shown in Tables 14 and 15 in the Appendix, giving the past results: 1) if the funds had not been rolled over, and 2) if they had been rolled over (*i.e.,* invested) in the Seminar Fund. I had the computer show a 9 percent withdrawal for 11 years, and, beginning in the twelfth year, used a 21-year self-liquidating program designed to exhaust the principal over the couple's combined expected lifetimes. I had the program done this way even though the couple did not need to start withdrawal immediately.

In the first printout, we assumed that they did not roll over and paid the tax of $14,056, leaving a net of $74,154 to invest in the Seminar Fund. From the 9 percent monthly withdrawals of $556.09, we have deducted 20 percent in taxes on all dividends and 10 percent on capital gains. As you can see, at the end of 11 years, their after-tax distributions would have been $73,403, and the remaining value $115,034. The printout shows a 21-year liquidation program starting in the twelfth year. During the entire 32-year period, the printout shows a withdrawal of $388,331 after taxes.

Now let's turn and look at the printout that assumed they had rolled over their pension distribution. As you will note, they had $88,201 to roll over, because they would not owe the $14,056 in taxes that year. Again, 9 percent was withdrawn, or $661.51 per month for 11 years. From these distributions shown under "Annual Total," 20 percent has been subtracted for federal income taxes. By the end of the eleventh year, $69,854 would have been withdrawn, after subtracting 20 percent for taxes, and the balance of $167,258, shown under the column "Total Value," would have still been in the account. Again, the printout shows a 21-year self-liquidating program starting in the twelfth year designed to exhaust the principal. At the end of that time, as you will note, a total of $520,789 was withdrawn. (Incidentally, you are not limited to withdrawing just the annual amount shown. You can make larger withdrawals, but not smaller.) In the period studied, they would have had an additional $132,458 in distributions by rolling over than if they had not rolled over. Needless to say, the couple decided to roll over—and fortunately there was still time to do so. And in reality, it made an even larger difference because this couple had other funds to use for retirement income and they have continued to let earnings compound tax deferred. They will not have to start their withdrawal until the man is age 70½, but at that time he will need to withdraw at a rate that will exhaust his account in 21 years.

TEN-YEAR FORWARD AVERAGING

Another choice that is now available for pension and profit-sharing distributions is ten-year forward averaging. If the amount of your "lump sum" retirement distribution is relatively small and you are advanced in years, it may be to your advantage not to use an IRA rollover but rather to use ten-year forward averaging. Have your financial planner or broker calculate both and then choose the plan that will best accomplish your financial objective.

Again, to make your calculations, begin with the amount of your distribution and deduct any contribution you made with after-tax dollars. The remainder is a combination of your employer's contributions, the earnings of your employer's contributions, and the earnings of your contributions.

Below is a table you can use to help calculate your tax:

SPECIAL TEN-YEAR AVERAGING FOR 1985

If the adjusted total taxable amount is:		The initial separate tax is:		
AT LEAST	BUT NOT OVER	THIS AMOUNT	PLUS THIS %	OF THE EXCESS OVER
$	$ 20,000	Zero	5.5	Zero
20,000	21,250	$ 1,100	13.2	$ 20,000
21,250	29,917	1,265	14.4	21,250
29,917	48,083	2,513	16.8	29,917
48,083	65,500	5,565	18.0	48,083
65,500	70,000	8,700	19.2	65,500
70,000	88,500	9,564	16.0	70,000
88,500	110,400	12,524	18.0	88,500
110,400	132,200	16,466	20.0	110,400
132,200	165,500	20,826	23.0	132,200
165,500	220,700	28,485	26.0	165,500
220,700	275,800	42,837	30.0	220,700
275,800	331,000	59,367	34.0	275,800
331,000	408,000	78,135	38.0	331,000
408,000	551,600	107,395	42.0	408,000
551,600	827,400	167,707	48.0	551,600
827,400	....	300,091	50.0	827,400

After you have done your arithmetic, are there any other factors you should consider? Your age, for one. For example, if you are 70 years of age and you opted for an IRA rollover, you would be required to start withdrawing at age 70½. The minimum amount of the required withdrawal would be based upon the life expectancy of you or you and your spouse. These withdrawals will be taxed to you at ordinary income rates, which could be higher than the amount you would have paid by using the ten-year forward averaging. If, however, you are 40 years of age, the IRA rollover may be a better choice, since your entire $50,000 can compound, tax deferred, until you are age 70½. You will also be free to move your investments around within your rollover without tax consequences. Regardless of which options you choose at retirement, upon your death any remaining assets in the plan are includable in your estate.

Company Termination of Retirement Programs

Perhaps you are not retiring but your company decides to terminate its retirement plan and makes a lump sum distribution to you. (This is occurring at an alarming rate since the passage of TEFRA and ERISA.) Under this type of rollover, the requirements are exactly the same as above. However, unless you are 59½ or have also terminated your employment, your benefits do not qualify for ten-year forward averaging. Therefore, the use of a rollover would be even more valuable. Rollovers based on such decisions may later be transferred into a new employer's retirement plan, if the employer's plan permits.

Non-Qualified Deferred Compensation Plans

A non-qualified deferred compensation plan is a commitment by an employer to pay an employee a predetermined amount of money for a specified period of years upon his retirement or termination of employment.

Let's assume that you are a highly paid executive. You could choose to have your income reduced and have the amount of the reduction become the substance of a deferred compensation plan. You could also have additional amounts deferred in lieu of a salary increase. This would allow you to reduce your current income tax and have an investment compounding under a tax shelter. When you reached retirement, you would begin to pay income taxes on your withdrawals, would no doubt be eligible for additional tax exemptions as a retiree, and would probably be in a lower tax bracket.

The non-qualified plan can be installed without prior approval of the IRS. The rules for adoption and maintenance are few, and the plan can be discriminatory. You may have a deferred plan in addition to a qualified profit-sharing or pension plan. Your corporation, however, cannot deduct its contributions from its federal income tax. As your taxes on this money come due, then the corporation begins to enjoy a corresponding tax deduction.

Tax-Sheltered Annuities for Employees of Non-Profit Institutions

If you work for a non-profit institution such as a school, charity, or hospital, you may also qualify for a tax-deferred retirement plan.

Let's assume that you are a schoolteacher. You may request that the school reduce your salary up to 16⅔ percent and have the school invest these funds in a qualified annuity program through a life insurance company or a mutual fund custodial account. You thereby avoid paying current taxes on the amount of your reduction, and you may also reduce your income sufficiently to reduce the taxes on the remainder.

There are two types of annuities: the fixed and the variable. Many of the older fixed annuities still pay a very low rate of return, many under 3 percent annually. Even with tax shelter, this is not progress at our present rate of inflation. Whether you consider inflation a destructive force or merely a normal way of life, you must recognize that it will forever be a part of the nation's economic environment.

Despite the foregoing, many people still think that conservative investment requires a "riskless" savings device such as a fixed annuity, and that any non-guaranteed equity investment is automatically speculative. This attitude is dedicated to the proposition that the long-range economy will be deflationary rather than inflationary, and that the world's economy will stand still waiting for one's retirement and will remain so after one's retirement. History indicates that basing your financial security on fixed guaranteed savings vehicles is a risky thing to do.

Investing Your Retirement Funds

If you are the trustee of your pension funds, you will have many potential investments to choose from. You will want to have investments that provide the following: safety (remember our definition of safety earlier), income, growth, a hedge against inflation, a certain amount of liquidity, ease of administration, professional management, and compliance with ERISA.

Let's look at some investments that could provide all or part of these requirements:

MUTUAL FUNDS

The professional management offered by a well-managed family of mutual funds should certainly be one of your first considerations. I personally prefer the growth funds offered by these families. The growth fund in my company's pension plan has averaged 24.4 percent per annum for the past ten years. Even if we had used one of their funds that has only stocks from the legal list of the Registry of Wills of the District of Columbia, we still would have had a 17.6 percent compound rate or $50,446 per $10,000 invested. I personally don't believe that ERISA requires you to be this conservative to fulfill your fiduciary capacities. Had we used the Seminar Fund, the results would have been 17.2 percent compounded. Of course, the next ten years may not produce results this favorable, or you may do better. We anticipate doing better.

There is an added advantage to using timing for your mutual funds inside your pension plan, since there are no tax consequences when moves are made. Over a 15-year period, the simulation of results using the mutual fund we have in our pension plan shows that on an investment of $100,000 bought and held our investment would have grown to $633,717. With the timing service, it would have grown to $2,916,679. In real life over the next 15 years, the fund might not show comparable results or the market could have a sideways movement over long periods with a negative or no impact. But timing is an approach you will want to consider; and remember, you are always free to cancel the service if it is not making you money.

REAL ESTATE

There are a number of registered limited partnerships designed especially for pension plans. Most of them I have discussed in the Real Estate chapter. You will want to reread certain sections to become familiar with them again. Some of the ones I discussed that you may want to consider are:

FHA Mortgages on Multifamily Housing. In this type of partnership, your principal and interest are guaranteed by the FHA arm of the government. It is anticipated that cash flow will begin at 8½ percent and increase ½ percent per year. During the holding period your plan would participate in 25 percent of any rental increases and on sale 25 percent of any appreciation. Liquidity is provided by the issue of Depository Receipts which are traded on the exchange.

All-Cash Commercial Real Estate. In these partnerships, cash flow is projected to begin at 7½ percent and increase approximately 1 percent per year. When the properties are sold, your pension plan participates in 85 percent of the gains.

Participating Mortgages and Loans. In this type of partnership, the pension plan would be investing in participating mortgage loans which produce a fixed income plus 25 percent of the increases in rental income and 25 percent of any property value increases when the property is sold. The objective is to provide a stable base yield and upside potential. Cash flow is projected at 8½ percent plus an increase of 1 percent a year. There are redemption features to provide liquidity.

Participating Mortgages and Equity Participation. In this program, 50 percent of the funds are invested in very high quality mortgages with high cash down payments and 50 percent in all-cash suburban office buildings. The pension plans have a preferred position on sale, with the original capital plus 12 percent being paid to them before others are eligible to participate.

Real Estate Investment Trusts. Some excellent real estate investment trusts designed especially for pension plans are also available. One that we use is managed by a team that has a long record of successful registered limited partnerships in real estate. The funds are invested in land sale or leaseback transactions and participating mortgage loans on improved, income-producing properties.

Miniwarehouses. Limited partnerships investing for all cash in miniwarehouses are another viable pension fund consideration. They should have a good cash flow, which can be reinvested in the mutual fund you have in your plan to keep your compounding going, and they also offer the potential for land appreciation. The partnerships may put a mortgage on these warehouses once you have received your original investment back through cash flow, return your original funds to you, which you will then have to reinvest in another miniwarehouse partnership or another viable investment vehicle.

MONEY MARKET MUTUAL FUNDS

Every pension plan should have a money market mutual fund. In periods of very high interest, it is a safe depository in which funds can compound at good rates. In periods of lower interest, the main portions of the account should be invested in other areas, but the account should be kept open for new contributions to your plan. It can serve as a depository for the quarterly distributions from your real estate partnerships in which you do not have reinvestment privileges, or for the proceeds from stock sales until you have decided when and where to invest. The money market fund also provides liquidity for a retiring or departing employee who has a vested interest in the plan.

OTHER INVESTMENTS

Be on the lookout for other "prudent" investments for your plan, whatever "prudent" may mean today. The racehorse Seattle Slew is in a pension plan, and all his tremendous earnings have accrued to the benefit of the plan holders and have not been taxed. Remember, however, that if you do use the more exotic investments, they may not turn out to be the bonanza that Seattle Slew has been and you may have the government sitting in judgment against you for not making a prudent investment.

Social Security

Do you really want to try to live on Social Security? You need to start thinking of Social Security as social insecurity. That way you won't be deceived into thinking that it will really take care of your retirement needs, because it won't. Social Security was never meant to provide financial independence for anyone. It was meant to prevent mass destitution, to provide a base on which you were to build. Even though Social Security is not in robust health today, you will, if you qualify, receive a check from the government when the time comes. The question is whether the proceeds will be sufficient to keep body and soul together. Remember too, depending on your other income, up to one-half of your Social Security benefits can now be taxable.

If your Social Security benefits are not sufficient (and they probably won't be) and you have to continue working, you may lose many of your benefits. If you are a Social Security beneficiary under age 65, $5,400 (increasing with the consumer price index) can be earned before benefits are reduced $1 for each $2 of excess earnings this year. If you are 65 or older, but not 70, the limit is $7,200 (also automatically adjusted). Beginning in 1990, the penalty will be reduced: you will only lose $1 for every $3 in earnings over the threshold. If you manage to keep from starving before you reach 70, you can work and not lose any benefits, no matter what you earn.

KEEP TRACK OF YOUR SOCIAL SECURITY ACCOUNT

The government does make mistakes in recording Social Security credits to the proper account. These mistakes can be corrected if they are discovered before three years have elapsed. To avoid future problems, you should write for a copy of your records every three years; and if there are errors, they can still be corrected. To do this, call your Social Security office and request Form OAR-7004. It is a postcard that you complete and return, and there is no charge for this service.

Should You Take Early Retirement?

The answer to the question of whether you should consider taking early retirement depends upon many things other than Social Security. If everything else is equal, and your income is sufficient with the lower benefits, then go ahead and take your benefits at age 62. It will take you many years to make up the income you missed from age 62 to age 65.

If you retire at age 62, your benefits will be reduced by 20 percent. The closer you are to 65, the smaller your reduction. At 63 you would receive 86⅔ percent, and at age 64 you would receive 93⅓ percent. If you wait until after age 65 to retire, you are entitled to an increase of 3 percent in your benefits for each year between 65 and 72. So if you wait until 70 to retire, you will get 15 percent more benefits. If you take early retirement, your benefits do not go up when you reach age 65. When you become entitled to Social Security benefits, your spouse can collect benefits equal to 50 percent of yours if your spouse is 65, or somewhat lower benefits as early as 62.

Make preparation for your retirement early so that if you receive Social Security it will only be the "butter on the bread—not the bread itself." Becoming financially independent will not be an unattainable goal if you begin early, use your intelligence, and don't allow yourself to be enticed by the words "guaranteed" and "no risk" when it comes to investments. Those that seem to have the least risk are often those that guarantee you losses.

The very least you can do—not that I consider this enough—is to begin an Individual Retirement Account today. As we have discussed earlier, the IRA provisions set up in our tax laws were an admission by Congress that you had better take some steps to fend for yourself if you want your golden years to have any semblance of sparkle and if you do not want to depend on Social Security.

Your Will

You should have a current will drawn by a competent attorney licensed in the state of your legal residence, and you should be conscientious in having it updated as our tax laws change. If you have a will but it was written before 1982, go back to your attorney and be sure it complies with your wishes and with ERTA and TEFRA. Obtain the services of an attorney with whom you are compatible and in whom you have confidence.

Summary

One of the great benefits of having been a financial planner for so many years is that I have had the privilege of designing retirement programs for clients, seeing the programs produce the hoped-for results, and observing them enjoy those beautiful golden years in financial dignity. This worthwhile predetermined goal is available to you too if you will just begin your retirement program early enough and skillfully combine the three ingredients for financial independence: time, plus money, plus American free enterprise. Time can be your most powerful ally, so start today to maximize your results.

APPLICATION

1. How many years before you retire? _____

2. How much income would you need per month to maintain your present standard of living if you were retiring today? _____

3. What do you think the rate of inflation will be between now and your projected retirement date?_____

4. How much income per month will you need by then?_____

5. What is your present age?_____

6. How many years have you worked?_____

7. What were your total earnings for those working years?_____

8. How much are your assets worth today?_____

9. Are your assets sufficient to allow you to retire?_____

10. If not, what action do you plan to take this week to correct the situation?

    1) _____

    2) _____

    3) _____

    4) _____

Chapter **15**

Investing in a College Education

Let's now consider the "Learning Period," the first of the three financial periods in almost every life. The purpose of this chapter is to discuss how you might finance the learning period if you have children who want to further their education by going to college. Second only to planning for your own retirement, planning for your children's college education may well be the largest financial challenge you will face.

You must realize that doing precise planning for a college education for one or more children could be even more difficult than planning your own retirement because there are so many unknowns. First, you do not know where, or even if, your children will want to go to college; second, since costs vary widely among the different types of postsecondary institutions, it is difficult to estimate the amount you will need to save; third, you will probably have fewer years in which to achieve this particular financial goal; and fourth, you do not know how fast the costs for a college education will escalate. But despite the many unknowns, it is possible to work out a plan to have dollars for those degrees.

I firmly believe that a college education is a good, prudent investment. Studies show that a college degree can add another $250,000 to $500,000 in earning power in an average lifetime. It can also be an investment in living, for the additional education and exposure to a wide variety of people can add a large dimension to life. Friendships made in college lend themselves to business connections later; there are fewer divorces among college graduates; and an appreciation for the arts and literature can also be developed there.

The mass college education that has been occurring over the past fifteen to twenty years has produced a new elite in America. This new elite consists of college graduates with skills honed by technology and rapid change. They are not only educated and articulate, but they are permeating every facet of American life, affecting our opinions, our policies, and our pleasures. Every day their influence is becoming more evident in government, business, industry, marketing, and research. "Think tanks" are producing studies for both government and industry. They especially affect the media, which in turn affect a vast number of people through news programs and documentaries.

Costs to Join the College-Educated "Elite"

Costs will vary according to the type of institution of higher learning your child attends and the time that will be required to complete his education. As a general rule, costs are usually lowest at publicly supported two-year community or junior colleges and highest at four-year private institutions. Four-year state-supported colleges and universities and private two-year colleges generally fall between the two extremes. The amount needed will also depend upon whether your child attends a nearby college and continues to live at home or attends a distant college (round-trip air fare several times a year can be expensive) and lives on campus or in housing in the surrounding community.

According to the College Board Annual Survey of Colleges, here are the components of average total college costs per annum per student for the year 1985–86:

Total average cost rose 8 percent at four-year public colleges for the year 1985–86 and, as you will note above, brought the annual costs to $5,314 for students who live on campus and to $4,240 for students who live at home. At four-year private colleges, this total

| | Two-Year | | Four-Year | |
PUBLIC COLLEGES	RESIDENT STUDENTS	COMMUTING STUDENTS	RESIDENT STUDENTS	COMMUTING STUDENTS
Tuition & fees	$659	$ 659	$1,242	$1,242
Books & supplies	355	355	373	373
Room & board	*	1,180	2,473	1,165
Personal expenses	*	729	836	800
Transportation	*	704	390	660
Total expenses	*	$3,627	$5,314	$4,240

| | Two-Year | | Four-Year | |
PRIVATE COLLEGES	RESIDENT STUDENTS	COMMUTING STUDENTS	RESIDENT STUDENTS	COMMUTING STUDENTS
Tuition & fees	$3,719	$3,719	$5,418	$5,418
Books & supplies	367	367	384	384
Room & board	2,591	1,132	2,781	1,250
Personal expenses	667	706	694	714
Transportation	351	546	382	581
Total expenses	$7,695	$6,470	$9,659	$8,347

* Sample too small to provide meaningful statistics.
Resident students live in college dormitories.
Commuting students live with their families and commute to campus.

average cost is $9,659 for resident students and $8,347 for commuting students, representing a one-year increase of 7 and 8 percent respectively. At two-year public colleges, total average costs were $3,627 for commuting students, a 5 percent increase over the previous year. Costs for resident students at two-year public colleges were not computed because the number of reporting institutions was too small for meaningful statistics.

Tuition and fees, which apply to all students regardless of their living arrangements, are estimated to rise slightly more than total costs for most students. The figures in the above charts represent the following increases over the previous year: four-year public colleges, 9 percent; four-year private colleges, 8 percent; two-year public colleges, 7 percent; two-year private colleges, 8 percent.

In addition, if your child chooses a school that is out of state, nonresident students may pay additional tuition costs averaging $2,104

Investing in a College Education   419

at public four-year colleges and $1,490 at public two-year colleges, signifying one-year increases of 16 and 9 percent respectively.

Some private schools will be even more expensive than those shown above. Below are the ten reportedly most expensive institutions of higher learning and their average total cost for tuition, fees, room and board, average personal expenses, and transportation for one year:

Massachusetts Institute of Technology	$16,130
Bennington	16,040
Harvard-Radcliffe	15,750
Princeton	15,625
Barnard	15,558
Yale	15,500
Brandeis	15,250
Tufts	15,236
Brown	15,190
Sarah Lawrence	15,180

CALCULATING THE COST OF COLLEGE EDUCATION

On page 421 I have assembled two columns of figures for you. The first is for a four-year public college resident student. The second is the same but for a private college. I have used the average costs today as reported by the College Board Annual Survey of Colleges and have used an inflation rate of 6 percent. You may want to study these projections. You can use the College Cost Worksheet to determine how much you will need for college expenses.

Paying for College

After you have made your calculations of how much will probably be required for college costs, and before you go into complete shock, let's look at the many ways you can soften the blow. The first rule is to start early to prepare for this known cost, because time can be your greatest ally. Also, you will not have to bear the burden alone if you put the greatest asset, time, and all the areas you have the privi-

Future College Costs with an Inflation Rate of 6 Percent

CHILD'S AGE	YEAR CHILD WILL ENTER COLLEGE	FOUR-YEAR PUBLIC COLLEGE RESIDENT STUDENT	FOUR-YEAR PRIVATE COLLEGE RESIDENT STUDENT
18	1986	$ 5,314	$ 9,659
17	1987	5,633	10,239
16	1988	5,971	10,853
15	1989	6,329	11,504
14	1990	6,709	12,194
13	1991	7,112	12,925
12	1992	7,538	13,701
11	1993	7,990	14,523
10	1994	8,469	15,394
9	1995	8,977	16,318
8	1996	9,516	17,297
7	1997	10,087	18,335
6	1998	10,692	19,435
5	1999	11,334	20,601
4	2000	12,014	21,837
3	2001	12,735	23,147
2	2002	13,499	24,536
1	2003	14,309	26,008

College Cost Worksheet

Entrance Year	Child: Age Now: Amount Needed	Child: Age Now: Amount Needed	Child: Age Now: Amount Needed	Child: Age Now: Amount Needed	Total Amount Needed For Year
Total					

Investing in a College Education   421

lege of investing in to work for you, plus various other programs that are available to you. Scholarships, grants, student aid, student loans, and jobs are some of the options that are available. About 60 percent of the students at private colleges and universities and about 30 percent of those at public institutions receive some form of financial assistance.

SCHOLARSHIPS

Today, colleges actively recruit top students, and you may find a surprising amount of scholarship money around. Many scholarships are not based on need but are awarded on intellectual ability, athletic skills, or vocational goals; while others are available to children whose parents are members of certain ethnic, religious, union, or other groups. There are even a few unusual scholarships for students who are left-handed, who are twins, or who have certain surnames or some unique characteristics.

Do not rule out a college just because of cost alone, because many of the higher-cost colleges have more financial aid resources to distribute than lower-cost colleges. As a result, your child may be eligible for financial aid at a more expensive college, even though he doesn't qualify for aid at a less expensive one.

If you think you are going to need help in paying for college, apply for it. Find out what you have to do to qualify and follow the guidelines set out. Information and advice on financial aid are available from high school guidance offices and college financial aid offices, and are detailed in *The College Cost Book,* an annual publication of the College Board covering over 3,000 schools. The book, in addition to listing the survey results, discusses various financial aid programs and eligibility requirements and explains how to estimate costs and needs. It also contains sample worksheets, a bibliography and glossary, and a financial aid application worksheet. *The College Cost Book* is available for $10.95 at local bookstores or by mail from College Board Publications, Department C77, Box 886, New York, N.Y. 10101.

Other excellent reference books include *Barron's Profiles of American Colleges* (Barron's Educational Series, Inc.), *Comparative Guide to American Colleges* (Harper & Row), *Peterson's Annual Guide to Undergraduate Study* (Peterson's Guides), *Lovejoy's College Guide* (Simon & Schuster), *The College Financial Aid Emer-*

gency Kit (Sun Features), *The A's & B's of Academic Scholarships, College Loans from Uncle Sam,* and *Don't Miss Out.*

The Horatio Alger Association of Distinguished Americans Scholarship Program. It has been my very great privilege to have received a number of honors, but none do I prize so highly as the Horatio Alger Award for Distinguished Americans.

Each year ten recipients from across the United States are chosen for this award. They are individuals who are living proof of success through triumph over adverse circumstances achieved under our free enterprise system. The awards are made each year at an inspiring ceremony and banquet; and the proceeds from this banquet, contributions by its members (all Horatio Alger recipients), and contributions by many others, provide twenty college scholarships each year to deserving high school seniors. The scholarships are awarded at the annual banquet to encourage similar efforts on the part of promising young people. In order to be eligible, the student must have participated in a Horatio Alger Day program at his high school and been chosen as one who best exemplifies the Horatio Alger characteristics, have severe financial limitations, proven character, ability, initiative, and exceptional promise.

My reasons for sharing this information with you are threefold:

1. You are invited to make nominations to the Association of potential recipients of the award who exemplify the Horatio Alger characteristics of hard work, individual initiative, honesty, adherence to goals, and community leadership.

2. If you are a high school counselor, may I suggest that you contact the Horatio Alger Association to inquire about the possibility of your having a Horatio Alger Day at your school. It will be one of the most inspiring and uplifting programs you could sponsor. Outstanding recipients of the Horatio Alger award will come to your school for the day and share an account of their inspiring and motivating lives with your students.

3. It is my privilege to contribute to this scholarship fund, and I want to invite you to make a tax-deductible contribution to it also. I do not know of a scholarship program where the recipients are more carefully chosen and hold as much promise.

For information, call or write the Horatio Alger Association of Distinguished Americans, Inc., One Rockefeller Plaza, Suite 1609, New York, N.Y. 10020; (212) 581-6433.

COOPERATIVE EDUCATION

Another way you and your children may want to consider for financing college costs is to attend a school with a five-year cooperative education program. The first year your child would take a basic freshman curriculum of math and English with courses in his major. Then the next four years he would alternate quarters of work and study, combining liberal arts with vocational training.

More than 1,000 colleges and universities offer co-op programs, but Drexel in Philadelphia ($5,225 for tuition), the University of Detroit ($2,385), and Northeastern University in Boston ($5,325) enroll the majority of their students in co-op education. Northeastern has the most extensive programs, providing its 18,000 undergraduates with a wide range of majors and jobs with more than 2,500 firms, including Raytheon, General Electric, Honeywell, and IBM. The university offers a first-rate education in such technical fields as computer science and engineering for an additional $300 in tuition per year.

The job experience obtained through cooperative education can be invaluable, and it can put your child far ahead of others in the job market at graduation.

Financial Aid Through the Federal Government

President Reagan's attempts to cut federal aid to college students made the headlines, but in reality the programs have not been greatly changed. There are two basic forms of government aid: grants and loans.

The U.S. Department of Education offers five major student financial aid programs. These include Pell Grants; the Guaranteed Student Loans (GSL) and PLUS loans; three campus-based programs called Supplemental Education Opportunity Grants (SEOG); College Work-Study (CWS); and the National Direct Student Loans (NDSL). Grants are awards that do not have to be paid back; loans are borrowed money and must be repaid with interest; and work-study gives the student a chance to work and earn money to help pay for school. Undergraduates may receive aid from all three types of programs, while graduate students may apply for any program except Pell Grants and Supplemental Education Opportunity Grants. Not all schools take part in all programs, so you will need to find out which ones are available at the school of your child's choice by contacting the school's financial aid office.

PELL GRANTS

These are awarded to help undergraduates pay for their education and provide a "foundation" of financial aid to which aid from other federal and non-federal sources may be added. The Department of Education processes these applications using a formula determined by Congress which produces a Student Aid Index. Awards will range up to $2,100, and most of these go to students with very limited means.

SUPPLEMENTAL EDUCATION OPPORTUNITY GRANTS

These grants are made for up to $2,000 a year, depending on the student's needs, the availability of the funds at the school, and the amount of other aid the student is receiving. Like the Pell Grants, they do not have to be paid back.

COLLEGE WORK-STUDY

The College Work-Study (CWS) program provides jobs for undergraduates and graduate students who need financial aid. The amount received will be at least the minimum wage and could be more, depending on the work done. The amount that will be awarded depends on the student's need, the amount of money the school has for the program, and the amount of aid the student is receiving from other programs.

NATIONAL DIRECT STUDENT LOANS

These are low interest (5 percent) loans that both undergraduate and graduate students can receive that are made through the school's financial aid office. Depending on need and availability, a student may borrow up to $3,000 if enrolled in a vocational program or if the student has completed less than two years of a program leading to a bachelor's degree, or $6,000 if the student is an undergraduate who has already completed two years of study toward a bachelor's degree and has achieved third-year status. This total includes any amount the student borrowed under NDSL for the first two years of study. A graduate student may borrow $12,000, which also includes any amount the student borrowed previously under NDSL. Repayment must begin six months after graduation and can continue over a ten-year period.

GUARANTEED STUDENT LOANS (GSL)

These are low-interest loans made to a student by a lender such as a bank, credit union, or savings and loan association to help pay for college costs. They are insured by the guarantee agency in the state and are reinsured by the federal government. For new borrowers, the interest rate is 8 percent. Each undergraduate student can borrow up to $2,500 per year, and in most states a graduate student can borrow up to $5,000 per year. The total GSL debt an undergraduate student can have is $12,500, while graduate or professional study students can have total debt of $25,000, including any loans made at the undergraduate level. Loan repayment must begin six months after the student leaves school for most loans, and they generally have ten years to repay. However, the minimum amount to be paid each month is $50. In some states there is also an origination fee for the loan.

These loans used to be available to virtually all students, but a 1981 change imposes a needs test that must be completed. The test is based upon your adjusted gross income; and if you are close to a cut-off point, IRA and Keogh contributions, business losses, and tax-shelter losses can be used to reduce your AGI. Families with rather high income can still qualify if they have two children going to expensive private universities. So if you have a need, you should go ahead and apply at a participating financial institution.

PLUS LOANS

If your child's needs for college expenses are not met by a GSL or your financial strength is too high to qualify for a GSL loan but you still have a cash flow problem, you may apply for a loan at 12 percent from the bank. This loan goes into repayment 60 days after you receive it, payments of a minimum of $50 must be made monthly, and the payout period can be for ten years.

Cautions. There are some deceptive insurance agents who reportedly are selling insurance policies on the life of prospective students, claiming that this type of policy will guarantee that the child will receive a GSL loan at college time. This is not true and has no connection whatsoever with these loans. As a matter of fact, there is no guarantee that there will even be a guaranteed loan program when it is time for your child to go to college.

MILITARY ACADEMIES

If your child has a patriotic bent, you might consider suggesting that he apply for admission to the U.S. Military Academy at West Point, the U.S. Naval Academy at Annapolis, or the U.S. Air Force Academy at Colorado Springs.

Each of these military academies awards a B.S. degree and an officer's commission for a five-year service obligation. Students get free tuition, room and board, plus a monthly stipend of $480. An equivalent four years at a private university—with the stipend and all other benefits considered—could come to $100,000 or more. Applicants have to be nominated by a member of Congress (a requirement not too difficult to meet) and must be academically bright and in prime physical health. Women are welcome too. West Point now has 498 women in its ranks, Annapolis has 325, and the Air Force Academy boasts 534.

Applications for admission are hitting a new high, probably because of the realization that a military college education makes good sense in terms of economics.

Working Part Time

Don't be reluctant to let your child work part time while in college to help meet some of the costs. A number of studies have shown that working students (probably because they have to budget their time more carefully) usually have better grade point averages than students who do not work. It seems that we humans have two speeds: full speed ahead and dead in the water. The work-study student can tailor his work schedule around his classes so as not to cut off time from study.

I worked my way through college and by trial and error came up with the jobs that best fit my needs. I chose jobs that I could do at times I would ordinarily waste and that required little or no concentration or intensive use of my eyes. By working as the cashier for the faculty and student dining room, I didn't have to stand in line waiting to get my food, but ate ahead of time. This job also provided me with a marvelous opportunity to get to know all the students and in turn led to my being elected president of my class. My other job was to represent the cleaners in my dormitory. This was done at night, right after the dorm closed, which was a good time to take a break from my studies. My first job was as a secretary, but this took up every afternoon and was tiring to my eyes. The less glamorous jobs were far superior for my purposes.

Even if your child can find part-time work, however, you will want to be able to help him meet those college expenses when that time comes.

Funding College Through Wise Tax Planning

Let's now look at the various ways you can fund your child or children's education with pretax dollars or at least lower-taxed dollars.

UNIFORM GIFTS TO MINORS

You are permitted to give $10,000 ($20,000 if given jointly with your spouse) to anyone each year without a gift tax. If you are in a fairly high tax bracket, you may want to make a gift to your child and then make an investment for the child by registering it in the name of a custodian under the Uniform Gifts to Minors Act. Under this arrangement the dividends and capital gains can compound without tax or at a lower tax if the child is in a low or no tax bracket. Each child can receive $1,040 per year tax-free from his own additional exemption plus a $100 dividend exclusion from American corporations. Until income exceeds $3,430, there should be little or no tax.

Under this program, you will still be entitled to the $1,040 exemption for your child, or for each child if you have more than one, as long as the child is either a student or under 19 years of age and if you supply over 50 percent of his support. You may not, however, use any of these funds for things that you are legally obligated to provide for your child such as food and clothing. But you may use the funds for college education.

If your estate is large, you may want to name as custodian someone other than yourself. In the event of your death, the value of the account could be considered a part of your estate for estate tax purposes if you are the custodian. At age 18, the funds in the account go to the child.

SPECIAL TRUST FOR MINORS

Perhaps you think it prudent that your child or children not have access to the principal until age 21. Under the Section 2503 (c) Trust, you may use your $10,000 per child annual gift exclusion ($20,000 if joined by your spouse). These assets and income can be used for the child before age 21, and if the trust's assets have not been spent by then, the principal must be paid to the child when he reaches age 21.

CLIFFORD REVERSIONARY TRUST*

As discussed in an earlier chapter, another tax savings technique you may want to consider is the Clifford Reversionary Trust. This is an irrevocable trust that must last for ten years and one day, or for the lifetime of the income beneficiary (whichever is shorter); and it can provide that the income be paid to your child or to a Uniform Gifts to Minors account for him. At the end of the trust, the capital would revert back to you. The net result of this arrangement is that the income from the trust can be used or accumulated for college expenses, it can be taxed in your child's lower bracket ($1,040 or more would be tax-free), and you can have your capital returned to you to fund your own retirement program.

If the amount that you place in the trust is $10,000 or less ($20,000

* Refer to the Tax Addendum in the Appendix for possible tax changes.

for split gifts), no gift tax is due. Each year the annual excludable amount may be added, and no tax will be due on the income if the trust is extended at least ten years beyond the date of the last gift. If your gift is in excess of the annual excludable amount, the IRS publishes a table to be used for determining this value and assumes a rate of 6 percent.

SPECIAL REMAINDER TRUST

You may also have a special trust drawn up by an attorney allowing your child to receive the income from property or money for a short term (say five years) and the remainder passing to your spouse. This arrangement can be for a shorter period than the Clifford Trust and shelters more principal, $54,618, than the ten-year-and-a-day Clifford Trust ($32,549) from gift tax.

APPRECIATED ASSETS

Another approach is to give appreciated stock to your child. Your child would assume your cost basis and when it is sold the capital gains would be at your child's lower tax bracket.

MATURED ASSETS

Let's assume you have invested in a registered real estate limited partnership and during the first five to six years have written off your entire investment and the property is now about to be sold for four times your original investment. Before the sale is made you may want to gift the units to your child and again let the capital gains be taxed at the child's bracket. The same could apply to registered limited partnerships and private placements in oil and gas programs, cable television, and miniwarehouses. There should be no major tax consequences for the child.

LEASING-PARTNERSHIP GIFTS

One of my favorite ways of accomplishing this technique is through the use of a leasing registered limited partnership. It might work something like this. Let's assume that you are in a 40 percent tax bracket and that you invest $10,000 and the general partner in turn borrows $20,000, non-recourse, for a tax basis of $30,000. During the first five years, you would probably write off the $10,000 you invested and the partnership may amortize (pay off) $11,000 of the borrowed funds, leaving $9,000 due. Since the rules say that the only time you must pay income tax is when the debt is greater than the tax basis, there would be no income tax due.

Now, let's assume that instead of $10,000 you have five times that amount, or $50,000, to invest and that over the next five years the partnership pays back to you approximately $42,500 after taxes in cash flow and tax benefits and you reinvest this at 8 percent. At the end of the five years you give the units of the partnership to your child or grandchild. Let's further assume that the partnership distributes over the next four years $80,000 in cash and that your child uses these distributions to pay for college costs. Your out-of-pocket cost would then be $7,500 for your child's $80,000 education.

EMPLOYING YOUR CHILD

As we discussed in the tax-shelter chapter, employing members of your family, especially your college-bound children, can be smart financial planning. Make sure your children do legitimate work for you or your company and that you pay them a fair wage as you would any other employee. If you pay your child $4,300 each year and your child opens an IRA account, contributing $2,000 each year, this would leave your child in a zero tax bracket. If your child does this for four years and averages only 10 percent return, the investment would grow to $10,210. Also, if he saved the remaining $2,300 he could have more than double that amount, or $11,742, for a combined amount of $21,952.

When your child withdraws his IRA account he will have a 10 percent penalty on the amount withdrawn that year. The amount still in the account continues to compound tax deferred until withdrawal.

I calculate that in a 35 percent bracket you would have had to earn over $30,000 to accomplish the same results as paying your child $17,200. In addition, his wages were tax deductible to the company.

Using Mutual Funds for College Expenses

You will find that a good growth mutual fund should be an excellent consideration for building up reserves for college, regardless of whether you place them inside a custodian or trust account.

Let's use the worksheet below and assume that you have two children, ages two and four, and that you want to plan to be financially able to send them to college when the time comes. Let's also assume that they will both choose to attend a public four-year college in the state in which you are a resident, that both of them will live on campus, and that they do not go on to graduate school but just attend college for four years. Using our worksheet, you will find that by the year 1998 you will need $10,692, by 1999 you will need $11,334, in the year 2000 you will have two children in college and you will need $24,028, the next year $25,470, the following year $13,499, and the last year $14,309, for a total of $99,332 over the six-year period.

Let's further assume that you can save $250 per month and that you begin today. You will have 14 years before you need your first funds and 16 years before you have the "double whammy." If you had invested $250 a month for 14 years in the middle-of-the-road Seminar Fund (I recommend a growth fund instead), you would have invested a total of $42,000 and it would have grown to $67,639 during this particular 14-year period. At the end of the 14-year period, let's assume that you began a monthly withdrawal program of $641 per

Entrance Year	Child: Jack Age Now: 4 Amount Needed	Child: Jill Age Now: 2 Amount Needed	Child: Age Now: Amount Needed	Child: Age Now: Amount Needed	Total Amount Needed For Year
1998	10,692				10,692
1999	11,334				11,334
2000	12,014	12,014			24,028
2001	12,735	12,735			25,470
2002		13,499			13,499
2003		14,309			14,309
Total	46,775	52,557			99,332

month. This amount, plus the $250 you have been saving, would produce $891 per month, or the $10,692 needed for the first year of college. Next year you withdraw $695 each month plus the $250 per month for a total of $945, or $11,334 for the second year of college. The next year you would withdraw $1,752 per month, plus your $250, which would produce $2,002 monthly or $24,028 for the year. The next year you would withdraw $1,878 per month, plus your $250, for $2,123 monthly or $25,470 for the year. The next year (with only one child still in college) you will withdraw $875 per month, plus your $250, giving you $1,125 monthly or $13,499 for the year. And the last year you would withdraw $942 per month, plus your $250, producing $1,192 monthly or $14,309 for the year. At the end of this six-year college period you would still have $34,960 left in the account, which you can use as the base for your retirement funds.

What if your budget would only allow you to save $200 a month during your investing period and through the six college years? You would have invested a total of $33,600 during the 14 years and it would have grown in that particular period to $54,618. In this assumption, you would need to have your withdrawal for $50 a month more than the program above because you will only be adding $200 a month to your withdrawal. Had you done this, you would have withdrawn $691 a month the first year, $745 a month the second year, $1,802 the third, $1,923 the fourth, $925 the fifth, and $992 a month for 11 months of the sixth year. There would only be $884 left in the account for the twelfth month, $108 short of what you need for that last month. However, if you have managed to fund this program for six years, I am sure you can handle this small shortage.

Summary

As you can see, funding the cost of your children's education may be a challenge. However, if you begin early and use some of the techniques we have looked at in this chapter, your task should be one that you should be able to accomplish.

APPLICATION

1. Use the worksheet on page 421 to calculate how much you will probably need for college expenses for each of your children.

2. What year will you need your first funds for college?_____

3. How many years from now will that be?_____

4. What will be your total anticipated college costs? $_____

5. How much do you presently have invested for that purpose? $_____

6. Will this amount be sufficient? _____ If not, how much

   more will you need? $_____

7. How much can you now invest for this purpose?

   Lump sum $_____ Per month $_____

8. What rate of return will you need to produce the amount needed?
   _____% (Use Table 5 in the Appendix to calculate lump sum; Table 6 to calculate monthly.)

Chapter 16

Taking Your Financial Inventory

Financial planning is akin to navigation. If you know where you are and where you want to go, navigation is not much of a problem. It is when you don't know the two points that it becomes difficult.

To find out where you are now with your personal financial planning, it is time for you to take a financial inventory. What follows is the simple personal Financial Planning Data Sheet that I distribute at the first session of my three-session financial planning seminars. After completing and returning this data sheet to us, each person in attendance at the seminar is entitled to a personal consultation in our office without charge. In addition to the data sheet, we ask that each person bring all of his life and disability insurance policies, his tax returns for the last three years, a printout of his retirement benefits, and any other related materials. This gives us an opportunity to do a preliminary analysis of his stocks, bonds, limited partnerships, retirement program, and tax situation prior to his initial office visit, thus allowing us to maximize the contribution that we can make to planning his financial future.

If we grant an appointment to someone who has not previously completed the data sheet, we then complete one together. Without this information, we are flying blind. If an individual refuses to give us this information, we usually will not accept him as a client. Without the information, it would be as if he had gone to his family doctor in pain and then refused to tell the doctor where the pain was located.

If the prospective client is married, we want the husband and wife to come in together for the planning session. We have found that love is not so much looking into each other's eyes as looking in the same direction—and that is doubly true when it comes to financial planning.

Please stop now and complete your Financial Planning Data Sheet.

FINANCIAL PLANNING DATA SHEET

DATE _____

NAME _____ AGE _____

ADDRESS _____ ZIP CODE _____

HOME PHONE NO. _____ BUSINESS PHONE NO. _____

EMPLOYER _____ OCCUPATION _____

NAME OF SPOUSE _____ AGE _____

EMPLOYER _____ SPOUSE'S BUSINESS PHONE NO. _____

OCCUPATION _____

DO YOU HAVE A CURRENT WILL? _____ DATE OF WILL _____
ARE YOU COVERED UNDER A PENSION PLAN? _____
DO YOU HAVE AN   IRA? _____ KEOGH? _____

MY FINANCIAL RESOURCES

I. LOANED DOLLARS:

A. Checking Account $_____

B. Amounts in Passbook Savings Accounts:

	Institution	Amount	
1.	_____	_____	
2.	_____	_____	$_____

C. Certificates of Deposit:

	Institution	Rate %	Maturity	Amount	
1.	_____	_____	_____	_____	
2.	_____	_____	_____	_____	
3.	_____	_____	_____	_____	$_____

D. Credit Union ____% $_____

E. Money Market Mutual Funds:

	Fund	Amount	
1.	_____	$_____	
2.	_____	$_____	$_____

F. Government Bonds & Instruments:

Description	% Rate	Maturity Date	Cost	Market Value
_____	_____	_____	_____	_____
_____	_____	_____	_____	_____
_____	_____	_____	_____	_____
				$_____

G. Bonds—Corporate and Municipals:

Name of Company or Municipality	No. of Bonds	Rate %	Maturity Date	Cost	Market Value
_____	_____	_____	_____	_____	_____
_____	_____	_____	_____	_____	_____
_____	_____	_____	_____	_____	$_____

H. Mortgage Receivable (Owed You) $_____

I. Loans Receivable (Owed You) $_____

J. Cash Value of Insurance Policies (Use Worksheet) $_____

K.   TOTAL LOANED DOLLARS $_____

II. WORKING DOLLARS:

L. Stocks and Mutual Funds

No. of Shares	Name of Company	Date of Purchase	Cost	Market Value
_____	_____	_____	_____	_____
_____	_____	_____	_____	_____
_____	_____	_____	_____	_____
_____	_____	_____	_____	_____
_____	_____	_____	_____	_____
_____	_____	_____	_____	_____
_____	_____	_____	_____	_____
_____	_____	_____	_____	_____
_____	_____	_____	_____	_____
_____	_____	_____	_____	_____

$_____

Total Market Value $_____

M. Real Estate:

Home (Market Value Less Mortgage) $_____

Other Real Estate (Net After Mortgages):

_____ $_____

_____ $_____

_____ $_____

_____ $_____ $_____

N. Vested Retirement Benefits Not Included Above:

	Amount	
Pension and/or Profit Sharing	$_____	
IRA	$_____	
Keogh	$_____	$_____

O. Limited Partnerships & Other:

_____	$_____	
_____	$_____	
_____	$_____	$_____

P. Investment Grade Tangible Assets:

_____	$_____	
_____	$_____	$_____

Q. Commodities:

_____	$_____	$_____

R.   Total Working Dollars $_____

S. Less Notes and Accounts Payable
    (Not already indicated) $_____

T. Total Loaned and Working Dollars $_____
    $(K + R − S)$

Financial Objectives Numbered in Order of Importance:

_____ Income Now

_____ Income at Retirement

_____ Maximum Tax Advantage

_____ Educate Children

_____ Travel

_____ Other _____
                     (SPECIFY)

Estimated Gross Income This Year $_____

Estimated Taxable Income $_____

Tax Bracket (Tax Table in Appendix)   _____%

Taxable Income Last 3 Years:

3 Years Ago	**2 Years Ago**	**Last Year**
$_____	$_____	$_____

Taxes Paid:

$_____	$_____	$_____

No. of Dependents _____

Amount You Could Save Each Month $_____

Retirement Data:

    No. of Years Before: _____

    Desired Monthly Income:
    1) If Retiring Today $_____
    2) Anticipated Inflation Rate per Year
       Between Now and Retirement   _____%

Children Educational Cost Data:

Name of Child	**Age**	**Years Before College**	**Estimated Cost**
_____	_____	_____	_____
_____	_____	_____	_____
_____	_____	_____	_____
	Total		_____
	Amount Set Aside		_____
	Additional Needed		_____

Present Life Insurance, & Annuities Worksheet

(to Complete Item J)

Company	**Type**	**Face Amount**	**Cash Value**	***Net Insurance**	**Annual Premium**
_____	_____	_____	_____	_____	_____
_____	_____	_____	_____	_____	_____

_____ _____ _____ _____ _____ _____
_____ _____ _____ _____ _____ _____

TOTAL   ══════ ══════ ══════ ══════ ══════
                * Face Amount Less Cash Value = Net Insurance

Disability Insurance

Company   **Monthly Coverage**   **Premium**

_____ $_____ $_____

Completing Your Data Sheet

YOUR WILL

You will note that I have asked if you have a will. This is a very important part of your financial planning. In reality, everyone has a will—either the one that you have written to accomplish your own wishes or the one the state will write for you after your death. However, the state's will most likely will not bear any resemblance to what you would have written had you done so during your lifetime.

I urge you to obtain a properly drawn will prepared by a competent lawyer in the state where you are living. If your will was drawn before September of 1981, because of changes in ERTA you should return to your lawyer to learn if your will fits your desires under our current tax laws.

I won't go into detail about all your will should contain. However, let me make this one suggestion as to what you should not do. Do not, for example, will so many shares of XYZ Corporation to your daughter Sally, nor your credit union account to your son Johnny. If you do, every time you change your investments (which you will need to do often with the rapid changes occurring in the New Economy), you will also need to change your will. Instead, if you plan to have your assets disbursed equally among your four children, specify that 25 percent of your assets should go to each. If you want a portion to go to charity, reduce these percentages in order to have some remaining for this purpose.

Men, if you are married, do prepare your wives to be widows, because most of them will be. Women do live longer than men. You have worked together a lifetime to accumulate your assets, and your death will be such a shock to your wife that she may not be able to make rational decisions about money and many other things. Yet, some of her most crucial financial decisions will have to be made at a time when she may be least prepared emotionally to make them.

Just as important, prepare for the disposition of your property should you and your spouse both die before your child (or children) reaches the age of majority. If only one of you dies, your spouse would automatically become guardian of your children; if you both die, then alternate provisions need to be made for a guardian and so forth.

If you are a woman and have been taught that it is "not nice to talk about money," let me assure you that it is "nice" not only to talk about money but also to learn as much about it as possible—or you won't have any!

LOANED DOLLARS

You have already learned many of the ways that you can loan money in a previous chapter. All of these ways of "lending" money to a savings institution, company, or individual offer you a reasonably good guarantee of return of principal and a stated rate of return, with the exception of the cash surrender value of your life insurance policies.

Checking Account. This item is self-explanatory. Just add up all your checking accounts and enter the total on your data sheet.

Passbook Savings Account. List these by institutions and amounts and then total.

Credit Union. List this amount.

Money Market Mutual Funds. List them. If your funds are there temporarily under a timing program and waiting to go back into a stock mutual fund, so indicate. If this account is for your liquid money, so indicate.

Government Bonds and Instruments. If you have a variety of them, be sure to give a description, the interest rate, how much you paid for them, and their current value.

Bonds—Corporate and Municipal. Be sure to describe the bonds fully, or your financial planner will not be able to get a current quote for you. List the bonds, their rate, maturities, cost, and if you know, their current value. If you have municipal bond trusts, list the issuer and the number of your series.

Mortgage Receivable. Have you carried back a mortgage when you sold some real estate? If so, list it here along with the payment schedule.

Loans Receivable. Have you loaned money that you anticipate will be repaid to you?

Cash Surrender Value of Life Insurance. In addition to this data sheet, there is the worksheet in Chapter 13 that you can use to calculate the cash surrender value of your life insurance. As we discussed earlier, these funds do not technically belong to you; they belong to the life insurance company as a part of its reserve. However, you can obtain that portion designated as cash surrender value by borrowing it from the insurance company and paying interest to do so, or by surrendering your protection. If it is left with the insurance company and death occurs, the beneficiary receives only the face amount of the policy, regardless of how much you have "saved" using this method.

HOW MUCH IN CASH RESERVES?

As you make a total of your "loaned dollars," you may be asking, "How much should I keep in cash reserve?" As I mentioned earlier, when I first started giving investment seminars, I suggested three months' expenses in cash reserve. Now I suggest that my clients leave as much money idle as it takes to give them peace of mind, for peace of mind is a good investment.

If you need cash and have your funds invested in good stocks, mutual funds, oil and gas income limited partnerships, commercial income real estate limited partnerships, etc., you can sell the first two any time you desire. If it is not the right time in the market to sell, you can always take your stock certificates to the bank and use them for collateral for a loan. You can rent a lot of time and deduct the rent (interest) on your income tax return. Therefore, I don't think I need to keep money idle, working for someone else, while waiting for an emergency. I have cash any time I need it.

WORKING OR "OWNED" DOLLARS

In this category you may have stocks, real estate through individual ownership or through limited partnerships, energy, cable television, leasing, investment-grade tangibles, and other areas of high demand.

Stocks. In this area you should list your common stocks, preferred stocks, convertible bonds, and any warrants or rights you may own. List the number of shares, the cost basis, date of purchase, and today's market value.

Knowing the cost basis of your stock is very important in doing good financial planning for two reasons. First of all, you need to take a good hard look at your performance in the market, and if you are not reaching the goals and objectives you set for each stock, you will need to consider making some changes in your investment program.

Another important reason for knowing your cost basis is that you need to know how much capital gains would be realized if you were to sell at a profit or capital loss if selling at a loss. You need to weigh how much you will have to gain from another investment to overcome the tax loss if you are selling at a profit to come out ahead. On the other hand, if you have a loss, you may need to know how much you could save on your income taxes by establishing the loss.

Many have difficulty figuring cost basis, usually because of poor recordkeeping or because they become confused by stock splits. It only takes a small amount of time to keep good records if this is done as transactions are made. Appendix Figure 1 shows a stock record sheet that you may want to consider using. I like to use this sheet in a loose-leaf notebook, and then pull and file the sheets after the stock has been sold. Both the buy and sell confirmations that you receive from your broker should be kept in your permanent files.

Real Estate. First list your home (its current market value less the mortgage). Then list your equity in other real estate holdings that are not limited partnerships.

Vested Retirement Fund Benefits. If you are covered by a pension and/or profit-sharing plan, vested means that you can take it with you if you move to another company. If you are self-employed or work with someone who has a Keogh plan under which you are covered, your vested interest can also be moved. Your IRA is yours, and you are free to transfer its assets to other custodians and investments or to cash it in (at a penalty if you are under 59½ years of age).

Limited Partnerships. List here your limited partnerships in real estate, oil and gas, cable television, leasing, and so on, and indicate whether they are registered or private placements. If your partnership publishes appraised values (which it probably does not), use that figure.

Investment-Grade Tangible Assets. List here your holdings in gold and silver bullion, gold coins, rare coins and stamps, investment-grade artworks, and any other collectibles.

Commodity Accounts. List each account, giving the cost basis and current market value.

TOTAL WORKING DOLLARS

Add up your working dollars.

MONEY YOU OWE OTHERS

Include here all your accounts and notes payable that you owe others (exclude your charge accounts unless they are a meaningful percentage of your assets) and subtract this amount from your working dollars.

TOTAL LOANED AND WORKING DOLLARS

This figure should be reasonably close to your net worth, exclusive of your personal assets.

YOUR FINANCIAL OBJECTIVES

This section is designed to make you do some "soul searching" as to what your true financial objectives are. Your investments should fit your objectives.

ESTIMATED GROSS INCOME

Determine early in the year what you estimate your income from all sources will be.

ESTIMATED TAXABLE INCOME

Now list all the deductions you will be entitled to make. Study last year's tax return, as this will help you list many that you may otherwise overlook. What is your estimated taxable income? Do you want to be taxed on this amount? If not, start early in the year to select tax-favored investments with good economic potential so that you can lower your taxable income. Always strive to turn your tax liabilities into assets.

YOUR TAX BRACKET

Look at the tax schedule in the Appendix (Table 13). I find that many do not understand what is meant by tax bracket. For example, it does not mean that if you earned $47,670 on a joint return, you lost 38 percent or $18,114.60 to taxes. Your tax would be $10,171.60. It means that if you had a taxable income of $47,671, you would lose 38 cents of that last $1. We have a progressive tax system beginning at 11 percent and rising up to 50 percent, and your income is taxed at these various levels.*

Your tax bracket is a very important item and should greatly influence your selection of investments. If you are in the lower brackets, you can afford to invest for income that is taxable. The higher your bracket, the more you should consider tax-sheltered and tax-favored investments.

* Refer to the Tax Addendum in the Appendix for possible tax changes.

TAXABLE INCOME LAST THREE YEARS

I ask this question for two reasons. I often find that estimates of current taxable income are too high or too low. This gives me a picture of what it has been and an opportunity to inquire about what has caused the change. Also, there are certain tax-favored investments that can be made that produce tax credits, energy tax credits, and certain business losses that, under certain conditions, can be carried back three years to allow us to recoup taxes paid.

NUMBER OF DEPENDENTS

This, of course, is a number each of us can calculate. However, if you are using some tax-favored investments with good write-offs, you should complete a W-4 form and claim a deduction for each $1,000 of write-off. Do this in January, or as early in the year as you know you will be making investments that entitle you to a write-off. Be sure to include your IRA contribution. After all, you are only required to send the IRS the taxes you owe, and if the money won't be owed, why send it to them and wait for them to send it back? Remember, money has fantastic earning power and it will either work for you or the IRS. Which do you choose?

AMOUNT YOU CAN SAVE MONTHLY

Sit down with your family and determine how much you can comfortably save each month—not too comfortably, or you won't save anything. However, don't set the amount too high, but establish an amount that you can actually save. If you set it too high, you may become discouraged, abandon the plan, and fail to reach your goal of financial independence.

IF RETIREMENT IS YOUR OBJECTIVE

Determine when you plan to retire and map out your financial strategy accordingly. I have counseled couples of 50 who solemnly tell me that they plan to retire at age 55. When I look at their assets, I realize that there is just no way. They are not being realistic; and regardless of how much they may want to retire in five years, they will not be able to do so with only the income from the assets they have accumulated. They didn't begin combining the three ingredients of time, money, and free enterprise early enough.

Desired Monthly Income. Decide what you feel would be adequate or a desired monthly income and adjust for inflation, using the inflation factor you feel is realistic. Do learn to look at circumstances the way they truly are, rather than the way you wish they were.

Sources of Monthly Income. I suggest that you call your local Social Security office and request their latest booklet to determine your projected income from this source. You may want to consider whether you think Social Security will be solvent when it is time for you to retire.

If your company has a pension or profit-sharing plan, find out how much your pension will be and/or what has been credited to your profit-sharing account. Also find out how much money is vested (meaning how much you could take with you if you should leave).

Be sure to read about the possible tax advantages of an IRA roll-over in an earlier chapter.

COLLEGE FINANCING NEEDS

Chapter 15 on financing a college education should be helpful in calculating how much you are going to need for college expenses.

How Did You Do?

By now you should have completed your personal financial planning data sheet. How did you do? How many years have you worked? How much have you earned? How much have you saved? How many years before retirement? What do you plan to do about your financial situation beginning today? Write down specific steps that you are going to take to reach your goal. Have a family council and plan your attack.

Financial planning should be a joint endeavor if a couple is involved and a family matter if there are children. If the whole family has financial vision, the chances for attaining financial goals are vastly improved.

(If your net worth is in excess of $500,000 and/or your yearly income is in excess of $150,000, you may want to consider a more in-depth written comprehensive plan done on a "fee" basis. The data required to do such a plan would be much more extensive and I will cover this more fully in the next chapter.)

APPLICATION

Now that you have completed your data sheet, study it carefully. Are you surprised at your net worth? Disappointed? Based on what you have learned so far in this book, do you feel that your assets are well positioned and are all working as hard as is possible for you?

1. How many dollars do you have idle in a "guaranteed" position?

   $_____

2. Should you have more of them idle?_____

3. Do you feel that these dollars are safe? (Safety means that you will be returned the same amount of purchasing power at a point of time in the future that you have today.)_____

4. Should you have more dollars working for you?_____

5. In what areas today is demand greater than supply?_____

   _____

6. Do these areas lend themselves to convenient and prudent investing?

   _____

7. Which are best for you?_____

8. What yield are you averaging on your fixed-dollar investments?

Fixed Dollar	Yield
_____	_____%
_____	_____%
_____	_____%

9. What rate of return are you averaging on your working dollars?

__Investment__	__Rate of Return__
$_____	_____%
$_____	_____%
$_____	_____%
$_____	_____%

Chapter 17

Selecting Your Financial Planner

Reaching your predetermined worthwhile goal of financial independence will require creativity, determination, a willingness to change courses often, agility, sublimation of your ego, a reduction of your prejudices, an open mind, and the ability to act quickly and accept the dynamic changes occurring in the New Economy.

If you are a success in your chosen profession, you are no doubt devoting many hours to keeping thoroughly informed and implementing that knowledge. This leaves little time for the very specialized and demanding area of financial planning. Therefore, to obtain the maximum performance on your investable dollars, you may want to consider retaining the services of a dedicated, creative, knowledgeable, and caring financial planner who is assisted by a team of professionals.

Financial planning as a profession is relatively new. The International Association for Financial Planning, the group's professional association, was formed in 1969, and their Registry was established in 1983. The College for Financial Planning was founded in 1972, with graduates awarded the designation of Certified Financial Planner and the right to add CFP after their names. I am very pleased to say that I have earned this coveted designation along with others in this profession. From all appearances, the profession of financial planning will mushroom during the New Economy—bolstered by deregulation, the growing complexity of the national and international money scene, and the rapid and far-reaching changes that will be occurring.

Many of the large Fortune 500 corporations now provide and pay for the professional services of financial planners for their top personnel. It is a good business practice, because it leaves their executives with more time to devote their full energy to the corporation's business. If these business people are worrying about the proper utilization of their money, they are being distracted from the maximum utilization of their concentration on corporate matters. An employee with his own financial house in order should be a more creative and happy individual who, in turn, can be more productive for his company. This service is becoming more and more entrenched as an executive "perk." If you are not fortunate enough to have this service provided for you, you will want to initiate the process of selecting a financial planner for yourself.

The financial planner that will best suit you and your particular needs will depend upon your personality, your temperament, your knowledge and expertise in money matters, the amount of your income and net worth, and the complexity of your financial affairs in the past and those anticipated in the future.

Characteristics to Look for in Your Financial Planner

You will want your financial planner to have a "sixth sense" about money. Understanding the many complexities of money comes naturally to many financial planners, and they have the innate ability to make a difficult and complicated subject appear simple and easy to understand, even to the novice investor.

More and more men and women who are knowledgeable, caring, and devoted people are entering the financial planning profession. You will want your planner to have the ability to stand back and analyze where demand is greater than supply today and is most likely to be in the near future. This is a talent that can only be developed from being in the "thick" of financial undertakings and having contacts with the people in this country who make the major decisions or influence those who do. You will want your planner to be well informed about the economy both here and abroad and to have the talent to predict megatrends before they occur, the acute perception to detect when the trends have changed, and the ability to act.

Your planner should be inquisitive and ask you lots of in-depth questions, similar to the ones you have just completed on the data sheet. He will want and need to learn your preferences, temperament, fears, prejudices, priorities, values, and goals. And if your planner is like our planners, once he or she has the data and learns about your assets, tax bracket, time frame, and goals, he or she will usually know what should be the best investments for you. But translating and applying these recommendations to fit your temperament will be a great challenge. And even though one investment would be better for you from a moneymaking standpoint than another, it will not be the best investment for you if it does not provide you with sufficient peace of mind.

Your planner should be a member of the International Association for Financial Planning. The IAFP has grown into an internationally prominent organization and I am pleased to have been a charter member and had the privilege of serving on the board of directors. The association is making a tremendous contribution to the field of financial planning, and its magazine, *The Financial Planner,* keeps planners current on new investment ideas, tax shelters, estate planning, and new tax laws.

Certified Financial Planners

In addition to being a member of the IAFP, you will probably want your planner to be a Certified Financial Planner (CFP). This accreditation is bestowed by the College for Financial Planning on those planners who have completed two years of advanced work and passed six rigorous examinations. In order to graduate, a financial planner must be proficient in such specialized areas as strategic tax planning, comprehensive investment planning, retirement and estate planning, risk management, and business planning.

The College for Financial Planning has graduated more than 3,500 certified financial planners who hold the CFP designation. Although this designation is not as well recognized by the public as is the CPA designation (certified public accountant), it is rapidly gaining respect in the industry. The CFP does not, however, take the place of your CPA, legal counsel, or other advisers. He collaborates with them to achieve the best results for you.

How Financial Planners Are Compensated

Financial planners are compensated in one of three ways: 1) commission only, 2) fee only, and 3) fee and commission. You should choose the arrangement that best fits your needs.

COMMISSION ONLY

The commission-only planner will provide you with recommendations but will make no charges for his services. If you make an investment that contains a commission, he will receive a portion of that commission and that is how he is compensated. If you do not make a commissionable investment with him, he will receive no compensation regardless of the amount of time, energy, and professional advice he has provided you.

FEE ONLY

A fee-only planner will provide you with a written comprehensive financial plan for a fee. His fee will vary with the expertise and reputation of his planning firm, your income, your assets, your past financial activities and anticipated future activities, but it is determined mainly by the number of hours that the planner feels the plan will require.

The planner will give you a range within which your fee should fall. If he runs into unforeseen complications and the time involved will be more than originally anticipated, he will come back to you before proceeding and discuss any increase in fee with you. As a general rule, one-half of your fee will usually be paid when the data collection session is arranged and the remainder when the plan is delivered.

Your planner will pay the professionals he has on retainer from what you have paid him. This will not include the preparation of legal documents, tax returns, or actuarial calculations. Your planner will also work with your other professional advisers, and you will be expected to pay them directly. If you do not have these professionals, your planner can usually recommend those he has found to be competent in the field.

When you receive your completed financial plan, you are free to take it to any broker you choose for implementation, or your "fee" planner may make recommendations and help facilitate your implementation.

FEE AND COMMISSION

The fee-and-commission planner will prepare a comprehensive written plan for you just as the fee-only planner does. In addition, he will have the capacity through another company, known as a broker/dealer, to actually implement your plan for you and continue to monitor its progress. As with the fee-only planner, you have the option to take your plan to another broker for implementation if you choose.

Can your planner be objective with you if he is receiving a commission? Of course he can, because a planner cannot retain his clients and maintain a long-term relationship with any client unless he performs well, nor will he receive any referrals from that client. Referrals are the greatest source of clients for a planner who performs well.

It is perfectly acceptable for the planner to receive both a fee and a commission, since it is quite costly for him to gather your data, process it, and make suitable recommendations. He deserves a fee just like any other professional for performing a valuable service. However, unless you implement your plan, it will not enhance your net worth. Most people prefer to have their planner implement their plan, since they have already developed confidence in him and he has access to all of their information. Since he will be responsible for making specific investment recommendations, he will also be thoroughly acquainted with all the products that may be available to accomplish your financial goals.

Your financial planner should be experienced in investments, life insurance, tax shelters, and estate planning, and should have a close working relationship with a competent and creative CPA and attorney. He should have the skills necessary to oversee your entire personal financial program, as all of these areas must be skillfully meshed in the complex money arena of the New Economy. He should also know when, how, and who to call to join him in making the overall financial plan come together.

Aggressively seek out a financial planner who has an excellent reputation and in whom you truly have confidence. Then follow his advice. Don't make the mistake of going from person to person asking their opinions, because this will only serve to confuse you and cause you to make poor decisions. You will always find those who are eager to give you free advice about your money; and often the more readily they give advice, the more miserable the job they have done with their own money.

The "No Obligation" Interview

If you are not sure which type of financial planning is best for you, you may ask for a no-obligation interview. Most fee planners will spend an hour with you, at which time you can discuss your assets, your general financial goals and objectives, and other special financial problems that may be concerning you. The planner can then assess what kind of help he can provide on your behalf and the amount of time involved, and he can indicate a range within which his fee will fall. This gives you an opportunity to see if both of you will be compatible and decide if you feel his services could enhance your wealth and overall financial situation.

The Comprehensive Financial Plan

Let's assume that you have made the decision to move ahead with utilizing the services of a financial planner and want a comprehensive written plan. What should you expect? Each planner will have a different approach and each can be equally valid. Since I am more familiar with the format that we use, let me describe some of the steps to you.

DOCUMENT ORGANIZER AND QUESTIONNAIRE

First, we give you a data questionnaire for you to complete and a document organizer for you to use to assemble the necessary documents that we will need to prepare your plan. If we stopped there, it would already be a good investment for many of our clients, for when they have all of their documents assembled in one place, their financial papers are usually better organized than they have ever been before. The compartments of our organizer include the following: marriage and divorce records, Social Security records, pension and retirement documents, will, budget, property records, auto papers, birth and baptism records, tax records, property insurance papers, military records, auto insurance, cemetery lot and instructions, safe-deposit box and bank accounts, disability insurance, life insurance, medical insurance, investments and agreements, loan records, important correspondence, and credit cards and miscellaneous.

We would also give you an Income Tax Organizer with compartments for: W-2 and 1099 forms, records of interest income, dividend income, other income, capital gains and losses, medical/dental expenses and insurance, taxes (state and local income), taxes (real estate), taxes (general sales and excise), taxes (personal property and other), interest expense, employee business expenses, miscellaneous deductions, residence improvements and utility records, brokerage account and life insurance statements, credit card and charge statements, bank statements and cancelled checks, current year returns and payments, contributions, and casualty and theft losses.

THE DATA GATHERING SESSION

After you have filled out a Financial Planning Data Sheet, completed a questionnaire designed to find out how you feel about numerous issues that affect your life, and brought us all your documents, then it is time for our data gathering session. Information necessary for your plan falls into two categories: objective and subjective. Each is essential for the production of an accurate, complete, and client-oriented plan. As a matter of fact, when you begin to do financial planning, you may be surprised to discover just how much of your life is touched by financial considerations.

The object of these sessions is to arrive at a set of data that everybody agrees on before specific financial recommendations are made. Your planner will often probe areas of importance with you to find out what some of your written responses really mean to you. Assumptions will play a large role in planning, and your discussions should clarify which assumptions you agree will be used, such as what you and your spouse both think and agree is a reasonable inflation rate, which expenses would be more or less affected by inflation, and which expenses would continue if you were disabled. Another topic to be covered is how to measure the future performance of your assets. If you own stocks, your planner will probably ask you how you think they will perform. Do you think the dividends will increase? If so, by how much? If you don't know, you both might agree to use past performance as a measure. You can always change your assumptions in succeeding years as your objectives and economic conditions change.

Your planner will ask you a number of questions about yourself, your aspirations, your future plans, how you feel about your job and your family relationships. In fact, in our process, we use two counselors in each session, with one taking notes as the other asks questions. This interview is necessarily one involving numerous personal questions which affect all areas of your financial plan and often these discussions get into very sensitive matters. And this is probably a good time to mention the issue of confidentiality. We take it very seriously, our clients take it seriously, and you should too. You should find out who has access to your files and documents and what security precautions the planner takes to protect the confidentiality of your data.

You should feel comfortable sharing the most sensitive information with your financial planner which is pertinent to the preparation of your plan. If you are not comfortable "opening up" with your planner, you may find that some of the planning recommendations you are paying for may make you uncomfortable. Your financial planner's time is quite valuable, and if he asks a question, it is because your answer may affect his advice. After the data-gathering session, your documents are copied and returned to you and the input of your data begins.

VERIFICATION OF DATA

Before your plan is completed, there should be some method used to determine if you agree with the planner's numbers and assumptions. Our data verification procedure provides our clients with all written interview notes, tax projections, net worth projections, cash flow projections, and all data assumptions used in their preparation. Thus our clients have a chance to review, reflect upon, and revise or correct data before it goes to the advisers. We do not proceed until our clients have sent back their corrections or a "no change" letter.

What Areas Should a Plan Include?

A comprehensive personal financial plan should include a detailed analysis of the following areas:

A. Setting objectives
B. Determining your current financial position
C. Evaluating and making recommendations as to strategies to solve problems in:
    1) Risk management (all insurances)
    2) Investment planning and risk analysis
    3) Tax planning with cash flow analysis
    4) Retirement planning with targets for financial independence
    5) Education planning
    6) Estate planning
    7) Business planning.

PLAN PRODUCTION

Now that all of your data have been gathered and verified, the work of the financial planning staff begins. They will start their in-depth review, probably in consultation with an estate planning attorney, a CPA, and a pension actuary on retainer. During this process they may also use other consultants and ask them for their input. The time that will be required to complete your plan will, of course, vary depending on the complexity of your financial affairs.

PLAN PRESENTATION

After your written plan has been completed, your planner will review it with you, and together you will analyze where you are now and where your present course may lead. The formats used for this step are varied, but your plan should present you with a clear-cut course of action. "Version 1" of your plan will contain projections (not guarantees) of where you will be if you continue on your present course, while "Version 2" projects where you may be in the future if you follow the plan of action proposed.

Your final plan will also include a written analysis of any outside professional advisers that your planner has used, and you should have the opportunity to consult with these advisers to enable you to ask any questions about their advice.

IMPLEMENTATION CHECKLIST

Our plans include an implementation checklist that will show what is desired, by whom, when the action should take place, and who is responsible for taking that action. Your planner should follow through with you in the implementation process, because a plan left on the shelf to gather dust will be of no value to you.

Perhaps the diagram on page 461 will be helpful to you in visualizing the initial and continuing financial counseling process.

Your plan will probably be assembled in a tabbed loose-leaf notebook and will cover the following areas: family information, interview notes, personal objectives, economic background, employer benefits, current financial position, income tax analysis, personal cash flow, projected financial position, disability analysis, retirement analysis, estate settlement, survivorship income analysis, legal analysis, investment analysis, insurance analysis, changes in financial condition and recommendations, additional material, implementation summary.

MONITORING AND TRACKING

You will want an ongoing relationship with your planner, for with the dynamic changes that will be occurring in the New Economy, a tremendous amount of agility will be required to keep your money working at its maximum efficiency.

Financial Counseling Process

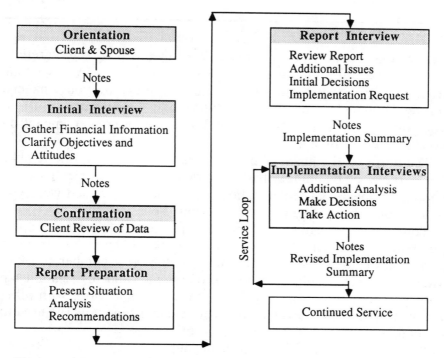

For continuous monitoring and tracking, your planner may charge you a yearly retainer which may be from 25 to 65 percent of the fee charged for your original plan. If you require a great amount of involvement on the part of the planner, your yearly fees could run about the same as your original plan fee. But remember, a good planner should earn much more for you than his fees, which are tax deductible.

It is smart financial management to call your planner any time you need financial advice. However, you should personally meet with him at least every six months. In the meantime, you should update him on your raises, savings, investments, sales, etc. And he should track your investments and provide you with a report. Most planners will have your information on computer and can give you a new financial statement and other updates upon request.

You would probably never consider starting a trip without carefully planning the route you plan to take. However, you may have gone from year to year without a plan to guide you toward your financial future. Obviously, your financial future and the financial future of your family are more important and will have a greater impact on your overall life than a single trip.

The purpose of a financial plan, professionally drawn, is much like the purpose of planning a trip. You determine your objective, you choose the best route for reaching it, and having planned well, you follow your plan until you reach your objective.

Your financial planner will be your personal adviser for helping you reach your secure financial future. He should have developed an expertise in investments, taxes, insurance, and a number of other vital areas. He should also be a professional, and his relationship with you should be a professional one. He should work with other talented professionals who advise you, using his input as required to execute your plan as skillfully as possible.

You should expect from your financial planner a breadth of knowledge, the confidential relationship customary among professionals, and understandable answers to your questions. You should also expect from him a comprehensive plan to maximize your assets, minimize your taxes, and allow you to reach your financial objectives. You should not expect him to perform miracles. But if you should find that you are not comfortable with your financial planner or have found his skills to be lacking, seek out another. Keep searching until you find the one that best fits you and your needs.

A good financial planner should be like a good growth investment that keeps paying for a lifetime, yet keeps growing in value. He should be one of your most valuable assets in projecting you down the road to financial independence.

APPLICATION

1. Contact the International Association for Financial Planning and get the names of members in your area. The address is: Two Concourse Parkway, Suite 800, Atlanta, Georgia 30328. Telephone (404) 395-1605.

2. For the names of Certified Financial Planners in your area and a copy of their Code of Ethics, contact the Institute of Certified Financial Planners, 3443 South Galena, Suite 190, Denver, Colorado 80231. Telephone (303) 751-3600.

3. For information about the scope of training to become a Certified Financial Planner, contact the College for Financial Planning. The address is 9725 East Hampden Avenue, Suite 200, Denver, Colorado 80231. Telephone (303) 755-7101.

4. Look in your local telephone directory for a listing of Financial Planners, Certified. Some cities now permit such a listing in the Yellow Pages.

5. Attend a local financial planning seminar. Try to appraise the speakers' knowledge and personality and determine if you may be able to work together.

6. Ask your friends and business associates if they know of a good financial planner in your area.

Chapter 18

Repositioning Your Assets for Maximum Gain in the New Economy

We have come a long way together since you began reading about the challenges of the New Economy in the Preface and Chapter 1 of this book, and now it is time to tie everything you have learned together and map out your financial plan. To help you accomplish this, I want to share with you my Diagram for Financial Independence, which I have designed, refined, tested, and embraced during my many years as a financial planner. The diagram has served my clients well over the years, and it is my sincere hope that it will be as helpful to you in your quest for financial independence. When we have counseled with clients, diversified their assets over the diagram in correlation with their tax bracket, and continually repositioned their assets within the diagram, their assets have grown toward their financial objective. I first published my diagram in *The Financial Planner* magazine in February 1977, and since that time it has been used by numerous financial planners with their clients.

Diagram for Financial Independence

Figure 18-1 is my Diagram for Financial Independence. Study it, see how it ties together many of the areas you have studied in this book, and then let's look at its implementation. All the knowledge that ever existed will not benefit you if you do not apply it to your own particular situation.

The Umbrella of Time

Across the top of the diagram you will find "Life Insurance—The Umbrella of Time." You learned earlier that the great mystery of life is the length of it, and since you don't know how long it will be, you will want to provide an umbrella over your dependents in order to protect them until you have had the time to substitute a living estate for a death estate. You have already discovered that the cost of buying time is not expensive if done properly and that the expense can be conveniently covered in the average family budget.

We also agreed that you want a living estate rather than a death estate. Once you have provided this living estate, you have fulfilled your obligation to those dependent upon you and are free to stop wasting your hard-earned after-tax dollars on life insurance premiums. (We also determined that if you wanted to pass on your estate intact, you could continue to carry sufficient life insurance for that purpose.)

After you have provided this umbrella or have become self-insured, you are free to devote your attention to making your assets grow. We have already concluded that although money will not bring you happiness, neither will poverty. Money will give you options in life that you will not have without it. No person is really free until he is financially independent. Until that time, he is an economic slave.

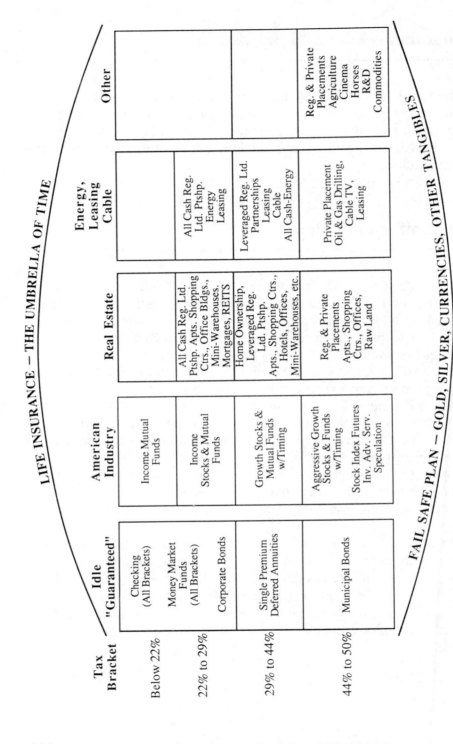

LIFE INSURANCE — THE UMBRELLA OF TIME

FAIL SAFE PLAN — GOLD, SILVER, CURRENCIES, OTHER TANGIBLES

Tax Bracket	Idle "Guaranteed"	American Industry	Real Estate	Energy, Leasing Cable	Other
Below 22%	Checking (All Brackets)	Income Mutual Funds			
	Money Market Funds (All Brackets)				
22% to 29%	Corporate Bonds	Income Stocks & Mutual Funds	All Cash Reg. Ltd. Ptshp. Apts. Shopping Ctrs., Office Bldgs., Mini-Warehouses. Mortgages, REITS	All Cash Reg. Ltd. Ptshp. Energy Leasing	
29% to 44%	Single Premium Deferred Annuities	Growth Stocks & Mutual Funds w/Timing	Home Ownership, Leveraged Reg. Ltd. Ptshp. Apts., Shopping Ctrs., Hotels, Offices, Mini-Warehouses, etc.	Leveraged Reg. Ltd. Partnerships Leasing Cable All Cash-Energy	
44% to 50%	Municipal Bonds	Aggressive Growth Stocks & Funds w/Timing Stock Index Futures Inv. Adv. Serv. Speculation	Reg. & Private Placements Apts., Shopping Ctrs., Offices, Raw Land	Private Placement Oil & Gas Drilling, Cable TV, Leasing	Reg. & Private Placements Agriculture Cinema Horses R&D Commodities

Figure 18-1.

Tax Bracket

Now that we have bought you time, let's proceed with the building of your living estate; or if you have already acquired sufficient assets, let's plot where they are located on the diagram and then see if some of them should be repositioned for greater growth, tax advantage, safety, diversification, or increased spendable income.

Every investment you will ever make should be carefully correlated with your tax bracket. If it is not, you are probably making the wrong investment. After all, the only money you will ever spend is what the government lets you keep. Therefore, you must learn to think in terms of "keepable" income or "after-tax" income, not pretax income.

Tax Equivalents

You must learn to think in tax equivalents. What would you have to earn on a taxable instrument, such as a certificate of deposit, to be equivalent to the after-tax, tax-sheltered, or tax-free return on an alternative investment? For example, if you are in the 33 percent tax bracket, you must earn $1,496 to have $1,000 left after taxes. If you are in a 44 percent bracket, you need to earn $1,786.

Tax Categories

You will note that the diagram has four tax categories going down the left side: below 22 percent, 22–29 percent, 29–44 percent, and 44–50 percent.* Because we have a progressive tax schedule, you will have some of your income in all of these brackets, beginning at 11 percent. By now you should have determined your top tax bracket. If not, look at Appendix Table 13 and do so now.

* Refer to the Tax Addendum in the Appendix for possible tax changes.

Idle "Guaranteed" Dollars

The next column in the diagram is for Idle "Guaranteed" Dollars. You need some liquid assets—we all do. As a matter of fact, I encourage you to keep as much money there as it takes to give you peace of mind. You may need what I call "patting money." Some people do, and you may be one of them, so you should keep some money in that position, since peace of mind is a good investment. However, throughout this book I have tried to educate you to the point where you will not have any peace of mind if you leave too many of your funds idle. The assets that you have in this column are "guaranteed" as to principal on maturity and rate of return. Unfortunately, in today's economy they may be guaranteed to lose! After inflation and taxation you may not be winning! You may be like the little frog we have already learned about, who is trying to get out of the financial well by hopping up one step and sliding back two. You may be losing the money game on the funds you have positioned in this column. Let's now analyze each category in the diagram.

CHECKING ACCOUNTS

Our first category under "guaranteed" dollars is a checking account. You will need one or more accounts for convenience and for a strong banking connection. Develop a superb relationship with the top people in the bank of your choice. Choose a bank large enough and progressive enough to fund any good bankable project that you may present to them. Your banking connections will be of immeasurable help to you in winning the money game. You will find that the wise use of leverage will be indispensable to you in the inflationary world in which we live. In addition, our tax laws subsidize a portion of this expense.

You may need more than one checking account to allocate your spending and investments properly. You will certainly need an account for the payment of your bills, whether for necessities or luxuries, but do not keep too large an amount there not earning interest. On the other hand, always keep enough there so that you can write a check whenever you want to. It is psychologically bad for you to feel poor, because you won't feel like a winner and you won't feel that you have options in life. You want to think, feel, and act like a winner at all times, because you are!

MONEY MARKET FUNDS

In my opinion, there are only three places to have "idle" dollars. These are in a checking account, or in one of the interest-paying accounts at your bank or savings and loan, or in one or more money market mutual funds or money market accounts at your bank. There will be times when you need liquid assets, such as when you are waiting for the right investment to become available, or when you have to set aside funds to pay taxes (not too many, I hope), or have temporarily withdrawn from the stock market and are waiting to return when conditions become more favorable. There are a number of money market instruments from which to choose; their rates vary slightly, but most will be comparable. A money market mutual fund gives you the convenience of opening an account for $1,000 or more with no cost to deposit the funds, no cost to take them out, and the privilege (if you request it) of writing checks for $500 or more (some smaller), while receiving approximately the same rate as a million-dollar certificate of deposit. Any time you need money in your checking account, just write a check on the fund and deposit it in your checking account. And if the amount you need is $500 or more, just write a check on the fund itself. I transfer funds from my money market fund to my checking account for ease of record-keeping.

CERTIFICATES OF DEPOSIT

Certificates can now be purchased for short periods of time. However, I still prefer the added flexibility and check-writing convenience of the money market mutual fund. You should think twice before tying your money up for long periods of time. If you want to use your funds before maturity of the certificate, you will suffer a penalty.

CORPORATE BONDS

I have placed corporate bonds in the guaranteed column. However, they are not guaranteed as to principal before their maturity date. If you should need your funds or find more attractive investments before that date and sell them, you will have a loss if interest rates have risen above the rate your bonds carry, or you may sell for a premium if interest rates have dropped below the rate your bond carries.

SINGLE-PREMIUM DEFERRED ANNUITY

You can use a single-premium deferred annuity if for your peace of mind you need to have your funds guaranteed and you are in a 33 percent tax bracket or higher and would like to defer taxes. This type of "loaned" dollar fits this requirement. Or perhaps you have invested in an aggressive tax shelter that has used accelerated depreciation, which creates a negative cost basis. When the property is sold or a foreclosure takes place, you may owe a capital gains tax. You can invest these tax dollars you have saved (you would not have had them anyway if you had not invested in the tax-favored investment and paid the tax) into an annuity where they can compound tax deferred. When and if the tax is due, you will have the funds with which to pay the taxes, and because the annuity has been earning interest on interest without the dilution of taxes, you may have funds left over. Until you withdraw the money from the annuity, there is no tax due.

Another possibility is that of refinancing your home and placing the funds in the annuity. (You can't do this if you live in Texas, because of its "homestead law.") You may not want to leave idle capital in the equity of your home if attractive financing is available. Your home doesn't know whether it has a small or large mortgage on it, and it can inflate just as much with a large mortgage as with a small one. Having a large equity in your home can be like having that much money in a checking account not drawing interest.

If you need the peace of mind of knowing that money is available and guaranteed if you should ever desire to pay on or off the mortgage, you could place these funds into an annuity and let them compound tax deferred. You can always withdraw them whenever you choose to pay off the mortgage or to pay for expenses such as a college education, starting a business, participating in an investment, and so on, and pay the tax at that time.

Cash is severely hurt by inflation and debt is the beneficiary. Also, you are entitled to deduct the interest while using the funds in alternative investments, and when you pay off the principal you can do so with cheaper dollars. Inflation does reward those who owe money, not those who pay cash. However, you must remember that unless your annuity rate is greater than the inflation rate, you are still not winning the money game.

MUNICIPAL BONDS

On the diagram under "idle" guaranteed dollars in the 44 to 50 percent bracket, I have placed municipal bonds. These can be municipal bond funds, municipal bond trusts, or individual municipal bonds that you have selected. At maturity, if you have chosen well, you will receive the face amount of your bonds. In the meantime, you will receive tax-free income. However, if you need your funds before maturity and interest rates have gone up, the amount you can sell your bond for will go down. Also, if inflation is high when you receive back your dollars, they will have lost a portion of their purchasing power.

American Industry

We now move into the area of putting your dollars to work for you as hard as you had to work to get them. You will definitely want to consider stock of American corporations and, if you have developed sufficient expertise, that of foreign corporations.

Equities in stocks should be a viable part of your asset distribution. However, you should probably never have more than 40 percent of your assets in that position, and there will be periods of time when none should be there. The only reason you should ever have money invested in the stock market is to make money. When you can't make money, and there will be times when this will be extremely difficult to do, get out and sit on the sidelines in money market mutual funds.

If you have the three T's and an M and find that the time spent selecting stocks is more enjoyable and more profitable than some leisure pursuits, select and manage your own portfolio. You will remember that the T's are: time to study the market and the information about current companies and national and international affairs; training to interpret and decipher financial reports; and the temperament to make rational decisions quickly. The M is for sufficient funds to diversify in order to spread your risks and broaden your base for profits.

MUTUAL FUNDS

If you do not have the three T's and an M, don't take an ego trip. Let the professionals help you, through either private professional management, using an investment advisory service if you have sufficient funds to obtain an excellent one, or public professional management, using a well-managed family of mutual funds.

You will note on the diagram that I have placed the income funds in the 29 percent or below category. If you are in these brackets, you usually need income and will not be sacrificing as much to taxes. As you move up in bracket, you will want to move more and more toward growth. Actually, above this 29 percent bracket, I like to jump all the way to an aggressive growth fund as my target fund, with a timing service superimposed to move my funds back and forth between its money market funds and aggressive growth fund. This allows your funds to be moved in and out of the market freely without commission and gives you a safe harbor to run to and stay in until the storm has passed. (You could have a capital gains tax, and the timing service will charge a fee.)

SPECULATION

In the 44 to 50 percent category, there is nothing wrong with speculating with some of your money that you can afford to lose. Approach this area intelligently. Try to predict a trend before it happens and move out of it before it runs out. Some of my most profitable investments (meaning I made money rapidly) have been in lower-priced silver, gold, computer, technology, and oil stocks.

REAL ESTATE

In the next column you will find real estate. Our tax laws in the past have unquestionably favored commercial and residential income-producing real estate, and ERTA gave it even greater advantages. Before we get into a summary of investment real estate, let's first look at home ownership.

HOME OWNERSHIP

Your first consideration may be the purchase of your own home. I have positioned your home in the 29 through 50 percent category in the real estate column. This does not mean that you should not consider owning your own home in the lower brackets. However, your tax advantage is not as great at the lower levels, and you will usually find it cheaper to rent than to buy.

In the ten-year period 1974 to 1984, the cost of home ownership increased from 21.9 percent of income for heads of household under age 35 to 35 percent of income. If you decide to buy a home, it will usually be to your advantage to obtain the maximum mortgage, for interest is deductible and you can probably pay off the mortgage in inflated dollars in the future. The difference between a large and small down payment, however, should not be spent but invested in order to pay the increased home payments.

Housing is one of the necessities of life and can also be an "investment in living" if it fits your lifestyle. A home, in most instances, has also been an excellent financial investment over the past few years, but may be less attractive in the future.

REGISTERED REAL ESTATE LIMITED PARTNERSHIPS

If you are in the 22 to 29 percent tax bracket or if you need cash flow now, you should probably choose registered limited partnerships that pay *all cash* and that invest in multifamily housing, with a sprinkling of selected shopping centers and office buildings. In most programs, you should begin with an 8 percent tax-sheltered cash flow, with it increasing in future years. Other partnerships will have combinations of mortgages and equity which you can review in Chapter 6.

If your tax bracket is above 29 percent, you should consider the *leveraged partnership*. Instead of just $1 working for you for every $1 invested as you will have in the all-cash programs, you could have $2 or $3 working for you for every $1 invested. Non-recourse financing can still be used, meaning that the lender looks to the value of the property rather than to you for his collateral.* You receive the appreciation on the total value of the property, not just on your cash contribution, and you are permitted to deduct the interest and at the same time you take depreciation on the total cost basis of the property, not just on your down payment.

* Refer to the Tax Addendum in the Appendix for possible tax changes.

There are a number of possibilities in real estate you will want to investigate. My favorite real estate investment for the last half of the 1980s is multifamily garden-type apartments, the reason for which I have discussed in the real estate chapter.

In deciding which is best for you currently—the all-cash or leveraged limited partnership—remember to use tax equivalents. (You may, however, want to use both investments.) Using tax equivalents, you may find that the leveraged partnership is best for you because of additional depreciation and interest expense, although the cash flow may be less than with the all-cash partnership. Your net keepable cash flow is the key to your decision. I often find that my clients forget about the tax dollars that they didn't have to send to Washington, and I have to remind them that if they didn't have to send them to Washington they would still have them in their pockets.

REAL ESTATE PRIVATE PLACEMENTS

You may want to consider real estate private placements for that portion of your income that is in the 44 percent and above bracket. If these are properly and fairly structured, with the right general partner buying, managing, and selling the properties, they can offer you excellent growth potential while providing you with write-offs going in and tax-sheltered cash flow during your holding period. You will give up the wide diversification of the registered program, for there will usually be only one property in the program. You will also not have the watchful eye of the Securities and Exchange Commission, nor will you have the added expense of registration costs. These offerings are usually structured so that you can use most or all "tax cash"! Your write-off can be 100 percent or more of your investment, and the properties may be apartment buildings, shopping centers, mini-warehouses, hotels, raw land, or office buildings. They may be new construction or second- or third-owner properties. If you invest in new construction, you could have more risk because you could have building overruns, interim financing rates could escalate while the buildings are under construction, and there could be a lag in rent-up time. You could also have added tax advantage and more profit when they are sold.

Suitability requirements on private placements usually run high. You usually have to be in a 42 percent tax bracket or above and/or have a substantial net worth.

RAW LAND

Raw land for investment purposes purchased on your own may not be a viable investment for you unless your bracket is very high and you anticipate having sufficient future income to service the mortgage and pay the taxes. You must be in a position to support the land over a period of time rather than the reverse situation. If you purchase a small bit of acreage in the country as a get-away retreat, you should consider it an investment in living rather than an investment for increasing your net worth. It may do the latter, but that's not your main purpose.

On the other hand, there are now both registered and private placement limited partnerships that offer you professional management, diversification, and the opportunity to participate in investments in raw land with only a modest investment.

Energy Investments

REGISTERED OIL AND GAS INCOME LIMITED PARTNERSHIPS

Oil is still black gold. There may be periods when demand may be less than supply, but the demand curve for energy should increase. A good way to participate in this demand is through registered oil and gas income limited partnerships. In the 22 to 50 percent bracket, these can be an excellent choice for some of your "serious" after-tax dollars. In most programs you will have the option to take the distributions in cash or to reinvest. If you are investing for later benefit, you should consider the latter so your funds will have an opportunity to compound.

The advantages of the limited partnership approach to investing in energy as compared to investing in oil and gas stocks is that it avoids double taxation of earnings, and the limited partner receives the tax advantage of being able to write off depreciation and depletion. The disadvantage is lack of liquidity.

REGISTERED OIL AND GAS DRILLING PROGRAMS

If you are in the 44 percent bracket or above, you may want to consider investing in a drilling program. You will have a wide range of programs from which to choose (exploration, development, royalty, etc.). For this approach to energy, you should use as much "tax cash" as you can, rather than "cash cash," meaning you should consider using some of your "soft" dollars—those that will be making that one-way trip to Washington if you don't invest in some tax-favored investment. Most registered drilling programs will have little or no leverage in them, so for each $1 you invest, you will write off nearly $1. This means that if you are in a 50 percent bracket, half of the money you invest will be yours and half will belong to the IRS.

PRIVATE PLACEMENT DRILLING PROGRAMS

I have seen some of the best and some of the worst drilling programs structured as private offerings. These offerings can usually be more creatively financed to provide first-year write-offs in excess of 100 percent using recourse financing for future payments. This means that you will be signing recourse notes that you will be required to pay if they aren't paid off out of production. Even if they are, any money paid on your loan is taxable to you.

Investments in Leasing

LEASING REGISTERED LIMITED PARTNERSHIPS

If you desire income now and you are in the 22 to 29 percent bracket, consider investing in the all-cash leasing programs. If you are in the 29 to 44 percent bracket, your need is for tax advantage and less income and you should consider the leveraged programs.

LEASING PRIVATE PLACEMENTS

If you are in the 44 percent bracket and above and your need is for maximum tax deferral, look at well-structured, highly leveraged programs offered by general partners with excellent track records and with blue chip corporations committed to the leases.

Investments in Cable Television

REGISTERED LIMITED PARTNERSHIPS

If you are in the 29 to 44 percent bracket, a registered cable program can offer you a write-off of your investment in five years, and when the systems are sold your profits should be taxed at the more favorable capital gains rate.

PRIVATE PLACEMENTS

If you need more tax advantage and are in a 44 percent or above bracket, these programs can be structured so that you can pay in over several years and your write-offs can be around 150 percent each year.

Other Investments

I have placed a wide variety of investments in this column. Each that is offered to you should be carefully weighed with your financial planner to determine if it fits your tax needs and temperament.

Fail-Safe Plan

As I have discussed earlier, I have used gold as my "fail-safe fire insurance" program in case my other areas of investing ran into difficulties. A portion of your funds could be in these types of hard assets that we discussed in Chapter 11. If we have inflation and worldwide economic and political instability, hard assets should play a more and more important role in your financial planning. However, I advise not being caught up in the near-hysteria of the "doom and gloom boys."

Application of What You Have Learned

All of the knowledge in the world will not increase your net worth if you do not apply it to your own particular assets, time schedule, tax bracket, and temperament.

It is now time for you to act and implement your own plan for financial independence. Where do you begin? You have already completed your Financial Planning Data Sheet—you have, haven't you? If not, why don't you stop right here and do it now. Your next step is to enter your own information on the blank Diagram for Financial Independence on the next page.

First, look up your tax bracket, then opposite your bracket enter where all of your assets are positioned now. When you have completed this, take a look at your diversification. Are you heavy on the side of "guaranteed" dollars? Are you betting your future on the likelihood that we will have deflation in the years ahead? Are you hedged against inflation? How does your diversification fit your tax bracket? Does it fit your financial objectives? How does it fit your "peace of mind" quotient? Should you do some repositioning? On the blank diagram, I have omitted hard assets. In that space, reposition your assets in the way that you feel will best accomplish your own financial objectives. These should be the best investments you can make in light of your present financial objectives and present economic conditions. However, never consider these to be written in stone. You are living in one of the most dynamic money climates the world has ever known and it will change rapidly in the New Economy. But remember that it is not change but your reaction to change that will determine where you will be financially in the years ahead.

You are indeed fortunate to be an investor at this moment in history as our economy moves from an industrial society to a communication and information society. As you will remember, any time a nation moves from one major era to the next, a parenthesis develops

DIAGRAM FOR FINANCIAL INDEPENDENCE

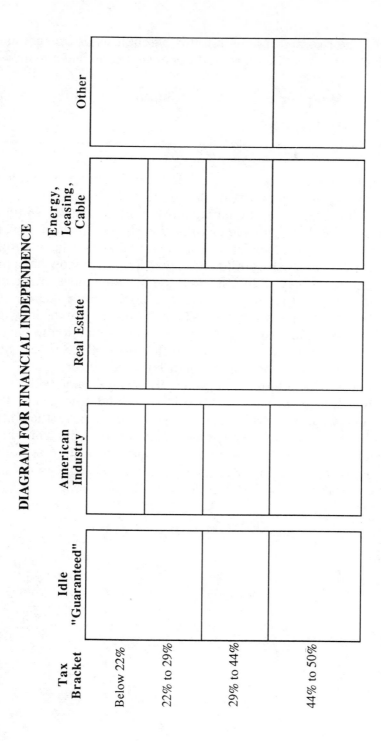

Tax Bracket	Idle "Guaranteed"	American Industry	Real Estate	Energy, Leasing, Cable	Other
Below 22%					
22% to 29%					
29% to 44%					
44% to 50%					

between the two and it is within this parenthesis of change that the knowledgeable have their greatest opportunities to make money.

The Money Game

Playing the money game can not only be fun but very profitable. Learn to play it well and reap the tremendous rewards that can be yours. It has been great fun taking this important journey with you. I sincerely hope that you have enjoyed the trip and that you now have the ingredients for financial independence, that you have sufficient time left to accomplish your financial goals, that you now have or can acquire some money to invest, that you are now more aware of the great privilege that is yours to invest in a good cross section of this great country of ours, and that this book has given you the knowledge of how to combine these ingredients and the motivation to do something about it now in order to make the most of the time that you have left. The world can truly be your financial oyster.

All you will need to do is approach the money game with enthusiasm, intelligence, a willingness to change, and true gusto! If you implement what you have learned, you should have the financial means by which to live the good life, enjoy the beautiful world around you, and someday be able to retire in financial dignity.

If you accomplish this worthy predetermined goal, you will say, "It was good that Venita passed my way." God bless!

Appendix

TAX ADDENDUM

Comparisons of Selected Provisions of Current Law, President Reagan's Proposal, and House Ways and Means Committee Proposals

INDIVIDUAL TAXES

	Current Law	President's Proposal	Ways-Means Bill
Individual tax rates	14 rate brackets from 11 percent to 50 percent, indexed	Three rate brackets set at 15, 25 & 35%, indexed	Four rate brackets set at 15, 25, 35, & 38 percent, indexed
Exemptions:			
Self, spouse	$1,080, indexed	$2,000, indexed	$2,000, indexed; $1,500 for itemizers
Dependents	$1,080, indexed	$2,000, indexed	$2,000, indexed; $1,500 for itemizers
Fringe benefits:			
• Health	Not taxed	Employee taxed on first $10 monthly of single coverage, $25 monthly for family	Not taxed
• Group-term life insurance, legal services, dependent care, education assistance	Not taxed, although subject to dollar limits in some cases	Not taxed	$50,000 exclusion for life continued; legal services, education assistance extended through 1987; $5,000 cap placed on dependent care.
Itemized Deductions:			
• State and local income, property, and sales taxes	Deductible	Repeal	Deductible
• Charitable contributions	Deductible (non-itemizer deduction expires after 1985)	Deductible for itemizers only	Deductible for itemizers; non-itemizers retain deduction above $100 floor

Mortgage interest	Deductible	Deductible for principal residences	Deductible for principal residences and second homes
Other personal interest	Personal interest deductible; investment interest limited to $10,000 over investment income	Limit to $5,000 over investment income (with expanded definition)	Limit to $10,000 individuals, $20,000 joint filers, plus net investment interest; cap includes limited partnership interest paid
Income shifting to children	Permissible	Tax unearned income of children under 14 at parents' rate	Generally same as President's proposal
Retirement savings:			
• IRA limit	$2,000	$2,000	$2,000
• Spousal IRA	$250	$2,000	$250
• 401 (K) plans	$30,000 annual deferred limit	Repeal tax-exempt status of contributions	$7,000 limit on employee deferrals, $25,000 combined limit, coordinated with IRA limit
Minimum tax	Alternative minimum tax of 20%, taxable amount includes preference items, $40,000 (joint) exemption	Alternative minimum tax of 20%, exemption amounts reduced, preference items tightened	25 percent rate with additional preferences, including tax-exempt interest on non-governmental bonds, losses from passive investments, and untaxed appreciation property contributed to charities
At-risk rules	Not applicable for real estate	Extend to real estate	Extend to real estate, but exempt third-party financing (as opposed to seller financing)

TAX ADDENDUM *(Continued)*

Comparisons of Selected Provisions of Current Law, President Reagan's Proposal, and House Ways and Means Committee Proposals

CORPORATE TAXES

	Current Law	*President's Proposal*	*Ways-Means Bill*
Corporate tax rate	Graduated, up to 46%	33% flat rate; graduated rates for small businesses	36% flat rate; graduated for small businesses
Depreciation	Accelerated Cost Recovery System (ACRS) with five (5) recovery periods for tangible property. Taxpayers elect straight line or accelerated	Capital Cost Recovery System (CCRS) with six (6) classes of assets, declining balance, indexed.	New system with 10 asset classes, ranging from three to 30 years; 200 percent declining balance for classes one through nine; straight-line deductions for class ten; partial indexing (over 5%) after 1987
Investment tax credit	6 percent to 10 percent	Repeal	Repeal
R & D tax credit	25% credit for qualified costs (sunset Dec. 31, 1985)	Extend for three years, revise and tighten definition of qualified costs	20% credit for qualified costs; tighten definition of qualified costs as under HR 1188
Capital gains	60% exclusion for individuals —20% effective rate (28% for effective rate for corporations)	50% individual exclusion— 17.5% effective rate; current law for corporations (optional indexing in 1991)	50% exclusion for individuals in 1986, 42% exclusion thereafter, creating 22% effective rate; repeal lower rate for corporations

Oil Industry:			
• Percentage depletion	Yes	Phase out with stripper exception	Phase out over three years, with stripper and royalty-owner exception
• Intangible drilling costs	Expense	Expense	Expense for costs prior to production casing installation
• Windfall profits tax	Will phase out in 1991	Same	Same
Deferral for life insurance and annuity income	Yes	No, except for existing policies	Yes
Municipal bonds	Tax-exempt	Only public purpose tax-exempt	Limit projects funded by private-purpose bonds; reduce volume caps but expand types of bonds under caps, including small-issue IDB's, mortgage revenue bonds; add new arbitrage restrictions

TABLE 1. $10,000 Lump Sum at Varying Rates Compounded Annually—End of Year Values

	5th Yr.	10th Yr.	15th Yr.	20th Yr.	25th Yr.	30th Yr.	35th Yr.	40th Yr.
1%	10,510	11,046	11,609	12,201	12,824	13,478	14,166	14,888
2%	11,040	12,189	13,458	14,859	16,406	18,113	19,998	22,080
3%	11,592	13,439	15,579	18,061	20,937	24,272	28,138	32,620
4%	12,166	14,802	18,009	21,911	26,658	32,433	39,460	48,010
5%	12,762	16,288	20,789	26,532	33,863	43,219	55,160	70,399
6%	13,382	17,908	23,965	32,071	42,918	57,434	76,860	102,857
7%	14,025	19,671	27,590	38,696	54,274	76,122	106,765	149,744
8%	14,693	21,589	31,721	46,609	68,484	100,626	147,853	217,245
9%	15,386	23,673	36,424	56,044	86,230	132,676	204,139	314,094
10%	16,105	25,937	41,772	67,274	108,347	174,494	281,024	452,592
11%	16,850	28,394	47,845	80,623	135,854	228,922	385,748	650,008
12%	17,623	31,058	54,735	96,462	170,000	299,599	527,996	930,509
13%	18,424	33,945	62,542	115,230	212,305	391,158	720,685	1,327,815
14%	19,254	37,072	71,379	137,434	264,619	509,501	981,001	1,888,835
15%	20,113	40,455	81,370	163,665	329,189	662,117	1,331,755	2,678,635
16%	21,003	44,114	92,655	194,607	408,742	858,498	1,803,140	3,787,211
17%	21,924	48,068	105,387	231,055	506,578	1,110,646	2,435,034	5,338,687
18%	22,877	52,338	119,737	273,930	626,686	1,433,706	3,279,972	7,503,783
19%	23,863	56,946	135,895	324,294	773,880	1,846,753	4,407,006	10,516,675
20%	24,883	61,917	154,070	383,375	953,962	2,373,763	5,906,682	14,697,715
21%	25,937	67,274	174,494	452,592	1,173,908	3,044,816	7,897,469	20,484,002
22%	27,027	73,046	197,422	533,576	1,442,101	3,897,578	10,534,018	28,470,377
23%	28,153	79,259	223,139	628,206	1,768,592	4,979,128	14,017,769	39,464,304
24%	29,316	85,944	251,956	738,641	2,165,419	6,348,199	18,610,540	54,559,126
25%	30,517	93,132	284,217	867,361	2,646,698	8,077,935	24,651,903	75,231,638

TABLE 2. $1,200 per Year at Varying Rates Compounded Annually—End of Year Values

	5th Yr.	10th Yr.	15th Yr.	20th Yr.	25th Yr.	30th Yr.	35th Yr.	40th Yr.
1%	6,182	12,680	19,509	26,686	34,231	43,359	50,492	59,250
2%	6,369	13,402	21,168	29,739	39,205	49,654	61,192	73,932
3%	6,561	14,169	22,988	33,211	45,063	58,803	74,731	93,195
4%	6,760	14,983	24,990	37,162	51,974	69,993	91,917	118,592
5%	6,962	15,848	27,188	41,662	60,135	83,713	113,803	152,208
6%	7,170	16,766	29,607	46,791	69,787	100,562	141,745	196,857
7%	7,383	17,740	32,265	52,638	81,211	121,287	177,495	256,332
8%	7,603	18,774	35,188	59,307	94,744	146,815	223,322	335,737
9%	7,827	19,872	38,403	66,918	110,788	178,290	282,150	441,950
10%	8,059	21,037	41,940	75,602	129,818	217,131	357,752	584,222
11%	8,295	22,273	45,828	85,518	152,398	265,095	454,996	774,992
12%	8,538	23,586	50,103	96,838	179,200	324,351	581,355	1,030,970
13%	8,786	24,976	54,806	112,164	211,020	397,578	741,298	1,374,583
14%	9,043	26,454	59,976	124,521	248,799	488,084	948,807	1,835,890
15%	9,304	28,018	65,660	141,372	293,654	599,948	1,216,015	2,455,144
16%	9,572	29,679	71,910	160,609	346,905	726,194	1,560,032	3,286,173
17%	9,848	31,440	78,778	182,566	410,115	909,004	2,002,792	4,400,869
18%	10,130	33,306	86,326	207,625	485,126	1,119,982	2,572,378	5,895,109
19%	10,419	35,284	94,620	236,216	574,117	1,380,464	3,304,696	7,896,595
20%	10,716	37,380	103,730	268,831	679,652	1,701,909	4,245,610	10,575,154
21%	11,019	39,601	113,736	306,021	804,759	2,098,358	5,453,622	14,156,310
22%	11,330	41,954	124,722	348,416	952,998	2,587,006	7,003,256	18,939,087
23%	11,649	44,446	136,779	396,727	1,128,558	3,188,884	8,989,333	25,319,371
24%	11,976	47,085	150,013	451,758	1,336,360	3,929,683	11,532,334	33,820,458
25%	12,310	49,879	164,530	514,417	1,582,186	4,840,641	14,666,342	45,132,982

TABLE 3. Approximate Annual Investment Required to Equal $100,000 at the End of a Specified Period—Varying Rates

	5 Yrs.	10 Yrs.	15 Yrs.	20 Yrs.	25 Yrs.	30 Yrs.	35 Yrs.	40 Yrs.
1%	19,380	9,464	6,151	4,497	3,506	2,768	2,378	2,026
2%	18,841	8,954	5,669	4,036	3,061	2,417	1,961	1,624
3%	18,290	8,470	5,220	3,613	2,663	2,041	1,606	1,288
4%	17,751	8,009	4,802	3,229	2,309	1,714	1,306	1,011
5%	17,236	7,572	4,414	2,880	1,966	1,433	1,054	788.39
6%	16,736	7,157	4,053	2,565	1,720	1,193	846.59	609.58
7%	16,254	6,764	3,719	2,280	1,478	989.39	676.08	468.14
8%	15,783	6,392	3,410	2,024	1,267	817.36	537.34	357.42
9%	15,332	6,039	3,125	1,793	1,083	673.06	425.31	271.52
10%	14,890	5,704	2,861	1,587	924.37	552.66	335.43	205.40
11%	14,467	5,388	2,618	1,403	787.41	452.67	263.74	154.84
12%	14,055	5,088	2,395	1,239	669.64	369.97	206.41	116.40
13%	13,658	4,805	2,190	1,070	568.67	301.83	168.00	87.29
14%	13,270	4,536	2,001	963.69	482.32	245.86	126.47	65.36
15%	12,898	4,283	1,828	848.82	408.64	200.02	98.68	48.88
16%	12,537	4,043	1,669	747.16	345.92	165.25	76.92	36.52
17%	12,185	3,817	1,523	657.30	292.60	132.02	59.92	27.27
18%	11,846	3,603	1,390	577.97	247.36	107.14	46.65	20.36
19%	11,517	3,401	1,268	508.01	209.02	86.93	36.31	15.20
20%	11,198	3,210	1,157	446.38	176.56	70.51	28.26	11.35
21%	10,802	3,030	1,056	392.13	149.11	57.19	22.00	8.48
22%	10,591	2,860	962.14	344.42	125.92	46.39	17.13	6.34
23%	10,301	2,700	877.33	302.48	106.33	37.63	13.35	4.74
24%	10,020	2,549	799.93	265.63	89.80	30.53	10.41	3.55
25%	9,749	2,406	729.35	233.27	75.84	24.79	8.18	2.66

TABLE 4. Lump Sum Required to Equal $100,000 at the End of a Specified Period—Varying Rates

	5 Yrs.	10 Yrs.	15 Yrs.	20 Yrs.	25 Yrs.	30 Yrs.	35 Yrs.	40 Yrs.
1%	95,147	90,529	86,135	81,954	77,977	74,192	70,591	67,165
2%	90,573	82,348	74,301	67,297	60,953	55,207	50,003	45,289
3%	86,261	74,409	64,186	55,367	47,761	41,199	35,538	30,656
4%	82,193	67,556	55,526	45,639	37,512	30,832	25,341	20,829
5%	78,353	61,391	48,102	37,689	29,530	23,138	18,129	14,205
6%	74,726	55,839	41,727	31,180	23,300	17,411	13,011	9,722
7%	71,299	50,835	36,245	25,842	18,425	13,137	9,367	6,678
8%	68,058	46,319	31,524	21,455	14,602	9,938	6,763	4,603
9%	64,993	42,241	27,454	17,843	11,597	7,537	4,899	3,184
10%	62,092	38,554	23,940	14,864	9,230	5,731	3,558	2,209
11%	59,345	35,218	20,900	12,403	7,361	4,368	2,592	1,538
12%	56,743	32,197	18,270	10,367	5,882	3,340	1,894	1,075
13%	54,276	29,460	15,989	8,678	4,710	2,557	1,388	753.12
14%	51,937	26,974	14,010	7,276	3,780	1,963	1,019	529.43
15%	49,718	24,718	12,289	6,110	3,040	1,510	750.89	373.32
16%	47,611	22,683	10,792	5,139	2,447	1,165	554.59	264.05
17%	45,611	20,804	9,489	4,329	1,974	900.38	410.67	187.31
18%	43,711	19,107	8,352	3,651	1,596	697.49	304.88	133.27
19%	41,905	17,560	7,359	3,084	1,292	541.49	226.91	95.10
20%	40,188	16,151	6,491	2,610	1,048	421.27	169.30	68.04
21%	38,554	14,864	5,731	2,209	851.85	328.43	126.62	48.82
22%	37,000	13,690	5,065	1,874	693.43	256.57	94.93	35.12
23%	35,520	12,617	4,482	1,592	565.42	200.84	71.34	25.34
24%	34,112	11,635	3,969	1,354	461.80	157.52	53.72	18.33
25%	32,768	10,737	3,512	1,153	377.78	123.79	40.56	13.30

TABLE 5. One Dollar Principal Compounded Annually

End of Year	2½%	3%	5%	6%	8%	10%	12%	15%
1	$1.0250	$1.0300	$1.0500	$1.0600	$1.0800	$1.1000	$1.1200	$1.1500
2	1.0506	1.0609	1.1025	1.1236	1.1664	1.2100	1.2544	1.3225
3	1.0769	1.0927	1.1576	1.1910	1.2597	1.3310	1.4049	1.5209
4	1.1038	1.1255	1.2155	1.2625	1.3605	1.4641	1.5735	1.7490
5	1.1314	1.1593	1.2763	1.3382	1.4693	1.6105	1.7623	2.0114
6	1.1597	1.1941	1.3401	1.4185	1.5869	1.7716	1.9738	2.3131
7	1.1887	1.2299	1.4071	1.5036	1.7138	1.9487	2.2107	2.6600
8	1.2184	1.2668	1.4775	1.5938	1.8509	2.1436	2.4760	3.0590
9	1.2489	1.3048	1.5513	1.6895	1.9990	2.3579	2.7731	3.5179
10	1.2801	1.3439	1.6289	1.7908	2.1589	2.5937	3.1058	4.0456
11	1.3121	1.3842	1.7103	1.8983	2.3316	2.8531	3.4785	4.6524
12	1.3449	1.4258	1.7959	2.0122	2.5182	3.1384	3.8960	5.3503
13	1.3785	1.4685	1.8856	2.1329	2.7196	3.4523	4.3635	6.1528
14	1.4130	1.5126	1.9799	2.2609	2.9372	3.7975	4.8871	7.0757
15	1.4483	1.5580	2.0789	2.3966	3.1722	4.1772	5.4736	8.1371
16	1.4845	1.6047	2.1829	2.5404	3.4259	4.5950	6.1304	9.3576
17	1.5216	1.6528	2.2920	2.6928	3.7000	5.0545	6.8660	10.7613
18	1.5597	1.7024	2.4066	2.8543	3.9960	5.5599	7.6900	12.3755
19	1.5987	1.7535	2.5270	3.0256	4.3157	6.1159	8.6128	14.2318
20	1.6386	1.8061	2.6533	3.2071	4.6610	6.7275	9.6463	16.3665
21	1.6796	1.8603	2.7860	3.3996	5.0338	7.4002	10.8038	18.8215
22	1.7216	1.9161	2.9253	3.6035	5.4365	8.1403	12.1003	21.6447
23	1.7646	1.9736	3.0715	3.8197	5.8715	8.9543	13.5523	24.8915
24	1.8087	2.0328	3.2251	4.0489	6.3412	9.8497	15.1786	28.6252
25	1.8539	2.0938	3.3864	4.2919	6.8485	10.8347	17.0001	32.9190

26	$1.9003	$2.1566	$3.5557	$4.5494	$7.3964	$11.9182	$19.0401	$37.8568
27	1.9478	2.2213	3.7335	4.8223	7.9881	13.1100	21.3249	43.5353
28	1.9965	2.2879	3.9201	5.1117	8.6271	14.4210	23.8839	50.0656
29	2.0464	2.3566	4.1161	5.4184	9.3173	15.8631	26.7499	57.5755
30	2.0976	2.4273	4.3219	5.7435	10.0627	17.4494	29.9599	66.2218
31	2.1500	2.5001	4.5380	6.0881	10.8677	19.1943	33.5551	76.1435
32	2.2038	2.5751	4.7649	6.4534	11.7371	21.1138	37.5817	87.5651
33	2.2589	2.6523	5.0032	6.8406	12.6760	23.2252	42.0915	100.6998
34	2.3153	2.7319	5.2533	7.2510	13.6901	25.5477	47.1425	115.8048
35	2.3732	2.8139	5.5160	7.6861	14.7853	28.1024	52.7996	133.1755
36	2.4325	2.8983	5.7918	8.1473	15.9682	30.9127	59.1356	153.1519
37	2.4933	2.9852	6.0814	8.6361	17.2456	34.0039	66.2318	176.1246
38	2.5557	3.0748	6.3855	9.1543	18.6253	37.4043	74.1797	202.5433
39	2.6196	3.1670	6.7048	9.7035	20.1153	41.1448	83.0812	232.9248
40	2.6851	3.2620	7.0400	10.2857	21.7245	45.2593	93.0510	267.8635
41	2.7522	3.3599	7.3920	10.9029	23.4625	49.7852	104.2171	308.0431
42	2.8210	3.4607	7.7616	11.5570	25.3395	54.7637	116.7231	354.2495
43	2.8915	3.5645	8.1497	12.2505	27.3666	60.2401	130.7299	407.3870
44	2.9638	3.6715	8.5572	12.9855	29.5560	66.2641	146.4175	468.4950
45	3.0379	3.7816	8.9850	13.7646	31.9204	72.8905	163.9876	538.7693
46	3.1139	3.8950	9.4343	14.5905	34.4741	80.1795	183.6661	619.5847
47	3.1917	4.0119	9.9060	15.4659	37.2320	88.1975	205.7061	712.5224
48	3.2715	4.1323	10.4013	16.3939	40.2106	97.0172	230.3908	819.4007
49	3.3533	4.2562	10.9213	17.3775	43.4274	106.7190	258.0377	942.3103
50	3.4371	4.3839	11.4674	18.4202	46.9016	117.3909	289.0022	1083.6574

TABLE 6. One Dollar per Annum Compounded Annually

End of Year	3%	5%	6%	8%	10%	12%	15%
1	$ 1.0300	$ 1.0500	$ 1.0600	$ 1.0800	$ 1.1000	$ 1.1200	$ 1.1500
2	2.0909	2.1525	2.1836	2.2464	2.3100	2.3744	2.4725
3	3.1836	3.3101	3.3746	3.5061	3.6410	3.7793	3.9934
4	4.3091	4.5256	4.6371	4.8666	5.1051	5.3528	5.7424
5	5.4684	5.8019	5.9753	6.3359	6.7156	7.1152	7.7537
6	6.6625	7.1420	7.3938	7.9228	8.4872	9.0890	10.0668
7	7.8923	8.5491	8.8975	9.6366	10.4359	11.2297	12.7268
8	9.1591	10.0266	10.4913	11.4876	12.5795	13.7757	15.7858
9	10.4639	11.5779	12.1808	13.4866	14.3974	16.5487	19.3037
10	11.8078	13.2068	13.9716	15.6455	17.5312	19.6546	23.3493
11	13.1920	14.9171	15.8699	17.9771	20.3843	23.1331	28.0017
12	14.6178	16.7130	17.8821	20.4953	23.5227	27.0291	33.3519
13	16.0863	18.5986	20.0151	23.2149	26.9750	31.3926	39.5047
14	17.5989	20.5786	22.2760	26.1521	30.7725	36.2797	46.5804
15	19.1569	22.6575	24.6725	29.3243	34.9497	41.7533	54.7175
16	20.7616	24.8404	27.2129	32.7502	39.5447	47.8837	64.0751
17	22.4144	27.1324	29.9057	36.4502	44.5992	54.7497	74.8364
18	24.1169	29.5390	32.7600	40.4463	50.1591	62.4397	87.2118
19	25.8704	32.0660	35.7856	44.7620	56.2750	71.0524	101.4436
20	27.6765	34.7193	38.9927	49.4229	63.0025	80.6987	117.8101
21	29.5368	37.5052	42.3923	54.4568	70.4027	91.5026	136.6316
22	31.4529	40.4305	45.9958	59.8933	78.5430	103.6029	158.2764
23	33.4265	43.5020	49.8156	65.7648	87.4973	117.1552	183.1678
24	35.4593	46.7271	53.8645	72.1059	97.3471	132.3339	211.7930
25	37.5530	50.1135	58.1564	78.9544	108.1818	149.3339	244.7120

26	$ 39.7096	$ 53.6691	$ 62.7058	$ 86.3508	$ 120.0999	$ 168.3740	$ 282.5688
27	41.9309	57.4026	67.5281	94.3388	133.2099	189.6989	326.1041
28	44.2189	61.3227	72.6398	102.9659	147.6309	213.5828	376.1697
29	46.5754	65.4388	78.0582	112.2832	163.4940	240.3327	433.7451
30	49.0027	69.7608	83.8017	122.3459	180.9434	270.2926	499.9569
31	51.5028	74.2988	89.8898	133.2135	200.1378	303.8477	576.1005
32	54.0778	79.0638	96.3432	144.9506	221.2515	341.4294	663.6655
33	56.7302	84.0670	103.1838	157.6267	244.4767	383.5210	764.3654
34	59.4621	89.3203	110.4348	171.3168	270.0244	430.6635	880.1702
35	62.2759	94.8363	118.1209	186.1021	298.1268	483.4631	1013.3757
36	65.1742	100.6281	126.2681	202.0703	329.0395	542.5987	1166.4975
37	68.1594	106.7095	134.9042	219.3158	363.0434	608.8305	1342.6222
38	71.2342	113.0950	144.0585	237.9412	400.4478	683.0102	1545.1655
39	74.4013	119.7998	153.7620	258.0565	441.5926	766.0914	1778.0903
40	77.6633	126.8398	164.0477	279.7810	486.8518	859.1424	2045.9539
41	81.0232	134.2318	174.9505	303.2435	536.6370	963.3595	2353.9969
42	84.4839	141.9933	186.5076	328.5830	591.4007	1080.0826	2708.2465
43	88.0484	150.1430	198.7580	355.9496	651.6408	1210.8125	3115.6334
44	91.7199	158.7002	211.7435	385.5056	717.9048	1357.2300	3584.1285
45	95.5015	167.6852	225.5081	417.4261	790.7953	1521.2176	4122.8977
46	99.3965	177.1194	240.0986	451.9002	870.9749	1704.8838	4742.4824
47	103.4084	187.0254	255.5645	489.1322	959.1723	1910.5898	5455.0047
48	107.5406	197.4267	271.9584	529.3427	1056.1896	2140.9806	6274.4055
49	111.7969	208.3480	289.3359	572.7702	1162.9085	2399.0182	7216.7163
50	116.1808	219.8154	307.7561	619.6718	1280.2994	2688.0204	8300.3737

TABLE 7. If You're Interested in a Retirement Program

Many shareholders who reinvest all of their income dividends and capital gain distributions while they are accumulating shares find it helpful to begin taking these dividends and distributions in cash when they retire.

Such was the case with John and Martha Thomas. This fictitious couple began an accumulation program by investing $250 on January 1, 1950. They added $100 each month thereafter until John retired 15 years later at the end of 1964. By this time, the value of their investment (as shown by the circled number below) had grown to $53,196.

Now John and Martha began to take all their dividends and capital gain distributions in cash. The right-hand table shows what they would have received each year and the fluctuations in the year-end value of their shares for the past 20 years. As you can see, over the past two decades they would have received $49,461 in dividends and $51,831 in capital gain distributions—a total of $101,292 in cash. And by the end of 1984 the value of their holdings would have grown to $100,198.

15-Year Share Accumulation Illustrations
Total Investments: $18,150

Jan. 1– Dec. 31	Dividends Reinvested	Total Cost (including dividends)	Capital Gain Distributions Taken in Shares*	Ending Value of Shares
1934–1948	$ 8,722	$26,872	$10,879	$39,313
1935–1949	8,613	26,763	9,989	37,673
1936–1950	8,592	26,742	9,107	39,599
1937–1951	9,153	27,303	9,737	43,433
1938–1952	9,928	28,078	10,915	46,488
1939–1953	9,942	28,092	10,359	41,889
1940–1954	9,949	28,099	11,599	59,097
1941–1955	9,997	28,147	14,336	65,869
1942–1956	9,810	27,960	16,509	63,802

20-Year Use of Investment
$53,196—Net asset value of shares accumulated as of December 31, 1964 †

Year Ended Dec. 31	Dividends in Cash	Capital Gains in Cash	Value at Year End
1965	$ 1,230	$ 3,962	$ 61,986
1966	1,412	4,646	56,657
1967	1,549	3,370	67,861
1968	1,731	2,869	73,919
1969	1,776	4,463	60,164
1970	1,776	2,642	57,067
1971	1,776	1,184	63,717
1972	1,776	2,141	69,729
1973	1,867	1,503	54,608

Year			
1943–1957	9,238	27,388	16,166	47,725
1944–1958	8,918	27,068	15,423	60,401
1945–1959	8,656	26,806	16,787	60,688
1946–1960	8,623	26,773	17,254	56,815
1947–1961	8,712	26,862	18,326	63,674
1948–1962	8,513	26,663	17,724	49,139
1949–1963	8,164	26,314	17,008	53,304
1950–1964	7,606	25,756	16,771	(53,196)
1951–1965	7,090	25,240	16,916	57,799
1952–1966	6,896	25,046	17,577	50,661
1953–1967	6,718	24,868	16,846	56,274
1954–1968	6,525	24,675	15,277	55,876
1955–1969	6,334	24,484	14,817	42,582
1956–1970	6,404	24,554	13,891	39,104
1957–1971	6,486	24,636	12,380	41,325
1958–1972	6,437	24,587	11,505	42,886
1959–1973	6,225	24,375	10,017	31,431
1960–1974	6,695	24,845	8,279	23,664
1961–1975	6,865	25,015	6,889	29,207
1962–1976	6,889	25,039	6,124	34,631
1963–1977	6,755	24,905	5,435	30,531
1964–1978	6,584	24,734	4,155	31,470
1965–1979	6,688	24,838	3,496	34,172
1966–1980	7,065	25,215	3,378	37,978
1967–1981	7,701	25,851	5,006	35,300
1968–1982	8,622	26,772	6,244	43,912
1969–1983	9,394	27,544	7,197	49,019
1970–1984	10,155	28,305	8,377	48,714

Year			
1974	2,733	—	42,174
1975	2,459	319	54,243
1976	2,186	1,048	66,905
1977	2,232	1,275	61,622
1978	2,368	—	68,226
1979	2,824	820	77,426
1980	3,461	1,822	87,901
1981	3,917	6,012	78,701
1982	4,372	5,010	92,820
1983	4,008	4,099	102,566
1984	4,008	4,646	100,198
Totals:	$49,461	$51,831	

* The value of the shares acquired with these capital gain distributions is reflected in "Ending Value of Shares."

† If all the shares had been purchased at offering price (which includes the sales commission as described in the prospectus) on December 31, 1984, instead of accumulated in the shareholder account, the cost would have been $58,160.

TABLE 8. If You're Interested in Investing Monthly

HERE'S WHAT WOULD HAVE HAPPENED IF YOU HAD INVESTED $250 AND ADDED $100 EVERY MONTH . . . .

. . . for 10 Years

(Total Investments: $12,150) Here's how you would have done in every 10-year period in the Fund's history:

Jan. 1–Dec. 31	Income Dividends Reinvested	Total Cost (including dividends reinvested)	Capital Gain Distributions Taken in Shares*	Ending Value of Shares
1934–1943	$2,808	$14,958	$2,113	$19,703
1935–1944	2,719	14,863	2,111	21,018
1936–1945	2,526	14,676	3,061	24,980
1937–1946	2,776	14,926	3,938	22,630
1938–1947	3,328	15,478	4,550	22,023
1939–1948	3,540	15,690	4,312	19,783
1940–1949	3,653	15,803	4,248	19,770
1941–1950	3,744	15,894	4,069	21,297
1942–1951	3,704	15,854	4,129	22,083
1943–1952	3,425	15,575	3,940	21,057
1944–1953	3,311	15,461	3,490	18,667
1945–1954	3,209	15,359	3,827	25,890
1946–1955	3,275	15,425	4,979	29,026
1947–1956	3,427	15,577	6,261	29,355
1948–1957	3,437	15,587	6,530	23,022
1949–1958	3,353	15,503	6,275	29,393
1950–1959	3,120	15,270	6,686	28,533
1951–1960	2,921	15,071	6,460	25,378
1952–1961	2,748	14,898	6,367	26,913
1953–1962	2,554	14,704	5,717	20,136
1954–1963	2,292	14,442	5,018	21,003
1955–1964	2,067	14,217	4,747	20,747
1956–1965	2,011	14,161	5,025	23,435
1957–1966	2,068	14,218	5,530	21,302
1958–1967	2,126	14,276	5,498	24,422
1959–1968	2,151	14,301	5,017	24,725
1960–1969	2,265	14,415	5,242	19,841

. . . for 20 Years

(Total Investments: $24,150) Here's how you would have done in every 20-year period in the Fund's history:

Jan. 1–Dec. 31	Income Dividends Reinvested	Total Cost (including dividends reinvested)	Capital Gain Distributions Taken in Shares*	Ending Value of Shares
1934–1953	$20,706	$44,856	$22,138	$ 76,013
1935–1954	19,967	44,117	23,135	103,655
1936–1955	19,635	43,785	27,075	113,533
1937–1956	20,533	44,683	32,583	116,063
1938–1957	22,022	46,172	36,166	98,643
1939–1958	21,860	46,010	35,720	124,788
1940–1959	21,782	45,932	39,722	128,003
1941–1960	21,555	45,705	40,827	118,964
1942–1961	20,772	44,922	41,451	128,247
1943–1962	19,302	43,452	38,380	94,830
1944–1963	18,394	42,544	36,623	101,930
1945–1964	17,742	41,892	37,189	104,552
1946–1965	17,455	41,605	39,302	118,599
1947–1966	17,924	42,074	43,082	109,020
1948–1967	18,047	42,197	43,149	124,915
1949–1968	18,207	42,357	41,487	128,493
1950–1969	17,814	41,964	41,043	98,650
1951–1970	17,257	41,407	37,648	87,183
1952–1971	16,780	40,930	33,092	88,925
1953–1972	16,068	40,218	30,012	89,317
1954–1973	15,153	39,303	25,994	63,756
1955–1974	15,176	39,326	20,983	45,341
1956–1975	15,385	39,535	17,956	55,258
1957–1976	15,367	39,517	16,215	64,995
1958–1977	15,187	39,337	14,755	57,235
1959–1978	14,728	38,878	11,993	58,273
1960–1979	15,037	39,187	10,666	63,355

. . . for 25 Years

(Total Investments: $30,150)

Here's how you would have done in every 25-year period in the Fund's history:

Jan. 1–Dec. 31	Income Dividends Reinvested	Total Cost (including dividends reinvested)	Capital Gain Distributions Taken in Shares*	Ending Value of Shares*
1934–1958	$41,888	$72,038	$67,212	$219,276
1935–1959	40,340	70,490	71,529	218,130
1936–1960	39,206	69,356	71,911	199,360
1937–1961	40,089	70,239	77,023	226,244
1938–1962	41,949	72,099	80,109	185,151
1939–1963	41,010	71,160	78,633	202,859
1940–1964	40,501	70,651	81,734	211,977
1941–1965	39,647	69,797	85,896	239,262
1942–1966	38,919	69,069	90,097	211,896
1943–1967	37,286	67,436	86,276	232,838
1944–1968	37,200	67,350	82,555	237,963
1945–1969	37,380	67,530	84,016	187,449
1946–1970	37,823	67,973	81,006	172,096
1947–1971	38,665	68,815	75,806	183,375
1948–1972	38,342	68,392	71,728	189,186
1949–1973	37,431	67,581	65,505	138,898
1950–1974	37,522	67,672	54,918	96,659
1951–1975	36,510	66,660	46,443	115,598
1952–1976	35,155	65,305	41,077	131,154
1953–1977	33,566	63,716	36,472	111,512
1954–1978	31,691	61,841	29,801	110,394
1955–1979	30,544	60,694	25,378	114,106
1956–1980	31,333	61,483	23,916	124,217
1957–1981	33,066	63,216	28,185	113,598
1958–1982	35,214	65,364	30,757	137,288
1959–1983	35,813	65,963	31,308	145,961
1960–1984	37,238	67,388	33,355	141,529
1961–1980	16,623	39,773	10,159	69,600
1962–1981	16,689	40,839	12,780	64,046
1963–1982	17,848	41,998	14,328	77,424
1964–1983	18,375	42,525	14,944	83,045
1965–1984	19,051	43,201	16,088	80,211

1961–1970	2,317	14,467	4,863	18,394
1962–1971	2,361	14,511	4,191	19,524
1963–1972	2,303	14,453	3,763	20,096
1964–1973	2,212	14,362	3,120	14,844
1965–1974	2,384	14,534	2,262	11,231
1966–1975	2,466	14,616	1,665	14,139
1967–1976	2,479	14,629	1,431	17,050
1968–1977	2,521	14,671	1,335	15,618
1969–1978	2,626	14,776	1,018	16,991
1970–1979	2,841	14,991	966	19,195
1971–1980	3,052	15,202	1,123	21,316
1972–1981	3,422	15,572	2,163	19,850
1973–1982	3,939	16,089	2,930	24,791
1974–1983	4,259	16,409	3,422	27,150
1975–1984	4,286	16,436	3,784	25,388

* The value of the shares acquired with these capital gain distributions is reflected in "Ending Value of Shares."

TABLE 9. All It Takes Is $250 to Start Your Investment Program Now

If you had invested $250 and then added $100 every month through the 51-year lifetime of the Fund, here's how you would have done . . . .

Total invested since January 1, 1934	$ 60,150
Income Dividends (reinvested)	1,060,286
Total Cost (including dividends reinvested)	$1,121,636
Value of Investment on December 31, 1984*	$3,371,100

* Includes value of shares taken as capital gain distributions

This table covers the period from January 1, 1934, through December 31, 1984. While this period, on the whole, was one of generally rising common stock prices, it also included some interim periods of substantial market decline. Results shown should not be considered as a representation of the dividend income or capital gain or loss that may be realized from an investment made in the Fund today. A program of the type illustrated does not ensure a profit or protect against depreciation in declining markets.

COST OF SHARES

Year Ended Dec. 31	Monthly Investments (cumulative)	Dividends Reinvested (cumulative)	Total Cost (including dividends)
1934	$ 1,350	—	$ 1,350
1935	2,550	—	2,550
1936	3,750	$ 97	3,847
1937	4,950	368	5,318
1938	6,150	425	6,575
1939	7,350	629	7,979
1940	8,550	1,005	9,555
1941	9,750	1,591	11,341
1942	10,950	2,200	13,150
1943	12,150	2,808	14,958
1944	13,350	3,533	16,883
1945	14,550	4,255	18,805
1946	15,750	5,370	21,120
1947	16,950	6,931	23,881
1948	18,150	8,722	26,872
1949	19,350	10,547	29,897
1950	20,550	12,768	33,318
1951	21,750	15,206	36,956
1952	22,950	17,789	40,739

VALUE OF SHARES ACQUIRED

Monthly Investments	Capital Gain Distributions (cumulative)	Dividends Reinvested (cumulative)	Total Value
$ 1,375	—	—	$ 1,375
4,305	—	—	4,305
6,389	$ 1,199	$ 127	7,715
4,428	743	286	5,457
6,681	1,271	414	8,366
7,549	1,493	603	9,645
8,087	1,533	947	10,567
8,086	1,374	1,389	10,849
10,094	1,644	2,188	13,926
14,002	2,312	3,389	19,703
17,316	3,583	4,651	25,550
22,778	6,971	6,564	36,313
21,149	8,516	6,858	36,523
20,584	9,607	7,859	38,050
20,169	10,137	9,007	39,313
21,528	11,762	10,989	44,279
25,126	14,688	14,532	54,346
28,354	18,723	18,193	65,270
30,453	22,627	21,407	74,487

Year							
1953	24,150	20,706	44,856	29,709	23,294	23,010	76,013
1954	25,350	23,797	49,147	44,206	39,285	36,671	120,162
1955	26,550	27,696	54,246	51,207	55,308	45,481	151,996
1956	27,750	31,995	59,745	52,381	67,453	49,730	169,564
1957	28,950	36,802	65,752	43,084	63,110	44,269	150,463
1958	30,150	41,888	72,038	59,765	93,713	65,798	219,276
1959	31,350	47,367	78,717	63,374	114,260	73,996	251,630
1960	32,550	53,756	86,306	62,082	124,556	77,651	264,289
1961	33,750	60,364	94,114	72,008	159,218	95,345	326,571
1962	34,950	67,585	102,535	59,495	140,389	84,626	284,510
1963	36,150	75,232	111,382	69,571	176,152	105,186	350,909
1964	37,350	83,770	121,120	75,712	212,351	121,139	409,202
1965	38,550	93,455	132,005	89,490	279,737	151,563	520,790
1966	39,750	105,889	145,639	82,932	293,444	150,729	527,105
1967	40,950	120,632	161,582	100,566	384,580	195,544	680,690
1968	42,150	138,839	180,989	110,831	454,226	232,444	797,501
1969	43,350	159,242	202,592	91,286	413,084	209,060	713,430
1970	44,550	181,280	225,830	87,866	423,511	222,071	733,448
1971	45,750	204,372	250,122	99,332	488,677	271,614	859,623
1972	46,950	228,591	275,541	109,930	564,827	322,403	997,160
1973	48,150	255,628	303,778	87,145	465,090	278,347	830,582
1974	49,350	298,002	347,352	68,318	359,194	255,094	682,606
1975	50,550	338,496	389,046	89,103	467,314	369,016	925,433
1976	51,750	376,298	428,048	111,167	595,230	494,245	1,200,642
1977	52,950	416,908	469,858	103,550	571,917	495,466	1,170,933
1978	54,150	462,558	516,708	115,883	633,209	595,172	1,344,264
1979	55,350	519,673	575,023	132,784	735,998	734,488	1,603,270
1980	56,550	594,267	650,817	152,065	876,757	916,232	1,945,054
1981	57,750	689,013	746,763	137,285	913,278	912,749	1,963,312
1982	58,950	808,514	867,464	163,371	1,241,666	1,222,837	2,627,874
1983	60,150	928,934	989,084	181,768	1,503,380	1,473,922	3,159,070
1984	61,350	1,060,286	1,121,636	178,829	1,612,803	1,579,468	3,371,100

The total cost column represents the initial investment of $250 plus the cumulative total of monthly investments of $100 plus the cumulative amount of dividends reinvested. A sales charge, as described in the prospectus, was included in the price of the shares purchased through periodic investments with right of accumulation reflected where applicable.

There is no sales charge on shares acquired through reinvestment of dividends and capital gain distributions.

Capital gain distributions taken in shares totaled $1,062,311.

TABLE 10. If You're Interested in Growth

SUMMARIES OF ASSUMED $10,000 INVESTMENTS

HERE'S WHAT WOULD HAVE HAPPENED IF YOU HAD INVESTED $10,000 AND TAKEN ALL INCOME DIVIDENDS AND CAPITAL GAIN DISTRIBUTIONS IN ADDITIONAL SHARES . . .

10-Year Periods

. . . here's how you would have done in any of these 42 periods:

Jan. 1–Dec. 31	Income Dividends Reinvested	Total Investment Cost	Ending Value of Shares	Capital Gain Distributions Taken in Shares*
1934–1943	$ 6,367	$16,367	$ 34,334	$ 6,853
1935–1944	6,038	16,038	33,734	6,640
1936–1945	3,801	13,801	25,192	5,337
1937–1946	3,005	13,005	16,853	3,598
1938–1947	5,545	15,545	27,612	6,993
1939–1948	5,273	15,273	21,577	5,779
1940–1949	6,006	16,006	23,416	6,297
1941–1950	7,002	17,002	28,746	7,154
1942–1951	8,421	18,421	36,562	9,256
1943–1952	8,026	18,026	35,134	9,383
1944–1953	6,783	16,783	26,579	7,691
1945–1954	6,106	16,106	33,648	7,482
1946–1955	5,072	15,072	30,844	6,976
1947–1956	5,805	15,805	34,995	9,056
1948–1957	6,351	16,351	30,558	10,432
1949–1958	6,935	16,935	44,084	11,638
1950–1959	6,959	16,959	46,002	13,339
1951–1960	6,404	16,404	40,139	13,026
1952–1961	5,938	15,938	41,912	12,831
1953–1962	5,801	15,801	32,421	12,945
1954–1963	6,286	16,286	39,662	13,821
1955–1964	4,407	14,407	29,537	10,119
1956–1965	3,834	13,834	29,872	9,225
1957–1966	3,870	13,870	27,238	9,741
1958–1967	4,968	14,968	39,877	12,382
1959–1968	3,956	13,956	32,214	9,400
1960–1969	3,985	13,985	25,196	9,333
1961–1970	4,334	14,334	24,736	9,495
1962–1971	3,966	13,966	23,508	7,660
1963–1972	5,102	15,102	31,400	9,352
1964–1973	4,645	14,645	21,257	7,795
1965–1974	4,734	14,734	14,994	6,177

15-Year Periods

. . . here's how you would have done in any of these 37 periods:

Jan. 1–Dec. 31	Income Dividends Reinvested	Total Investment Cost	Ending Value of Shares	Capital Gain Distributions Taken in Shares*
1934–1948	$15,397	$25,397	$ 57,089	$ 20,336
1935–1949	14,332	24,332	49,772	17,919
1936–1950	9,162	19,162	32,569	10,739
1937–1951	7,149	17,149	26,303	7,323
1938–1952	12,808	22,808	47,929	13,854
1939–1953	11,428	21,428	37,573	11,524
1940–1954	12,638	22,638	58,174	13,894
1941–1955	14,538	24,538	74,744	19,262
1942–1956	17,453	27,453	89,365	27,177
1943–1957	16,695	26,695	67,439	27,353
1944–1958	13,996	23,996	73,532	23,037
1945–1959	12,569	22,569	68,078	22,827
1946–1960	10,263	20,263	52,022	18,862
1947–1961	11,563	21,563	65,590	22,118
1948–1962	12,512	22,512	56,391	24,019
1949–1963	13,557	23,557	69,051	26,499
1950–1964	13,540	23,540	73,362	28,102
1951–1965	12,370	22,370	77,732	27,859
1952–1966	11,723	21,723	66,593	28,299
1953–1967	11,794	21,794	76,532	28,446
1954–1968	13,422	23,422	89,115	31,288
1955–1969	9,820	19,820	50,985	23,062
1956–1970	8,844	18,844	41,685	19,525
1957–1971	8,935	18,935	44,049	17,770
1958–1972	11,265	21,265	57,963	21,332
1959–1973	8,654	18,654	33,301	15,298
1960–1974	8,864	18,864	23,928	12,795
1961–1975	9,615	19,615	30,992	11,927
1962–1976	8,649	18,649	32,616	9,707
1963–1977	11,010	21,010	36,636	11,520
1964–1978	9,923	19,923	34,198	8,997
1965–1979	9,588	19,588	35,032	7,563

Period				
1966–1975	4,260	14,260	16,002	4,411
1967–1976	4,646	14,646	20,523	3,986
1968–1977	3,949	13,949	15,523	2,972
1969–1978	3,682	13,682	15,215	2,209
1970–1979	4,583	14,583	20,299	2,060
1971–1980	5,113	15,113	23,992	2,084
1972–1981	5,120	15,120	20,673	3,014
1973–1982	5,284	15,284	23,876	3,468
1974–1983	7,369	17,369	34,497	5,196
1975–1984	10,158	20,158	44,833	8,235

20-Year Periods

. . . here's how you would have done in any of these 32 periods:

Period				
1934–1953	$31,576	$41,576	$99,201	$35,435
1935–1954	28,345	38,345	123,418	33,970
1936–1955	17,651	27,651	84,521	24,379
1937–1956	13,615	23,615	64,174	20,149
1938–1957	24,579	34,579	91,846	38,256
1939–1958	21,625	31,625	103,944	33,217
1940–1959	23,815	33,815	117,703	40,426
1941–1960	27,120	37,120	126,064	48,064
1942–1961	32,157	42,157	167,493	60,535
1943–1962	30,292	40,292	124,450	57,336
1944–1963	25,040	35,040	115,177	47,824
1945–1964	22,806	32,306	108,571	44,673
1946–1965	17,996	27,996	100,743	38,084
1947–1966	20,616	30,616	104,215	46,325
1948–1967	22,934	32,934	133,109	51,763
1949–1968	25,980	35,980	155,150	56,909
1950–1969	26,986	36,986	126,637	60,252
1951–1970	25,406	35,406	108,473	54,662
1952–1971	24,105	34,105	107,694	47,929
1953–1972	23,878	33,878	111,244	45,624
1954–1973	26,417	36,417	92,123	47,606
1955–1974	19,692	29,692	48,421	30,068
1956–1975	17,741	27,741	52,228	23,623
1957–1976	17,710	27,710	61,116	21,606
1958–1977	22,171	32,171	67,632	25,334
1959–1978	16,921	26,921	53,573	17,181
1960–1979	16,609	26,609	55,905	15,008
1961–1980	18,156	28,156	64,841	15,124
1962–1981	17,121	27,121	53,116	15,406
1963–1982	23,233	33,233	81,924	21,253
1964–1983	21,764	31,764	80,117	19,863
1965–1984	21,381	31,381	73,466	19,669

Period				
1966–1980	8,669	18,669	33,480	6,062
1967–1981	9,977	19,977	33,424	7,574
1968–1982	9,128	19,128	34,709	7,097
1969–1983	8,949	18,949	35,645	7,044
1970–1984	11,416	21,416	42,567	9,075

25-Year Periods

. . . here's how you would have done in any of these 27 periods:

Period				
1934–1958	$58,378	$68,378	$274,006	$92,456
1935–1959	51,959	61,959	249,340	90,027
1936–1960	31,827	41,827	142,370	56,830
1937–1961	24,140	34,140	120,145	44,024
1938–1962	43,042	53,042	169,326	78,968
1939–1963	37,238	47,238	162,816	68,257
1940–1964	40,650	50,650	187,710	78,196
1941–1965	45,860	55,860	244,133	94,648
1942–1966	55,276	65,276	266,129	122,350
1943–1967	53,293	63,293	293,762	118,563
1944–1968	45,761	55,761	258,788	98,548
1945–1969	42,202	52,202	187,411	92,252
1946–1970	34,891	44,891	140,585	72,821
1947–1971	39,993	49,993	168,537	77,045
1948–1972	43,951	53,951	193,484	81,640
1949–1973	48,604	58,604	160,386	85,318
1950–1974	51,507	61,507	120,265	77,652
1951–1975	48,559	58,559	135,906	65,323
1952–1976	45,560	55,560	149,420	57,308
1953–1977	44,809	54,809	129,796	53,306
1954–1978	49,288	59,288	148,202	52,814
1955–1979	35,366	45,366	113,131	34,544
1956–1980	32,134	42,134	109,270	29,012
1957–1981	33,585	43,585	99,531	32,286
1958–1982	44,734	54,734	151,233	43,303
1959–1983	35,470	45,470	125,513	34,204
1960–1984	35,428	45,428	117,237	34,327

51-Years Lifetime

Period				
1934–1984	$1,273,117	$1,283,117	$3,997,274	$1,283,391

12.46%
Lifetime compound growth rate

* The value of the shares acquired with these capital gain distributions is reflected in "Ending Value of Shares."

TABLE 11. $10,000 Initial Investment in the Fund—20 Years

Date	Initial Investment	Sales Charge Included	Offering Price	Shares Purchased	Net Asset Value Per Share	Initial Net Asset Value
1/1/55	$10,000.00	8.50%	$4.55	2,197.802	$4,165	$9,154

MONTHLY INVESTMENTS OF $100.00—SAME DAY AS INITIAL INVESTMENT
DIVIDENDS AND CAPITAL GAINS REINVESTED
CUMULATIVE VOLUME DISCOUNT REFLECTED WHERE APPLICABLE IN THIS ILLUSTRATION

	COST OF SHARES					VALUE OF SHARES					
Date	Cumulative Investment	Annual Income Dividends	Cumulative Income Dividends	Total Investment Cost	Annual Capital Gain Distribution	From Investment	From Capital Gains Reinvested	Subtotal	From Dividends Reinvested	Total Value	Shares Held
12/31/55	11,100	314	314	11,414	850	11,401	881	12,282	323	12,605	2,676
12/31/56	12,300	374	688	12,988	1,075	12,477	1,950	14,427	689	15,116	3,206
12/31/57	13,500	447	1,135	14,635	866	10,963	2,400	13,363	953	14,316	3,777
12/31/58	14,700	502	1,636	16,336	751	16,186	4,065	20,251	1,865	22,116	4,307
12/31/59	15,900	566	2,202	18,102	1,715	17,970	5,968	23,938	2,510	26,448	4,948
12/31/60	17,100	687	2,889	19,989	1,517	18,427	7,313	25,740	3,116	28,856	5,619
12/31/61	18,300	734	3,623	21,923	1,883	22,183	10,254	32,437	4,309	36,746	6,276
12/31/62	19,500	827	4,451	23,951	1,448	19,072	9,603	28,675	4,335	33,010	6,957
12/31/63	20,700	903	5,353	26,053	1,713	23,096	12,796	35,892	5,922	41,814	7,672
12/31/64	21,900	1,031	6,384	28,284	2,838	25,866	16,571	42,437	7,363	49,800	8,527
12/31/65	23,100	1,191	7,575	30,675	3,859	31,371	23,291	54,662	9,859	64,521	9,481
12/31/66	24,300	1,554	9,129	33,429	4,986	29,772	25,999	55,771	10,536	66,307	10,660
12/31/67	25,500	1,869	10,998	36,498	4,076	36,855	35,341	72,196	14,522	86,718	11,640
12/31/68	26,700	2,337	13,335	40,035	3,675	41,396	43,004	84,400	18,313	102,713	12,657
12/31/69	27,900	2,646	15,980	43,880	6,220	34,746	40,603	75,349	17,482	92,831	14,055
12/31/70	29,100	2,886	18,867	47,967	4,089	34,202	42,648	76,850	19,695	96,545	15,410
12/31/71	30,300	3,056	21,923	52,223	2,067	39,393	49,719	89,112	25,123	114,235	16,331
12/31/72	31,500	3,233	25,156	56,656	3,949	44,314	58,436	102,750	30,852	133,602	17,453
12/31/73	32,700	3,640	28,796	61,496	2,971	35,740	48,837	84,577	27,644	112,221	18,719
12/31/74	33,900	5,765	34,561	68,461	0	28,597	37,717	66,314	26,810	93,124	20,113
				Total	50,548						

TABLE 11. (Continued)

Date	Initial Investment	Offering Price	Sales Charge Included	Shares Purchased	Net Asset Value Per Share	Initial Net Asset Value
12/31/74	$93,124.00	$4.63	0.00%	20,113.174	$4.630	$93,124

SYSTEMATIC WITHDRAWAL PLAN
DIVIDENDS AND CAPITAL GAINS REINVESTED
MONTHLY WITHDRAWALS OF $465.87 (6.0% ANNUALLY) BEGINNING 1/31/75

	AMOUNTS WITHDRAWN					VALUE OF REMAINING SHARES			
Date	From Income Dividends	From Principal	Annual Total	Cumulative Total	Annual Capital Gain Distribution	Remaining Original Shares	Capital Gain Shares	Total Value	Shares Held
12/31/74	0	0	0	0	0	93,124	0	93,124	20,113
12/31/75	5,353	238	5,590	5,590	691	119,452	694	120,146	20,176
12/31/76	4,798	792	5,590	11,180	2,294	146,425	3,211	149,636	20,373
12/31/77	4,948	642	5,590	16,770	2,822	134,247	5,801	140,048	20,702
12/31/78	5,338	252	5,590	22,360	0	148,311	6,422	154,733	20,659
12/31/79	6,439	−849	5,590	27,950	1,859	169,016	9,291	178,307	20,977
12/31/80	8,143	−2,552	5,590	33,540	4,195	194,725	15,128	209,853	21,746
12/31/81	10,066	−4,475	5,590	39,130	14,353	178,768	27,385	206,153	23,860
12/31/82	12,383	−6,792	5,590	44,720	13,123	219,249	49,575	268,824	26,381
12/31/83	12,198	−6,608	5,590	50,310	11,872	248,927	68,215	317,142	28,165
12/31/84	13,052	−7,462	5,590	55,900	14,364	251,131	81,109	332,240	30,204
Totals	82,718	−26,818	55,900		65,573				

TABLE 12.   Investing in Common Stocks Requires Skill

The Difficulty of Selecting Individual Stocks is Illustrated by the Wide Variation in the Results of Assumed Investments Made 51 Years Ago in Each of the 30 Stocks Now in the Dow Jones Industrial Average.

	Market Value of Investment*		
Dow Jones Industrial Stocks	Dec. 31, 1933	Dec. 31, 1984	Percent Change
Minnesota Mining & Manufacturing ..	$10,000	$9,435,000	94,250%
International Business Machines.....	10,000	5,854,164	58,442
Merck	**	4,230,003	42,200
International Paper	10,000	669,094	6,591
American Express	10,000	604,085	5,941
Eastman Kodak	10,000	575,538	5,655
United Technologies	10,000	464,975	4,550
Sears, Roebuck..................	10,000	365,796	3,558
Procter & Gamble	10,000	350,769	3,408
General Electric	10,000	348,462	3,385
Exxon	10,000	283,606	2,736
Texaco	10,000	255,836	2,458
Westinghouse Electric.............	10,000	228,659	2,187
Goodyear Tire & Rubber	10,000	212,352	2,024
Chevron	10,000	189,186	1,792
Aluminum Company of America.....	10,000	180,003	1,700
General Foods	10,000	137,538	1,275
General Motors..................	10,000	136,046	1,260
Du Pont	10,000	108,586	986
Owens-Illinois..................	10,000	79,506	695
American Brands	10,000	76,148	661
Bethlehem Steel	10,000	56,757	468
United States Steel	10,000	49,241	392
Union Carbide	10,000	46,421	364
American Telephone & Telegraph ...	10,000	39,749	297
Allied Chemical	10,000	32,050	221
INCO	10,000	28,125	181
Woolworth, F. W.	10,000	25,665	157
American Can	10,000	20,404	104
International Harvester............	10,000	12,188.	22

 * It was assumed that the entire $10,000 was invested in each stock and that fractional shares were purchased where required to use up the full amount.
   No brokerage charges were included in the cost. Adjustments were made for all stock splits and stock dividends.
** This $10,000 investment was made one year later, December 31, 1934, when the stock of this company was first available for purchase by the public.

TABLE 13. Federal Income Tax Rates PREPARED: DECEMBER 1985

FOR TAX YEAR 1985   SCHEDULE X—SINGLE TAXPAYERS

Taxable Income		Tax				On Excess
Over	Not Over	Pay	+	Rate %	×	Over
—	$ 2,390	—		—		—
$ 2,390	3,540	—		11		$ 2,390
3,540	4,580	$ 126.50		12		3,540
4,580	6,760	251.30		14		4,580
6,760	8,850	556.50		15		6,760
8,850	11,240	870.00		16		8,850
11,240	13,430	1,252.40		18		11,240
13,430	15,610	1,646.60		20		13,430
15,610	18,940	2,082.60		23		15,610
18,940	24,460	2,848.50		26		18,940
24,460	29,970	4,283.70		30		24,460
29,970	35,490	5,936.70		34		29,970
35,490	43,190	7,813.50		38		35,490
43,190	57,550	10,739.50		42		43,190
57,550	85,130	16,770.70		48		57,550
85,130	—	30,009.10		50		85,130

SCHEDULE Y—MARRIED FILING JOINTLY, SURVIVING SPOUSES

Taxable Income		Tax				On Excess
Over	Not Over	Pay	+	Rate %	×	Over
—	$ 3,540	—		—		—
$ 3,540	5,720	—		11		$ 3,540
5,720	7,910	$ 239.80		12		5,720
7,910	12,390	502.60		14		7,910
12,390	16,650	1,129.80		16		12,390
16,650	21,020	1,811.40		18		16,650
21,020	25,600	2,598.00		22		21,020
25,600	31,120	3,605.60		25		25,600
31,120	36,630	4,985.60		28		31,120
36,630	47,670	6,528.40		33		36,630
47,670	62,450	10,171.60		38		47,670
62,450	89,090	15,788.00		42		62,450
89,090	113,860	26,976.80		45		89,090
113,860	169,020	38,123.30		49		113,860
169,020	—	65,151.70		50		169,020

SCHEDULE Z—HEADS OF HOUSEHOLDS

Taxable Income		Tax				On Excess
Over	Not Over	Pay	+	Rate %	×	Over
—	$ 2,390	—		—		—
$ 2,390	4,580	—		11		$ 2,390
4,580	6,760	$ 240.90		12		4,580
6,760	9,050	502.50		14		6,760
9,050	12,280	823.10		17		9,050
12,280	15,610	1,372.20		18		12,280
15,610	18,940	1,971.60		20		15,610
18,940	24,460	2,637.60		24		18,940
24,460	29,970	3,962.40		28		24,460
29,970	35,490	5,505.20		32		29,970
35,490	46,520	7,271.60		35		35,490
46,520	63,070	11,132.10		42		46,520
63,070	85,130	18,083.10		45		63,070
85,130	112,720	28,010.10		48		85,130
112,720	—	41,253.30		50		112,720

$88,201 Distribution
$14,056 Taxes Due
$74,145 Balance Invested in The Fund
9% Withdrawal for First 11 Years
January 1, 1944–December 31, 1954
Self-Liquidating for the Next 21 Years
January 1, 1955–January 1, 1976

TABLE 14. Without IRA Rollover

Date	Initial Investment	Offering Price	Sales Charge Included	Shares Purchased	Net Asset Value Per Share	Initial Net Asset Value
1/1/44	$74,145.00	$4.75	4.50%	15,609.470	$4.532	$70,742

SYSTEMATIC WITHDRAWAL PLAN
DIVIDENDS AND CAPITAL GAINS REINVESTED
MONTHLY WITHDRAWALS OF $556.09 (9.0% ANNUALLY) BEGINNING 1/31/44

	AMOUNTS WITHDRAWN					VALUE OF REMAINING SHARES			
Date	From Income Dividends	From Principal	Annual Total	Cumulative Total	Annual Capital Gain Distribution	Remaining Original Shares	Capital Gain Shares	Total Value	Shares Held
12/31/44	1,920	4,753	6,673	6,673	2,536	76,330	2,609	78,939	15,116
12/31/45	1,640	5,033	6,673	13,346	6,235	89,410	9,567	98,977	15,245
12/31/46	2,243	4,430	6,673	20,019	5,407	75,400	13,751	89,151	15,509
12/31/47	2,869	3,804	6,673	26,692	3,446	65,696	16,086	81,782	15,448
12/31/48	2,854	3,819	6,673	33,365	2,108	57,444	17,047	74,491	15,152
12/31/49	2,556	4,117	6,673	40,038	2,311	53,652	19,522	73,174	14,752
12/31/50	2,715	3,958	6,673	46,711	2,134	55,373	23,854	79,227	14,378
12/31/51	2,668	4,005	6,673	53,384	3,327	55,971	29,189	85,160	14,276
12/31/52	2,550	4,123	6,673	60,057	3,514	53,577	33,694	87,271	14,167
12/31/53	2,637	4,036	6,673	66,730	1,956	46,278	33,551	79,829	13,811
12/31/54	2,526	4,148	6,673	73,403	4,844	61,744	53,290	115,034	13,809
Totals	27,178	46,225	73,403		37,818				

Note: 20.0% subtracted from dividends and 10.0% subtracted from capital gain distributions as paid to reflect liability for federal income taxes.

TABLE 14. (Continued)

Date	Initial Investment	Offering Price	Sales Charge Included	Shares Purchased	Net Asset Value Per Share	Initial Net Asset Value
1/1/55	$115,034.00	$8.33	0.00%	13,809.600	$8.330	$115,034

SYSTEMATIC WITHDRAWAL PLAN
DIVIDENDS AND CAPITAL GAINS REINVESTED
MONTHLY WITHDRAWALS BEGINNING 1/31/55 BASED ON A 21-YEAR SELF-LIQUIDATING PROGRAM
DESIGNED TO EXHAUST PRINCIPAL

	AMOUNTS WITHDRAWN					VALUE OF REMAINING SHARES			
Date	From Income Dividends	From Principal	Annual Total	Cumulative Total	Annual Capital Gain Distribution	Remaining Original Shares	Capital Gain Shares	Total Value	Shares Held
12/31/55	2,875	3,313	6,188	6,188	8,659	126,629	8,995	135,624	14,397
12/31/56	2,958	4,240	7,198	13,386	9,286	122,702	18,229	140,931	14,945
12/31/57	3,080	4,083	7,164	20,550	6,642	95,234	21,012	116,246	15,335
12/31/58	3,035	4,692	7,727	28,277	5,028	123,528	33,939	157,467	15,332
12/31/59	3,034	6,923	9,956	38,233	10,188	121,668	45,649	167,317	15,651
12/31/60	3,265	6,917	10,182	48,415	8,273	109,723	52,479	162,202	15,793
12/31/61	3,110	9,242	12,352	60,767	8,904	115,628	68,904	184,532	15,758
12/31/62	3,113	8,187	11,300	72,067	6,286	85,837	61,439	147,276	15,519
12/31/63	3,015	9,746	12,761	84,828	6,304	88,472	77,080	165,552	15,188
12/31/64	3,055	12,318	15,373	100,201	9,260	82,725	91,923	174,648	14,952
12/31/65	3,116	14,800	17,916	118,117	11,159	80,791	118,649	199,440	14,653
12/31/66	3,563	16,289	19,852	137,969	13,120	58,249	120,820	179,069	14,394
12/31/67	3,739	20,086	23,825	161,794	9,036	49,174	154,042	203,216	13,638
12/31/68	3,992	22,827	26,819	188,613	7,572	28,944	177,080	206,024	12,694
12/31/69	3,815	23,521	27,336	215,949	10,930	1,893	153,972	155,865	11,798
12/31/70	3,483	20,319	23,802	239,751	5,988	0	131,831	131,831	10,521
12/31/71	2,957	25,919	28,876	268,627	2,044	0	122,503	122,503	8,756
12/31/72	2,386	30,509	32,895	301,522	2,899	0	105,567	105,567	6,895
12/31/73	1,862	28,842	30,704	332,226	1,447	0	58,008	58,008	4,838
12/31/74	1,582	24,489	26,071	358,297	0	0	23,515	23,515	2,539
12/31/75	414	29,620	30,034	388,331	14	0	0	0	0
Totals	61,451	326,880	388,331		143,040				

Note: 20.0% subtracted from dividends and 10.0% subtracted from capital gain distributions as paid to reflect liability for federal income taxes.

TABLE 15. With IRA Rollover

$88,201 Invested in The Fund
9% Withdrawal for 11 Years
Self-Liquidating for the Next 21 Years
January 1, 1955 through January 1, 1976

Date	Initial Investment	Offering Price	Sales Charge Included	Net Asset Value Per Share	Shares Purchased	Initial Net Asset Value
1/1/44	$88,201.00	$4.75	4.50%	$4.532	18,568.630	$84,153

SYSTEMATIC WITHDRAWAL PLAN
DIVIDENDS AND CAPITAL GAINS REINVESTED
MONTHLY WITHDRAWALS OF $661.51 (9.0% ANNUALLY) BEGINNING 1/31/44

	AMOUNTS WITHDRAWN					VALUE OF REMAINING SHARES			
Date	From Income Dividends	From Principal	Annual Total	Cumulative Total	Annual Capital Gain Distribution	Remaining Original Shares	Capital Gain Shares	Total Value	Shares Held
12/31/44	2,864	5,074	6,350	6,350	3,367	91,396	3,464	94,860	18,165
12/31/45	2,471	5,467	6,350	12,701	8,365	107,664	12,790	120,454	18,554
12/31/46	3,425	4,513	6,350	19,051	7,346	91,560	18,498	110,058	19,147
12/31/47	4,451	3,487	6,350	25,402	4,766	80,893	21,769	102,662	19,392
12/31/48	4,506	3,432	6,350	31,752	2,969	71,941	23,185	95,126	19,350
12/31/49	4,112	3,826	6,350	38,102	3,319	68,577	26,728	95,305	19,214
12/31/50	4,459	3,479	6,350	44,453	3,126	72,437	32,869	105,306	19,111
12/31/51	4,469	3,469	6,350	50,803	4,980	75,002	40,618	115,620	19,383
12/31/52	4,363	3,575	6,350	57,154	5,375	73,777	47,378	121,155	19,667
12/31/53	4,621	3,317	6,350	63,504	3,064	65,961	47,488	113,449	19,627
12/31/54	4,527	3,411	6,350	69,854	7,764	90,907	76,351	167,258	20,078
Totals	44,267	43,051	69,854		54,442				

Note: 20.0% subtracted from total amounts withdrawn to reflect liability for federal income taxes.

TABLE 15. (Continued)

Date	Initial Investment	Offering Price	Sales Charge Included	Shares Purchased	Net Asset Value Per Share	Initial Net Asset Value
1/1/55	$167,258.00	$8.33	0.00%	20,078.990	$8.330	$167,258

SYSTEMATIC WITHDRAWAL PLAN
DIVIDENDS AND CAPITAL GAINS REINVESTED
MONTHLY WITHDRAWALS BEGINNING 1/31/55 BASED ON A 21-YEAR SELF-LIQUIDATING PROGRAM
DESIGNED TO EXHAUST PRINCIPAL

	AMOUNTS WITHDRAWN					VALUE OF REMAINING SHARES			
Date	From Income Dividends	From Principal	Annual Total	Cumulative Total	Annual Capital Gain Distribution	Remaining Original Shares	Capital Gain Shares	Total Value	Shares Held
12/31/55	5,248	3,797	7,236	7,236	14,050	185,168	14,592	199,760	21,205
12/31/56	5,462	5,180	8,514	15,750	15,259	180,421	29,767	210,188	22,289
12/31/57	5,762	4,972	8,587	24,337	11,050	140,959	34,508	175,467	23,148
12/31/58	5,744	5,975	9,376	33,713	8,466	183,947	55,963	239,910	23,360
12/31/59	5,796	9,447	12,194	45,907	17,312	182,044	75,792	257,836	24,119
12/31/60	6,320	9,472	12,633	58,541	14,201	165,071	87,615	252,686	24,604
12/31/61	6,076	13,249	15,461	74,002	15,462	174,631	115,644	290,275	24,788
12/31/62	6,146	11,712	14,286	88,288	11,005	130,332	103,523	233,855	24,642
12/31/63	6,001	14,332	16,266	104,554	11,161	134,828	130,432	265,260	24,335
12/31/64	6,134	18,581	19,772	124,326	16,541	126,264	156,428	282,692	24,203
12/31/65	6,324	22,786	23,288	147,614	20,138	123,137	203,093	326,230	23,969
12/31/66	7,324	25,342	26,133	173,748	23,910	88,313	208,183	296,496	23,834
12/31/67	7,762	31,838	31,680	205,428	16,683	73,127	266,570	339,697	22,798
12/31/68	8,387	36,714	36,081	241,509	14,064	40,049	307,617	347,666	21,421
12/31/69	8,103	38,361	37,171	278,679	20,493	0	266,168	266,168	20,148
12/31/70	7,475	33,447	32,737	311,417	11,362	0	227,621	227,621	18,166
12/31/71	6,395	43,606	40,001	351,418	3,937	0	213,107	213,107	15,232
12/31/72	5,198	52,185	45,907	397,324	5,625	0	185,164	185,164	12,094
12/31/73	4,091	49,925	43,213	440,537	2,832	0	102,684	102,684	8,564
12/31/74	3,513	42,802	37,052	477,588	0	0	42,129	42,129	4,549
12/31/75	929	53,073	43,201	520,789	27	0	0	0	0
Totals	124,190	526,796	520,789		253,578				

Note: 20.0% subtracted from total amounts withdrawn to reflect liability for federal income taxes.

STOCKS

Company _____

Date Bought	No. of Shares	Price Per Share	Total Cost	Date Sold	No. of Shares	Price Per Share	Total Net Proceeds

FIGURE 1. **Recordkeeping form for stocks.**

DIVIDEND RECORD

Company _____

Date Dividend Paid	Number of Shares	Rate Per Share	Total Amount of Dividend

FIGURE 2. **Dividend record.**

Program:

Investment Schedule: _____ _____ _____   TOTAL _____

TAX SAVINGS WORKSHEET

WITHOUT INVESTMENT:

   1. Taxable Income $_____   Bracket ____%

   2. Tax Due $_____

WITH INVESTMENT:

   3. Amount of Investment $_____ $_____ $_____

   4. Write-off   _____   _____   _____

   5. Net Taxable Income after Investment _____   _____   _____

   6. Tax Due   _____   _____   _____

   7. Net Tax Savings $_____ $_____ $_____

   8. Investment Tax Credit   _____   _____   _____

   9. TOTAL TAX SAVINGS   _____   _____   _____

  10. Amount Invested $_____ $_____ $_____

  11. Less Tax Saved   _____   _____   _____

  12. Net Cost of Investment   _____   _____   _____

FIGURE 3.

ALTERNATIVE MINIMUM TAX

Regular Adjusted Gross Income (AGI) _____

Deduct: Medical Expense Over 5% of AGI _____

    Contributions _____

    Casualty and Theft Losses _____

    Interest on Residence _____

    Other Interest Deductions _____

    Net Investment Income _____

    Smaller of Preceding Two Lines _____

    Allowable Gambling Losses _____

    Allowable Estate Tax Deduction _____

TOTAL _____

SUBTRACT DEDUCTIONS FROM AGI _____(1)

Add: Tax Preference Items:

    Dividend Exclusion _____

    60% Capital Gains Deduction _____

    Accelerated Depreciation Preferences _____

    Excess Depletion _____

    Incentive Stock Options _____

    Intangible Drilling Costs _____

    Other Preference Items _____

TOTAL _____(2)

Sum of (1) and (2) Alternative Minimum Taxable Income

Exemption: $40,000 Married Filing Jointly

      $30,000 Single or Head of Household _____

      $20,000 Married Filing Separately

Subtract Exemption from Amount (1) (If zero or less, no amt.)

$\times$ 20% = Alternative Minimum Tax _____*

* *Excess over tax computed in the regular way is added to your tax.*

FIGURE 4.

Glossary of Investing

Accrued Interest: Interest accrued on a bond since the last interest payment was made. The buyer of the bond pays the market price plus accrued interest.

Accumulation Plan: A plan for the systematic accumulation of mutual fund shares through periodic investments and reinvestments of income dividends and capital gains distributions.

ACRS: Accelerated Cost Recovery System, liberalized depreciation schedules introduced by the Economic Recovery Tax Act of 1981.

AMEX: The American Stock Exchange, located in New York City.

Amortization: Accounting for expenses or charges as applicable rather than as paid. Includes such practices as depreciation, depletion, write-off of intangibles, prepaid expenses, and deferred charges.

Annual Report: The formal financial statement issued yearly by a corporation. The annual report shows assets, liabilities, earnings, standing of the company at the close of the business year, performance of the company profit-wise during the year, and other information of interest to shareowners.

Appreciation: The increase in value of an asset.

Arbitrage: Dealing in differences. Example: Buying on one exchange while simultaneously selling short on another at a higher price.

Asked Price: The price asked for a security offered for sale. Quoted, bid, and asked prices are wholesale prices for interdealer trading and do not represent prices for the public.

Asset: On a balance sheet, that which is owned or receivable.

Auction Market: Dealings on a securities exchange where a two-way auction is continuously in effect.

Authorized Stock: The total number of shares of stock authorized for issue by a company's shareholders.

Averages: Various ways of measuring the trend of stocks listed on exchanges. Formulas, some very elaborate, have been devised to compensate for stock splits and stock dividends and thus give continuity to the average. In the case of the Dow Jones Industrial Average, the prices of the thirty stocks are totaled and then divided by a figure that is intended to compensate for past stock splits and stock dividends and that is changed from time to time.

Balance Sheet: A condensed financial statement showing the nature and amount of a company's assets, liabilities, and capital on a given date. The balance sheet shows in dollar amounts what the company owns, what it owes, and its stockholders' ownership in the company.

Balanced Fund: A mutual fund that is required to keep a specified percentage of its total assets invested in senior securities.

Bear: One who believes the stock market will decline.

Bear Market: A declining stock market.

Bearer Bond: A bond that does not have the owner's name registered on the books of the issuing company and that is payable to the holder.

Bid and Asked: Often referred to as a quotation or quote. The bid is the highest price anyone has declared that he wants to pay for a security at a given time; the asked is the lowest price anyone will take at the same time.

Big Board: A popular term for the New York Stock Exchange, Inc.

Block: A large holding or transaction of stock, popularly considered to be 10,000 shares or more.

Blue Chip: A company known nationally for the quality and wide acceptance of its products or services, and for its ability to make money and pay dividends.

Blue Sky Laws: A popular name for laws enacted by various states to protect the public against securities frauds. The term is believed to have originated when a judge ruled that a particular stock had about the same value as a patch of blue sky.

Bond: Basically an IOU or promissory note of a corporation, usually issued in multiples of $1,000. A bond is evidence of a debt on which the issuing company usually promises to pay the bondholders a specified amount of interest for a specified length of time, and to repay the loan on the expiration date. In every case, a bond represents debt—its holder is a creditor of the corporation and not a part owner, as is the shareholder.

Bond Fund: A mutual fund invested completely in bonds.

Book Value: An accounting term for the value of a stock determined from a company's records by adding all assets and then deducting all debts and other liabilities, plus the liquidation price of any preferred issues. The sum arrived at is divided by the number of common shares outstanding, and the result is book value per common share. Book value of the assets of a company or a security may have little or no significant relationship to market value.

Broker: An agent who handles the public's orders to buy and sell securities, commodities, or other property. A commission is charged for this service.

Bull: One who believes the stock market will rise.

Bull Market: An advancing stock market.

Business Cycle: The long-term boom-recession cycle that has been characteristic of business conditions not only nationally but on a worldwide basis.

Call: An option to buy a specified number of shares of a certain security at a definite price within a specified period of time.

Callable: A bond issue, all or part of which may be redeemed by the issuing corporation under definite conditions before maturity. The term also applies to preferred shares, which may be redeemed by the issuing corporation.

Capital Gain or Capital Loss: Profit or loss from the sale of a capital asset. A capital gain, under current federal income tax laws, may be either short-term (six months or less) or long-term (more than six months). A short-term capital gain is taxed at the reporting individual's full income tax rate. A long-term capital gain is subject to a lower tax.

Capital Market: The market that deals in long-term securities issues of both debt and equity.

Capital Shares: When referring to a dual- or leveraged-type closed-end investment company, those shares to which all gains or losses accrue and which have no claim on dividends.

Capital Stock: All shares representing ownership of a business, including preferred and common.

Capitalization: Total amount of the various securities issued by a corporation. Capitalization may include bonds, debentures, preferred and common stock, and surplus.

Cash Flow: Cash distributions from an investment. Negative cash flow occurs when expenses exceed income.

CBT: Chicago Board of Trade, the oldest and largest commodites exchange in the United States.

Certificate: The actual piece of paper that is evidence of ownership of stock in a corporation. Loss of a certificate may cause, at least, a great deal of inconvenience; at worse, financial loss.

Certificate of Deposit (CD): Receipt for funds deposited with a financial institution payable to holder at some specified date and bearing interest at a fixed rate.

Certified Public Accountant (CPA): A professional license granted by a state board of accountancy to an individual who has passed the Uniform CPA Examination (administered by the American Institute of Certified Public Accountants) and has fulfilled that state's educational and professional experience requirements for certification.

CFP: A Certified Financial Planner. A designation granted by the College for Financial Planning (Denver, Colorado) to individuals who complete a six-part curriculum in financial planning (including risk management, investments, tax planning, employee benefits, and estate planning).

Clifford Trust: A short-term living trust created for a period of the lesser of ten years and a day or the life of the beneficiary, at which time the assets revert to the original owner.

Closed-End Investment Company: An investment company that issues a fixed number of shares and does not redeem them. It may also issue senior securities and/or warrants.

Collateral: Securities or other property pledged by a borrower to secure repayment of a loan.

Collectibles: Tangible goods often purchased as investments, including coins, stamps, books, antiques, art, oriental rugs, and pottery.

Commercial Paper: Short-term notes issued by corporations which can be purchased either at a discount or on an interest-bearing basis.

Commission: The broker's basic fee for purchasing or selling securities or property as an agent.

Common Stock: Securities that represent an ownership interest in a corporation. If the company has also issued preferred stock, both common and preferred have ownership rights. Claims of both common and preferred stockholders are junior to claims of bondholders or other creditors of the company. Common stockholders assume the greater risk, but generally they also exercise the greater control and may gain the greater reward in the form of dividends and capital appreciation.

Common Stock Fund: A mutual fund that has a stated policy of investing all of its assets in common stocks. The term is also applied to funds that normally invest only in common stocks, though are not restricted to them by charter.

Confirmation: A written description of the terms of a transaction in securities supplied by a broker/dealer to his customer or to another broker/dealer.

Conglomerate: A corporation that has diversified its operations, usually by acquiring enterprises in widely varied industries.

Constructive Receipt: A doctrine of the Internal Revenue Service that requires the reporting of income (including capital gains) in the year in which it could have been received had the taxpayer so wished. Thus, dividends of a mutual fund automatically reinvested are taxable in the year in which reinvested on the basis that the taxpayer could have received them by check and then reinvested them or not at his option.

Convertible: A bond, debenture, or preferred share that may be exchanged by the owner for common stock or another security, usually of the same company, in accordance with the terms of the issue.

Convertible Bond Fund: A mutual fund that invests in convertible bonds.

Corporate Bond: An evidence of indebtedness issued by a corporation, rather than by the U.S. government or a municipality.

Corporate Bond Fund: A mutual fund that invests in corporate bonds.

Corporation: An organization chartered by a state government. When the term is used without qualification, it generally refers to an organization carrying on a business for profit. However, there are non-profit corporations and municipalities, which differ from corporations organized for profit in that they do not issue stock.

Coupon Bond: Bond with interest coupons attached. The coupons are clipped as they come due and are presented by the holder for payment of interest.

Cumulative Preferred: A stock with a provision that if one or more dividends are omitted, the omitted dividends must be paid before dividends may be paid on the company's common stock.

Cumulative Voting: A type of shareholder voting in which the number of shares held is multiplied by the number of directors to be elected to determine the number of votes a shareholder may cast. He may cast all votes for one director or may allocate them in any way he sees fit.

Current Assets: Those assets of a company that are reasonably expected to be realized in cash, or sold, or consumed during the normal operating cycle of the business.

Current Liabilities: Money owed and payable by a company, usually within one year.

Custodian: The corporation, usually a bank, charged with the safekeeping of an investment company's portfolio securities.

Dealer: An individual or firm in the securities business acting as a principal rather than as an agent. Typically, a dealer buys for his own account and sells to a customer from his own inventory. The dealer's profit or loss is the difference between the price he pays and the price he receives for the same security. The dealer's confirmation must disclose to his customer that he has acted as principal. The same individual or firm may function, at different times, as either a broker or dealer.

Debenture: A promissory note backed by the general credit of a company and usually not secured by a mortgage or lien on any specific property.

Depletion: Natural resources, such as metals, oils and gas, and timber that conceivably can be reduced to zero over the years, present a special problem in capital management. Depletion is an accounting practice consisting of charges against earnings based upon the amount of the assets taken out of the total reserves in the period for which accounting is made. A bookkeeping entry, it does not represent any cash outlay, nor are any funds earmarked for the purpose.

Depreciation: Normally, charges against earnings to write off the cost, less salvage value, of an asset over its estimated useful life. A bookkeeping entry, it does not represent any cash outlay, nor are any funds earmarked for the purpose.

Director: A person elected by shareholders to establish company policies. The directors elect the president, vice-president, and all other operating officers. Directors decide, among other matters, if and when dividends will be paid.

Discount: The amount of money by which a preferred stock or bond may sell below its par value.

Discretionary Account: An account in which the customer gives the broker or someone else discretion, either complete or within specific limits, as to the purchase and sale of securities or commodities, including selection, timing, amount, and price to be paid or received.

Diversification: Spreading investments among different companies in different fields. Another type of diversification is also offered by the securities of many individual companies because of the wide range of their activities. Diversification can also be accomplished by investing in areas outside of the stock market, such as registered limited partnerships or private placement limited partnerships in real estate, energy, leasing, and cable television.

Diversified Investment Company: An investment company which, under the Investment Company Act of 1940, must invest 75 percent of its total assets so that not more than 5 percent of total assets are invested in the securities of any one issuer. Also, the company may not own more than 10 percent of the voting securities of any one issuer.

Dividend: The payment designated by the board of directors to be distributed pro rata among the shares outstanding. On preferred shares, it is generally a fixed amount. On common shares, the dividend varies with the fortunes of the company and the amount of cash on hand, and it may be omitted if business is poor or the directors determine to withhold earnings to invest in plant and equipment. Sometimes a company will pay a dividend out of past earnings even if it is not currently operating at a profit.

Dividend Reinvestment Plan: A mutual fund share account in which dividends are automatically reinvested in additional shares. With this type of account, capital gains distributions are also automatically reinvested. Dividends (but not capital gains) may be invested at offering price (i.e., with a sales charge), but are more commonly reinvested at asset value.

Dollar-Cost-Averaging: A system of buying securities at regular intervals with a fixed dollar amount. Under this system the investor buys by the dollars' worth rather than by the number of shares. If each investment is of the same number of dollars, payments buy more when the price is low and fewer when it rises. Temporary downswings in price thus benefit the investor if he continues to make periodic purchases in both good times and bad, and the price at which the shares are sold is more than their average cost.

Double Taxation: The federal government taxes corporate profits once as corporate income; any part of the remaining profits distributed as dividends to stockholders may be taxed again as income to the recipient stockholder.

Dow Jones Average: Widely quoted stock averages computed regularly. They include an industrial stock average, a transportation stock average, a utility average, and a combination of the three.

Dow Theory: A theory of market analysis based upon performance of the Dow Jones industrial and transportation stock price averages. The theory says that the market is in a basic upward trend if one of these averages advances above a previous important high, accompanied or followed by a similar advance in the other. A dip in both averages below previous important lows is regarded as confirmation of a basic downward trend. The theory does not attempt to predict how long either trend will continue, although it is widely misinterpreted as a method of forecasting future action.

Dual Fund: A closed-end investment company with two classes of shares: income and capital outstanding. Also designated as a *leveraged fund*.

Equity: The ownership interest of common and preferred stockholders in a company. Also refers to excess of value of securities over the debit balance in a margin account. Also, the value of a property that remains after all liens and other charges against the property are paid. A property owner's equity generally consists of his or her monetary interest in the property in excess of the mortgage indebtedness. In the case of a long-term mortgage, the owner's equity builds up quite gradually during the first several years because the bulk of each monthly payment is applied, not to the principal amount of the loan, but to the interest.

ERISA: Employee Retirement Income Security Act of 1974.

ERTA: Economic Recovery Tax Act of 1981.

Exchange Privilege: The right to exchange shares in one mutual fund for shares in another mutual fund offered by the same company at little or no cost.

Ex-Dividend: A synonym for "without dividend." The buyer of a stock selling ex-dividend does not receive the recently declared dividend. Every dividend is payable on a fixed date to all shareholders recorded on the books of the company as of a previous date of record. For example, a dividend may be declared as payable to holders of record on the books of the company on a given Friday. Since five business days are allowed for delivery of stock in a "regular way" transaction on the stock exchange, the exchange would declare the stock "ex-dividend" as of the opening of the market on the preceding Monday. That means anyone who bought it on or after Monday would not be entitled to that dividend. When stocks go ex-dividend, the stock tables include the symbol "x" following the name.

Ex-Rights: Without the rights. Corporations raising additional money may do so by offering stockholders the right to subscribe to new or additional stock, usually at a discount from the prevailing market price. The buyer of a stock selling ex-rights is not entitled to the rights.

Extra: The short form of "extra dividend." A dividend in the form of stock or cash in addition to the regular or usual dividend the company has been paying.

Face Value: The value of a bond that appears on the face of the bond, unless the value is otherwise specified by the issuing company. Face value is ordinarily the amount the issuing company promises to pay at maturity. Face value is not an indication of market value. It is sometimes referred to as par value.

FDIC: Federal Deposit Insurance Corporation, the federal agency that insures deposits of up to $100,000 in member banks.

Fiduciary: One who acts for another in financial matters.

Floor: The huge trading area of a stock exchange where stocks and bonds are bought and sold.

Floor Broker: A member of the stock exchange who executes orders on the floor of the exchange to buy or sell any listed securities.

FSLIC: Federal Savings and Loan Insurance Corporation, the federal agency that insures deposits of up to $100,000 in member savings and loan associations.

Fully Managed Fund: A mutual fund whose investment policy gives its management complete flexibility as to the types of investments made and the proportions of each. Management is restricted only to the extent that federal or blue sky laws require.

Gilt-Edged: High-grade bond issued by a company that has demonstrated its ability to earn a comfortable profit over a period of years and pay its bondholders their interest without interruption.

Good Delivery: Certain basic qualifications must be met before a security sold on the exchange may be delivered. The security must be in proper form to comply with the contract of sale and to transfer title to the purchaser.

Good till Cancelled Order (GTC) or **Open Order:** An order to buy or sell that remains in effect until it is either executed or cancelled.

Government Bonds: Obligations of the U.S. government, regarded as the highest-grade issues in existence.

Government Securities Fund: A mutual fund that invests in government securities.

Growth Fund: A fund whose rate of growth over a period of time is considerably greater than that of business generally. An average rate of 10 percent per year is used by some analysts as definitive.

Growth Stock: Stock of a company with a record of relatively rapid growth earnings.

Holding Company: A corporation that owns the securities of another, in most cases with voting control.

Income Fund: A mutual fund with a primary objective of current income.

Indenture: A written agreement under which bonds and debentures are issued, setting forth maturity date, interest rate, and other terms.

Individual Retirement Account (IRA): A retirement plan available to all workers under the age of 70½ who may contribute earned income of up to $2,000 to a qualified IRA account, deduct the contribution from taxable income, and have the investment compound tax deferred until withdrawal.

Institution: An organization holding substantial investing assets, often for others. Includes banks, insurance companies, investment companies, and pension funds.

Interest: Payments made by a borrower to a lender for the use of his money. A corporation pays interest on its bonds to its bondholders.

Investment: The use of money for the purpose of making more money: to gain income or increase capital or both.

Investment Banker: Also known as an *underwriter*. The middleman between the corporation issuing new securities and the public. The usual practice is for one or more investment bankers to buy outright from a corporation a new issue of stocks or bonds. The group forms a syndicate to sell the securities to individuals and institutions. Investment bankers also distribute very large blocks of stocks or bonds (perhaps held by an estate).

Investment Company: A company or trust that uses its capital to invest in other companies. There are two principal types: the closed-end and the open-end, or mutual fund. Shares in closed-end investment companies are readily transferrable in the open market and are bought and sold like other shares. Capitalization of these companies remains the same unless action is taken to change, which seldom occurs. Open-end funds sell their own new shares to investors, stand ready to buy back their old shares, and are not listed. Open-end funds are so named because their capitalization is not fixed; they issue more shares as people want them.

Investment Company Act of 1940: An act passed by the Congress for the specific purpose of empowering the Securities and Exchange Commission to regulate investment companies.

Investment Counsel: One whose principal business consists of acting as investment adviser, and a substantial part of whose business consists of rendering investment supervisory services.

Investor: An individual whose principal concerns in the purchase of a security are regular dividend income, safety of the original investment, and, if possible, capital appreciation.

Issue: Any of a company's securities, or the act of distributing such securities.

Keogh Plan: A retirement plan available to self-employed workers.

Legal List: A list of investments selected by various states in which certain institutions and fiduciaries, such as insurance companies and banks, may invest. Legal lists are often restricted to high-quality securities and, if possible, capital appreciation.

Leverage: The effect on the per-share earnings of the common stock of a company when large sums must be paid for bond interest or preferred stock dividends, or both, before the common stock is entitled to share in earnings. Leverage may be advantageous for the common stock when earnings are good, but may work against the common stock when earnings decline. Leverage also refers to mortgage funds used in financing limited partnerships in real estate, oil and gas, leasing, cable television, etc.

Liabilities: All the claims against a corporation. Liabilities include accounts and wages and salaries payable, dividends declared payable, accrued taxes payable, fixed or long-term liabilities such as mortgage bonds, debentures, and bank loans.

Lien: A claim against property that has been pledged or mortgaged to secure the performance of an obligation. A bond may be secured by a lien against specified property of a company.

Limited Order: An order to buy or sell a stated amount of a security at a specified price, or at a better price.

Limited Partnership: A partnership composed of one or more general partners with professional expertise willing to assume unlimited liability and several or a large number of limited partners, usually without expertise, with investable funds but unwilling to assume liability beyond the extent of their investment. There are registered limited partnerships, registered with the SEC, and private placement limited partnerships that are exempt from registration. For tax purposes and cash distributions the limited partners are treated as individuals, with all the benefits flowing directly through to them as certain IRS criteria are met. This is called the conduit principle.

Liquidating Value: When referring to the shares of an open-end investment company, the value at redemption. Usually the net asset value.

Listed Stock: The stock of a company that is traded on a securities exchange.

Locked In: An investor is said to be locked in when he has a profit on a security he owns, but does not sell because his profit would immediately become subject to the capital gains tax.

Management: The board of directors, elected by the stockholders, and the officers of the corporation, appointed by the board of directors.

Management Fee: The fee paid to the investment manager of a mutual fund. It is usually about one-half of one percent of average net assets annually. Not to be confused with the sales charge, which is the one-time commission paid at the time of purchase as a part of the offering price.

Manipulation: An illegal operation. Buying or selling a security for the purpose of creating false or misleading appearance of active trading or for the purpose of raising or depressing the price to induce purchase or sale by others.

Margin: The amount paid by the customer when he uses his broker's credit to buy securities.

Margin Call: A demand upon a customer to put up money or securities with the broker. The call is made when a purchase is made or when a customer's equity in a margin account declines below a minimum standard set by the exchange or by the firm.

Market Order: An order to buy or sell a slated amount of a security at the most advantageous price obtainable.

Market Price: In the case of a security, market price is usually considered the last reported price at which the stock or bond sold.

Maturity: The date on which a loan or a bond or a debenture comes due and is to be paid off.

Member Firm: A securities brokerage firm organized as a partnership or corporation and owning at least one seat on the exchange.

Money Market: The market created by the sale or purchase of short-term financial instruments, including commercial paper and government securities.

Money Market Fund: A mutual fund that invests in money market instruments.

Mortgage Bond: A bond secured by a mortgage on a property. The value of the property may or may not equal the value of the so-called mortgage bonds issued against it.

Municipal Bond: A bond issued by a state or a political subdivision, such as a county, city, town, or village. The term also designates bonds issued by state agencies and authorities. In general, interest paid on municipal bonds is exempt from federal income taxes and from state and local income taxes within the state of issue.

Municipal Bond Fund: A mutual fund that invests in municipal bonds.

Mutual Fund: An open-end investment company that continuously offers new shares to the public in addition to redeeming shares on demand as required by law. While in common use, the term mutual fund has no meaning in law.

NASD: The National Association of Securities Dealers, Inc. An association of brokers and dealers in the over-the-counter securities business. The association has the power to expel members who have been declared guilty of unethical practices. NASD is dedicated to, among other objectives, "adopt, administer and enforce rules of fair practice and rules to prevent fraudulent and manipulative acts and practices, and in general to promote just and equitable principles of trade for the protection of investors."

NASDAQ: An acronym for National Association of Securities Dealers Automated Quotations. An automated information network that provides brokers and dealers with price quotations on securities traded over the counter.

Negotiable: Refers to a security, title to which is transferrable by delivery.

Net Asset Value: A term usually used in connection with investment companies, meaning net asset value per share. It is common practice for an investment company to compute its assets daily by totaling the market value of all securities owned. All liabilities are deducted, and the balance is divided by the number of shares outstanding. The resulting figure is the net asset value per share.

Net Change: The change in the price of a security from the closing price on one day to the closing price on the following day on which the stock is traded. The net change is ordinarily the last figure on the stock price list. The mark + 2⅛ means up $2.125 a share from the last sale on the previous day the stock traded.

New Issue: A stock or bond sold by a corporation for the first time. Proceeds may be issued to retire outstanding securities of the company, for new plant or equipment, or for additional working capital.

Non-Cumulative: A preferred stock on which unpaid dividends do not accrue. Omitted dividends are, as a rule, gone forever.

NYEX: The New York Stock Exchange, the largest securities exchange in the United States.

NYSE Common Stock Index: A composite index covering price movements of all common stocks listed on the "Big Board." It is based on the close of the market December 31, 1965, as 50.00 and is weighted according to the number of shares listed for each issue. The index is computed continuously and printed on the ticker tape each half hour. Point changes in the index are converted to dollars and cents to provide a meaningful measure of changes in the average price of listed stocks.

Odd Lot: An amount of stock less than the established 100-share unit or 10-share unit of trading: from 1 to 99 shares for the great majority of issues, 1 to 9 for so-called inactive stocks. Odd-lot prices are geared to the auction market. On an odd-lot market order, the odd-lot dealer's price is based on the first round-lot transaction that occurs on the floor following receipt at the trading post of the odd-lot order. The differential between the odd-lot price and the "effective" round-lot price is 12½ cents a share. For example: You decide to buy 20 shares of ABC common at the market. Your order is transmitted by your commission broker to the representative of an odd-lot dealer at the post where ABC is traded. A few minutes later there is a 100-share transaction in ABC at $10 a share. The odd-lot price at which your order is immediately filled by the odd-lot dealer is $10.125 a share. If you had sold 20 shares of ABC, you would have received $9.875 a share.

Offer: The price at which a person is ready to sell. Opposite of bid, the price at which one is ready to buy.

Open Account: When referring to a mutual fund, a type of account in which the investor may add or withdraw shares at any time. In such an account, dividends may be paid in cash or reinvested at the account holder's option.

Open-End Investment Company: By definition under the 1940 act, an investment company that has outstanding redeemable shares. Also generally applied to those investment companies which continuously offer new shares to the public and stand ready at any time to redeem their outstanding shares.

Option: A right to buy or sell specific securities or properties at a specified price within a specified time.

Overbought: An opinion as to price levels. May refer to a security that has had a sharp rise or to the market as a whole after a period of vigorous buying which, it may be argued, has left prices "too high."

Oversold: An opinion, the reverse of overbought. A single security or a market that, it is believed, has declined to an unreasonable level.

Over-the-Counter: A market for securities made up of securities dealers who may or may not be members of a securities exchange. Over-the-counter is mainly a market made over the telephone. Thousands of companies have insufficient shares outstanding, stockholders, or earnings to warrant application for listing on an exchange. Securities of these companies are traded in the over-the-counter market between dealers who act either as principals or as brokers for customers.

Paper Profit: An unrealized profit on a security still held. Paper profits become realized profits only when the security is sold.

Par: In the case of a common share, par means a dollar amount assigned to the share by the company's charter. Par value may also be used to compute the dollar amount of the common shares on the balance sheet. Par value has little significance so far as market value of common stock is concerned.

Penny Stocks: Low-priced issues, often highly speculative, selling at less than $1 a share. Frequently used as a term of disparagement, although a few penny stocks have developed into investment-caliber issues.

Point: In the case of shares of stock, a point means $1. If ABC shares rise three points, each share has risen $3. In the case of bonds, a point means $10, since a bond is quoted as a percentage of $1,000. A bond that rises three points gains 3 percent of $1,000, or $30 in value. An advance from 87 to 90 would mean an advance in dollar value from $870 to 900 for each $1,000 bond. In the case of market averages, the word point means merely that and no more. If, for example, the Dow Jones Industrial Average rises from 1535.21 to 1536.21, it has risen a point. A point in this average, however, is not equivalent to $1.

Portfolio: Holdings of securities by an individual or institution. A portfolio may contain bonds, preferred stocks, and common stocks of various types of enterprises.

Preferred Stock: A class stock with a claim on the company's earnings before payment may be made on the common stock and usually entitled to priority over common stock if the company liquidates. Usually entitled to dividends at a specified rate, when declared by the board of directors and before payment of a dividend on the common stock, depending upon the term of the issue.

Premium: The amount by which a preferred stock or bond may sell above its par value. In the case of a new issue of bonds or stocks, premium is the amount the market price rises over the original selling price.

Price-Earnings Ratio: The price of a share of stock divided by earnings per share for a twelve-month period. For example, a stock selling for $100 a share and earning $5 a share is said to be selling at a price-earnings ratio of 20 to 1.

Primary Distribution: Also called *primary offering*. The original sale of a company's securities.

Principal: The person for whom a broker executes an order, or a dealer buying or selling for his own account. The term "principal" may also refer to a person's capital or to the face amount of a bond.

Profit Taking: Selling stock that has appreciated in value since purchase to realize the profit that has been made possible. The term is often used to explain a downturn in the market following a period of rising prices.

Prospectus: The document that offers a new issue of securities to the public. It is required under the Securities Act of 1933.

Proxy: Written authorization given by a shareholder to someone else to represent him and vote his shares at a shareholders' meeting.

Proxy Statement: Information required by the SEC to be given to stockholders as a prerequisite to solicitation of proxies for a security subject to the requirements of the Securities Exchange Act.

Prudent Man's Rule: An investment standard. In some states, the law requires that a fiduciary, such as a trustee, may invest the fund's money only in a list of securities designated by the state—the so-called legal list. In other states, the trustee may invest in a security if it is one that a prudent man of discretion and intelligence, who is seeking a reasonable income and preservation of capital, would buy.

Put: An option to sell a specified number of shares at a definite price within a specified period of time. The opposite of a call.

Quotation: Often shortened to *quote*. The highest bid to buy and the lowest offer to sell a security in a given market at a given time. If you ask your broker for a quote on a stock, he may come back with something like "45¼ to 45½." This means that $45.25 is the highest price any buyer wanted to pay at the time the quote was given on the floor of the exchange, and that $45.50 was the lowest price any seller would take at the same time.

Rally: A brisk rise following a decline in the general price level of the market or in an individual stock.

Record Date: The date on which you must be registered as a shareholder on the stock book of a company to receive a declared dividend or, among other things, to vote on company affairs.

Red Herring: A preliminary prospectus used to obtain indications of interest from prospective buyers of a new issue.

Redemption Price: The price at which a bond may be redeemed before maturity, at the option of the issuing company. Redemption value also applies to the price an open-end investment company must pay to call in certain types of preferred stock. It is usually the net asset value per share—it fluctuates with the value of the company's investment portfolio.

Registered Bond: A bond that is registered on the books of the issuing company in the name of the owner. It can be transferred only when endorsed by the registered owner.

Registered Representative: A full-time employee who has met the requirements of an exchange as to background and knowledge of the securities business. Also known as an *account executive* or *customer's broker*.

Registrar: Usually a trust company or bank charged with the responsibility of preventing the issuance of more stock than authorized by a company.

Registration: Before a public offering may be made of new securities by controlling stockholders, through the mails or in interstate commerce, the securities must be registered under the Securities Act of 1933. Registration statement is filed with the SEC by the issuer. It must disclose pertinent information relating to the company's operations, securities, management, and purpose of the public offering. On security offerings involving less than $300,000, less information is required. Before a security may be admitted to dealings on a national securities exchange, it must be registered under the Securities Exchange Act of 1934. The application for registration must be filed with the exchange and the SEC by the company issuing the securities. It must disclose pertinent information relating to the company's operations, securities, and management.

Regulation T: The federal regulation governing the amount of credit that may be advanced by brokers and dealers to customers for the purchase of securities.

Regulation U: The federal regulation governing the amount of credit that may be advanced by a bank to its customers for the purchase of listed stocks.

REIT: Real estate investment trust, an organization similar to an investment company in some respects, but concentrating its holdings in real estate investments.

The yield is generally liberal, since REIT's are required to distribute as much as 90 percent of their income.

Return: Another term for *yield*.

Rights: When a company wants to raise more funds by issuing additional securities, it may give its stockholders the opportunity, ahead of others, to buy the new securities in proportion to the number of shares each owns. The piece of paper evidencing this privilege is called a right. Because the additional stock is usually offered to stockholders below the current market price, rights ordinarily have a market value of their own and are actively traded. In most cases they must be exercised within a relatively short period. Failure to exercise or sell rights would result in actual loss to the holder.

Round Lot: A unit of trading or a multiple thereof. On most exchanges the unit of trading is 100 shares in the case of stocks and $1,000 par value in the case of bonds. In some inactive stocks, the unit of trading is 10 shares.

Seat: A traditional figure of speech for a membership on an exchange. Price and admission requirements vary.

SEC: Securities and Exchange Commission, established by Congress to help protect investors. The SEC administers the Securities Act of 1933, the Securities Exchange Act of 1934, the Trust Indenture Act, the Investment Company Act, the Investment Advisers Act, and the Public Utility Holding Company Act.

Secondary Distribution: Also known as a *secondary offering*. The redistribution of a block of stock some time after it has been sold by the issuing company. The sale is handled off the exchange by a securities firm or group of firms, and the shares are usually offered at a fixed price that is related to the current market price of the stock. Usually the block is a large one, such as might be involved in the settlement of an estate. The security may be listed or unlisted.

Sinking Fund: Money regularly set aside by a company to redeem its bonds, debentures, or preferred stock from time to time as specified in the indenture or charter.

Special Offering: Occasionally a large block of stock becomes available for sale that, due to its size and the market in that particular issue, calls for special handling. A notice is printed on the ticker tape announcing that the stock will be offered for sale on the floor of the exchange at a fixed price. Member firms may buy this stock for customers directly from the seller's broker during trading hours. The price is usually based on the last transaction in the regular auction market. If there are more buyers than stock, allotments are made. Only the seller pays a commission on a special offering.

Specialist: A member of an exchange who has two functions. The first is to maintain an orderly market, insofar as reasonably practicable, in the stocks in which he is registered as a specialist. The exchange expects the specialist to buy or sell for his own account, to a reasonable degree, when there is a temporary disparity between supply and demand. The specialist also acts as a broker's broker. When a commission broker on the exchange floor receives a limit order, say, to buy at $50 a stock then selling at $60, he cannot wait at the post where the stock is traded to see if the price reaches the specified level. So he leaves the order with the specialist, who will try to execute it in the market if and when the stock declines to the specified price. The specialist must put his customers' interest above his own at all times.

Specialty Fund: A mutual fund that invests in stocks of related industries or other areas, such as insurance, utilities, electronics, and gold.

Speculator: One who is willing to assume a relatively large risk in the hope of gain. His principal concern is to increase his capital rather than his dividend income. The speculator may buy and sell the same day or speculate in an enterprise he does not expect to be profitable for years.

Split: The division of the outstanding shares of a corporation into a larger number of shares. A 3-for-1 split by a company with 1 million shares outstanding results in 3 million shares outstanding. Each holder of 100 shares before the 3-to-1 split would have 300 shares, although his proportionate equity in the company would remain the same; 100 parts of 1 million are the equivalent of 300 parts of 3 million.

Spread: The difference between the bid price and the offering price. Also, the combination of a put and a call "points away" from the market.

Statement of Policy: The SEC's statement of its own position as to those things considered "materially misleading" in the offer of shares of open-end investment companies.

Stock: Ownership shares of a corporation.

Stock Certificate: A certificate that provides physical evidence of stock ownership.

Stock Dividend: A dividend paid in securities rather than cash. The dividend may be additional shares of the issuing company or shares of another company (usually a subsidiary) held by the issuing company.

Stock Exchange: An organization registered under the Securities Exchange Act of 1934 with physical facilities for the buying and selling of securities in a two-way auction.

Stock Power: An assignment and power of substitution separate from a stock certificate authorizing transfer of the stock on the books of the corporation.

Stockholder of Record: A stockholder whose name is registered on the books of the issuing corporation.

Stop Order: An order to buy at a price above or to sell below the current market. Stop buy orders are generally used to limit loss or protect unrealized profits on a short sale. Stop sell orders are generally used to protect unrealized profits or limit loss on a holding.

Street Name: Securities held in the name of a broker instead of his customer's name are said to be carried in a street name. This occurs when the securities have been bought on margin or when the customer wishes the security to be held by the broker.

Suitability Rule: The rule of fair practice that requires a member to have reasonable grounds for believing that a recommendation to a customer is suitable on the basis of his financial objectives and abilities.

Tax Shelter: A means by which taxable income may be decreased, deferred, or, in some cases, eliminated. Tax-advantaged investments are legal incentives to encourage investment in areas of social need.

TEFRA: Tax Equity and Fiscal Responsibility Act of 1982.

Tenants in Common: A form of registration of property, frequently used with securities. An undivided estate in property where, upon the death of the owner, the undivided estate becomes the property of his heirs or divisees and not of his surviving co-owner.

Tenants by the Entirety: A form of registration of property, usually real estate.

Timing Service: A professional service which, for a fee, moves the investor's funds in and out of the market within a family of funds from equities or bonds into money market funds in an effort to have funds in a cash position when it is anticipated that the market will go down and in an invested position when it is anticipated that the market will go up.

Tips: Supposedly "inside" information on corporation affairs.

Trader: One who buys and sells for his own account for short-term profit.

Transfer: This term may refer to two different operations. For one, the delivery of a stock certificate from the seller's broker to the buyer's broker and legal change of ownership, normally accomplished within a few days. For another, to record the change of ownership on the books of the corporation by the transfer agent. When the purchaser's name is recorded on the books of the company, dividends, notices of meetings, proxies, financial reports, and all pertinent literature sent by the issuer to its securities holders are mailed directly to the new owner.

Transfer Agent: One who keeps a record of the name of each registered shareowner, his or her address, and the number of shares owned, and sees that certificates presented to his office for transfer are properly cancelled and that new certificates are issued in the name of the transferee.

Treasury Bill: Short-term U.S. government paper with no stated interest rate. It is sold at a discount in competitive bidding and reaches maturity in ninety days or less.

Treasury Bond: U.S. government bonds issued in $1,000 units with maturity of five years or longer. They are traded on the market like other bonds.

Treasury Note: U.S. government paper, not legally restricted as to interest rates, with maturities from one to five years.

Treasury Stock: Stock issued by a company but later reacquired. It may be held in the company's treasury indefinitely, reissued to the public, or retired. Treasury stock receives no dividends and has no vote while held by the company.

Underwriter's Fee: In the sale of mutual funds shares, the difference between the total sales charge and the underwriter's reallowance to the dealer.

Unlisted: A security not listed on a stock exchange.

Voting Right: The stockholder's right to vote his stock in the affairs of his company. Most common shares have one vote each. Preferred stock usually has the right to vote when preferred dividends are in default for a specified period. The right to vote may be delegated by the stockholder to another person.

Warrant: A certificate giving the holder the right to purchase securities at a stipulated price within a specified time limit or perpetually. Sometimes a warrant is offered with securities as an inducement to buy.

When Issued: A short form of "when, as, and if issued." The term indicates a conditional transaction in a security authorized for issuance but not yet actually issued. All "when issued" transactions are on an "if" basis, to be settled if and